Shelter in a Time of Storm

How Black Colleges Fostered Generations of Leadership and Activism

• •

JELANI M. FAVORS

The University of North Carolina Press Chapel Hill

This book was published with the assistance of the John Hope Franklin Fund
of the University of North Carolina Press.

Set in Charis by Westchester Publishing Services
The University of North Carolina Press has been a member of the
Green Press Initiative since 2003.

Library of Congress Cataloging-in-Publication Data
Names: Favors, Jelani Manu-Gowon, 1975– author.
Title: Shelter in a time of storm : how black colleges fostered student activism /
    Jelani Favors.
Description: Chapel Hill : University of North Carolina Press, [2019] |
    Includes bibliographical references and index.
Identifiers: LCCN 2018031170| ISBN 9781469648330 (cloth : alk. paper) |
ISBN 9781469661445 (pbk. : alk. paper) | ISBN 9781469648347 (ebook)
Subjects: LCSH: African American universities and colleges—History. |
    African American student movements—History. | African American college
    students—Political activity—History. | African Americans—Race
    identity—History.
Classification: LCC LC2781 .F34 2019 | DDC 378.7308996073—dc23
    LC record available at https://lccn.loc.gov/2018031170

Cover illustration: Elizabeth Catlett, *A Second Generation*, from the portfolio
For My People (1992). The Museum of Fine Arts, Houston, museum purchase
funded by the family of Dr. Mavis P. Kelsey Sr. in honor of the African
American Art Advisory Association, 99.4.6, © Catlett Mora Family Trust/
VAGA at Artists Rights Society (ARS), NY.

Epigraph: Excerpt of Margaret Walker's "For My People," used with
permission of the University of Georgia Press.

Portions of this book were previously published in a different form.
Chapter 3 appeared as "Race Women: New Negro Politics and the Flowering
of Radicalism at Bennett College, 1900–1945," *North Carolina Historical Review*
94 (October 2017): 391–430. Chapter 5 appeared as "Trouble in My Way:
Curriculum, Conflict, and Confrontation at Jackson State University,
1945–1963," in *The Civil Rights Movement in Mississippi*, ed. Ted Ownby
(Jackson: University Press of Mississippi, 2013), 90–122. Both used here
with permission.

Shelter in a Time of Storm

To Paris Eva Favors

May kindness, wisdom, justice, and love guide you all your life.

Let a new earth rise. Let another world be born.
Let a bloody peace be written in the sky. Let a second
generation full of courage issue forth; let a people
loving freedom come to growth. Let a beauty full of
healing and a strength of final clenching be the pulsing
in our spirits and our blood. Let the martial songs
be written, let the dirges disappear. Let a race of men
now rise and take control.

—Excerpt of Margaret Walker's "For My People"

Contents

Graph and Illustrations

Shelter in a Time of Storm

Introduction

Enroll for Freedom: The Long History of Black College Student Activism

· ·

For the South believed an educated Negro to be a dangerous Negro.
And the South was not wholly wrong; for education among all kinds of
men always has had, and always will have, an element of danger and
revolution, of dissatisfaction and discontent.

—W. E. B. DuBois, *The Souls of Black Folk*

In April 2010, the Student Nonviolent Coordinating Committee (SNCC) celebrated its fiftieth anniversary on the campus of Shaw University, where it
was founded. Thousands arrived to celebrate and honor the founding of the
most important civil rights organization of the 1960s. Among the attendees were numerous youths from across the country, many imbued with a
desire to channel the energy of SNCC and perhaps reignite the spark that
had transformed the social and political landscape of America.

Veterans of the civil rights struggle and scholars of the movement sat on
panels and were peppered with questions from the crowd. One of the inquiries that continued to surface, particularly from the youths, focused on
the origins of the movement. How and why did SNCC come together when
it did? Much to the chagrin of some of the young people in attendance, the
panelists seemed to be stymied by the question. Fifty years before, as college students, they had initiated the sit-in movement, signaling the emergence of youth as a potent weapon against white supremacy. Yet producing
a blueprint for social revolution can be difficult. How exactly does one go
about the process of reproducing an Ella Baker, Stokely Carmichael, Ruby
Doris Smith, or Diane Nash? Additionally, and perhaps most importantly,
how does one re-create the activist energies that propelled an entire generation and transformed the world?

Toward the end of the conference, longtime activist and living patriarch
of the movement Harry Belafonte grew frustrated. Launching into an impromptu speech that was half tongue-lashing, half pep talk, Belafonte re-
pudiated the tone of a conference where so many sessions praised past

triumphs but few offered guidance to today's youths on the prodigious challenges plaguing the marginalized and downtrodden communities of the world. "Why can't our children find us?" asked Belafonte. "Why can't they hear us more clearly? What are we so busy doing that we can afford to abandon them and then have the arrogance and the nerve to accuse them of being lost?"[1]

Some of the youths in attendance shared in his frustration and organized informal side sessions to share their concerns and contact information. The failure to pass the torch of dissent seamlessly from one generation to the next befuddled conference attendees, largely due to a failure to acknowledge one immutable truth: activists are not born; they are made.

In the shock troops that came together on April 15, 1960, to create SNCC, there was one common ingredient: they were almost all products of historically Black colleges. Given this obvious reality, it seems odd that there were no panel discussions at the conference that identified the environment that produced the original veterans of the movement, save one session that focused on the role of Shaw University as the host of the initial meeting of SNCC. Black colleges produced a wave of foot soldiers unlike anything the burgeoning movement had ever seen. The explosion of student activism in 1960 was no accident or anomaly. It was indeed a development long in the making.

To date, there have been few book-length studies that provide an intimate and detailed view of the long movement at historically Black colleges and universities (HBCUs).[2] It took more than mere fate or a string of isolated local protests to generate the energy to move thousands of students into action across the South. The shared space that housed SNCC students had previously and successfully produced generations of activists and was essential in advancing the freedom dreams of countless Black Americans. Indeed, Black colleges form a vital crossroads in the broader struggle for liberation. We can begin to understand their importance by looking to the founding of one college whose role in the nascent stage of the long movement for Black liberation proved critical to its success.

· · · · · ·

Nestled at the confluence of the Potomac and Shenandoah Rivers lies Harpers Ferry, a town permanently etched in the narrative of American history. On October 16, 1859, the militant abolitionist John Brown famously led a biracial coalition of eighteen men determined to bring a bloody end to the peculiar institution of slavery. An advancing force of the U.S. Marines soon cut Brown's men to shreds. Only a handful escaped capture. Brown's plans were foiled, but he became a hero in the social imagination of African Americans.[3]

Storer College was founded in Harpers Ferry in 1867, a fitting memorial to Brown's raid. This newly constructed educational enclave attracted scores of freemen who sought training and, above all, hope. Slavery had fallen, but white repression and violence were on the rise. Blacks confronted the ever-pressing question of "What now?" Churches, lodges, and schoolhouses where African Americans frequently met to seek resolutions for this dilemma were habitually attacked and set aflame. Ministers and community activists who dared to be outspoken on the issue of race relations were often violently eliminated. With terrorism against Blacks rapidly increasing and with virtually no protection from local or federal authorities, Storer offered a vital sanctuary for African Americans looking for a new beginning.

In the decades after the founding of both Storer and the modern civil rights movement, Black colleges provided the only noncollapsible space for African Americans. The founders of Black colleges employed no special strategy to escape the terrorism afflicting other Black spaces.[4] The white power structure simply saw Black education, if administered properly, as a formidable control mechanism that would pacify Black youths. William H. Watkins suggests that "Black education invited Blacks to participate in, without disrupting, the social order. . . . It taught conformity, obedience, sobriety, piety, and the values of enterprise."[5] With Black colleges assuming a nonthreatening posture and the notion of *higher* education evoking momentary civility from aggressive whites, it appeared that no community, southern or otherwise, found reason to annihilate Black college campuses or lynch faculty and administrators who seemingly kept Black youths in step with the white supremacists' agenda.

Institutions like Storer College would use this precious gift of space to their advantage. John Robert Clifford came to Storer as a veteran of the Civil War. After his graduation in 1875, Clifford became deeply engaged with the struggle for Black liberation. He accepted his calling as an educator, like so many of his fellow classmates, and later became the principal of the Sumner School in Martinsburg, West Virginia. In 1882, Clifford founded the *Pioneer Press*, the state's only African American newspaper, and utilized its pages to champion the cause of justice for Blacks. He became the lead plaintiff in a case argued before the West Virginia Supreme Court in 1898 when he pressed for equality in the field of education, a harbinger of things to come. Yet his and Storer's relationship to the broader struggle of African

Americans was never clearer than in the chain of events Clifford set in motion in 1906.

The year before, in July 1905, W. E. B. DuBois had convened a meeting of twenty-nine radicals seeking justice and equality for African Americans. They called themselves the Niagara Movement in recognition of their first gathering place in Fort Erie, Ontario, on the banks of the Niagara River.[6] But before they could meet again and create plans for action, they needed a foothold on American soil, and DuBois sought out an appropriate setting that could provide asylum for his militant group. Clifford, who was affiliated with the Niagara Movement, quickly steered them to Storer. Its most salient virtue was as a safe haven for movement participants to debate freely and argue passionately about the future of the race. There were few environments where such undertakings could be carried out in the United States without reprisal. Thus, on August 15, 1906, Storer College hosted the first meeting on American soil of what would eventually become the National Association for the Advancement of Colored People (NAACP).[7] It was not the first or last time Black colleges would utilize their space in pursuit of the freedom dreams of African Americans.

Contrary to Watkins's ideas about Black education, Clifford was anything but a conformist: he dedicated his life to disrupting the social order on behalf of African Americans. So did scores of other Black college graduates seeking their place in a hostile society. While many of their life stories and accomplishments have been well documented by historians, the spaces that shaped their lives and gave many of them direction have largely gone unexamined.[8] At best, much of the research has yielded incomplete studies that fail to weave together the vital contributions that Black colleges have made to the long movement for civil and human rights. Too few of them have successfully linked the historic insurgency of the 1960s with previous generations that emerged from Black colleges that also engaged in dissent. The same spirit of defiance that guided the actions of Clifford at Storer is evident in the training that Ella Baker received as a student at Shaw University, and in the vision of a beloved community that dawned on Martin Luther King Jr. at Morehouse College. The dominant interpretations of these spaces have tended to depict Black colleges as bastions of conservatism, constructed either through white philanthropic efforts or by the order of white politicians.[9] Many of these studies have confined their analysis to contrasting vocational training with the liberal arts, usually paralleling these models with the figures of Booker T. Washington and DuBois. Yet, legendary though these figures may be, this only tells a partial story of what was taught at these institutions.

Beyond the written course of study, at Black colleges, an unwritten *second curriculum* thrived. This second curriculum defined the bond between teacher and student, inspiring youths to develop a "linked sense of fate" with the race.[10] This second curriculum was a pedagogy of hope grounded in idealism, race consciousness, and cultural nationalism. More importantly, within the noncollapsible space of Black colleges, this instruction and mentoring was beyond the reach of outsiders. Emerging from the teacher-student relationship, the second curriculum was shielded from the hostilities of whites who, despite their best efforts, remained unaware of how fruitful this association would eventually become.

While the bond shared between teachers and students was critical in the development of the second curriculum, it was not the only way or means in which it was delivered. The space where freedom dreams were shared was just as important. Peers emboldened each other as they swapped stories of Black liberation, challenged each other in the classroom, and bantered back and forth in the privacy of their dormitories. Students were exposed to a virtual who's who of the Black literati who traveled the Black college lecture circuit and espoused messages of idealism and race consciousness. Black colleges sporadically offered classes on African American history and became some of the foremost champions and promoters of Carter G. Woodson's Negro History Week. As their confidence and self-esteem grew, so too did their ability to muster critiques against white supremacy.

Within their fortified interstitial spaces, African American students established what cultural anthropologist Victor Turner has termed "communitas."[11] Turner used the term to describe the sense of unity found in religious pilgrimage. Though other critics have deepened and criticized aspects of this idea, this book seeks to recast Turner's term. Here, communitas offers a conceptual framework to describe the vital space that Black colleges provided, offering shelter from the worst elements of a white supremacist society that sought to undermine, overlook, and render impotent the intellectual capacity of Black youths. Turner argues that the Latin term *communitas* implies the practice of building "social relationship" as opposed to "an area of common living." Furthermore, Turner's theories on communitas highlight "symbolic rites of passage" that are transferred within the "open society," a development that Turner argues could not take place within the "closed society." Numerous students and faculty saw it as their duty to inculcate the second curriculum in their peers, students, or colleagues who resided within the same space. As the tradition and ritual of embracing their social responsibilities emerged, it did so within a racialized space that was intentional in its technique and deliberate in its methodology. Black colleges would be unequivocally linked to the freedom of African Americans and carry out this mission for several generations. The college itself was but a space of brick and mortar where various disciplines and academic lessons were passed along to youths in preparation for their transition into the workforce. However, the communitas embodied by Black colleges was much more. Black students and faculty did not simply replicate the routine carried out at white institutions. The relationships that were built and the lessons learned through a second curriculum buoyed the hopes and dreams of the entire race. Much more would be expected of the products of this space. While it is certain that numerous shoulders proved unwilling to carry this burden, the larger narrative of HBCUs relays the story of those who welcomed the challenge of creating a blueprint for Black liberation—a vision and a charge that was crafted and fortified within the walls of Black institutions.

· · · · · ·

At times, the growth and vitality of Black colleges waned, like most aspects of Black life that were dependent on white benefactors, public funds, or federal support. Yet as HBCUs struggled on and a deliberate space dedicated to building relationships and a mission for uplift was formed, most white Americans considered them benign and nonthreatening to the white supremacist social order. In this regard, HBCUs were unique. While other African American spaces, institutions, and organizations were vigorously interrogated and subjected to racial violence, the communitas of Black colleges provided a covering for anyone who sought to radicalize youths within their midst. This produced various forms of dissent and activism as generations of students passed through the Black college communitas and departed to seek ways to improve the conditions and collective experiences of the race. The racialized space that enveloped them sharpened their critiques of white supremacy and provided them with the training and tools to reintegrate themselves into the larger society as agents of social and political change. Regarding the education and mission he received as a student at Atlanta University, the future NAACP leader James Weldon Johnson recalls, "This knowledge was no part of classroom instruction—the college course at Atlanta University was practically the old academic course at Yale; it was simply in the spirit of the institution; the atmosphere of the place was charged with it. Students talked 'race.' It was the subject of essays, orations and debates. Nearly all that was acquired, mental, and moral, was destined to be fitted into a particular system of which 'race' was the center."[12] A race-centered mission became the core of the second curriculum and an essential component of the communitas, as it existed at HBCUs. Alumni carried it with them as they entered the world as teachers, ministers, doctors, civil servants, military servicemen, lawyers, professors, and typical, everyday citizens. Commenting on the transformative power of those who are products of shared experiences, Turner notes, "Communitas, or the 'open society,' differs in this from structure, or the 'closed society,' in that it is potentially or ideally extensible to the limits of humanity."[13] While Black colleges were particularly paternalistic and notoriously closed on issues related to socializing and fraternizing among coeds for most of the twentieth century, the proliferation of the second curriculum flourished relatively unencumbered, thus directing the goals and initiatives of untold students.

Thus the second curriculum formed the heartbeat of the Black college communitas. Unlike other scholars, who reference the implementation of race consciousness and holistic education as a "hidden curriculum," I contend that under most circumstances there was nothing hidden in the way that Black faculty and students infused race consciousness into the curriculum and extracurricular activities of their day-to-day campus life.[14] In doing so, Black colleges became a significant progenitor of race men and women who tackled Jim Crow and white supremacy by utilizing various strategies that differed based on local or regional political conditions, the national current of Black militant thought, and the energy that flowed throughout their specific communitas. One can therefore conclude that the generations of insurgency that emanated from Black colleges in the nineteenth and twentieth centuries were impacted by the ebb and flow of dissent and radicalism in the same way that most social movements typically are.[15]

The fostering of activism in the communitas of Black colleges was directly linked to the embrace of identity and cultural nationalism encountered by African Americans in both churches and schools. One of America's preeminent theologians, Benjamin E. Mays, recalls of his training at South Carolina State College, "It did my soul good in 1911 to find at State College an all Negro-faculty and a Negro President. They were good teachers, holding degrees from Benedict College, Biddle University (now Johnson C. Smith), Lincoln University in Pennsylvania, Fisk University, and other colleges. . . . The inspiration which I received at State College was and is of incalculable value."[16] As the future dean of religion at Howard University and the president of Morehouse College from 1940 to 1967, Mays poured identity and purpose into countless students, none more notable than Martin Luther King Jr., a 1948 graduate of Morehouse. For Mays and countless other educators, a pedagogy steeped in the second curriculum gave the youths they taught potent tools to articulate the concerns and demands of an oppressed people.

Mays's colleagues in academia also found their place at the vanguard of Black education. Howard Thurman, a former student of Mays, reflected on the obligation impressed on him by Black educators: "I was profoundly affected by the sense of mission the college inculcated in us. . . . We understood that our job was to learn so that we could go back into our communities and teach others. . . . But over and above this, we were always inspired to keep alive our responsibility to the many, many others who had not been fortunate enough to go to college."[17] This is not to discount the existence of elitism and classism among Blacks, which at times was amplified by the respectability awarded by Black colleges. Indeed, the reality of these factors contributed to tension and further stratification within the Black community.[18] However, the complete narrative of educated Blacks who composed a growing middle class in the twentieth century reveals the efforts of politically conscious Black college alumni who entered their communities with the goal to eliminate the destructive effects Jim Crow had on *all* African Americans. Therefore, our interpretations of class conflicts are far more complex than the arguments that many scholars have previously asserted. In his brilliant study on politics and class in Atlanta, historian Maurice J. Hobson documents Mays's creation of a partnership with a local number runners kingpin to ensure that needy students had the money to stay in school, as well as the efforts of students from Spelman College to align themselves with "the brothers on the streets" during the fallout of the Rodney King verdict in 1992. Both Morehouse and Spelman represent the pinnacle of the Black academic experience in America, yet these crucial institutions were never so removed from the masses that they could not retain a critical nexus or stand in solidarity with the brothers and sisters on the block.[19]

Class divisions were even more permeable at HBCUs that mostly enrolled students from the poor and working-class communities that often surrounded them. Although tension, schisms, and even fisticuffs occurred between the Black masses and the so-called talented tenth, those ruptures were never so deep or permanent as to create perpetual discord. Former North Carolina A&T student Clarence Fisher recalled a critical moment when those local and superficial tensions gave way in order to unite around a common foe. "In the 1960s when I was at A&T we fought with the "block boys" (local non-students) but when the riots broke they were on campus breathing tear gas and throwing rocks with us at the National Guard." For students like Fisher, class fissures between local folks and students like him were virtually nonexistent—particularly in the heat of battle against the forces of white supremacy. Such was the case for many first generation students who attended state supported institutions that recruited heavily from mill and farming towns in the Deep South. "We were all poor and trying to get somewhere" remembered Fisher.[20]

These vital inroads created to and from the Black community were important passageways that civil rights workers from Black colleges would later use to move seamlessly through the neighborhoods of the Deep South in an effort to solicit support for the movement. Many of these students were products of these environments, and their connections with the communities from which they originated provided them a sense of service and a linked sense of fate with the Black masses. One can only imagine how quickly their operations would have been terminated if Black college students representing SNCC had wandered into impoverished communities such as Lowndes County, Alabama, or Sunflower County, Mississippi, with an air of elitism and aloofness to the plight of the local folk. They were all too familiar with the radiance of their smiles, the aroma of the local cuisine, and the tales of suffering under racial violence and Jim Crow that had marginalized Black life across class lines. *Their* struggles were the same.

Black youths were saddled with weighty expectations as they moved from the sheltered communitas into the unrelenting intimidation, violence, and repression of Jim Crow. Some of the elders of the Black community expressed disappointment at the failure of a long awaited insurgency to emerge from the enclave of southern Black colleges. Kelly Miller, the venerable dean of Howard University's College of Liberal Arts and New Negro activist, declared in 1923, "Our intelligentsia does not effectually grasp the actualities of racial life and uplift as the founders of our colleges hoped they would do. How to reinvigorate our collegians with the sense of racial responsibility and the quickening power of racial motive is the great task that devolves upon us."[21] Much of Miller's response was undoubtedly shaped by both the surge of Black militancy emanating from urban centers such as Harlem, Baltimore, Chicago, and Atlanta and the bitter realities confronting Blacks in 1923. Despite the intensification of radicalism and protests in cities that provided buffer zones against the worst of Jim Crow, the majority of Black Americans grappled with severe bouts of violence and terrorism and a rising tide of race hatred that was enshrined by both de facto and de jure policies.[22]

It would take close to forty more years for massive direct action to gather sufficient strength to emerge from Black colleges, and so the broadsides against the quiescent Black youths would continue unabated. Visiting Alabama in 1934 as a correspondent for the *Crisis* and documenting the fallout from the Scottsboro Boys trial, Langston Hughes composed one of the most stinging of these condemnations. In an article entitled "Cowards from the Colleges," Hughes expresses dismay that no Tuskegee students claimed knowledge of the event, nor had any attended the trial, despite Tuskegee's relatively short distance from Scottsboro. Hughes writes, "American Negroes in the future had best look to the unlettered for their leaders, and expect only cowards from the 'colleges.'"[23] Himself an alumnus of historically Black Lincoln University in Pennsylvania, Hughes shared with other activists high expectations for African American youths.

W. E. B. DuBois launched criticism of his own, albeit for lighter transgressions. "The greatest meetings of the Negro college year like those of the white college year have become vulgar exhibitions of liquor, extravagance, and fur coats," writes the esteemed scholar-activist. "We have in our colleges a growing mass of stupidity and indifference."[24] DuBois's denunciation reflected both a prudish nature and the impossibility of the situation Blacks faced. Race leaders expected teenagers and young adults to emerge as political dissidents and potential martyrs, a herculean task for which even the majority of Black southern adults were not prepared. As historian Steven Hahn has pointed out, overt protests and more militant expressions were easier to achieve for those who "had already fled the South," or for those who were already "a safe distance from the worst of it."[25] The most outspoken critics often hailed from the relatively safe confines of urban centers, away from the more far-flung, often southern communities where Black youths were growing up and going to school.

In the Deep South, open activism was unthinkable for most students in the first half of the twentieth century. Recalling this hostile environment, Mays writes, "It was difficult, virtually impossible, to combine manhood and Blackness under one skin in the days of my youth. To exercise manhood, as white men displayed it, was to invite disaster."[26] The communities that surrounded Black colleges were often fearsome. Richard Wright depicts the challenge of mounting open rebellion against such a closed society: "If I fought openly I would die and I did not want to die. News of lynchings were frequent. . . . My days and nights were one long, quiet, continuously contained dream of terror, tension, and anxiety. I wondered how long I could bear it."[27] Wright would soon escape his Mississippi home and head north to Chicago, but it would take several more decades for African Americans in the Deep South to marshal their political strength and to chip away at the white power structure.

Black colleges' role in advancing the movement in the first half of the twentieth century was muted, drawing from the legacy of hidden education that African Americans mastered during slavery.[28] Yet though these institutions may not have made the significant splash that early twentieth-century race leaders expected, the second curriculum was spreading race consciousness among Black youths. In the decades that led up to the more turbulent 1960s, frustration grew, and HBCUs began to bear radical fruit. Commenting on the radicalism that slowly unfolded during the New Deal era, historian James Gregory notes, "The Negro colleges would become staging grounds for all sorts of projects that would transform the South over the coming decades. . . . Some of the political boldness that showed up in Black southern communities in the 1940s and the civil rights era would also emanate from those same institutions."[29]

The politicization of students, a rise in militancy against white supremacy and imperialism, and gradual political transformations on the home front were significant steps in priming the struggle for liberation. On February 1, 1960, the struggle emerged into the open as students from North Carolina A&T State University launched a wave of sit-ins from a Greensboro lunch counter, catalyzed the modern civil rights movement, and forever altered the political destiny of the United States.

· · · · · ·

Black colleges were complex institutions facing prodigious political and economic challenges. Yet from one generation to the next, HBCUs served as the most important space for sheltering budding activists, inculcating a second curriculum of racial consciousness, and providing the communitas necessary to generate the sense of solidarity and connections sufficient to launch a full frontal assault on white supremacy. To tell this multigenerational story, the narrative of *Shelter in a Time of Storm* spans the founding of the very first HBCU, the apex of the Black Power movement on campus, and beyond. Examining the inner workings of Black college life, the political leanings and philosophies of HBCU administrators and faculty, and the role these institutions' communitas played in advancing the freedom dreams of all African Americans, in this book I seek to capture the development from graduates' careful activism in the mid- to late 1800s to overt and enthusiastic protest in the second half of the twentieth century.

The following chapters chronicle the communitas of seven Black colleges at specific moments in their history. These institutions represent a diverse cross section of Black colleges: northern and southern, private and public, conservative and liberal. At the time of this writing, there are 105 institutions that are designated as HBCUs. Numerous other schools have since closed, mostly due to financial hardship. It is virtually impossible to compose a study that highlights the social and political significance of all these colleges and their roles as seedbeds for activism. Analysis of the long movement at schools such as Howard University, Virginia Union University, South Carolina State University, Florida A&M University, and countless others would greatly add to our understanding of activism at Black colleges, and they all present compelling narratives that other scholars will hopefully one day examine. The institutions, taken together, offer dynamic illustrations of the significant role these colleges played in formulating collective and individual responses from faculty, students, and alumni to the historical crossroads confronting African American life.

The story begins with the oldest Black college, Cheyney State University, following its growth through the end of Reconstruction. Founded in 1837 as the Institute for Colored Youth (ICY), Cheyney faced arduous challenges exacerbated by the forces of white supremacy in Philadelphia. Nevertheless, the ICY produced a host of young students who proved to be exemplars of Black college communitas and the second curriculum that thrived within. The school was targeted as a threat to the white establishment and social order, accused of sheltering militants who sought to do away with slavery, and fettered with financial constraints. Yet Cheyney survived, and armed with a pedagogical vision of social, political, and economic liberation, its faculty took in the masses. The story of the ICY demonstrates the fact that the second curriculum was at work long before missionaries headed south to begin the effort to educate former slaves.

Turning south, the second chapter looks to Tougaloo College from its founding in 1869 through the Nadir of race relations. Though most accounts of Mississippi's only safe haven focus on the turbulent 1960s, this longer view demonstrates that this private institution had a long history of serving as a shelter in a time of storm. Located on the grounds of an old slave plantation, Tougaloo managed to exorcise the ghosts of the peculiar institution and provide a much-needed space for Black youths who faced severe repression during America's lowest point. This chapter illustrates how Tougaloo, as an institution exposed to unprecedented levels of race hatred and white terrorism, struggled against a color line that was strictly and violently enforced. School administrators navigated this tightrope, maintaining a space that nurtured a sprouting culture of tolerance and race consciousness. In time, this would become an oasis supporting countless soldiers of SNCC's campaign to exterminate white supremacy in the Magnolia State.

Chapter 3 examines the history of Bennett College from the turn of the century through the end of World War II. Although Bennett did not become an all-female school until 1926, its transformation in the midst of an outgrowth of Black radicalism exposed female students to increased levels of race consciousness that they used to launch an attack against Jim Crow policies in Greensboro. The protest objectives that sprang from Bennett in the 1930s would have been unthinkable in Mississippi's harsh political climate, suggesting that the relatively more moderate culture of North Carolina facilitated more militant expressions. Also aiding Bennett's role as a seedbed for activism was the presence of administrators who were open and supportive of student demonstrations against Jim Crow policies. The intersection of gender and class at Bennett foreshadows how both components would play out in later movement-related events and organizations.

The dawning of the 1960s was essential to the growth and development of radicalism among Black college youths, and to encompass the varied responses to the color line in the Deep South during this time span, the narrative branches in three directions. The fourth chapter provides an intimate and detailed analysis of Alabama State University. Crucial to the long movement was the long presidency of Harper Councill Trenholm, who, over the course of thirty-six years, constructed a dynamic communitas, embraced radical faculty members, and trained students who went on to become some of the most important figures in the burgeoning civil rights movement. Trenholm's story illustrates the complexity of Black college leadership in an environment teeming with idealism and race consciousness within while confronting hostility from southern whites without. As Black colleges emerged as one of the principle catalysts for the assault against segregation, leaders such as Trenholm were confronted with an extraordinary moral dilemma: allow the freedom dreams of Blacks to manifest through the overt protests of students, or yield to forces that controlled the purse strings. The dominant narrative has most often portrayed Black college presidents as traitors to the struggle for Black liberation who gave in to financial pressure. A longer view complicates that assessment, particularly given the presidents' long-standing contributions to the communitas that produced widespread insurgency among Black students. By these benchmarks, Trenholm proved to be one of the most important facilitators of campus dissent in the long history of Black colleges.

Chapter 5 returns to Mississippi and documents the unfolding movement at Jackson State University. Even amid the preeminent closed society, a communitas developed on campus that encouraged and supported the flowering of radicalism—to an extent. Jacob L. Reddix is a perfect example of a president who embraced radical expressions on campus in the years leading up to overt direct-action protests. However, at the critical juncture between rhetoric and action, Reddix turned on a dime and yielded to the demands of state politicians in grand fashion. His duplicity provided fodder for the writings of famed poet Margaret Walker Alexander, who taught English at Jackson State for over thirty years. Her unpublished and hitherto undocumented memoirs provide a fascinating view of the struggle confronting faculty members. Nevertheless, Walker and a handful of her colleagues braved the raging tempest of life in Mississippi to find their voice and make meaningful contributions to the student protests that emerged in Jackson.

Chapter 6 illustrates the history of an extremely active communitas found at Southern University. Located in Baton Rouge, Louisiana, where local Black leadership was known for moderation, capitulation, and incremental negotiations with the white establishment, the students of Southern nevertheless developed a movement that grew to become the largest of its kind—and then dissolved fairly quickly. The outgrowth of militancy at Southern was years in the making and illustrates a long history of radical expression supported by the campus community. However, much like Jackson State, Southern was under the control of a college president who quickly obeyed the white legislature when student activism intensified at the dawn of the 1960s. Cracking down on students, President Felton Grandison Clark fell in line with the stereotypical depiction of the intolerant, insensitive Black college president. Nevertheless, the story of Southern University's developing communitas and the flowering of activism on campus from the interwar era up to the unveiling of Black Power provides a detailed view of both the promise and the limitations of Black colleges as nerve centers of the movement.

The final chapter moves forward in time to outline the rise of the Black Power movement in one of the most involved and active environments for student insurgency, North Carolina A&T. The epicenter of the student movement of the 1960s, A&T was the birthplace of the sit-ins that launched the direct-action phase of the struggle for civil and human rights. Not only did students there trigger a domino effect with the sit-ins that swept across the South, but toward the middle of the decade they also spearheaded the mass jail-ins that became a protest method employed by other southern activists, and in the latter half of the decade they transformed Greensboro, North Carolina, into the primary headquarters for the Black Power movement below the Mason-Dixon Line. Telling the story of the latter part of this transformation, this chapter details how A&T's centrality to the movement made it a magnet for grassroots support for Black Power initiatives with national implications. The reputation and track record of A&T directly led to the founding of the Student Organization for Black Unity, the relocation of Malcolm X Liberation University from Durham to Greensboro, and the establishment of the Greensboro Association of Poor People—one of the most effective local organizations championing Black Power ideologies and advancing the concerns of marginalized people in the city and throughout the nation. This chapter discusses how the communitas at A&T paved the way for these important transformations and how its development in the Black Power era mirrored changes that were taking place at other Black colleges.

As Black Power activism shifted away from campuses, HBCUs continued to be important staging grounds for race consciousness and idealism and enjoyed a renaissance aided by popular culture in the 1980s and 1990s. Yet the curriculum and culture were shifting, and the voices of dissent that once emanated from Black colleges throughout the twentieth century grew relatively quiet. The social sciences departments that had served as storehouses for activist energies that pushed students to think critically and act locally against white supremacy receded in importance. Increasingly dominant were the science, technology, engineering, and mathematics fields essential for drawing much-needed research funds into schools that had been chronically underfunded for decades. This book's final pages explore the prospects of student insurgency arising from Black colleges in light of this transformation. As students shun academic fields that challenge them to reckon with the continued marginalization of the Black masses, the reservoir of Black radical thought grows shallower. Worsening matters is the "brain drain" of young, talented, and politically radicalized faculty who were drawn to new employment opportunities at white institutions. Without the fresh voices of intellectually gifted and militant faculty rubbing shoulders with students within the HBCU communitas, Black youth dissidence is less and less likely to achieve a critical mass.

Ultimately, *Shelter in a Time of Storm* zeroes in on life on Black college campuses to understand the long movement that produced generations of insurgency. To accomplish this, the book draws inspiration from Kidada E. Williams's brilliant study on violence from Reconstruction to the New Negro era, and its methods for interpreting and measuring protests, particularly in closed societies. Williams looks to discursive resistance, "vernacular history," and "speech acts" to see activism and resistance in the power of prose.[30] With this framework in mind, this book's most important sources for documenting rising militancy and radicalism on campus are the students' newspapers, which have received scant attention by movement scholars. As essential platforms articulating students' freedom dreams, these papers capture the communitas in action as numerous scholars and activists visited campus and challenged youths to deeply examine their commitments to the race. Within the pages produced by the student press, Black youths worked out their angst; rallied their peers to various social, political, and economic causes; and demanded democracy and full citizenship.

Their written words have seldom been regarded as a form of activism, but in a society that habitually and severely punished overt and demonstrative forms of protest, written communication was a key index of rising radicalism and dissent. In addition to student newspapers, this book draws from oral histories, particularly in the later chapters, and supplements its findings wherever possible with the private diaries and personal papers of administrators, faculty, and activists who were on the front lines of the struggle.

Shelter in a Time of Storm certainly does not suggest that *all* students at Black colleges were trained as militants and immediately placed their hands on the freedom plow. Nor does it advance the idea that *all* Black college faculty and administrators were willing partners in radicalizing Black youths. Indeed, a significant portion of the history surrounding HBCUs during the turbulent 1960s involves the numerous students who were expelled from Black colleges. In most cases, these expulsions were carried out in an effort to preserve the longevity of institutions whose fates were often in the hands of conservative white legislatures or racist white benefactors. Nevertheless, these sporadic crackdowns on campus rebellion were noteworthy developments that provide another level of complexity in understanding Black colleges as seedbeds for activism. Yet this book also emphasizes the immutable fact that Black colleges were an essential, and noncollapsible, space that oriented and trained Black youths to serve as agents for justice.

Black colleges were a crucial waypoint for the freedom struggle, as the institutions that produced teachers and ministers who emphasized self-determination, racial responsibility, and service; exposed countless youths to idealism, race consciousness, and cultural nationalism; and provided a space where students could engage with their own peers, administrators, or faculty who challenged them to embrace the vision of opportunity and democracy for all.

1 A Seedbed of Activism

Holistic Education and the Institute for Colored Youth, 1837–1877

· ·

And the Lord answered me, and said, Write the vision, and make it plain upon tables, that he may run that readeth it.

—Habakkuk 2:2

Octavius Catto was only thirty-two when he was murdered in the streets of Philadelphia. The students from the Institute for Colored Youth (ICY) called him Professor, a title warmly bestowed on many Black educators by community members as a show of respect, regardless of academic rank.[1] Indeed, Catto was well beloved throughout the Black community of Philadelphia, and at the time of his murder, he was on the cusp of becoming one of the most recognized activists for the freedom of African Americans throughout the country. Something of a renaissance man, he was the most popular instructor at the ICY, a political organizer, a soldier of the Pennsylvania National Guard, and captain and standout second baseman for the all-Black Pythian Baseball Club in Philadelphia. But the legend of Octavius Catto was grounded in his role as one of Philadelphia's most assertive Black militants. He was greatly admired and respected by the city's growing Black community, and his popularity as an activist and outspoken leader of the race was increasing up and down the East Coast. In one observer's words, he was "the rising Catto."[2]

October 10, 1871, was Election Day in Philadelphia. Much to the chagrin of white democrats, African Americans were making use of newly secured Fifteenth Amendment rights, of which Catto had been one of the most prominent champions. The streets of Philadelphia had long been marred by ethnic conflicts and racial antipathy, both before and after the Civil War. Historian Roger Lane describes the City of Brotherly Love as "marked by a kaleidoscopic series of clashes in which Irish immigrants 'hunted the nigs' in their little enclaves, nativist bigots attacked Catholic churches, and displaced workingmen resisted the new industrial technology."[3] The elections

The murder of Octavius Catto in 1871 was a major event in the early civil rights movement and was a significant blow to the ICY. Catto was targeted by assassins for being an outspoken proponent of the Fourteenth and Fifteenth Amendments. "Scene of the Shooting of Octavious V. Catto, on October 10, 1871," from the pamphlet entitled *The Trial of Frank Kelly, for the Assassination and Murder of Octavius V. Catto, on October 10, 1871* (ca. 1871). Courtesy of the Historical Society of Pennsylvania (call # Wk* .799 v. 1).

that year marked the first opportunity for Blacks to exercise their political voices, and they faced unprecedented backlash as a result. As the sun rose, a cacophony of violence transformed Philadelphia's streets into a war zone. Black citizens sought shelter from frenzied whites who assaulted would-be Black voters, block by block, ward by ward, in an effort to intimidate them and reduce any semblance of Black political power.

Late that afternoon, Catto had a chance encounter with a young Irish hooligan named Frank Kelly. Recognizing Catto as he passed him on a crowded Philadelphia street, Kelly spun around and squeezed off three shots, one fatally piercing the young professor's heart. Catto landed in the arms of a police officer who witnessed the murder as it unfolded. Nevertheless, Kelly was declared innocent of all crimes six years later in a highly publicized trial, despite numerous witnesses. One of those eyewitnesses was also shot by Kelly and, in the words of a local paper, "had no doubts of the identity of Kelly, who wore on his hat the badge of a deputy sheriff."[4]

After being apprehended by city police, Kelly was quickly escorted from town by local law enforcement. He found refuge in Cincinnati, where he went to work for the Democratic city bosses.[5] Upon his capture and return to Philadelphia in 1877, a local newspaper, the *Philadelphia Press*, characterized the culture of the city that produced such events by concluding that the die was cast "when the police force appointed by Mayor Fox suffered desperadoes of the Kelly stamp to override law, to escape arrest, and to permit the criminal classes to hold high carnival."[6]

This miscarriage of justice was a harbinger of things to come. One Black observer of the court proceedings noted, "The acquittal of Frank Kelly, in Philadelphia, on a charge of murder, which was clearly proven, shows that no white man can be convicted in that city of murdering a colored man, no matter how clear the proof may be."[7] Without the ability to lean on the rights guaranteed to all American citizens, which were supposedly protected by the country's most cherished institutions, African Americans would have to construct their own enclaves and refuges to regroup and launch new campaigns to demand justice.

Tributes to Catto poured in from across the country. Mourners at his funeral reflected the diverse cross section of people whose lives the fallen activist had touched. Catto's biographers Daniel R. Biddle and Murray Dubin write, "Crying students from the Institute for Colored Youth were part of the procession, as were Pythians, military officers, members of the City Council and the state legislature, literary-society friends, one infantry brigade, three regiments, eight other military detachments, and 125 horse-drawn carriages."[8] Drawing more than five thousand people, Catto's funeral had an attendance that was on par with that for President Abraham Lincoln's funeral procession, which had come through the city just six years earlier. The solemn service memorializing the slain leader was, as W. E. B. DuBois writes, "perhaps the most imposing ever given to an American Negro."[9] Local schools, city government, and many city businesses shut down for the day in an attempt to properly honor a man who, despite his young age, had established himself as a titan in the early movement for Black liberation and civil rights. His friends and contemporaries eulogized him, both in Philadelphia and across the country. But few had any inkling of how quickly the dialogue on Black citizenship and the enfranchisement of Blacks' freedom rights would deteriorate.

Black institutions would be essential to protecting communities from assault and generating space for organizing, education, and the creation of counternarratives. Drawing from antebellum traditions of resistance, communities would rely on vital Black institutions such as churches, lodges, and, most importantly, schools.

· · · · · ·

Institution building was an enterprise of the utmost necessity for Blacks in antebellum America, and Philadelphia was teeming with various enclaves. Northern Blacks utilized what little space was afforded to them to create mutual aid societies, churches, fraternal organizations, civil rights organizations, literary societies, and schools. The Black enclaves of Philadelphia opened themselves to escaped slaves looking to reunite with loved ones or those seeking rest and shelter before continuing their push farther northward. Mutual aid societies doled out resources to the poor and marginalized Black citizens of the city while Masonic and fraternal groups sharpened the leadership of the Black community by providing rites of passage and rituals that emboldened members, who were presented with forums for spirited debate on the future of the race. The formation of these Black institutions laid the groundwork for Black independence and ensured the cultivation of resistance and activism.

One of the more unique and significant channels for the articulation of Black personhood was found in the numerous literary societies spreading throughout the North. Through the collective efforts of these organizations, literacy was directly connected to both the cause of emancipation and the recognition of freedom rights. Scholar Elizabeth McHenry notes, "Their organized literary activities were a means of educating individuals who would be prepared to perform as and would consider themselves capable, respected citizens."[10] Perhaps the most significant of the Philadelphia literary societies was the Banneker Literary Institute, founded in 1854. While the membership of this organization was a literal who's who of Black men in Philadelphia, there were also a number of students from the ICY who were in attendance. Members were drilled in various topics, and a rotating lecture circuit existed in the organization. Topics of discussion included metaphysics, logic, mathematics, natural history, and of course the present condition and future of African Americans. On March 10, 1858, William Henry Johnson, a veteran supporter of the Underground Railroad and Banneker Literary Institute member, stood before the brotherhood and delivered a stirring lecture titled "The Right of Suffrage." The minutes of the meeting state that Johnson "lectured last evening before the Banneker

Literary Institute, Walnut Street, above Sixth, on the principles of suffrage in the application to the African race. His address was eloquent and argumentative, and was frequently interrupted by prolonged and cordial applause."[11]

More than any other initiative, the pursuit of education represented the pregnant potential of both the present and the immediate future. Both adults and children filed into makeshift schoolrooms to do more than simply gain skills that would help them integrate into American society. Theirs was a search for voice, identity, and justice. In one of his many tours through Pennsylvania, nationally known activist and race leader Martin Delany expressed his belief in the necessity of Black education and what it could become. Delany reported to Frederick Douglass his findings on the topic of education as a traveling correspondent for the abolitionist newspaper the *North Star*, writing that in meetings he held with local Blacks, he was "endeavoring to awaken an interest among our brethren in their own welfare, by showing them the necessity of acting and doing for themselves—that we must, in fact, become our own representatives in presenting our own claims, and making known our own wrongs."[12] Black activists like Delany understood that whatever slice of heaven on earth was obtainable for Blacks would be secured by those men and women who were equipped with the literary and rhetorical skills to articulate their call for justice. Thus, the distinction between the mission of the Black church and that of Black schools was quite clear.[13]

Yet African Americans were aware that they would not easily be admitted into the emerging American middle class. Blacks who suffered under the great weight of slavery and the entrenchment of racism in the North knew through their blood-stained experiences that America had no intention of freely parting the seas of democracy or opening the lucrative coffers of capitalism. Whether they were the children of slaves or the offspring of members of the Black aristocracy, Black youths had no inroads to American citizenship, a reality that was reinforced by the proliferation of white supremacy. Consequently, powered by the tools of literacy, they called for the recognition of both their civil and human rights and started a battle that would be waged through the construction of schools and the training of youths to serve as foot soldiers for a growing movement.

This crusade was of the highest priority for men such as Abraham Shadd. A veteran conductor on the Underground Railroad and one of the most respected activists in America, Shadd became one of the principal organizers of the country's first national gathering of African Americans, held in

Philadelphia in 1830. At the third national convention, held on June 13, 1833, Shadd served as the keynote speaker and addressed the crowd on the topic of creating schools, declaring, "The most meritorious institution, in the vindication of the natural, civil, and political rights of the coloured people, ought, and we trust does, occupy a distinguished place in the feelings and affections of our people."[14] Shadd set the tone for the future demands of African Americans, emphasizing the importance of creating Black educational institutions that crafted a holistic vision of liberation and imparted that vision to youths who would serve this cause. The mission of these schools was not simply to prove the self-worth of Black youths, and it certainly was not to beg for their placement in the brotherhood of mankind. It was, rather, to defend the "natural, civil, and political rights" African Americans knew belonged to them as children of God.

With Black activists elevating the demands for justice in the North and feverishly working to weaken the stranglehold of slavery in the South, the 1830s opened as a challenging decade for the burgeoning movement. There was a lot of work to do. The dawn of the Jacksonian Era and the ascendency of the "common man" meant very little to marginalized African Americans. As James Horton and Lois Horton write, "This 'age of the common man' was the age of the common white man, as Black men (and all women) lost their franchise in many states. . . . As race became a more powerful determinant of political participation among common people, it became more difficult for nonwhite Americans to assert their rights."[15] Blacks launched a counterattack grounded in moral suasion, though David Walker initiated a more aggressive tone with his publication of *An Appeal to the Colored Citizens of the World* in 1829, while activists such as Maria W. Stewart, Lydia Maria Child, and William Lloyd Garrison employed their religious convictions to convince America of its sins. "We have been imposed upon, insulted and derided on every side," writes Stewart of the Black race. "These things have fired my soul with a holy indignation, and compelled me thus to come forward, and endeavor to turn their attention to knowledge and improvement; for knowledge is power."[16]

The long road to justice and citizenship would be paved with education. The articulation for and defense of Black rights was a primary function of Black institutions, a fact not lost on white detractors who attacked these establishments. African Americans rallied together to fend off the rising aggression. Clearly the North was no promised land for African Americans. Hollow professions of democracy, which were rising as working-class whites cast their ballots for the first time in the young republic's history, only served to agitate African Americans who were frustrated to the point that many pondered withdrawal to foreign lands. White abolitionist Oliver Johnson recalled one Black youth saying, "What's the use in my attempting to improve myself when, do what I may, I can never be anything but a nigger?"[17] Nevertheless, African Americans remained faithful to the potential of education, their resolve to defend their humanity, and the confidence they held in each other to continue lifting upward in spite of such conditions. To achieve these goals, they began to carve out space from which they could mount the necessary crusade.[18]

In 1837, storm clouds gathered swiftly for African Americans in Pennsylvania. Whatever claims they may have had on the democracy being professed by the young nation were being placed up for debate at a constitutional convention being held in the state's capital of Harrisburg. Pennsylvania was one of only five free states out of twelve that actually gave voting privileges to Black males at the beginning of the decade. New York added property requirements for would-be Black voters.[19] Concerned African Americans observed the convention with great interest, knowing that removal of voting rights would strike a mighty blow to the future of the race. Historian Julie Winch documents how the proposal to disenfranchise Blacks moved quickly from a casual suggestion to a deliberate and swift act. "When the delegates to the Reform Convention assembled in Harrisburg on May 2, 1837, it was not with the intention of regulating the political status of Blacks," writes Winch. "As in other states, a constitutional convention had been called in Pennsylvania to remedy what were seen as abuses in the existing constitution, particularly the restrictions barring poorer whites from the polls. However, the question of Black voting rights was raised almost immediately with a proposal to exclude Blacks from the franchise while lowering the property qualification for whites."[20] To be certain, there was no widespread utilization of the ballot by African Americans anywhere in Pennsylvania. Many did not vote due to their belief that there were more pressing issues for the Black community to focus on, and others were suppressed by various acts of intimidation, which had become a constant reality of Black life in the North. In Philadelphia alone, there were three separate race riots, in 1834, 1838, and 1842. The attempt to crush every hint of Black political power, which had not yet manifested into any real threat, bespoke how effective white supremacy would become in shaping the political, social, and economic landscape of America. By October 9, 1838, the new state constitution was successfully ratified, effectively denying Blacks in Pennsylvania the right to vote for the next thirty-two years.

African Americans were distraught. The reform convention, as Martin Delany conveyed to Frederick Douglass, "despotically wrested from the colored citizen his citizenship, degrading him to the condition of an alien! Thus we are stripped and disarmed of our manhood, and left to the mercy of the most consummate demagogue."[21] As the tent of the new republic was broadening, the definition of citizenship was being rewritten to cut Black citizens out. Yet in the years that followed, work was under way to create a new institution that would lend Black Americans new means of seizing their rights.

Just as the reform convention was coming together to disenfranchise the state's Black population, the manifestation of Richard Humphreys's will was beginning to unfold. Humphreys, a Quaker who was born on the island of Tortola in the British Virgin Islands, left in his will a sum of $10,000 for the founding of a future school dedicated to the "descendants of the African Race."[22] Humphreys, who was born a slave owner, came to Philadelphia as a young boy with his family, who judged the climate in Tortola too harsh for the sustained living of Englishmen. Before he passed in 1832, Humphreys left his mark on the city as a successful goldsmith and craftsman, leaving behind a modest but handsome estate. It is likely that his support for initiatives to aid Blacks in the city was triggered by his boyhood memories of the cruel life of slaves on Tortola and the increased hostilities against Blacks that he undoubtedly witnessed as an artisan in Philadelphia. Additionally, the Society of Friends to which he belonged supported a number of efforts to assist the Black community. Encouraged by that spirit of charity, Humphreys also made a financial provision for the Shelter for Colored Orphans in his will.[23] But it was the money that Humphreys left in his will to be administered by his appointed trustees for the building of a school that would leave an indelible impact on the African race. In the spring of 1837, those wheels were set in motion.

First known as the African Institute, then renamed the Institute for Colored Youth, the school faced difficulties from the very beginning. The thought of providing space dedicated to the education of Black youths rankled local whites, many of whom sought to prevent trustees from securing land to build the institution in the first place. Farmland was at last purchased from Oliver Watson on June 11, 1839, for the purpose of establishing space for the school, and on October 5, 1840, the ICY would hold its first classes.

In its early years, the school's pedagogical philosophy remained unfocused. At the same time as the early teachers taught students about the ins and outs of farm life, they also tried to implement a curriculum that provided basic training in reading, writing, and arithmetic. These fields of study failed to catch on. As Biddle and Dubin note, "Neither teachers nor pupils had their hearts in it."[24] In the early stages of the ICY, the need to put forth a curriculum that resonated with the attendees' marginalized positions in society was an essential component of what both parents and students desired. Students would need to not only learn but learn for a purpose that served the social, political, and economic needs of the race. To achieve this, it was imperative to hire teachers who could transmit and translate a second curriculum that expressed race consciousness and applied daily instruction that was expressly connected to the uplift of the race. Without this pedagogy, the school began to flounder. As historian Roger Lane astutely notes, "The executors discovered predictably that farmers couldn't teach and teachers couldn't farm, and that boys brought out from the city rebelled against all of them."[25] The school closed its doors in 1846 to retool its efforts and reopened in 1852 with a new formula that captured the support of the Black community by finding teachers who spearheaded a new curriculum that brought a fresh motive and a renewed momentum.

Charles Lewis Reason enjoyed problem solving. As one of the foremost Black mathematicians in the country, Reason became the first African American to teach at a white university, receiving an appointment as an adjunct professor of mathematics at New York Central College in 1849. His ascension to that point was aided by the communitas that shaped him in his formative years. Reason, a native of New York City, was educated at the city's African Free School (AFS) and competed academically with childhood friends who included future activists and race leaders Alexander Crummell and Henry Highland Garnet. The school's administrators thought so highly of their young graduate that they hired him to begin teaching at the AFS at the tender age of fourteen. The friends of his youth grew up to become some of the strongest voices in the abolitionist movement, as did Reason. Historians James Horton and Lois Horton note, "Encouraged by their teacher Charles Andrews to believe that they 'had as much capacity to acquire knowledge as any other children,' the students were proud of their accomplishments and outspoken in their beliefs."[26] Those beliefs included suffrage for Black men, emancipation for the race, and access to an education that would empower and uplift the masses. Reason was undoubtedly a *race man*, and like many of his fellow graduates of the AFS, he was proficient and talented in numerous fields. As a poet, Reason penned an ode to the liberation struggle of Black people in 1849 that he aptly entitled "Freedom." The poem's last stanza reads,

We pray to see Thee, face to face: To feel our souls grow strong and
  wide:
So ever shall our injured race, By Thy firm principles abide.[27]

With his unwavering commitment to justice and his love for all things mathematical, the thirty-four-year-old Reason was named the new principal of
the ICY on May 26, 1852, and arrived in Philadelphia ready to tackle the
troubles plaguing the new school.

The board of trustees for the ICY jettisoned the idea of farm life for their
students and looked for a suitable place in the city where they could implement an education grounded in the classics. They settled on a three-story
building located on the corner of Seventh and Lombard Street. It is unclear
whether it was the sole decision of the board of trustees or whether they
yielded to suggestions made by Reason, but the faculty of the ICY was all
Black, a fact that made the ICY stand out from all other schools admitting Black youths in Philadelphia.[28] Sarah Mapps Douglass and her cousin
Grace Mapps joined Reason, who also invited additional visiting lecturers
to supplement certain courses. Douglass and Mapps were members of established abolitionist families in the city and brought their fervor for activism to the classroom. Douglass, who previously was the head of her own
school for girls, was invited to integrate her students into the ICY, thus making the school coeducational in February 1853. As scholar Eric Gardner
contends, the addition of the cousins "helped make the institute into the
flowering center of Philadelphia's free Black community and pushed parents to become more active in their children's education."[29] In spite of the
egalitarian rhetoric often associated with the Quakers, Douglass had her
own run-in with the segregationist policies observed by the religious group,
which strengthened her resolve to oppose bigotry wherever she found it.
Writing to William Basset, an English Quaker, she noted, "There is a bench
set apart for our people, whether officially appointed or not I cannot say,
but my mother and myself were told to sit there and a Friend sat at each
end of the bench to prevent white persons from sitting there. Even when a
child my soul was made sad with hearing five or six times during the course
of one meeting, 'This bench is for Black people.' Oftentimes I wept, at other
times felt indignant."[30] One can imagine how the bitter sting of white supremacy affected the countless Blacks who were mocked by the open
spaces that beckoned to them, only to be openly rejected and routinely
denied by the color line. Douglass channeled this anger and the energy it
generated into her work with youths. As the communitas of the fledgling

school grew, so too did the rise of an activist agenda that was driven by race-conscious faculty who were determined to sharpen their students with a second curriculum.

At the beginning of the 1854 school year, the courses being offered at the ICY ranged from bookkeeping and physiology to natural philosophy and elocution.[31] Charles Reason's arrival had strengthened the profile of the young institution and increased its standing in the Black community, causing more students to enroll. Between 1852 and 1866, the enrollment ballooned from 6 to 181. Indeed, the Black community turned out in droves to applaud and receive the newly crowned alumni of the school; in one instance, three thousand of them packed into a concert hall to watch nine students graduate.[32] The reputation of the ICY was linked to more than its promotion of education to a people starved for the written word. The ICY was becoming increasingly known for nurturing pupils who proved more assertive with the forces of white supremacy. The Black community of Philadelphia was intrigued and emboldened by the faculty of the school, which was quickly becoming the talk of the town. As discriminatory policies continued to bar African Americans from enjoying full citizenship and as many refugees from slavery lived their lives in the shadows while eluding capture in the city, the ICY was a beacon of hope. Its blossoming second curriculum espoused a rhetoric tinged with hope, determination, and defiance. Much of this can be attributed to Headmaster Reason, who was quickly becoming a seasoned activist. Biddle and Dubin write, "He began a tradition for ICY principals: Be subversive, keep one hand in the equal-rights fight at all times."[33]

The faculty of the ICY had at their disposal a roster of sharp, disciplined, and eager youths. Students such as Robert Adger Jr., Mary Ayers, Octavius Catto, Martha Farbeaux, and Jacob White Jr. quickly emerged as some of the institute's most talented stars. White made quite a splash in the city, delivering a lecture entitled "The Inconsistency of Colored People Using Slave Produce" in 1852 when he was just fifteen years old. The purchase and consumption of slave produce such as rice, sugar, and cotton became a target of the abolitionist movement, with Philadelphia becoming ground zero for the boycott initiative. Although historian Benjamin Quarles documents that attempts to place an economic stranglehold on the peculiar institution failed in gaining mass appeal as a tactic, the free produce movement exhibited yet one more form of resistance to the spread of slavery that facilitated the maturation of young activists such as White.[34] The outspoken teenager reproached those who decried the evils of slavery yet continued in their economic support of agrarian products from Southern planters. White declared, "They utter maledictions against the slaveholders, and cry against the system of slavery as an infernal system; they at the same time encourage the slave holder to continue his business."[35]

White's most famous act of defiance came on May 24, 1855, when the governor of Pennsylvania paid a visit to the school with the growing reputation. James Pollock was elected as the thirteenth governor of the commonwealth earlier in the year and was conducting a tour of schools through the state. Assuredly he was taken off guard when White, now eighteen years old and on the cusp of manhood and graduation, rose to greet him on behalf of his peers at the ICY. White eloquently yet forcefully pressed Pollock on the issue of Black citizenship and served notice to the governor that the noble work of the institute was training him and his cohorts "for a future day, when citizenship in our country will be based on manhood and not on color."[36] This product of the second curriculum stood in the gap for his marginalized race and proudly announced the steadfast resolve of Black youths to apply pressure on the powers that be, a tactic that would continue to outline the objectives of the liberation movement for years to come.[37] All the while, the communitas that produced a young man like White seemed satisfied that their work led to a monumental moment such as this. Biddle and Dubin write of the incident, "Reason and the school's other Negro teachers had not lifted a finger to halt the pelting. Had Pollock detected in the principal's broad brow an effort to smother a smile? What sort of school *was* this?"[38]

However effective Reason was in bringing energy and vision to the ICY, it did not stop him from being enticed to pursue professional opportunities back in his home state. He resigned from his post on November 1, 1855, to become the principal of a public school in New York. Before he departed, he recruited Ebenezer Bassett into the fold of the ICY, a move that would pay huge dividends for the freedom struggle. Bassett was born free in the state of Connecticut on October 16, 1833. In that same year, the idea of educating Black folks came under violent attack in his home state. Mobs attacked Prudence Crandall's newly founded school for "coloured females" in Canterbury, Connecticut, creating an overt threat to present and future attempts of Blacks to educate themselves. At the Colored Convention of 1833 held in Philadelphia, the abolitionist Abraham Shadd commented on those future endeavors and continued attempts to build schools and colleges for Blacks by noting, "Notwithstanding the persecution and opposition to the establishment of Miss Prudence Crandall's School . . . it was in a flourishing condition, and only required the encouragement and support of those for whom it was opened, to triumph over the opposition."[39]

The Bassett family was able to navigate the treacherous waters of racism and find education for their son, largely due to young Ebenezer's being the only Black student in his town of Derby, Connecticut, and seemingly a nonthreat. Historian Christopher Teal writes, "Though the community of Derby had been racially tolerant of this family of free Blacks, the Bassetts understood that real barriers existed all across the country because of race, and they knew that only a good work ethic and education would potentially provide an avenue to overcome this prejudice."[40] Thus, Bassett's formative years were punctuated by a sense of race consciousness that was embedded by his family and certainly utilized by Bassett as the only Black student admitted to Connecticut State Normal College, where he graduated in 1855. Bassett sharpened that consciousness as a member of the Convention of Colored Men in Connecticut, where his level of political awareness increased as he came into contact with Black men in his community who fought vigorously for suffrage, abolition, and civil rights. He was more than ready to unleash his swelling sense of activism and advocacy when he received the invitation from Reason to join the faculty of the ICY in 1855.

Bassett was quickly promoted to replace Reason as principal. His graduation from a four-year college and the additional training he received by taking courses at Yale more than qualified him in the eyes of the ICY trustees. Yet however well versed Bassett was in Greek, Latin, and mathematics, his interest in such subjects paled in comparison to his belief that it was the second curriculum that should be increasingly stressed at the institute. A carousel of activists that included Henry Highland Garnet, Frederick Douglass, and Alexander Crummell were soon making their way through the ICY on a constant basis, lecturing students on the emerging civil rights movement and the role they should assume in the struggle. As the communitas became more infused with idealism and race consciousness, students increasingly lifted their voices and dedicated their actions to various social and political causes. Teal notes, "Bassett knew that he was doing more than just teaching young boys and girls the traditional reading, writing, and arithmetic. He was exposing those Black boys and girls to the greatest minds of the day and to the radical idea that they were every bit as good as the white children down the street, but he was also opening their minds to the fact that real wrongs existed in the United States—wrongs that those same children would one day be called upon to correct."[41] ICY alumni soon joined the seedbed of activism that Bassett was cultivating. He brought on

White as faculty in 1856. White, whose championing of the rights of his people in the presence of the governor had occurred just one year before his appointment at the ICY, would remain with his alma mater for eight years, resigning from his position in 1864 to become principal of a Black primary school in Philadelphia. Added to the faculty roster along with White was Octavius Catto, the fourth graduate of the school and valedictorian in 1858, and Martha Farbeaux, the first female graduate of the ICY in 1859.

Not counted among alumni but certainly influential in the establishment of a second curriculum at ICY was Robert Campbell, a Jamaican-born scholar who arrived in 1855 along with Bassett to fill the void left by Charles Reason. Before arriving, Campbell traversed the African diaspora with an upbringing in Jamaica and stints in Nicaragua and Panama.[42] As the free-born son of a mulatto woman and a Scotsman, his ethnic background was just as diverse as his travels. Campbell's feet, however, were firmly planted in the struggle for Black liberation. Undoubtedly moved by the plight of African peoples that he observed in his travels throughout the hemisphere, Campbell felt his Blackness even more when he was subjected to racism as a professor at the ICY. When seeking admittance to a lecture series being offered by the Franklin Institute in Philadelphia, one of the foremost centers of science in the country, Campbell was initially rebuffed due to his race. The institute's attempt to smooth things over by offering Campbell a complimentary ticket resulted in the jilted professor declining the offer on "principle" and writing one of the trustees of the ICY to explain his position. "If the Managers of that institution deem it wrong for respectable men of different complexions to partake of knowledge in common, then let them as scientific men, let them as the assured instructors of the people, fearlessly proclaim it," wrote Campbell. "I could then pity the distortion of their judgment, but would respect their honesty. On the other hand, if they do not, why cater to the weakness and prejudice of the vulgar—why on any pretense evade a direct issue in this matter?"[43] The crash course in white supremacy that Campbell received in Philadelphia motivated him to take up the banner of Black nationalism. In 1858, just three years after he joined the faculty of the ICY, he joined forces with one of the architects of the ideology, Martin Delany, and charted a new course for West Africa.[44] Nevertheless, his impact on the communitas of the ICY proved so great that the students threw him a going-away party. Historian R. J. M. Blackett writes, "The students organized a farewell meeting in his honor, and to express their appreciation for his work, they presented him with a gold watch and chain and a copy of *Cosmos: Sketch of a Physical Description of the Universe*, the five-volume work by Alexander von Humboldt."[45] Campbell boarded a ship that set sail for what is now southwest Nigeria, taking with him the profound appreciation and respect of the students whose freedom dreams he continued to represent.

The convergence of young faculty members like Campbell, forthright in their drive to uplift the race, created a powerful communitas in the small and intimate space that was the ICY. Such a community proved useful as the tensions related to slavery and growing sectional differences threatened to rip the country in two and captured the attention of curious Black youths. Social and political powder kegs abounded throughout the turbulent decade of the 1850s. The turmoil first unfolded with the Compromise of 1850 and its most notorious provision, known as the Fugitive Slave Law, which sent refugees of the peculiar institution scrambling throughout the city and all over the North. In an attempt to acquiesce to the demands of the southern aristocracy, the U.S. government opened the floodgates for slave owners to pursue their "property" or anyone who resembled their "property" with few restrictions. In yet another by-product of the Compromise of 1850, the idea that popular sovereignty could settle the slavery question on the western frontier resulted in white men clashing with other white men in a violent episode that news headlines referred to as Bleeding Kansas. Beginning in 1854, the question raised in Kansas with bullets and bayonets would not be resolved until after the nation itself erupted in war. One of the decade's most controversial events reached the highest court in the land in 1857 with Supreme Court justices ruling in a lopsided seven-to-two decision against Dred Scott. The court concluded not only that Scott, a slave who filed suit on the grounds that extended time spent with his master in Illinois and the Wisconsin territory made him a free man, was the absolute property of his former owner's family but that the suit itself had no legal grounds due to the widely held belief that Blacks were noncitizens, slave or free.

African Americans across the country were outraged. In a gathering at the Israel Church in Philadelphia on April 3, 1857, veteran Black abolitionists Robert Purvis and Charles Remond drafted a resolution that read in part, "The only duty the colored man owes to a Constitution under which he is declared to be an inferior and degraded being, having no rights which white men are bound to respect, is to denounce and repudiate it, and to do what he can by all proper means to bring it into contempt."[46] As the drumbeats of war grew louder, students at the ICY had front-row seats as militant voices in both the community and their own school defied the enslavement and marginalization of African Americans. Exposure to the growing rhetoric of liberation was uniquely facilitated by the communitas fashioned at the ICY, a development that failed to transpire at city schools where Black youths were taught exclusively by whites unsympathetic to the cause of full emancipation. With the benefit of such a space, ICY youths sharpened and directed their own voices toward the decade's most volatile issues. Historian Roger Lane records, "In the late 1850s . . . the managers had felt some unease about student orations which smacked of 'war, hatred, and revenge.'"[47] The trustees' concerns about the growing militancy of students reflected the presence of a second curriculum. Whether the ICY's instructors deliberately suspended their daily lessons on physiology or Homer's *Odyssey* and substituted them for discussions concerning the Fugitive Slave Law or the Dred Scott decision is uncertain. What is clearly evident is that students who were products of this environment achieved higher levels of race consciousness and political awareness, which many would use in later years as agents of social change themselves. On the eve of the bloodiest conflict in American military history, the reputation of the school as an enclave for radicalism was so strong that it attracted the attention of the fiercest warriors for abolition in the country.

John Brown was no stranger to Philadelphia. The city's strong roots in the abolitionist movement made the city headquarters for many of the top names associated with the crusade against slavery. Robert Purvis, Lucretia and James Mott, William Still, and Charlotte Forten were just some of the heavy hitters in the movement that called Philadelphia home. But Brown was not interested in merely lecturing. His hands were already stained with the blood of proslavery men whom he and his sons had personally cut down on the battlefield of Bleeding Kansas. Moving far beyond the rhetoric of gradual abolition or moral suasion, Brown sought to start a fight with the peculiar institution of slavery, a position that put him at odds with both leading abolitionists and the federal government. Nevertheless, Brown traversed the country seeking support for a plan to overthrow slavery by igniting a rebellion in the heart of the slavocracy. His efforts led him to Philadelphia, which in turn put him in the intimate company of those who had ties to one of the city's most important institutions that served the cause of liberation: the ICY.

In 1859 Ebenezer Bassett was still relatively new in his role as principal, but he had jumped into the position headfirst and proceeded full steam ahead with the design of politicizing his students. His reception in the community was so warm that he received a rare invitation for honorary membership in the exclusive Banneker Debating Society, where learned

Black men matched wits and intellect, sparring over the hottest political and social issues of the day.[48] His own deep involvement with the abolitionist movement provided his students with firsthand knowledge of and personal access to everyone connected with the cause. But nothing could have prepared him for Brown's radical and risky scheme that would bring the country to the brink of war. Although the sources do not fully establish the extent of the two men's relationship, it is clear that Bassett and Brown were familiar with each other and apparently shared some meaningful relationship. Robert Adger, a leading Black abolitionist in the city, and his son Robert Adger Jr. were members of the Banneker Literary Institute, and Adger Sr. would later send many of his other children to school at the ICY. Adger Jr. wrote to a friend years later of the chance encounter he had with Brown at a meeting that took place with other Black abolitionists in the days leading up to Harpers Ferry. Adger noted, "I can recall vividly everything about it. I had the pleasure of seeing him [Brown] the night before he went to Harper's Ferry. Prof. [Ebenezer D.] Bassett was present but he was nearer to him than I, that is he knew of his plans."[49] As Brown made his way down into Dixie to launch his attack on October 16, 1859, his diary contained a short list of men he could turn to should something go wrong with his plot. Scribbled among the names was "E.D. Bassett, 718 Lombard Street, Philadelphia."[50] Of the seven people named by Brown, Bassett was the only one whose full address appeared—and it happened to be the address of the ICY itself. Bassett must have been gripped with fear as federal authorities and angry white locals tried to piece together how Brown could have mounted such an unthinkable raid and who may have been connected with it. Teal suggests that the larger political events related to the divisive presidential election in 1860 were the distraction Bassett needed to shrink from the spotlight of the explosive event.[51]

Throughout the turbulent 1850s, several Black youths from the ICY and throughout the city had already engaged in fisticuffs with local and federal authorities over issues related to slavery. Robert Adger Jr. wrote, "I remember the distressing position Bassett was in, but we had at that time a lot of young fellows who stood together and . . . gave good account in many broils [involving] fugitive slave cases."[52] It is quite possible that this same sense of militancy would have emerged at the sight of their leader in handcuffs. As for Brown, following his infamous trial and subsequent hanging, his body traveled back north, making its way through the streets of Philadelphia, although not in the way that devoted Blacks in the city had hoped. Sensing that Brown's followers would turn out in great numbers and perhaps even make a political demonstration, Mayor Alexander Henry used a decoy coffin that the large crowd of African Americans followed, believing that it carried the body of their fallen martyr. Historian Benjamin Quarles writes, "As the wagon that bore it pulled out of the station and moved rapidly through the streets, it was followed by a stream of Blacks, many of them in a highly emotional state. Most of them were on foot but some rode in the several carriages that formed a part of the procession. The Blacks had been led to believe that the wagon was on its way to the anti-slavery office where the body would lie in state for a few hours."[53] Brown's real coffin was already on the move to its final resting place in New York.

In 1861 Abraham Lincoln declared war, he claimed, to save the Union. But for Black people in bondage and those who were free, it was always a war to end slavery. For the previous two centuries, slavery had profoundly shaped the political economy of the British colonies and what would become the United States of America. In the process, it left an indelible impact on West Africa, created severe physical and psychological trauma for enslaved Africans, and carved a path through the North American continent that simultaneously plundered the lands of America's indigenous population and created tension between white Americans who favored soil free from slavery and those who desired land where the peculiar institution would be unfettered in its growth. The reckoning resulted in a national showdown of epic proportions, and the young men from the ICY jumped at the opportunity to lead the charge. Not only did the ICY become the chief recruiting center for Black soldiers, but the faculty themselves lent their hand to rallying young men to the cause, with Catto in the center of it all.

For the firebrand professor, the opportunity to strike a blow against slavery was too irresistible to pass up. Catto led the graduating class of the ICY, nine young men in total, to the railroad station, where they boarded a train headed to the state capital of Harrisburg. When they arrived to enlist, Major General Darius Couch manufactured a technicality that thwarted the eager youths' effort to take up arms on behalf of their race. Couch's real reason reflected the white supremacist tendencies of many white soldiers, who shuddered at the idea of the war to save the Union being transformed into a war to end slavery. Not only were Black men being turned away from enlisting across the country, but the tide of white supremacy seemed to be increasing. Jacob White Jr. received letters from his friend William Parham, a teacher in Cincinnati, documenting the violent response to Black men's attempts to volunteer for the war. Parham wrote, "Meetings were held at which ardent speeches were made calling upon all colored Americans to rally under the stars and stripes . . . Judge the surprise of these patriotic individuals when waited upon by the Chief of Police and informed that all that kind of thing must be stopped, that they had nothing to do with the fight. It was a white men's fight with which niggers had nothing to do."[54] Both Pennsylvania and Ohio were states that held extraordinary places in the Black imagination. They were, after all, considered part of the promised land that Blacks dreamed of when thoughts of escaping slavery raced through their minds. But reports from more and more Blacks in both states attested to anything but hope, opportunity, and promise, even as the Civil War unfolded. Writing again from Cincinnati, Parham conveyed to White, "Our troubles with the Irish are not yet at an end. On Friday a party of them attacked a house occupied by a colored family."[55] Random violence such as this had consumed the lives of Blacks in the North for years. However, many Blacks believed the war placed America on the cusp of change. How disappointing it must have been to see those whom they believed would act as liberators lashing out violently at their very presence. Catto and his would-be soldiers returned to Philadelphia dejected but still determined to move forward with their fight for emancipation and equality.[56]

Shortly after Catto and his ICY recruits returned to town, the Black community came out in full force against the rejection of Black troops. Bassett described the War between the States as Black America's "golden moment" before a gathering of citizens on July 6, 1863. Speaking to the crowd, Bassett declared, "Our enemies have made the country believe that we are craven cowards, without soul, without manhood, without the spirit of soldiers. Shall we die with this stigma resting on our graves? Shall we leave this inheritance of shame to our children? No! A thousand times no! We will rise!"[57] Bassett's passion for justice was growing stronger. Perhaps it was the Civil War that continued to rage on or the passage of the Emancipation Proclamation at the very beginning of that year, but something was moving the celebrated principal to become more forceful and outspoken for the freedom rights of Black people.

In the summer of 1864, the school was once again packed for its annual commencement address, which was preceded by a rather vigorous and customary public examination of the students on various academic subjects. Catto gave a keynote address that proved so popular it was published and circulated throughout the country. But Bassett also addressed the overflowing crowd that morning and commanded their attention for one and a half hours with a speech titled "Elements of Permanent Governments and Societies." It is not certain how familiar Bassett was with the address that

Lincoln delivered at Gettysburg in November 1863, but in his speech that morning, the leader of the ICY seemed to invoke the tenets of Lincoln's oration. Building on the concepts of what constitutes a true republic, Bassett declared that "neither form, territory, population, commerce, wealth, physical well being, military nor intellectual greatness . . . was sufficient to constitute permanent governments. . . . While all the aforesaid characteristics of well ordered society were essential . . . there must be added virtue, liberty, and a high moral and religious development."[58] While Lincoln considered it a foregone conclusion that the nation was "conceived in liberty" and that there would emerge a "new birth of freedom," Bassett declared that America's professions of freedom and virtue were hollow. According to Bassett, if America was to stand as a true beacon of freedom before the world, living up to its avowed principles was essential. He was not alone. Countless other Black activists had long since made the hypocrisy of America the very cornerstone of their protest agenda and would continue to do so as the country sought to reconstruct itself in the aftermath of the bloody and bitter conflict.

About the same time that Lincoln was unleashing Generals Ulysses Grant and William Tecumseh Sherman on the South and effectively placing a stranglehold on the crumbling Confederacy, African Americans in the North were attempting to seize the day. In early October 1864, a call went out to gather in Syracuse, New York, for the express purpose of "promot[ing] the freedom, progress, elevation, and perfect enfranchisement of the entire colored people of the United States."[59] As the meeting got under way on October 4, the delegates were reminded of the delicate nature of the espousal of freedom rights for African Americans. The town of Syracuse, only forty miles from the Canadian border, came out to greet the conference-goers with jeers and violence. Historian Hugh Davis notes, "Shortly after the delegates arrived in the city, local toughs indeed sought to intimidate them by chanting 'Here comes the niggers, here comes the moaks, they can't have any convention here' and by assaulting [Henry Highland] Garnet and two other African Americans. . . . Most delegates were determined to stay the course, no matter the obstacles that confronted them."[60] The overt hostilities of white ruffians were not the major obstacle confronting the activists. It was the ideology of white supremacy that served as the theoretical underpinning of American society that marginalized African Americans and effectively denied their humanity in the North and the South. The saturation of white supremacy throughout America's foreign and domestic policies and its acceptance by those it benefited the most would continue to haunt the objectives of Blacks long after the attendees successfully drafted their positions, organized their agendas, and returned to their respective cities. How to dissolve such a nefarious belief system confounded Black activists. Nevertheless, African Americans quickly resolved to form local organizations that targeted manifestations of white supremacy and institutions that produced a counternarrative capable of generating self-reliance and self-love. The conference concluded with the birth of the National Equal Rights League, and the Pennsylvania delegation returned home with new marching orders that once again found the ICY in the middle of the fight.

With associates of the ICY at the helm, the Philadelphia branch of the league immediately got to work in an effort to address racist policies throughout the city. Bassett, who was a member of the Pennsylvania delegation that traveled to Syracuse, continued to use his position and influence to promote the freedom rights of African Americans. The establishment of the Pennsylvania Equal Rights League (PERL) presented him with yet another instrument for delivering his message. The principal in fact tried to make Philadelphia the center of the National Equal Rights League movement by proposing that the newly formed organization be headquartered in the city.[61] Convention delegates settled on Cleveland instead; nevertheless, the Philadelphia chapter boasted a team of Black civil rights all-stars, many of whom had direct ties to the ICY. Faculty members such as John Quincy Allen, Jacob White Jr., James Needham, Bassett, and Catto all lent their voices to the PERL, whose headquarters in the city was located at 717 Lombard Street—directly across the street from the ICY. With the fall of slavery imminent, Black activists focused their crosshairs squarely on the goal of citizenship. Having been denied personhood by their tormentors for generations, African Americans seized on the opportunity presented by the reconstruction of America to reassert their claims for both empowerment and enfranchisement. The PERL's constitution framed the objectives of Blacks in the Keystone State. The organizers wrote, "We declare the objects of the League are to unite the entire colored people of our State in a common brotherhood, for the promotion of morality, education, temperance, industry, and the encouragement of everything that pertains to a well ordered and dignified life, and to obtain by appeals to the conscience of the American people, or by legal process, a recognition of the rights of the colored people of the United States."[62]

The constitution of the PERL reflected a growing generational divide. While older members of the Black elite favored the tactics of moral suasion that defined the objectives of the early abolitionist societies throughout the city, the new wave of Black militants embraced a more direct approach that reflected a cadre of youths who were unwilling to cringe or beg for their "unalienable rights." Tired of white apathy on the issue, young activists such as Catto and White stood poised to be more forthright in their articulation of the freedom dreams of *all* Blacks. While historians such as Julie Winch have documented the strong presence of a Black elite in Philadelphia, it appears that the emerging liberation struggle in the wake of the Civil War cannot simply be categorized as a case of the haves speaking on behalf of the have-nots.[63] Working-class Blacks in Philadelphia supported the efforts of the PERL in the same way that they had supported the work of the ICY. Although their sons or daughters may not have enrolled in the school, Blacks throughout the city and indeed the state fully recognized the centrality of the ICY to their own freedom dreams. Moreover, every positive step the institution took elevated the entire race and sent waves of delight throughout the community. As historian Hugh Davis notes, the PERL achieved that same recognition and garnered the support of the race. "The evidence indicates that farmers, mechanics, factory workers, porters, waiters, maids, and other non-elites supported, and were involved in, the cause in a number of capacities. . . . Men, women, and children also donated to the cause in their churches and engaged in acts of civil disobedience on the school and transportation issues."[64] This latter concern gained serious traction in the Black community and soon became the first public target of the PERL and the activist faculty of the ICY that composed its ranks.

A torrential downpour greeted Fanny Jackson Coppin when she arrived in Philadelphia in September 1865. Her growing reputation as a talented educator led to her recruitment by the trustees of the ICY. She left Oberlin College in Ohio, where she had earned a bachelor's degree in 1865, and headed for Philadelphia, where she was asked to assume the duties of principal in the Female Department. Before her formative years in Massachusetts and Rhode Island, Coppin was a slave in the District of Columbia for the first twelve years of her life, making her intimately familiar with the forceful and oppressive hand of white supremacy.[65] The City of Brotherly Love promptly reintroduced her to the racism that she was partially shielded from in her adolescence and as a student in the liberal environment of Oberlin. She wrote, "I had been so long in Oberlin that I had forgotten about my color, but I was sharply reminded of it when, in a storm of rain, a Philadelphia street car conductor forbid my entering a car that did not have on it 'for colored people,' so I had to wait in the storm until one came in which colored people could ride. This was my first unpleasant experience in Philadelphia."[66]

When Coppin finally arrived at the ICY, she found a communitas fervently working to eradicate the color line and colleagues who emboldened their students to carry on the fight for justice. In the same year her offer letter arrived for employment at the ICY, the PERL held a meeting to discuss the case of Sergeant Major Alfred Green, a militant youth who served his country in the Civil War and previously defended Black refugees in the streets of Philadelphia by fighting off fugitive slave catchers.[67] Green, like so many activists, was engaged in willfully challenging the Jim Crow restrictions of Philadelphia streetcars and now sought to take his case to court. Green leaned on the assistance of the newly formed PERL. The minutes of the meeting, recorded by Jacob White Jr., showed, "Mr. Green made a statement concerning his ejectment from a car on the P.W. & B. Rail Road. He has commenced a (law) suit and his lawyer a portion of his fee. To carry on the suit would require more means than he can command. He asked for a loan to enable him to prosecute the case. On motion of Mr. Bassett, a loan of thirty dollars was made to Sargent Major A.M. Green to enable him to prosecute his suit."[68] "Mr. Bassett" was none other than Ebenezer Bassett, in the thick of things, pushing the cause forward and keeping the ICY at the center of it all.

The move to eliminate Blacks from public spaces intensified throughout the country as slavery fell. W. E. B. DuBois adequately described the tense situation by writing, "No sooner had Northern armies touched Southern soil, than this new question, newly guised, sprang from the earth,—What shall be done with the Negroes?"[69] That question increasingly perplexed white Americans as they pondered and debated exactly what space should be reserved for Blacks in this newly reconstructed America. In Congress and the other corridors of power, politicians were much more willing to at least discuss the subject. The general white public offered up an immediate and resounding answer: white supremacy would not falter as America's ruling ethos and doctrine. As that reality played itself out in the streets, schools, churches, and businesses of America, Blacks confronted it with defiance. As would be the case in every American military conflict, African Americans displayed their patriotism with a dual purpose: to prove their manhood and to appeal to the moral conscience of those who denied them their humanity in an effort to soften their position. Now that men such as Sergeant Green were still being deprived of their dignity in public, the confrontation with the city's Jim Crow policies on streetcars became a major front in the war against white supremacy. Biddle and Dubin write, "Men deemed citizen enough to fight for the nation but not to sit inside its streetcars? That was an argument. In car after car, riders saw conductors unseat Negroes visiting relatives who were drilling at Camp William Penn or convalescing at army hospitals."[70]

Leading the fight against segregation on Philadelphia's streetcars were ICY alumni White and Catto. Their exposure to the second curriculum and time spent within the communitas of the school prepared them for a moment such as this. After years of being exposed to the most militant Black voices, buffered from hostilities that surely would have crushed their self-esteem, and given a vision of liberation wrapped in idealism and race consciousness, the two friends were more than prepared to articulate the concerns of their marginalized race. Catto was dispatched along with other members of the PERL's Committee of Railroads to the state legislature in Harrisburg during the latter part of 1865 to lobby on behalf of the race. At the second annual meeting of the PERL in Pittsburg, it was reported that "the committee had been to the Legislature twice, and had succeeded in getting the desired bill passed by the House, but on account of the lateness in the session, and the defection of a member who pretended to be a friend of the bill, it was not voted on in the Senate."[71] In order to gain a foothold in the struggle for equal rights, it was imperative that pressure be placed at both the state and federal levels. While the state legislature in Harrisburg must have resembled a den of wolves to the PERL, the prospect of finding friends of the movement in Washington, D.C., was only slightly improved. Nevertheless, the Radical Republicans held significant sway in Congress as Reconstruction gained steam. Soliciting their support became a crucial step in the crusade for equal rights, and Catto and White pounced on the opportunity to display the power of the pen, a weapon they picked up as students at the ICY.

The appeal offered by Catto and White was one of the most moving petitions composed in the Reconstruction era. The lengthy requisition, which was submitted on February 20, 1866, read in part, "What we desire at your hands, Gentlemen, is simply JUSTICE. We wish to be secure in our persons wherever we may go throughout this Union; we wish to be allowed to travel unmolested in railroad cars, in steamboats and by all other modes of public conveyance, and we wish to be politically and legally equal with our white fellow citizens." Catto and White specifically referenced the decision to rob African Americans of the right to vote in the state of Pennsylvania in 1838, a move that was made when both were only one year old. They wrote, "We have been disfranchised twenty-eight years, and suffered all the insults and outrage consequent upon it—which legitimately flow from an act disfranchising us, and determining our right by the texture of our hair, and our citizenship by the color of our skin." As the petition read on, not only was the boldness of a new generation clearly on display, but so too were the effects of the ICY. These were clearly young men who were taught to stand defiantly and defend their race. While theirs was a generation that was certainly still open to the idea of working with whites who were sincere in their efforts to assist African Americans, they used a militant tone that escaped the previous generation. They wrote, "Hate us as you will, turn from us at your pleasure—this you may claim a perfect right to do, but in the name of God, we ask you not to allow us to be robbed of the price of our blood, our sufferings, and that which is ours by birth-right and taxation. On the Constitution of our Common Country we stand, and in its name demand justice."[72]

On June 13, 1866, just four months after the PERL submitted the petition crafted by Catto and White, the U.S. Congress proposed the Fourteenth Amendment, which recognized the citizenship of *all* Americans. It took two more years for ratification. Whatever joy may have been expressed for the hard-fought victory quickly dissipated. The amendment, along with subsequent pieces of legislation that followed at both the state and federal levels, rang hollow without a groundswell of support from the American people. The body politic, overwhelmingly white in both the North and the South, mustered token levels of sympathy for the plight of a race that many were convinced was inherently inferior, licentious, and shiftless. No public relations campaign or federal decrees could uproot how deeply entrenched white supremacy had become in all facets of American life. In documenting the position of the white public, Davis writes, "The most formidable obstacle that the crusade against Jim Crow in transit systems and the public schools confronted during these years, apart from exclusion from the political process in Pennsylvania and many other northern states, was the pervasive racism among employers, public officials, and the white public generally. Their support for racial segregation and exclusion was clearly manifested in the political arena, where Democrats consistently opposed any attempt to modify or repeal racist policies, while many Republicans were ambivalent, cautious, and opportunistic in their stance on equal rights for African Americans."[73] The Republican "friends" who did support the efforts of the PERL managed to finally push through a new statewide law on February 5, 1867, that desegregated streetcars throughout the state. It appeared that the Pennsylvania legislature was moving in lockstep with Congress's attempt to address the citizenship question. However, the herculean effort to achieve the political milestone was weakened by continuous efforts to undercut Black advancement. In coming years, African Americans in the Keystone State continued to seek advocates for their cause at the highest level. In a "special dispatch" to the *New York Times* in 1872, the paper reported an exchange between a delegation of the PERL and President Ulysses Grant in which the PERL's members argued yet again for the protection of citizenship rights that should have been upheld by the Constitution four years ago. The paper ominously reported, "Their earnest recommendation in regard to his message, however, might properly belong to the next administration."[74] It appeared that in an election year, no one was willing to pledge themselves to something so controversial as upholding the rights of African American citizens. The decision of those in positions of power to move at all deliberate speed effectively arrested the social, political, and economic development of Black America. In 1874, an aging and increasingly bitter PERL president William Nesbit reported, "Our children are still denied decent treatment in the school system; and, by reason of prejudice alone, we are debarred from many of the rights precious to us, and to which citizenship properly entitles us."[75]

In August 1868, the same year the Fourteenth Amendment was finally ratified, members of the PERL gathered yet again to collectively raise their voices against the rising tide of racism, this time targeting what many believed to be the last great hurdle in the uplift of the race: suffrage for Black men. Nesbit yet again turned to the ICY professors Catto and White, asking the two young men to collectively compose a "stirring appeal" that would draw Blacks throughout the state together on behalf of suffrage. He wrote to White, "I sincerely trust that yourself and Mr. Catto will no longer delay."[76] As Catto and White got to work, they framed a protest agenda that invoked the memories of those who made the ultimate sacrifice to end the evils of slavery. "Come, then, all whose rights are denied!" they wrote. "Pennsylvanians! Remember that you have given 10,000 braves to fight the battles of the Republic against treason in the form of State Rights. Fifty thousand of our brothers sleep in death, and thousands walk about maimed and crippled in defence of our country and its flag, and still we are disfranchised."[77] In this crucial moment, the ICY was not the only Black school working to empower African Americans. Students at nearby Lincoln University also got in on the act. Founded in 1854 as Ashmun Institute, the school changed its name in 1866 to honor the recently slain president whose efforts had put America on a path toward finally settling the issue of slavery. While delivering the commencement address in 1866, Lincoln University student William Decker Johnson declared that the institution and its students would uphold a "pledge of universal and complete emancipation" for African Americans.[78] By underscoring the idea that the goal of Black liberation was still unrealized by millions of former slaves and northern Blacks who were the victims of discrimination, Johnson sharply brought into focus the need for African Americans to gain access to the one weapon that mattered most in a democracy—the ballot. In 1868, both faculty and students of Lincoln University sent petitions to Washington calling on Congress to deliver the vote to Black men.[79] It took two more years before the Fifteenth Amendment was ratified in 1870, giving African American men the right to vote.

In the context of such a bitter reality, the significance of a space like the ICY was indisputable. With Reconstruction in full swing, Black activists fought hard to ensure that the agenda of a nation moving toward reconciliation would include the long list of concerns and problems confronting the race. However, as Black America stood on the verge of transitioning, so too was the ICY heading in a new direction. In a move that reflected the influence of the school and the stature of its leader, Principal Bassett was appointed by newly elected president Ulysses Grant to the position of envoy for Haiti, becoming the first African American to represent the country abroad. While it was the opportunity of a lifetime for the ambitious Bassett, the move was also an attempt by the Republican Party to appease African Americans whose votes they would count on in the next political cycle. Historian and Bassett biographer Christopher Teal notes, "Appointing leading African Americans to visible positions would ensure a gratitude that paid dividends at the election."[80] Nevertheless, Bassett's new promotion offered an important commentary on the seeds of Black nationalism and Black colleges' role in their dissemination. Black schools generated a transnational dialogue across the African diaspora by exchanging students and creating passageways for administrators and faculty members like Bassett. Former ICY faculty member Robert Campbell's arrival from Jamaica in 1855 and departure to West Africa three years later were part of a diasporic trend that Bassett and countless others would continue. Moreover, the space provided by Black colleges and the existing communitas developed by Bassett at the ICY reflected the tones of Black nationalism by asserting autonomy and self-sufficiency. Perhaps no administrator reflected these freedom dreams more than Bassett's replacement, Fanny Jackson Coppin.

Coppin labored in the vineyard of the ICY for four years until she was appointed head principal. Many outside supporters of the institution believed that the dynamic and outspoken Catto would be the natural successor. But if the Quaker trustees who made the appointment were counting on Coppin to be any less forthright and visible in the liberation struggle, they were quickly proved wrong. As the nation was rebuilding, Coppin believed the ICY could play a distinct role in creating a pluralistic society where Black hands were set to work to build the infrastructure of a nation within a nation. In her work at the institute, Coppin espoused ideas of self-sufficiency and Black economic power, thus reflecting the themes that would make Booker T. Washington a household name in the last decade of the nineteenth century. To provide African Americans with the necessary tools that would aid in their ascent, Coppin fought with the school trustees over issues such as the continued radicalization of the ICY youth (a development that did not stop with Coppin's appointment) and the establishment of an industrial department at the ICY, eventually winning her battle and creating a curriculum that was popular with both students and benefactors.[81] For Coppin, the victory was a necessary and critical step in the quest for Black independence. In a move that she called "a matter of painful anxiety," Coppin strategized for Black youths to possess the power of self-sufficiency and establish a culture of interdependence in a Black community that was increasingly rebuffed by racist employers and businesses. In her autobiography, Coppin wrote, "Frederick Douglass once said, it was easier to get a colored boy into a lawyer's office than into a Blacksmith shop; and on account of the inflexibility of the Trades Unions, this condition of affairs still continues, making it necessary for us to have our own Blacksmith shop. The minds of our people had to be enlightened upon the necessity of industrial education."[82]

Under her leadership, the ICY escaped many of the ideological debates juxtaposing a liberal arts curriculum to vocational training. Such disputes have infamously become the lens through which many scholars and students view the Washington-DuBois dichotomy of the early twentieth century. In the midst of Reconstruction, Coppin gravitated toward the idea of implementing industrial training while simultaneously teaching rhetoric, German, logic, music theory, poetry, and a litany of sciences, to name a few subjects.[83] Coppin's holistic approach was a trademark of Black education, but it was her cunningness in implementing her own pedagogy that became the foundation on which many teachers and professors covertly advanced a second curriculum underpinned with the freedom dreams of Black people. Historian Linda Perkins notes that when Coppin was told by the ICY trustees that she could only teach German to students after the school day had ended, "she quietly included the course in the regular curriculum of the high school during the day."[84] Such subversiveness created valuable space within the ICY to continue its long legacy of politicizing its students and crafting a vision imbued with the two most important components of the second curriculum, idealism and race consciousness. As the attention of northern Black activists such as Coppin turned toward the millions of Black southerners emerging from slavery, the need to create noncollapsible spaces where uplift could commence down in Dixie became preeminent. As she later wrote, the new objectives of the liberation movement focused on the effort to "teach the millions of poor colored laborers of the South how much power they have in themselves."[85] To achieve this act of self-determination, Coppin and the ICY began the process of sending waves of alumni down South to fight the good fight by putting their training to use, most notably as teachers themselves.

While the northern Black experience proved to be frustratingly encumbered by the hostilities of white supremacy, during Reconstruction, the part of the country below the Mason-Dixon Line had descended into an active warzone that targeted Blacks as enemies of the state. Historian Leon Litwack writes, "With Black men and women no longer commanding a market price, the value placed on Black life declined precipitately, and the slaves freed by the war found themselves living among a people who had suffered the worst possible ignominy—military defeat and 'alien' occupation."[86] It was open season on African Americans and their beloved institutions that were struggling to serve the masses. Churches, schools, and any space that was dedicated to Black uplift faced the looming threat of extermination. Into this environment ICY students boldly came to serve. One unidentified female alumna of the school proceeded to the mountains of East Tennessee in 1868 and corresponded with northern supporters about her rewarding yet dangerous work. In a letter that she entitled "Yours for the Uplifting," the ICY graduate revealed a community under siege when she described how nightriders, under the cover of darkness, had torched the school where she served as the head teacher. She wrote, "It was a sad spectacle to behold the little ones this morning, having come to Sunday School, gathered around the spot where we have loved to meet, and to see the tears running down their cheeks, disappointed, yea, sorely disappointed, at finding no [school] house."[87] Joining with her heartbroken students and the community that welcomed her, she ultimately and courageously rebuilt the school.

The early founding of the ICY placed it in a unique position among historically Black colleges. While the Reconstruction era gave birth to numerous Black schools, it was the antebellum triumvirate of the ICY, Lincoln University, and Wilberforce that provided a unique source of many Black educators. ICY alumni descended on Dixie, joining the caravan of white missionary-teachers who also promoted education for newly freed slaves.[88] The products of the ICY brought with them an academic training that made them equal to and often better than their white contemporaries.[89] More importantly, they had been thoroughly drilled in the concept of nation building and considered themselves fitting ambassadors of the ICY's second curriculum. Sheryll Cashin, a descendant of Herschel Cashin, noted that Herschel left the ICY in 1869 as a student to make his way south and begin work as a teacher among the freedmen. Herschel would later go on to serve in the Alabama state legislature and become a prominent champion of civil rights in the state, but it was during his tenure at the ICY that he accepted his charge for racial uplift. In her family memoirs, Sheryll Cashin wrote, "It is quite probable that Herschel's passion for Republican politics and the education and social uplift of African Americans was incubated during his five years under Catto's wing."[90]

Throughout the school's history, there had always been a spirit of self-sufficiency. While the Quakers provided the structural space and dollars to keep the ICY's doors open, the Black leadership that created a vision for the school and the Black youths who poured through its doors concretely understood that as it was one of the nation's first schools for Black youths, all eyes would be trained on them. What could these Blacks do for themselves in the arena of education? Could they possibly rewrite America's central thesis, underpinned with white supremacy, that Blacks were inherently inferior and incapable of progress without the beneficent hand of slavery? Reconstruction was a pivotal crossroads in advancing the freedom dreams of Black America, and the institutions that they crafted out of this sense of self-sufficiency and self-determination framed the pathway toward liberation for years to come. As America quickly retreated from promises to uphold their newfound citizenry and protect their humanity, institutions like the ICY promoted solutions steeped in pluralistic Black nationalism. ICY principal Fanny Coppin wrote, "The people of the South, it is true, cannot produce hundreds of dollars, but they have millions of pennies; and millions of pennies make tens of thousands of dollars. By clubbing together and lumping their pennies, a fund might be raised in the cities of the South that the poorer classes might fall back upon while their crops are growing, or else by the opening of co-operative stores become their own creditors and so effectually rid themselves of their merciless extortioners."[91] Moving forward,

Black colleges would continue to provide policy recommendations to alleviate the ills of white supremacy. While several of these efforts would be enveloped in elitism, Black colleges provided fruitful ground for intellectual debates that mapped the future of Black America.

Figures like Charles Lewis Reason, Ebenezer Bassett, Sarah Mapps Douglass, Jacob White Jr., Octavius Catto, and Fanny Jackson Coppin not only founded and advanced the ICY but also played crucial parts in a larger struggle to secure the freedom rights of African people in the United States. By harnessing the transformative power of education, the men and women of the ICY transformed the space in which they worked into a seedbed of activism and harvested youths who found their place in the crusade for Black liberation. As teachers, ministers, activists, and conscientious citizens, ICY alumni utilized their training and exposure to a second curriculum to agitate a power structure that would continue to marginalize the lives of African Americans for years to come. By the time Reconstruction abruptly concluded in 1877, it was clear that if African Americans were going to make advancements in a hostile environment, enclaves such as the ICY would be essential in providing hope, vision, and purpose.

2 Black and Tan Academia

Tougaloo College and the Nadir, 1869–1900

. . . .

The young activists of the 1960s trying to work within the organizing
tradition were bringing back to the rural Black South a refined, codified
version of something that had begun there, an expression of the historical
vision of ex-slaves, men and women who understood that, for them,
maintaining a deep sense of community was itself an act of resistance.

—Charles Payne, *I've Got the Light of Freedom*

M. W. Whitt rose in the pulpit of the Tougaloo chapel on a hot Tuesday evening during the summer of 1889. A small crowd of alumni, students, and
faculty had gathered to hear him speak during a meeting of the newly
founded Alumni Association. A Tougaloo alumnus, Whitt was now studying theology at Howard University, and his words that evening gave evidence of a charge he shared with future generations of students. In
discussing Tougaloo, Whitt acknowledged that "no students have passed
through its consecrated walls without having been deeply impressed with
the fact of their responsibility to God, as well as their duty to their fellow
man; and the result is, that nearly all of those who have gone from here with
the testimony and confidence of the Faculty, have met the difficulties of life
with courage and success."[1]

As graduates entered society to serve in various professional capacities,
what awaited them bordered on the inconceivable and the impossible. In
the coming years, it would be the responsibility of institutions like Tougaloo to convince Black youths that the future of the race was intrinsically
linked with their ability to wade carefully into the deep waters of despair
and racial violence that defined the everyday lives of African Americans
living in a state that would soon become synonymous with intolerance and
terrorism. Therefore, whatever "success" Tougaloo students were able to
muster in confronting such odds would prove vital in uplifting the social,
political, and economic conditions of the race.

Founded in 1869, Tougaloo was still in its infancy at the time of Whitt's
address. Mississippi was still recovering from the Civil War, which left the

region ravaged and in desperate need of renewal and modernization. The Reconstruction era had brought the promise of a new age as African Americans briefly tasted the fruits of freedom, citizenship, and democracy, which instilled former bondsmen and bondswomen with unbridled joy. Yet that bliss was quickly replaced with dread as nightriders, vigilantes, and mobs fiercely sought to arrest the progress of Blacks throughout the state. By the time Reconstruction came to an abrupt close in 1877, it was already clear for millions of Black southerners that any pursuit of justice would be arduous and dangerous. Howard University professor Rayford Logan would call the period that followed the Nadir—the lowest point of race relations in American history.[2] In 1889, the same year that Whitt addressed his fellow alumni, there were twenty-five known Black Mississippians who fell victim to lynch mobs, a state record for lynching at that point that was well ahead of the national average.[3] Those numbers and the horrific acts of violence and intimidation that accompanied them would escalate dramatically as the years wore on. Black folks in the state of Mississippi were left to reckon with a pressing question: How would they survive in the face of such realities, let alone mount a resistance?

For institutions that were dependent on white support, a frontal attack on Mississippi's white power structure would be suicide. State legislators were comfortable funding education for Black students, but only within limits. Vocational schools and religious education were deemed acceptable as the most appropriate prescription for a race perceived to be inherently devoid of morals and lacking the benevolent institution of slavery to provide direction and discipline. Liberal studies were frowned on, even though their antecedents were developing.[4]

For African Americans to endure in Mississippi, refuge from the violent tempests that swirled around them was essential to their immediate survival and critical to the advancement of a liberation struggle that would not openly manifest itself until future generations. In the Magnolia State, no other institution would defend the civil and human rights of African Americans more than Tougaloo College, and its slow development into an oasis of Black liberation is emblematic of the prodigious challenges Black colleges in the Deep South would undergo.

· · · · · ·

During the fall of 1869, the American Missionary Association (AMA) transformed the once sprawling and lucrative cotton plantation of John Boddie into an institution that would nurture the freedom dreams of Black

Mississippians. The AMA designated the plantation, located on the outskirts of Jackson, as the future site of a normal and agricultural school for Blacks. On May 13, 1871, the institution was renamed Tougaloo University and finally changed its name to Tougaloo College in 1916. At the height of the modern civil rights movement, Student Nonviolent Coordinating Committee (SNCC) activists identified the college as one of its few safe spaces of operation and a true enemy of the Jim Crow state. Tougaloo became a key meeting place for civil rights activists and sparked the indignation of white legislators who lacked power and direct oversight over the privately controlled institution.[5]

The school's beginnings were meager in the extreme. Conceived in paternalism and molded in the fashion of northern white colleges in regard to pedagogy and curriculum, Tougaloo and its students were never expected to challenge the dominant paradigm of white supremacy in the South. It was expected to produce "good" Christian citizens with an industrial or vocational background who understood their role and place in the southern caste system.[6] For African Americans to defy those expectations and craft an environment that fostered idealism, race consciousness, and cultural nationalism, the presence of an active communitas was imperative. Institutions such as Tougaloo carved out interstitial space that cultivated strong aspirations in its students and alumni to challenge the aggressive tide of white supremacy in the Magnolia State.

The historical backdrop of Tougaloo's formative years was nothing if not chaotic. Five different men were appointed to preside over the school in the first decade of its existence. Like most fledgling Black institutions in the late nineteenth and early twentieth centuries, Tougaloo was saddled with debt, mired in inner turmoil, buffeted by periods of low enrollment, and riven with debate over what sort of education it should provide. However, these issues were minor compared to the violent atmosphere that both consumed and defined the action and direction of African Americans throughout the Magnolia State.

The ratification of the new state constitution in 1868 was the by-product of the first biracial political cooperation in the state. Of the ninety-four politicians who gathered in Jackson to craft the new document, only sixteen were African American. Nevertheless, that fact did not prevent white claims of "Negro rule," and animosity was directed toward a constitution that recognized former slaves as citizens and provided them access to education funded by Mississippians—white and Black. The state press derisively referred to the motley crew of legislators as the "Black and Tan Convention," as white Democrats throughout the state almost immediately plotted their violent demise. In vain, federal troops positioned themselves throughout the state in an attempt to abate the violence and uphold the rule of law, yet over a dozen riots and massacres ensued during Mississippi's Reconstruction era that stymied the progress of race relations and undermined the efforts of Tougaloo alumni, who found their work for uplift confronted by prodigious challenges on all sides. The fledgling institution discovered that state-sponsored terrorism directly impacted its growth. Enrollment dropped precipitously in 1875, as students dared not be found navigating back roads or secluded pathways on their way to school, lest they too become victims of the widespread assaults that swept the region.[7]

Nevertheless, the AMA maintained its small investment in Black education. In doing so, the association proceeded to craft a vital space that welcomed young Black minds that dared to build and dream. Almost immediately, the concerns and interests of the AMA and the young Black students it recruited ran into serious conflicts of purpose arising from the contrast between what whites expected of Blacks and what Blacks expected and desired for themselves.

Unlike Philadelphia's Institute for Colored Youth, the administrators and many of the faculty attached to Tougaloo were white at the inception of the school, and a great deal of them expressed paternalistic and short-sighted views about the future of Black America.[8] This reality sparked concern among some Black Mississippians who, just one year after Tougaloo's founding, pressured the state legislature to open a school run by African Americans. The result was the creation of Alcorn College, which was headed up by Hiram Revels, who left his esteemed position as the first elected Black senator in the U.S. Congress in order to lead the fledgling institution located in the southwest corner of the state.[9]

Yet the presence of militant faculty was not the sole ingredient that enabled the flowering of radicalism on campus. While students often sought out those faculty and administrators who were sympathetic to their impulses for racial uplift, they also leaned on each other, sharpening the views of their peers and orienting their fellow students in the national current of militant idealism that slowly leaked into Mississippi's closed society via newspapers and campus visitors.

Youths who gathered on a former slave plantation could listen to one of their own, like Whitt, who had gone off into the world and come back ready to put his training from both Howard and Tougaloo to work. Three years after addressing his fellow Tougalooans, Whitt eventually settled in New

Iberia, Louisiana, as the pastor of the Belle Place Congregational Church and brought with him an ardent belief in cultural nationalism that was nurtured as a student at Tougaloo. Leaning heavily on that former guidance, Whitt galvanized his congregation, which subsequently grew from three to eighty-five parishioners. The young pastor taught the value of property ownership, investment, and community building, which led historian Harlan Paul Douglass to conclude, "It is doubtful if many ministers have been of more economic value to the community than this American Missionary Association product." One of Whitt's parishioners and a disciple of his teachings steeped in cultural nationalism also chimed in, stating, "Today I have a home that cost $1000, paid for, and Elder Whitt is the cause of it."[10] The efforts of Whitt and countless other African Americans engaged in the work of uplift were often perceived as a danger to white dominance. Consequently, Black churches and the ministers who led them were habitually vandalized and targeted for assassination in the hostile South. This bitter reality caused fledgling Black colleges located deep within Dixie to proceed cautiously as they trained mostly ministers and teachers who worked in an environment that held a zero-tolerance policy for overt Black militancy.

In this setting, cultural nationalism and the social gospel movement collided. The former philosophy was underpinned with a spirit of self-help, race pride, cultural pluralism, and nation building that had circulated in African American communities, organizations, and institutions since the emergence of various free Black communities in the North toward the beginning of the nineteenth century. In cities such as Philadelphia and New York, the philosophy of cultural nationalism aided in the development of Black schools such as the Institute for Colored Youth and the African Free School, where Black students intrinsically associated their matriculation with the uplift of the race. Additionally, the creation of mutual relief and benevolent organizations, scores of African-centered churches, and numerous secret societies offered northern Blacks opportunities to advance the struggle for liberation and craft a vision that supported a "nation within a nation" for years to come.[11] These same concepts materialized in Mississippi as former students such as Whitt equipped artisans, farmers, and sharecroppers with the tools to construct their own properties and thus further cultivate an appreciation for the work being carried out by the first generation of Black college alumni. In an environment where the work of Black-controlled and Black-operated institutions was increasingly appreciated, several Tougaloo students entertained the same stream of thought that created an institution such as Alcorn, where Black teachers and administrators took the reins of leadership—unlike the white-controlled and white-operated Tougaloo. The question of how that particular environment aided or impeded the progress of the race produced editorials in the student-run newspaper that broached the subject. "It is a question discussed very frequently that we should attend schools conducted and taught by our own color," declared Tougaloo alumnus E. H. Haynes Jr. "I am in the affirmative too, at the same time I think that whoever is doing good should be highly appreciated."[12]

Although Haynes tipped his cap to the white faculty and administrators who had made his matriculation at Tougaloo possible, it was clear that the young alumnus understood the properties of cultural nationalism and the redeeming value that Black youths received from seeing African Americans in positions of authority as the arduous work of uplift in the midst of the Nadir began. Moreover, considerable evidence documents the fact that Tougaloo's white administrators and faculty members eschewed the idea of including African Americans within the ranks of the faculty due to their own sense of racial superiority.[13] This further demonstrates the vitality of the Black college communitas that could thrive and generate a spirit of Black solidarity and race consciousness in spite of the indifference of its white staff.

As new Black-owned and Black-operated institutions, businesses, churches, and schools emerged throughout the South, African Americans often bristled with pride as they found their own at the helm of leadership. Haynes boldly professed in his letter to the student newspaper that he was a "lover" of his race, "proud of the color of [his] skin," and "glad that [he was] a Negro."[14] Such affirmations provide testimony to the power and purpose of a Black college communitas that was undergirded by race consciousness and cultural nationalism, if for no other reason than to expose and deter the strong current of defamation and self-hate that particularly targeted and victimized the psyche of African American youths. Thus, the counternarratives of self-love and dignity were essential components of a second curriculum that flowed through Tougaloo.

While the stirring of Black self-esteem was a critically important seed of insurgency, nothing surpassed Black dreams of self-sufficiency and empowerment as the Reconstruction era descended into the Nadir. For the millions of African Americans who had known nothing but dispossession and heartbreak during slavery, the idea of building their own properties, businesses, and community institutions and using them as platforms for the advancement of the race was sacrosanct. The very thought of accessing the

American dream of property, voting, and first-class citizenship had fueled migration patterns of Black folks to Liberia, Kansas, and all points north since the end of slavery and the onset of southern redemption. But the vast majority of Black southerners remained in Dixie. This was due in large part to a lack of resources that prevented many families from packing up and exploring other parts of the country. Additionally, in the rural South, the idea of Black migration was violently suppressed by roving militias, vigilante groups, and white plantation owners in order to keep their docile labor force intact. Yet there were also scores of Black folks who loved the land of their birth, feared the uncertainty of unknown and foreign regions, and, perhaps most importantly, fiercely defended their right for unfettered access to the fruits of their labor. For this last group, the philosophy of cultural nationalism was incredibly appealing. It gave them stake in their own lives by generating a feeling of pride and independence not readily available to them during their years as bondsmen and bondswomen. Cultural nationalism announced a new beginning where Black folks would be in control of their own destinies and institutions that served their freedom dreams. It catered to identity politics and further underscored a genuine distrust in white endeavors on behalf of Blacks. The future of the race, according to scores of young Black activists who were emerging throughout the South, should be prescribed and administered by the efforts of its own people. In 1889, Whitt clearly outlined his plan for the salvation of African Americans, six years before Booker T. Washington would gain national acclaim during his Atlanta Exposition Speech. "We must be educated, we must get property, we must get power," declared Whitt in his talk before the students, faculty, administrators, and local observers. Whitt continued, "Not education alone, not property alone, not power alone. For neither of these by itself will bridge the chasm over which we are to pass. But to become such a factor in the political problems of today as to deeply and lastingly affect public affairs, the three things must be combined. . . . It is to be done by stimulating within them the spirit of industry, economy, ambition, and pride. And this spirit must be planted largely by those who have had years of training in schools like our own Alma Mater."[15]

The administration and faculty of the institution may have been white at the outset, but Black students took advantage of the shelter to raise critiques of white supremacy itself. Their world was slowly and violently changing. Whatever advancements Blacks had achieved in the Magnolia State during Reconstruction were gradually whittled away by southern Democrats who stood on the verge of upending the country's first experiment in biracial democracy. In 1890 the newly devised state constitution ushered in poll taxes and literacy tests that were underpinned with violence in order to mitigate the Black vote throughout the state. In such an environment, Tougaloo was conceived as a shelter in which its apolitical white administration and faculty could mold Black youths with their own Victorian, middle-class beliefs, which were solidly rooted in strict religious training. From their perspective, such an endeavor was the perfect remedy to placate the white aggression that threatened to consume and devour any semblance of Black militancy. Tougaloo historians Clarice Campbell and Oscar Rogers write, "Seldom did Tougaloo's administrators cross social or political swords with the white power structure. . . . Young Negro men were taught they could do little to protect their women from the white man's lust other than to respect black women themselves. The school and the A.M.A. usually stood aloof from politics and sometimes acquiesced in them."[16] In spite of this adopted policy on southern white aggression, Black students found their own voice within the Tougaloo communitas. While their teachers and caretakers sought to suppress signs of Black radicalism in order to preserve the school and curry local favor with the white power structure, they could not completely corral the militant expressions of young students who utilized Tougaloo's space to envision freedom dreams. In their casual time students spoke of their growing concerns with the repressive political changes that were sweeping across the state, and in the pages of their school newspaper they spoke of righteousness in the face of wrongdoing and debated what solutions seemed most pragmatic in an effort to ameliorate the worsening condition of their people.

From the pages of the *Tougaloo Quarterly* in 1889, student Marion Jones encouraged his fellow students by declaring, "We are to be outspoken against anything that keeps us from prospering. But take into consideration that it will make one enemies for taking a stand for the right, and there will be hard blows and discouragement on every side."[17] Jones's comments were couched in his promotion of ministry as a viable profession for the uplift of the race, but they also reflect cultural nationalist leanings.

Subtle jabs at white supremacy did not go unnoticed in the closed society of Mississippi. Indeed, an article from the June 1886 edition of the *Tougaloo Quarterly* had so startled local whites in its open critique of white supremacy that Tougaloo president G. Stanley Pope promised that future editions of the student paper would face greater scrutiny from him and the faculty responsible for editing its content. However, students understood that institution building was vital to the struggle for Black liberation, and, regardless of what detached and often insensitive faculty thought of their political musings, they believed the space could and should be used explicitly for their empowerment and the elevation of the race. Jones declared, "We young men who go out from these institutions are to be leaders of the race, and we should strive to be well equipped, so that the standard of justice, truth and morality shall be raised in the communities where we labor."[18]

Following the terse exchanges that Tougaloo administrators had with local white community leaders who were wary of the school's influence and potential for stimulating discontent, a handful of students left the school in protest against the university's capitulation with Jim Crow policies. While Jones's comments showed a faith in the power and usefulness of the institution, they also illustrated the future path and tone that the arduous work of racial uplift would take. It could at one moment promote cultural nationalism and racial justice, and in the next moment be fraught with a sense of exclusivity and elitism that would become characteristic of Black town and gown relationships for generations to come.[19]

· · · · · ·

As cultural nationalism inspired visions of Black autonomy and empowerment, another philosophy weaved its way into the training of African American youths that tapped into the long tradition of Black spirituality while simultaneously containing elements of elitism that would fuel class conflict. Beginning in the second half of the nineteenth century, white ministers in the North increasingly spoke out against the vices of city life. The underlying economic tension that defined urban America introduced yet another explosive problem—competition over jobs. America's dependency on cheap labor resulted in a massive influx of European and Asian immigrants who gravitated toward the same cities that housed swelling populations of African Americans who had also flocked to the North in search of employment. What many northbound Blacks found instead of the paradise that they had imagined was the same racial violence that they had sought to escape in the South. Race riots were common in urban centers, and their proliferation in the latter half of the nineteenth century was yet another factor that escalated a call among a handful of "social gospel prophets" who sought to apply the teachings of Christ to address the race problem.[20] As historian Ralph Luker has argued, the AMA became a powerful agent of this religious movement and "held that religion was the only resource powerful enough to assimilate diverse groups into a cohesive social community."[21] As the association continued its work in the advancement of Black education down South, schools such as Tougaloo became willing adherents to the social gospel message that embraced temperance, clean living, and strict discipline while also stressing the importance of a Christ-centered life. Scores of Black youths being trained at AMA schools such as Tougaloo saw religion as a tonic for ignorance, immorality, and racism. While the last proved more difficult to uproot, the first two "problems" called for the widespread embrace of education as a figurative messiah and a heavy-handed approach to moralizing against the "sins" of Black folks who often did not see eye to eye with the more "enlightened" students of Tougaloo who entered into their communities to serve.

At the heart of the social gospel mission was the eradication of alcohol. While northern advocates of temperance believed that banishment of the "devil's drink" would prevent the abuse of women and children in homes across the industrialized North, numerous southerners endorsed the convenient mythology that Black men's intoxication with spirits and ale added fuel to their sexual appetites for white women, thus making organizations such as the Ku Klux Klan and numerous other vigilante groups necessary for the security of the South. Southern newspapers were rife with such stories, and white southerners embraced them as true, thus leading to an orgy of violence throughout Dixie. The real story behind white anxiety was more consistent with social and economic trends that swept across the nation. With the fall of the peculiar institution, Black men and women entered the lists as economic competitors, vying for jobs and the same commercial opportunities that whites across the country coveted. Whether it was newspaper magnets seeking to sell salacious stories or missionary teachers employed at schools such as Tougaloo, many whites asserted that alcohol was one of the primary sources of Black criminality, justifying the work of "Judge Lynch" throughout the South.

To eschew the threat of violence, Tougaloo administrators promoted godly living that would keep their students, and particularly their males, from falling under suspicion by mobs who mustered whatever arbitrary excuse they needed to justify racial violence. In documenting the work of Tougaloo's temperance society for male students, known as the White Cross, Campbell and Rogers note, "Knowing that if a black man attempted to defend a Negro woman by word or weapon he courted death or something worse, the White Cross taught that the best defense of the Negro woman was in the Negro man's virtue."[22] Such teachings suggested that the onus for preventing abuse or violence from whites rested with Black folks, who were expected to pursue virtue, and not with southern whites, whose neglect of Blacks' civil rights and humanity went unchallenged. Neverthe-less, scores of Black youths being educated at institutions such as Tougaloo subscribed to such beliefs, many because they devoutly and fervently de-sired to follow the will of God—and, undoubtedly, others embraced the phi-losophy of temperance with the hopes of keeping the hellhounds of the South off their backs.

Tougaloo students fanned out into the Mississippi countryside to spread a message of temperance, but what they found was a class of Black folks who embodied the pervasive paradoxes characterizing church life. The sharecroppers, domestics, and day laborers they worked with and preached to were God-fearing people who held fast to the teachings of Christ and be-lieved in the importance of the Black church as an institution, and these beliefs were often sprinkled with indigenous African traditions and prac-tices that dismayed Tougaloo alumni, as their newly acquired biblical train-ing eschewed such rituals. But while many Black Mississippians offered praise on Sunday, they turned to other coping devices to get them through their struggles during the week. Snuff, chewing tobacco, and alcohol were prevalent throughout the state, and both Blacks and whites partook of such vices quite liberally. Nevertheless, Tougaloo students saw a danger in this consumption among Black folks, particularly as it mixed with the violent tendencies of white southerners. Speaking on the conditions of the embat-tled masses, one Tougaloo student wrote, "The highest ambition of this class of people is to avoid incurring the displeasure of the white people who may shoot or hang them on the first occasion for complaint against them. They rejoice that matters are no worse than they are and hope for something bet-ter in Africa or Heaven."[23] Such passages reveal the crucial nature of elud-ing the lawless horrors of the Nadir. Countless Tougaloo students and alumni embraced the idea that escaping racial violence proved easier when sober. Thus they set out on a mission to indoctrinate the masses with the same mes-sage of abstinence from social vices that they had embraced at Tougaloo.

Temperance maintained its hold on campus. By 1884, the number of Tou-galoo students who had taken the pledge of sobriety and those they had recruited had reached four hundred. Tougalooans were charged with can-vassing the countryside with tracts and newspapers and arming themselves with the "Sword of the Spirit" in order to slay the sin of hedonism that en-gulfed their people. They signed up repented sinners and children who pledged to swear off drinking for their entire lives. The student newspapers from this era reveal the struggles that many of them faced in their recruit-ment efforts. One Tougalooan reported that during one incident, "the children came twenty-six in all, without being asked or encouraged by their parents to sign the pledge. The parent would not sign—drinking was their only pleasure."[24] Such a response underscores how drinking and other social vices became an outlet for numerous working-class Blacks who had been cheated out of their wages, endured daily physical and psychological abuse, and grew more hopeless by the day that their lowly social conditions were immutable. The students' stubbornness, insensitivity, and inability to empathize with the various ways working-class Black folks struggled to cope with white supremacy only served to widen the chasm between the so-called enlightened and the masses. The cultural impasse spoke to competing visions. While generations of African Americans would proudly send their daughters and sons off to institutions such as Tougaloo with hopes that it would result in their upward mobility, many chaffed at any move by alumni that could be perceived as judgment against the working-class ethos or the unorthodox traditions and vices that helped countless survive through relaxation, pleasure, and delight. However, many Tougaloo students and alumni saw their work as a vital part of nation building.

With the Nadir in full stride, young Tougalooans readily adhered to the concept of respectability politics. Black youths, and Black folks in general, desperately wanted respect from a society that stripped them of their humanity at every opportunity. As historian Evelyn Brooks Higginbotham so brilliantly outlines, many Black college alumni saw "the development and growth of black-owned institutions" and "the black community's support of its middle class" as a vital part of the struggle for liberation.[25] For those who clung tightly to the principles of cultural nationalism, racial uplift required economists, lawyers, engineers, and upright citizens who were disciplined and race conscious. These were to be the foot soldiers of the movement toward the liberation of the race, and from the perspective of numerous Tougaloo students and alumni, it was wholly impossible to occupy a space in the movement if one was inebriated, aloof, and a ragged example of Black manhood and womanhood. Writing in the *Tougaloo Quarterly*, student Frank W. Sims opined on the evils of Jim Crow and embraced respectability politics as part of the solution. "The negro problem is yet being agitated and will not be settled until he is given justice," wrote Sims. "I can see many hopeful signs of better things in the future for the sons of Ham. . . . Let us be at work, trying to get money and property, improve our morals and religion, and other races will be bound to respect us."[26] The reflections of Tougaloo students expose the fact that they did not view respectability politics alone as a panacea for white supremacy. They openly discussed the social and political conditions of the race and frequently denounced the injustice of Jim Crow. This did not prevent them from imploring Black folks to take greater control over their lives when and where they could. Whether it was promoting temperance or advocating for Black-owned institutions, Tougalooans entered the communities that they served with an aggressive agenda for racial and moral uplift that unquestionably offended the sensibilities of certain working-class Blacks. In this atmosphere, disdain for those who appeared not to be on board with the uplift program was perhaps influenced by the anxiety of a people who felt the promise of the Reconstruction era slipping away from them. While such advice carried a tone of exclusivity and snobbery, it is also true that the goals of building Black institutions, amassing wealth, and placing Black people in positions of social, political, and economic influence reflected the tenets of a Black Power movement that would hold full sway over the imaginations and freedom dreams of Black folks in the years to come.

A letter by Joseph C. Aaron Jr., a Tougaloo graduate who found his way to northern Louisiana on a teaching assignment in 1889, offers strong evidence for what was at stake for both Black laborers who were tied to the land and Black educators sent to do the work of uplift while among them. Aaron's letter, which was printed in the student newspaper, smacked of elitism. He referred to the Black laborers in Morehouse Parish as "ignorant," suggested that the people had few cares or concerns, and mocked the field songs that the community workhands depended on to ease their troubles during their tedious and backbreaking work. But while Aaron outlined the day-to-day challenges that he faced in recruiting schoolchildren, working with few resources, and selling the people on temperance and clean living, a deadly subtext lay hidden within his letter. Aaron was working in one of the most violent places in the South, and North Louisiana proved to be particularly notorious for lynching.[27] His description of the state as "barbarous" and his suggestion that the mere mention of Louisiana was enough to conjure ominous feelings among other Blacks were vague and did not truly contextualize the hostility that defined Black life in that portion of the state. In 1882, three Black men had been lynched simultaneously in Morehouse Parish, and the year after that another lynching followed. Memories of those ghastly encounters and the additional mob violence that defined North Louisiana effectively worked to undermine Black progress. It is unclear whether white landowners in the parish had given Aaron a stern warning about the goals and aims of his work, but it is clear that Aaron had established contact with those men, who authorized his presence. Nevertheless, his correspondence bore a menacing warning concerning the fragile state of race relations. "Some people try to do things which don't concern them, hence they bring trouble on themselves," wrote Aaron. "I think if we attend to our duties, as we ought, there will be no time for other things which don't concern us. We know that the privileges of the colored man are limited here. We can't express our thoughts as free men yet, for we are too weak and scattering."[28] Aaron continued in his letter to attempt to persuade his fellow Tougalooans to conquer their fears about branching out into the more violent arenas of the South, but it was abundantly clear that Black students and alumni treaded cautiously as they worked in environments such as Morehouse Parish.

Within the shelter of the institution, cultural nationalism and the social gospel were at times in deep conflict with each other, particularly when cultural nationalists embraced immigration to Africa as a cure for the cancer of Jim Crow. With Tougaloo students venturing into increasingly hostile environments, discussions concerning the colonization of Africa as a way to achieve unfettered liberation were still on the table. However, social gospel prophets across the country castigated the idea of emigration, which was a notion that Black folks had flirted with since the early nineteenth century.[29] Indeed, by the end of the nineteenth century, there had been several attempts at colonizing Liberia. While there was no mass exodus of African Americans, the violence and terrorism that Black folks experienced in places like northern Louisiana, Texas, Georgia, and Mississippi were more than enough to keep the thought of immigration to Africa fresh within the imaginations of millions who were marginalized by the surge of white supremacy.

The emigration question was not lost on Tougaloo students. Writing in the campus newspaper in 1889, L. S. Jefferson interrogated the subject in an article titled "Shall We Emigrate?" Jefferson reflected the position taken up by the leading social gospel prophets and their objective of moralizing among "heathens" at home. As historian Ralph Luker suggests, many constituents of the social gospel movement considered emigration as "a cruel hoax," a position that stood in direct contrast with that of outspoken proponents of Black relocation such as famed ministers Alexander Crummell and Henry McNeal Turner.[30] Jefferson's assessment clearly advocated for Blacks to wait out the storms of oppression; however, his interpretation of the domestic conditions confronting African Americans offered a mixed bag of criticisms. He presented a sly reprimand of white-controlled institutions and initiatives, arguing that the scheme of colonization would have whites in the lead. "I say what the American negro needs is education and not emigration," declared Jefferson. "Shall we not have the courage to stand up and battle for our rights here, rather than give up all and go somewhere else, where we would have to begin over again?"[31] But Jefferson's obvious regard for respectability politics and heavy-handed moralizing of African Americans undermined his argument. He referred to Blacks as unintelligent, inferior, and imitative of whites. Additionally, his assessment of Black folks' conditions stateside was saturated with concern for what others thought of African Americans and not what African Americans thought of themselves. Furthermore, in the coming years, students from Tougaloo would revisit the idea of emigration and arrive at far different conclusions, thus illustrating the fluidity of Black militancy on campus, which was shaped by worsening political conditions, local and national episodes of racial violence, and, of course, the influential power of the communitas itself.

Moving forward, the path toward Black liberation for many Tougaloo students remained rooted in temperance, racial uplift, and the politics of respectability, and they professed as much in the pages of their student newspaper. Students recorded conversations about their commitment to service while documenting their own politicization through exposure to various ideas. "Much is being done for the interest of our people at the University here," wrote Tougaloo student Alexander Lawrence Eans. Eans's comments were in praise of the widespread industrial training that occurred on campus, giving young men and women skills that accompanied their preparation as teachers and ministers. Those skills, coupled with their future occupations, could help them build communities and simultaneously assist them in the propagation of more radical ideas. The latter was further accentuated by new developments on campus. In November 1890 the student newspaper reported the circulation in the campus reading room of the *A.M.E. Church Review*, which was touted as "the leading exponent of the best Negro thinking and writing on great subjects of the day." In that same academic year, students who gathered in Tougaloo's humble library to peruse the magazine would have stumbled on the first entry, which was submitted by Thomas McCants Stewart, a civil rights activist and champion of emigration. In it, Stewart considered the evolution of discontent throughout world history and prophetically warned of growing tension that would soon find its way into even the most suppressed venues of American life. "But there is another form of discontent with existing conditions which is part and parcel of the unfolding plan of the universe itself," argued Stewart. "A discontent that does not mutter, but that protests, agitates, presents remedies and persists until sooner or later it reforms. It is not simply iconoclastic. It is architectural. It constructs. It builds. It develops. It is the pioneer of destiny. . . . And wherever it goes, it blesses." Stewart's powerful prose undoubtedly resonated with Tougaloo students. As many of them ventured into the hinterlands of Mississippi and beyond, they took with them dreams of building a better world. To do so, they would have to plant seeds of discontent among their students, parishioners, and colleagues—a task many of them embraced.[32]

Tougaloo ultimately became a critical space in which Black Mississippians could be exposed to a second curriculum that espoused militant ideas that were unlikely to be produced by those living in the closed society of the Magnolia State. One of the ways in which these ideas were advanced was through the proliferation of literary societies. Beginning in the fall of 1891, Tougaloo founded two such societies, one for men and women that met every Friday.[33] This development was paramount in the advancement of the second curriculum. As Wilson Jeremiah Moses argues in his classic study on Black Nationalism, literary societies were one of the three principal ways in which the Black masses "received information about Africa and sometimes even Pan-Africanist political indoctrination."[34] While scholarship covering Black history failed to make its way into the main curriculum being taught at Tougaloo, the second curriculum wholly embraced its discussion as topics pulled from magazines such as the *A.M.E. Church Review* and other sources covering the Black experience were widely debated.[35] Furthermore, utilization of these sources filled the void that Black historians struggled to address as their scholarship was hampered by limited funding and distribution issues.[36] Literary societies on Black college campuses blossomed in the latter half of the nineteenth century and continued into the early part of the next. African American youths considered reading and debate as an important form of entertainment. Recalling his matriculation at Morehouse College in Atlanta, National Association for the Advancement of Colored People activist and cofounder James Weldon Johnson notes, "They thrilled the large audiences that filled the chapel on special occasions; and the applause they received was without question a higher approbation than the cheers given to players on the baseball field."[37]

As literary societies exposed students to a variety of opinions concerning the desperate condition of African Americans during the Nadir, the second curriculum began its work at Tougaloo. According to the *American Missionary*, there were over three hundred "pupils" attending Tougaloo by 1895.[38] Many of them darted in and out of regular attendance, taking a class or two between the demands of an agrarian life that often beckoned them to the fields to assist their own families. As the century was drawing to a close, the tone and tenor of the education that they received were evolving. Tougaloo professor E. C. Moore acknowledged the shifting approach, which was undoubtedly a response to the great weight that Black youths bore. While Tougaloo alumni made their pitch for lessons undergirded by cultural nationalism and moral uplift, the daunting task of reeling in youths who saw little room for progress in a closed society was a formidable challenge. "The old education sought to give knowledge," wrote Moore. "The new education seeks to give life." Moore's comments reflect a position that would be both promoted and derided in the coming years.[39]

Nevertheless, educators and students affiliated with Tougaloo held fast to the belief that the second curriculum could serve in a messianic capacity—delivering them from a society that deemed them inherently inferior while outfitting their students with the power to counter the effects of white supremacy. Moore declared, "We believe that education is the force which shall reform iniquitous conditions, which shall drive out the poison, which shall give a better life."[40] The social gospel movement influenced countless Tougaloo students to contemptuously view various social vices as sinful, but it also provided the space for students to view racial violence and the trappings of white supremacy with just as much scorn, if not more.

As Tougaloo alumni departed, they approached their work courageously yet pragmatically. On an intensely hot day in May 1896, Tougaloo alumni briefly returned to their dear alma mater for an alumni conference and reported on their service in the field. One alumnus provided an ominous warning that illustrated the confinements that defined the lives of young Black teachers. "When you are thirty or forty miles from the railroad you must get along the best way you can, and find out how to make friends. If you know more than a white man, you needn't argue with him and try to show it," avowed the Tougalooan. "You just keep quiet and do your work."[41] The conference continued with other alumni ascending the podium to share their experiences, as well as their warnings of how to survive their demoralizing conditions. Having been forced to table any overt pursuit of liberation, Tougaloo's finest envisioned their work as teachers and ministers as a vital yet humble role in advancing the race. As the twentieth century drew to a close, a new terrorist organization known as the Whitecaps appeared in Mississippi and particularly threatened Blacks who lived in rural communities and those who were "sober, industrious, and reliable"—the very men and women whom Tougalooans were molding across the state.[42] Tougaloo students such as Rachel Pepper Scott answered the call to serve in these types of communities, and her response adequately framed how many Tougalooans saw their work. "I try in a quiet way to do what I can for the people and the Master," declared Scott. "I'll never be able to do any great work for others but I will be content to fill in the small cracks."[43] The work of women such as Scott cannot be overlooked, as they sought to patch together the torn and tattered lives of southern Blacks. While they understandably lacked the type of radicalism that many scholars and readers would expect in social activism, her efforts, and those of her fellow Tougalooans, were crucial in the effort to patch the millions of small cracks and fissures that tore at the souls of Black folks struggling to survive through the Nadir. Years later, Scott delivered a talk before the Illinois Woman's Home Missionary Union, and her comments there perhaps best summed up the prospects for the immediate future. With a spirit of despondency, Scott announced to the crowd, "It is dark for my people in Mississippi."[44]

With the full weight of Jim Crow bearing down on them, Black Mississippians tapped into every possible resource they could muster in an effort to improve their conditions. A full decade had passed since Tougaloo student L. S. Jefferson first excoriated the idea of emigration in the campus newspaper. As white supremacy crystallized into unrelenting public policy and orgies of blood and flames became normalized throughout the South, new positions emerged in the Tougaloo press that illustrated a philosophical shift within the communitas. Although the era of the New Negro was still a few years off, Tougaloo student S. W. Polk championed a rhetoric that called for immediate action and embraced the spirit of cultural nationalism that had emanated throughout the campus for years. Writing in 1900, Polk declared, "We cannot say that the present Negro is just like the Negro of 35 years ago. The American people must deal with a new Negro, new in every sense of the word!" Polk's rallying cry reached new heights two years later when he advocated the internal colonization and formation of independent communities, a move that Polk believed was the "only salvation" of African Americans marginalized by the color line.[45] Polk was not alone in his position. When the all-Black town of Mound Bayou, Mississippi, was inaugurated in 1887, former Tougaloo student George Lee was among the town's first aldermen.[46] The presence of Tougaloo alumni in the town's early years did not stop with Lee. Several notable Tougaloo alumni counted themselves among the first denizens of Mound Bayou. There was Clyde Lee, who studied at Tougaloo and went on to become one of the first doctors in town after receiving his medical degree from Meharry College in Tennessee. Samuel Hood, after studying at Tougaloo, became a teacher in the adjoining Washington County. And his father, R. W. Hood, who attended Tougaloo in its very first year of existence, also called Mound Bayou home. The senior Hood had four other children, and all went on to attend his alma mater, including one who in 1909 published one of the first histories of the all-Black town.[47]

As the twentieth century unfolded, Mound Bayou captured the attention of Booker T. Washington. The headman at Tuskegee and the most influential and powerful Black figure in the United States, Washington proceeded to interpret Black Mississippians' attempts at self-sufficiency and Black nationalism as the blueprint for Black salvation. Echoing the sentiment previously expressed by numerous Tougalooans, Washington referred to thrift, industry, and property ownership as the keys to "a door of hope" that "the South has no disposition to close."[48] Yet Washington's vision of a Mississippi that offered ample opportunity for Blacks and a door of hope that swung open without white resistance was a mirage. Much like Tougaloo itself, Mound Bayou faced deep challenges to its economic prosperity at the dawn of the twentieth century, and it never fully transformed into the Black Mecca that Washington and others had hoped it would become.[49] The town's development was closely aligned with the cultural nationalist leanings of numerous Tougaloo students, and as white supremacy prevailed by choking off the town's assets and undermining its institutions, Tougalooans were confronted with yet another hurdle in the race to distance themselves from the very worst of the Nadir. Indeed, symbols of Black empowerment were under attack throughout the state at the dawn of the century. When Minnie Cox, a Black postmistress serving in the Mississippi Delta town of Indianola, was forced from her position by white townspeople who saw her employment as a threat to white supremacy, they also attacked B. F. Fulton, an 1892 graduate of Tougaloo who ran a lucrative medical practice in the city. "Fulton has secured a large practice there and for this reason has been ordered away," reported the campus newspaper. Threats to Fulton's life must have been severe. The *Tougaloo News* reported that he "mysteriously disappeared from the place," but went on to announce that he resurfaced safely in Nashville, Tennessee.[50]

Such events further illustrate the fact that there were few strategies that could successfully take on white supremacy in the Deep South during the Nadir. In spite of Blacks' economic standing, level of education, or Christian humility, their original sin of Blackness was unpardonable in the eyes of hostile white Mississippians. In light of these deteriorating events, African Americans increasingly looked toward Black institutions such as Tougaloo to continue in the articulation of their freedom dreams and to defend their humanity. If Black education was to serve as the primary catalyst for a people ascending from the ashes of slavery, then it would have to be composed of much more than lessons in agriculture and industry, or even a curriculum patterned after that of the finest New England schools. Both the social gospel prophets and the cultural nationalist warriors had occupied the thoughts and imaginations of Tougaloo students in its earlier days, and both philosophies were deeply influential and informed various attempts by Tougalooans to ameliorate the oppressive conditions that defined Black life in Mississippi. However, as the Mississippi state legislature shed itself of its official oversight of the institution in 1892, it gradually provided the space for Tougaloo students to be exposed to more radical professors, an increase in the flow of militant ideas, and a relatively safe space to debate and determine the careful steps the students would take as the era of the New Negro emerged.[51]

Thus, the second curriculum blossomed at Tougaloo, and as the twentieth century unfolded, the campus and its leaders were abhorred by local whites for the school's deliberate practice of integration among its faculty, and Tougaloo was rechristened by many as "Cancer College."[52] Through its teachers, ministers, and other conscientious alumni, Tougaloo became a prominent force in the struggle for Black liberation and one of the most important seedbeds for activism in the state.

While the story of "activism" during the embryonic stage of Tougaloo's development is not nearly as sensational as the overt protests that would become the university's calling card in the second half of the twentieth century, it is a critical part of the Black college narrative. Historically Black colleges and universities located in the Deep South during the Nadir were faced with the same set of challenges that confronted the Black masses down in Dixie. Survival was paramount. In a closed society where Black life could be extinguished quickly and with impunity, alternative methods for advancing the freedom rights and dreams of African Americans developed. As historian Neil R. McMillen notes in his brilliant study on life under Jim Crow in Mississippi, "Tougaloo was unambiguously dedicated from the beginning not to 'negro education,' as that patronizing term was understood in the Jim Crow era, but to the education of Negroes."[53]

As Tougaloo's history bears out, administrators and faculty members were not the only ones who had a say in the composition of the second curriculum. In the years during which white paternalism and moralism were deeply influential, so too were the private musings and campus interchanges that Tougalooans shared with each other. The powerful communitas that they cultivated helped to sharpen their criticisms of Jim Crow and deepen their resolve to develop a linked sense of fate with the masses of African Americans suffering during the Nadir. The creative tools that they developed to endure and teach generations of young people to believe in themselves and their talents were just as important as other strategies and tactics employed by the early civil rights movement. Tougalooans' determination should remind the reader of sociologist Charles Payne's observation that even in the most violent and closed societies, "maintaining a deep sense of community was itself an act of resistance."[54]

3 Race Women

New Negro Politics and the Flowering of
Radicalism at Bennett College, 1900–1945

. . . .

> If there is one thing more than another which stands out in the present
> race situation in America, possibly it is that we have to-day a new
> Negro; a Negro who is very unlike the Negro of the past and whom
> it is very easy to misunderstand. . . . The fawning "hat-in-his-hand"
> Negro belongs to another generation; the alert, intelligent, capable,
> self-reliant Negro characterizes the present. The danger, and without
> doubt there is real danger, arises when we insist on treating the second
> as though he were still the first.
>
> —Jay S. Stowell, *Methodist Adventures in Negro Education*

Hattie Bailey was not known for being timid. She was loquacious, brilliant,
and driven when her peers elected her as the student government president
of Bennett College in 1937. She did not arrive at Bennett that way. Her parents in Pennsylvania had been nervous about her attending the private,
Black institution for women, given that it was in the South, but she fondly
recalled that she "learned to speak at Bennett."[1] By senior year, she had
learned quite a bit else.

In October 1937, she represented the Bennett Belles alongside 1,149 other
attendees at the Second National Negro Congress (NNC) in Philadelphia and
came away a convert.[2] The Communist-linked organization had been
founded on Howard University's campus in 1935.[3] Describing the meeting
of the NNC in the City of Brotherly Love, the famous sociologist Gunnar
Myrdal claimed that "nothing important happened."[4] Bailey disagreed,
boldly announcing upon her return to campus, "It is the genius of unity
alone that can save the race." The youth session Bailey had attended at the
Philadelphia meeting was titled "How to Develop Youth Movements in the
United States." Less than two months later, Bailey joined with her fellow
Belles in waging a successful boycott against white-owned downtown the-
aters for their decision to censor movie scenes that depicted whites and
Blacks as equals.[5]

It is clear to see how radical groups such as the NNC facilitated the politicization of scores of youths who joined the organization. Labor organizers, scholars, and activists were an integral part of the group's founding and deeply influenced youths who attended the national and local meetings. However, evidence strongly suggests that students like Bailey were heavily influenced and politically oriented by the communitas of Black colleges. Once disseminated, critical seeds of insurgency helped students like Bailey to find their voice and encouraged them to devote their time, talent, and efforts to improving the social and political condition of the race.

Bennett was founded in 1873 by the Methodist Episcopal Church and supported by the Freedmen's Aid and Southern Education Society, and its trajectory as a source of racial uplift was formally launched with the appointment of Rev. Charles N. Grandison as the first Black president of the institution in 1889. Grandison cast a long shadow across the country, and he was well known as one of the best orators on the Black lecture circuit.[6] He was also known as an uncompromising and unwavering Black nationalist. When Grandison convinced future literary giant James Corrothers to leave his studies at Northwestern University in order to attend the fledgling school briefly, he did so by expressing to Corrothers his vision of establishing a new Black Christian republic on the African continent.[7] The revelation left Corrothers in such awe of Grandison that the kindred spirits set out immediately for North Carolina, where they were quickly besieged by the harsh realities of the color line. Corrothers watched with great fear and fascination as Grandison defiantly refused to abandon his first-class seat. The train pulled into a station in Knoxville, Tennessee, and a brief yet physical exchange with the conductor left Grandison and Corrothers in the Jim Crow car, but it further bolstered Corrothers's admiration for Bennett's new chief administrator. The young scribe could not help but wonder: who was this man, and exactly what kind of school was he building in Greensboro?

After arriving in Greensboro, Corrothers had yet another harsh encounter with Jim Crow policies, this time in the neighboring city of High Point. After refusing to obey the conductor's request to move to the segregated part of the train car, the young men exited in protest and made the fourteen-mile walk back to campus. A group of female Bennett students who were also on the train had already delivered news of the young men's impromptu protest. When the weary students finally made it back to school, they were hailed as heroes and treated as guests of honor at a banquet-like feast where they relayed stories of their encounter and faculty delivered "stirring speeches" celebrating their efforts to defend the dignity of the race. One faculty member who was known to be inept at public speaking rose and boldly stated, "Let us say to the whites who would impede our progress and trample us in the mire; 'The nobility of *my* house begins in *me*; *yours* ends in *you*!'" Bennett College was well on its way to becoming a storehouse of knowledge and dissent.

Exhausted by his southern ordeals, Corrothers soon returned to Chicago to continue his studies at Northwestern. The man who first recruited him to share in his visions of Black nationalism had a harder road ahead of him. The hostility and psychological trauma of white supremacy would take their toll on Grandison.[8] His dream of returning his people to Africa was not to be, and daily emasculation and denigration steadily wore Grandison down. To manage the pressures of forced subservience, the minister, who was revered across the country, increasingly drowned both his troubles and his career in rum. He was removed from his position as Bennett's president in 1892 and lived out the rest of his life in relative obscurity.[9]

Nevertheless, Grandison's administration was critical in setting the political tone on campus, and the groundwork that he laid paved the way for future presidents of Bennett to craft a communitas that advanced the freedom dreams of Black America. Jordan Chavis (1892–1905) and Rev. Silas Peeler (1905–13) followed Grandison as the new leaders of Bennett, and both men were alumni of the school when it was still under Grandison's watch. Most likely the future campus leaders developed their own political values there on campus, with Chavis embracing the emerging philosophies of W. E. B. DuBois and his theories on the "talented tenth" and Peeler following the steps of Grandison and Booker T. Washington into ideas of racial solidarity and economic nationalism.[10] While Chavis was still president of Bennett, Peeler was selected as one of the key speakers at a conference held in Atlanta in 1902 entitled "The United Negro: His Problems and His Progress."[11] By the time Peeler succeeded Chavis, he was so deeply influenced by the principles espoused by Washington that he established Bennett as one of the institutions in the Tuskegee Machine's extensive network of supporters. The school was among the stops that Washington made during his 1910 tour of the Tar Heel State, and upon the news of Washington's death in 1915, the Black community of Greensboro gathered on campus to memorialize the nation's most prominent race leader.[12]

The varying political ideologies that swirled about campus were all focused on the survival and advancement of a race that witnessed a complete betrayal of the principles expressed in the American dream. In the coming years, Bennett students reimagined and refashioned those ideals in order to give them true meaning and purpose. A counternarrative grounded in race consciousness would prove essential. Literary societies such as the Cornelian Ring and the Bennett Literary Society were established on campus and provided an open forum to debate social issues, engage in the latest articles and readings related to racial uplift, and affirm students' sense of self.[13] Peeler, a disciple of the fallen Grandison, carried on his mentor's dream for a greater tie to the motherland when he rebooted the Samuel Crowther Friends of Africa Society on campus in 1913. Much as in Grandison's original vision, the organization supported missionary work in Africa while simultaneously encouraging students to take pride in their African roots.[14] Perhaps most critical to the development of racial consciousness among students was the addition of African American history to the curriculum itself. Long before Carter G. Woodson established his campaign to educate the masses on the contributions of the race, Bennett chartered a course entitled "The American Negro" in 1915. Among other things, the course required upperclassmen to engage in "organized efforts for improving the conditions of living and the social conditions of the American Negro."[15]

There were numerous white southerners who resented the rising tide of self-consciousness among Blacks. As if educational initiatives promoting such concepts were not enough to stoke the wrath of the white public, the increasing competition over jobs created a cauldron of violence as World War I came to a close in 1919. Perhaps Bennett's board of trustees sensed the problems associated with the growing zeal among educated Blacks. They removed Peeler in 1913 for being too "aggressive" and "outspoken." In his place they brought in the older James E. Wallace, who only remained president for two years before he was succeeded by Rev. Frank Trigg, who served as president from 1915 to 1926. A former slave from Virginia who lost his arm in a farming accident, Trigg displayed accomodationist values that went far beyond those of his predecessors. Presiding over Bennett as the New Negro rose in America, he sought to suppress any semblance of militancy on campus. His approach resembled that of many cautious administrators, which historian Sarah Thuesen summarizes: "Black educational advancement hinged on keeping black 'agitation' at bay." In the wake of the Red Summer of 1919, Trigg banned the circulation of *Crisis* magazine, a publication of the National Association for the Advancement of Colored People (NAACP), on campus in an effort to court continued support from white benefactors.[16] Trigg's politics were perhaps still greatly informed by fresh memories of slavery, but while he was willing to bend campus policies to accommodate his overseers on the board of trustees, a more defiant generation of youths was soon to emerge.

· · · · · ·

The embers of the Red Summer had barely cooled by the time Trigg left office in 1926. That very year, Bennett College would make a critical pivot, transitioning to a women's college.[17] Even before the opening of this new chapter, the campus was making its mark in the arena of educating Black women. Wilbur Steele, who served as Bennett's principal from 1881 to 1889, briefly highlighted the increased impact of educating women when he recalled former students' professional accomplishments. "Ten of these old students have been members of the General Conference, nine of them as delegates and nearly all of them as alternates," noted Steele. "As many more are nearly as notable in their communities and in the elevation of their race, not to mention as many of the girls."[18] By 1910, North Carolina far outpaced the nation in the amount of bachelor of arts degrees awarded to African American women. Of the 168 degrees awarded in the state, Bennett had granted 71. The next-highest total among southern states was Tennessee, which had awarded a total of 91 degrees.[19] As the era of the New Negro dawned, the question (at least in North Carolina) was not whether Black women would become the beneficiaries of increased opportunities for education but whether that education would fit within the paradigm of Black radicalism sweeping across the country.

DuBois joined a chorus of other Black scholars and activists of the New Negro era when he observed the potential of a young, informed, and radicalized intelligentsia. The esteemed scholar declared, "If the college can pour into the coming age an American Negro who knows himself and his plight and how to protect himself and fight race prejudice, then the world of our dream will come and not otherwise."[20] Other scholars were more blunt in their evaluation. In assessing the need to stimulate activism among Black college students in 1923, Howard University dean Kelly Miller declared that there was "no problem that is more practical and pressing than this." A year later, his colleague E. Franklin Frazier shared his sentiments by writing "the product of Negro education has become a spectator of civilization incapable of participation."[21]

The students were apparently listening. Beginning in 1923, protests swept across various Black college campuses, targeting a diverse set of issues encompassing the paternalism of white administrators, the need for new curriculum offerings, and deplorable campus conditions.[22] Off-campus protests targeting Jim Crow policies were practically nonexistent for college students residing below the Mason-Dixon Line. In this regard they were no different from the majority of Black southerners, whose pathways toward overt protests were obstructed by psychological barriers created by decades of racial violence and institutionalized white supremacy. The women of Bennett College continued in their studies that reinforced their sense of self, listened intently to the steady stream of Black scholars and activists who were brought to campus, and bided their time while waiting for the right place and opportunity to take a stand. They also welcomed a new president who would be instrumental in increasing their politicization.

When David Dallas Jones was appointed to the Bennett presidency in 1927, he was returning home. Jones was born and raised in Greensboro and left his Dixie roots behind to pursue degrees at Wesleyan and Columbia. When he finally returned home to the Tar Heel State, he brought first-hand experience in the politics of racial reconciliation, having served on the Atlanta Inter-racial Commission. This was a rather conservative organization that tiptoed around volatile issues of race rather than tackling them head on, but it nevertheless soon spread throughout the South, acting as a council of the enlightened, hoping to prevail over the ever-percolating racial tension that defined the southland. Jones was not the only college president to participate in the various interracial commissions established during the interwar period and beyond. As historian Raymond Gavins correctly observes, these organizations were created to "meliorate grievances and ease tensions" but were never designed to dismantle the racial hierarchy that imprisoned Blacks in a permanent state of inequality.[23] Black college presidents such as Jones were welcome additions to a group that provided the illusion of gradualism, race cooperation, and peace—but Jones soon offered more than just a token nod toward the idea of Black liberation.

For Jones, the pursuit of racial justice was becoming a family tradition. While he went off to attend college outside North Carolina, his older brother Robert Elijah Jones quickly emerged as a race leader in the arena of religion. Robert scaled the ranks of the Methodist Episcopal Church and was appointed as the church's first African American bishop. He was the chief editor of the *Southwestern Christian Advocate*, a news bulletin dedicated to covering the details of the Black Methodist church, and later founded the Gulfside Assembly in Waveland, Mississippi, one of the few retreat and vacation spaces for African Americans throughout the South. His baby brother David made sure that he would not be the only Jones brother engaged in uplifting the race.

When David Dallas Jones took over at Bennett in 1927, he did so as the college was entering a new phase. It had just made a transition from co-ed to single sex, and Jones welcomed the challenge of leading one of only two institutions in the country dedicated to serving African American women. As Jones stepped into his new role, it provide him an opportunity to exert his brand of politics across campus—and as the New Negro era unfolded, Jones increasingly refused to soft-pedal his increasing irritation with Jim Crow.

As the headman of Bennett, he deliberately passed his frustration with racial subjugation along to his students. He routinely instructed the women of Bennett to avoid shopping in downtown stores that physically or verbally abused them, and much to the chagrin of white laborers, he consistently hired Black contractors to complete work around campus.[24] When the Black community of Greensboro called for a mass meeting at the nearby Trinity African Methodist Episcopal Zion Church to encourage patronage of home merchants as opposed to supporting hostile white businesses that employed Jim Crow policies, Bennett students not only attended the meeting in great numbers, they also "enlivened" the crowd with a musical performance from a Bennett choir.[25] As the nation struggled through the Great Depression, Jones continued to cultivate a campus community where education and race consciousness worked hand in hand. Bennett women formed campus organizations such as the Phyllis Wheatley Literary Society and the Charlotte Hawkins Brown Club, where they debated topics such as "Will Education Solve the Race Problem?" Gladys Whitefield, a 1931 graduate of Bennett, noted that the presence of such forensic groups offered "valuable educational service in that they quickly bring a student to measure her capacities and give the student an ambition to test and develop her powers . . . based on worthwhile knowledge of current history." By the end of the 1931 academic year, Bennett women had also organized the first Student Inter-racial Movement on campus. They welcomed student visitors from across the state and discussed topics such as education, health, and economics. However, one can only wonder whether more sensitive and controversial conversations on race also surfaced among the youths as students from Duke, Elon, and the University of North Carolina at Chapel Hill gathered on the quaint and lovely campus.[26] What is certain is the fact that Bennett students were slowly fanning out into the surrounding communities and were impacted by the growing radicalism of the emerging left during the Depression while simultaneously leaving their impression on those they encountered. Years later, when left-wing activist Junius Scales briefly left the all-white campus of the University of North Carolina at Chapel Hill in 1938 to attend an interracial student-labor conference in Durham, he was awestruck by the young Bennett Belle who boldly took a seat beside him for an integrated dinner in the basement of the local YMCA. Her name was Frances—the daughter of David Dallas Jones.[27]

Militant expressions increasingly surfaced in the campus newspaper, the *Bennett Banner.* Jones used his connections to bring politicians such as Illinois congressman Oscar De Priest and former NAACP head James Weldon Johnson to campus. Johnson delivered the spring commencement speech in 1934 and lectured students on "the stern conditions of life" they would face upon departing. But it was the nurturing they received at Bennett that taught them how to confront Jim Crow. In his first year as president, Jones introduced the Annual Home Making Institute. The yearly program trained young women in domestic responsibilities while also imparting an element of race consciousness and dissent. In May 1934 the ladies heard from Forrester Washington, the director of Negro Work with the Federal Emergency Relief Association, who suggested that an increasing number of Blacks were escaping the bleak economic times by changing "religious faith, politics, and even breaking away from the color line."[28] Such was the nature of college life at Bennett. One could enjoy playful banter with friends, learn about the best practices in domestic homemaking, and receive a stirring rally to defend the race all in a week's time on campus.

Students took their cues from those who worked within the communitas, whether those were the political leanings of friends, the radical musings of faculty, or visions of liberation crafted by administrators like Jones, whose commitment to racial justice went beyond just casual lip service. In the year before the Bennett women launched the boycott of Greensboro theaters in 1937, Jones joined together with a titan of Black education, Mary McLeod Bethune, to protest the governing body of their respective schools—the Methodist Church. At a national convening of the church held in Columbus, Ohio, the organization enforced the color line in order to accommodate white attendees from their southern jurisdictions. Jones and Bethune walked out, leaving in their wake numerous Black ministers who were too timid to challenge the Jim Crow policy embraced by their own church.[29]

Jones walked the tightrope of race relations with care. He was never reckless, but he delighted in provocation—a tactic he used more with his students than he did with the white establishment.[30] Provoking local whites had consequences that Jones well understood. Nevertheless, he also was heading an institution where his students were constantly drilled in the importance of citizenship and democracy—two concepts whose benefits African Americans were robbed of on a daily basis. In the eyes of many local whites, Jones and his students were expected to be paragons of virtue, docility, and compliance with the laws of the land, thus serving as an example to poor and working-class Black folks. Much to their disappointment, by 1937 the effects of Jones's influence, coupled with daily reminders of his students' role in the burgeoning struggle for Black liberation, manifested themselves in a public protest that pierced the placid conformity and racist underpinnings of life in the Jim Crow South.

Portraits of Black dignity and accomplishment were repeatedly brought to the forefront for those on Bennett's campus. One week before Hattie Bailey took the train to Philadelphia to represent Bennett at the NNC, faculty members on campus were drilling students in the works of DuBois, Paul Laurence Dunbar, and James Weldon Johnson during the weekly chapel sessions that were held.[31] Courses on Black history were offered at Bennett on a regular basis. Beyond the curriculum itself, a spirit of resistance was in the air. In 1937, the Southern Negro Youth Congress (SNYC) was formed as an offshoot of the NNC to encourage race consciousness and to continue "fighting against racism and of achieving political and cultural progress."[32] These ideals and experiences reinforced the growth and development of Bennett women, and it was not surprising that students demanded that Southern Theaters Incorporated reverse its new policy to cut out film scenes in which Blacks and whites were portrayed as equal.

The scene that triggered consternation and panic among the collective of white theater owners was frivolous by most standards and was so heavily draped in minstrelsy and racial caricature that it is a wonder that theater owners such as Greensboro's Montgomery S. Hill were not pacified by the overt racial stereotypes fully on display. Yet it also displayed the warped fascination with racial politics during the era. The movie in question featured vaudeville and minstrel era star Eddie Cantor and was entitled *Ali Baba Goes to Town*. The plot centered on a young drifter (played by Cantor) who finds his way onto a movie set, eventually taking a small role in the production. Suffering from an injury, the directors of the film provide him with painkillers that soon induce him into a dreamlike state where he hallucinates about taking an even larger role in the film set in the fanciful world of *Arabian Nights*. It is here that the racial absurdities embedded and portrayed within a specific scene invoked the fear of Montgomery Hill and his fellow theater owners.

Cantor, desirous to speak the "swing" language of the Sultan's all-Black musicians who are conveniently and idly laying about the palace grounds, quickly dons minstrel era blackface and transitions into a musical number entitled "Swing Is Here to Stay." Enter Black vaudeville dancing star Jeni LeGon, who descends the stage stairs wearing a grass skirt and performing a commanding and virtuoso tap number that witnessed her flowing effortlessly across the stage and stoking the desire and approval of Cantor. For southern white theater owners, this proved to be too much. Had LeGon exhibited a typical minstrel era shuffling routine that failed to display her full prowess and genius as a performer, perhaps their anger and fears would have been mitigated. From their perspective, such mastery and talent was reserved for the likes of Eleanor Powell or Ginger Rogers, the most prominent white female dance stars of their era. "The negro in the southern theaters as a character will always be accepted," declared Hill. Yet not only was LeGon's character not subservient or submissive enough, but the real crime was that she shared the stage with Cantor who fawned and followed her every graceful move. "People will always resent," continued Hill, "a mixed chorus or any chorus where a negro and a white person appear, as it were, on the same plane." This scene was deliberately cut from the Greensboro showing, drawing the ire and protest of Bennett students who chaffed at the thought of Black excellence being censored to appease those who catered to white supremacist sensibilities. Ironically, one of the dominant concerns at the three-day conference of southern theater owners was the threat of federal regulation of their industry and how "communists sought to use the screen for propaganda."[33]

News announcing the theater company's decision spread quickly among both the Belles and the students attending the larger North Carolina Agricultural and Technical State College located directly across the street from Bennett. The *Carolina Times*, a Black newspaper serving citizens across the state, reported that one thousand students joined in the boycott. It also reported that the North Carolina Inter-racial Committee had also registered a stern protest with Southern Theatres—a move that showed David Dallas Jones working behind the scenes.[34] Jones's daughter Frances, who would go on one year later to inspire Junius Scales as they shared dinner at a student-labor conference, was a freshman at Bennett during the boycott, and the chief organizer of the uprising.

To be certain, boycotting a theater company for removing scenes that fortified the dignity of Black folks could not be compared to direct-action protests that targeted policies barring Black communities from basic civil and human rights. Those types of overt protest were still over two decades away. However, the theater company capitulated to the students' demands, running Hollywood productions unedited. With this victory, the women of Bennett demonstrated their resolve to tackle larger issues that belittled their humanity and the power of the communitas that surrounded them. Not only that, but Jones also displayed his willingness to nullify the unofficial social contract between him and the white city fathers of Greensboro. To be sure, peace was preserved, and the boycotts were nonviolent. However, the women of Bennett defiantly broke the public silence on Jim Crow with poise, with grace, and with Jones unequivocally standing behind them.

To most of the white community outside campus, Jones was looking more and more like an agitator. Following the boycott of 1937, Frances Jones learned that her father was targeted by the Federal Bureau of Investigation and was visited by agents who "tried to force him to get us to stop."[35] The FBI did not typically conduct surveillance in small southern cities and devoted most of its resources to fighting radicalism in northern cities. There, Black urban enclaves provided enough shelter from racial violence that supporters of labor activism and Pan-Africanist movements could speak out freely against racial injustice. Moreover, the type of work unfolding at historically Black colleges such as Bennett was viewed as largely benign. Historian Theodore Kornweibel Jr. notes that even New Negro–era moderates "must have been inhibited by the fact that the Bureau had no tolerance for civil rights advocacy."[36] While activists of the New Negro era who were associated with Black colleges were acutely aware of the scrutiny and even danger that they faced in openly questioning the power structure, they were afforded a certain measure of stealth—a fact that many, but not all, used to their advantage. Bennett women were not stockpiling weapons, openly courting communism, or repudiating capitalism on street corners. Nevertheless, as seeds of rebellion were planted in their campus culture, they, along with scores of other Black college students across the South would eventually become the shock troops that catalyzed the movement to dismantle Jim Crow, a fact that FBI director J. Edgar Hoover and his army of agents completely underestimated during the interwar years. The Bennett-led boycott dissolved after students found a suitable resolution; however, Jones continued to cultivate an environment that generated political consciousness and activist impulses among his students.

Administrators like Jones could never publically admit to the fact that the rebellion against the theaters resulted directly from the communitas he had helped to shape. But his fingerprints were all over the protest that was unlike anything the South had seen from Black college youths.[37] Moreover, the 1937 boycott brought forth a groundswell of support from heavily politicized youth across the city, confirming that Greensboro had the potential to host massive student-led protests. Students like Harriet Bailey returned to campus with dispatches from the burgeoning Black labor movement in the North. Frances Jones organized boots on the ground to take down the offensive policies of the Southern Theaters Incorporated. The women of Bennett College were clearly dissatisfied with the status quo and prepared to protest white supremacy as they encountered it.

To accomplish the task of politicizing his students, Jones exposed them to faculty linked to the burgeoning New Negro movement. In a paper that he published in the *Bulletin of the Association of American Colleges,* Jones specifically outlined the "cultural obligations" of faculty teaching at historically Black colleges and noted that one of their chief roles was to empower their students to tackle the social and political problems that they encountered. Perhaps most telling in Jones's article is the fact that he did not simply see the role of faculty as passive coconspirators in this struggle. Instead, he envisioned faculty as hands-on players in the full-court press against Jim Crow. "Perhaps in our day we shall see a decisive struggle and perhaps the 'coming victory' of culture as we understand it in our democratic land," declared Jones. "At least you may be sure we Negro teachers greatly desire to become a part of the force which struggles to bring about this victory."[38]

The faculty that Jones assembled at Bennett did not stray from the course that he charted. As Frances Jones organized the boycott of the local theater, not only did she lean on her father to support her efforts, but she also received counsel from Bennett faculty such as Willa Player and nationally known music composer Robert Nathaniel Dett. The former would proceed to play a vital role in the liberation movement as the future president of Bennett. Only three years before the boycott, William Edward Farrison, a formidable professor of English, was corresponding with DuBois as he sought to rally youths and adults across the state to join the NAACP. "Let me say that I am very deeply interested in the youth movement," wrote Farrison. "As plans for the movement go forward, I shall greatly appreciate being informed concerning them, and also to give whatever help I may be able to give in the making of them." Farrison continued to be a force for change on Bennett's campus as he influenced countless women to take up the fight against Jim Crow. As the New Negro era gave way to New Deal activism, it was clear that the faculty of Bennett embraced Jones's vision of fulfilling their obligations to advance the movement.[39]

. . . . . .

Jones increasingly used his position of influence to publicly laud the contributions women were making to the fledgling freedom struggle. Shortly after the boycott, Jones took to the airwaves on a nationally syndicated radio show entitled *Wings over Jordan*. Based out of Cleveland, *Wings over Jordan* featured a choir of the same name and served as a platform through which various leaders of the Black community addressed diverse issues of interests to African Americans. Students reported that "the campus chest swelled ten additional inches after hearing President Jones' talk."[40] The mother of the show's founder, Rev. Glenn Settle, was an alumna of Bennett and thus Jones was a frequent guest, and his use of radio to advance the causes of the freedom movement soon inspired his students to do the same.

Produced by the women of Bennett College, a program entitled *Bennett College on the Air* began airing on radio station WBIG (We Believe in Greensboro). In an era when radio was still the primary method by which information and entertainment were disseminated, the advent of this program was a remarkable achievement by the women of Bennett. It is astonishing and indicative of the moderate politics of the city that WBIG was Greensboro's first radio station, with its content and primary market focus on the larger white community, yet the station owners saw fit to carve out space for Bennett students to address Black and white listeners alike on topics that surely shocked and perhaps angered some of their white audience.[41]

The women of Bennett regularly packed their fifteen-minute show full of inspiration, with the hopes to establish a counternarrative that commended the contributions of African Americans to daily life in America. A transcript from one show apprising their audience of the importance of Carter G. Woodson's Negro History Week reads, "Mr. Woodson . . . felt that the colored group here in America needed something for its own internal racial growth. They thought that as people learned more about the achievements of the Negro, this would help destroy some of the misconceptions about his native ability, which seem to exist, even among Negroes. They hoped that learning about the Negro, both in the past and present, would prove an inspiration to colored people everywhere."[42] The Bennett students in charge of the program, Carol Lynn Booker and Cassandra Moore, proceeded to discuss a course titled "Negro History" that was offered at Bennett by Frances Johnson, and they also acquainted the audience with

The Bennett College radio program provided the women of Bennett with a platform to broadcast lessons on Black history to their listeners. It also allowed them to deepen their ties with the surrounding Black community. Image courtesy of the Bennett College Archives at Thomas F. Holgate Library.

the resources that were available through the campus library. The young ladies also took the time to promote a modest pamphlet on the history of the "American Negro" entitled *America's Tenth Man: A Brief Survey of the Negro's Part in American History*. If there were any question as to whether Jones played a role in the content of the radio production, this pamphlet suggests an answer—it was a product of the Commission on Interracial Cooperation out of Atlanta, the very organization of which Jones was a member.

The Bennett radio program demonstrates not only the critical role Black colleges played in edifying the students enrolled in the institutions but also the commitment schools such as Bennett made to uplifting the surrounding African American communities to which they were inextricably linked. Black colleges such as Bennett sought to fortify the self-esteem of Black youth through cultural nationalism and a counternarrative that celebrated the achievements of African Americans. Decades later, at the height of the civil rights movement, Freedom Schools established in Mississippi to educate and provide political literacy to both the young and the old adopted into their curriculums the same concepts of civic education and race consciousness that Black colleges had offered for years.[43] As products of a more radical New Negro era, this particular generation of Bennett College women saw no need to hide their intentions, nor were they under any pressure to do so from their administration. Students were encouraged to share their lessons as far as the airwaves would take them. The creation of the radio program ensured that they could reach fellow citizens across the city and the nearby rural areas and, more importantly, disseminate a message to young and old alike that illustrated the beauty and power embodied in the Black experience.

The radio program also provided a platform for the further construction of Black womanhood. Radio was then, as it still is largely today, a male-dominated industry that provided little room for female voices or on-air personalities. It was highly unusual for women in the 1930s and 1940s to write their own scripts and produce their own show, but Bennett students shattered whatever notions the listening public had about who should be given on-air publicity or what topics should be broached. On one broadcast, a segment entitled "Great Names in History" featured all African American women who had served as powerful change agents in American history: Sojourner Truth, Harriet Tubman, Phillis Wheatley, Mary McLeod Bethune, and Marian Anderson. Their Negro history class instructor for that semester—John Hope Franklin—must have surely been proud of his students.[44] Just two years after witnessing his students promote African American history on the Greensboro airwaves, he finished a manuscript that would become a seminal contribution to the field, entitled *From Slavery to Freedom: A History of Negro Americans.*

The influence of such developments were far reaching. As Bennett students were exposed to visiting scholars and molded by the women and men who were essential to their vibrant communitas, they were empowered to carry the gospel of social justice and equality with them into the communities they were charged to serve. One such example was Eva De Journette, who matriculated at Bennett and by 1942 had made her way to Greenville, South Carolina, where she started a teaching career in math and science at Greenville Colored High School. At Bennett, she had worked on the radio series, serving as an announcer, working behind the boards, and developing a recurring segment called "The Negro Too Has Achieved." De Journette remained so connected with this work that she volunteered to continue writing the script for the show after she graduated, making sure to "send it in each week before the deadline set by the Federal Communications Commission." When she arrived in South Carolina she was determined to continue the training in cultural nationalism she received at Bennett. She was invited to launch a replica of "The Negro Too Has Achieved" at radio station WGTC in Greenville. One can only imagine the far-reaching effect that Journette had on both her students at Greenville Colored High School and those who fell under the spell of the sound of her voice proudly emanating from the radio in the Greenville community.[45]

A rising militancy reverberated through Black America during World War II. Like Journette, Jones took to the local airwaves to rally the African American community, promote movement activity, and enlist the support of all those who were interested in reshaping American democracy. Jones urged his listeners to become stewards of cultural nationalism by backing churches, schools, and Black-owned businesses. For Jones, the upkeep of Black institutions that were dedicated to improving the social, political, and economic conditions confronting African Americans was a paramount objective intrinsically linked with the future success of the race. "Let us make history by building, through loyalty and co-operation, a firm foundation on which tomorrow's generations may advance even further than we have come," implored Jones.

Most distinctively, Jones defied the conservatism of his fellow college presidents by openly embracing activist organizations. Whether because they were beholden to racist southern legislators for funding or cowed by the hostile and often violent culture of the Deep South, many of the heads of Black colleges steered clear of activism. Jones spoke freely and publicly of the need to support the initiatives of organizations such as the NAACP and the Urban League. In a local radio address in 1942, Jones urged his listeners to join both organizations. "We can contribute financially to their upkeep," he declared, "and we can give some of our free time to the furtherance of their aims and objectives in our particular communities." Jones concluded his comments by also urging the support of Black media and the celebration of Negro History Week. "For information and for inspiration, we owe this to ourselves," noted Jones.[46]

The Second World War marked a watershed moment in the struggle for liberation. The *Bennett Banner* was brimming with stories that illustrated a surging determination to address social inequality, and the campus buzzed with activity that focused on the emerging movement. A summer institute was held on campus in 1942 entitled the Home Defense Workshop in Community Leadership. Among its goals was the desire to achieve "a world where the walls of racial prejudice and intolerance will not exist." The senior class of 1944 voted the Supreme Court's decision to overturn the Texas white primary in the landmark case *Smith v. Allwright* as the most important news story of that year. A student interracial conference was held in Greensboro and cohosted by Bennett and Greensboro College, a same-sex school for white females. Hosting delegates from thirty-four colleges in North Carolina and Virginia, the conference reached its peak when a resolution was drafted that pledged students' dedication to end segregation in North Carolina's public transportation. But the most consistent theme that emerged was democracy. It was the topic of class discussions and addresses by visiting speakers, and editorials concerning America's hypocrisy in failing to extend it fully and fairly to Blacks were constantly present in the Bennett campus press.[47]

The women of Bennett took their cue from Jones, who highlighted the paradox of America again claiming to fight a war to preserve freedom and democracy while once again depriving its own citizens of those rights. In 1943 Jones delivered a speech entitled "The Negro and the Postwar World" before the Institute of Human Relations at the Woman's College of the University of North Carolina, and in it he displayed the political militancy that increasingly defined him as a social agitator. "It would be amusing if it were not so tragic how little the Negro's situation is understood," Jones declared. "We are segregated, we are separated, and yet that very separation causes us to be sensitive to the ideas which are rampant in the world. And when

The staff of the *Bennett Banner* in action. Black college newspapers were essential outlets for dissent. Students ran stories and editorials that reflected their growing militancy throughout the twentieth century. Image courtesy of the Bennett College Archives at Thomas F. Holgate Library.

our great leaders talk of the worth of individuals, the struggle for freedom and democracy, those ideas penetrate into our sphere of life and we are fired with the hope that it may mean that these rights and privileges shall be extended to all people."[48]

To be certain, Jones's assessment of the struggles and contradictions confronting Black America was not shared by all of his peers. As veterans returned home ready to pursue their rights aggressively, Jones's counterpart fifty-four miles east at the historically Black and state-controlled North Carolina College for Negroes adopted a position that was diametrically opposed to Jones's. James E. Shepard, president of the state's second-largest Black college, was clearly not a public firebrand. Unlike Jones, Shepard used the radio airwaves to caution against unlimited freedom for African Americans, arguing in a national debate against Langston Hughes that "unqualified freedom" could be a dangerous outcome.[49] Many Black elites did not share Shepard's assessment, but a growing militancy in Black America meant that African Americans were faced with uncomfortable choices. Battle lines were being drawn between those who supported Shepard's cautious, accommodationist approach and those who spoke out boldly and unequivocally against white supremacy. Pressure to choose sides bubbled over into daily life at Bennett.

The social and political commentary in the *Bennett Banner* during the Second World War reflects the growing support for civil rights organizing and public protests against Jim Crow. Historian Raymond Gavins chronicled this transformation, noting that NAACP operatives such as Roy Wilkins sensed a surge in wartime radicalism in the Tar Heel State, with Greensboro having the fourth-highest membership among NAACP chapters, just slightly behind Raleigh.[50] Additionally, the political climate of the city had as much to do with an increase in public expressions of dissent, as did the changing mindset of Black youth. As historian William Chafe documents in his classic study *Civilities and Civil Rights*, Greensboro's culture of moderation enticed Black youth, who were revitalized by the burgeoning movement to take more risks with breaking the color line. There were no great barriers to African American voting, and the city had made tremendous strides toward voter registration in the 1940s that resulted in the election of the first Black city councilman in 1951.[51] However, the public spectacle of breaking Jim Crow policies was still taboo.

During the war, Bennett had formed a Contemporary Affairs Committee to keep students informed on current issues connected with the war effort and local politics, but some students still complained of apathy on campus and publicly questioned the commitment of their fellow Belles. "What are your ideas and opinions concerning our national problems—our race problems?" wrote one disgruntled student. Although Bennett administrators decided to dedicate one day out of the week for discussions of "current events and history" in chapel, apparently some students were not as tuned in or invigorated as their peers had hoped they would be.[52] Perhaps they disliked the mandatory daily chapel sessions or, like many young people, were indifferent to world events. A few Bennett women, however, including Valena E. Minor, editor of the student newspaper, attempted to stoke the fires of dissent in their fellow students.

Minor was the daughter of Norman Minor, a prominent and legendary Cleveland lawyer and prosecutor known for his toughness as a prosecutor. As a student leader, she brought that same work ethic and tenacity to campus as the editor of the *Bennett Banner*. In January 1943, Minor wrote an editorial, "Through the Eyes of a New America," that sharply condemned Jim Crow but also criticized those who were unprepared to protest against the American caste system. Her upbringing in the Midwest had insulated her from the more demeaning public policies that defined life in Dixie, but living in the Tar Heel State exposed her to the realities of life under Jim Crow. The tone of the editorial made it unclear whether she actually experienced the events she described or whether she was satirizing white supremacy. Her opening salvo, aimed at students who neglected to become politically engaged, was inflammatory to say the least. "Hail cohorts of Hitler!" wrote Minor. "You brandish your swastika most effectively. No, no, my 'friend,' why do you turn to look at your neighbor? . . . You, dear compatriots, are the most obvious evidence of fifth columning I've seen in a long time. Yet you rest smug assured of the fact that no F.B.I. can ever harm you. Irony . . . how funny." Minor juxtaposed Nazism and Jim Crow, as did other detractors of white supremacy in the New Negro era.[53] She went on to describe a bus ride in which she or a fictional character lodged a small personal protest against the unjust policies of segregation. Never had a writer within the pages of the *Bennett Banner* written such an acerbic, yet witty denunciation of America's racial shortcomings.

Toward the end of her editorial, Minor turned her attention to the countless African Americans who were sidelined by fear or apathy—a reality that became a hallmark of the civil rights movement to come. African Americans who were psychologically conditioned to accept their own denigration, or feared the injurious and often violent backlash that accompanied overt protests, marveled at conscientious objectors of Jim Crow. They boldly drank out of "white only" fountains, stubbornly took their seats in "white only" sections of restaurants, or in the case of the person represented in Minor's editorial, refused to comply with segregation on public transportation. Some members of the Black community who vowed to uphold the color line frowned upon or even threatened these "trouble makers." The defiant bus rider in Minor's editorial encountered "giggles" from those who thought her foolish to challenge what they believed to be the sacrosanct policies of the Jim Crow South. Minor admonished them by leaning upon her teachings from Bennett. "I can't be too critical of the attitude you take," she declared. "It's engrained in you—this fear of the "superior race." But stand up for your rights—and stand by those who do stand up for your rights if you can't stand up for them yourself. . . . The next time you're in a similar situation, think twice before you sniggle . . . and then be PROUD to be a

Negro." In a final rhetorical flourish targeting white supremacy, she warned, "You'll see hundreds more like me, Hitlerites," declared Minor. "Maybe they can make Americans out of you yet."[54]

Minor was a graduating senior the year that she wrote the explosive piece for the *Bennett Banner*. As the editor of the paper, she had the latitude to publish what she wanted, but most importantly, she was the beneficiary of four years within a communitas that nurtured her sense of self and emboldened her to use the power of print media to express her frustrations and angst with American racism. The era of the New Negro slowly bled over into the flowering of radicalism during World War II, and students like Minor were the by-product of that nexus. History has seldom recorded their names or venerated their deeds, but scores of young women and men who were exposed to environments like Bennett entered their respective communities as race women and race men and used that foundation to nurture, mold, and produce the student activists of the 1960s who would soon reshape American democracy and transform a nation. Upon graduating from Bennett, Minor returned to her hometown of Cleveland, married a local bandleader, and kicked off a long and prominent career in local radio. She became a fixture at station WABQ and later helped to launch the Community Action for Youth, a Cleveland-based organization dedicated to providing job training and social services for the city's poor.

· · · · · ·

The spring semester of 1944 was busy, displaying the full panorama of the second curriculum that a Black college like Bennett had to offer—including service to the broader community, lectures on Black history, and guests with perspectives uniquely valuable to the student body. Early that semester, the Woman's Division of Christian Service, an extension of the Methodist Church, invited Jones to a seminar titled "Christianity and the Race Problem," which was to culminate in a conference entitled "Racism and World Order." According to the correspondence, Jones was invited because the conference organizers knew he not only would be a vital asset in presenting his expertise on the subject but also would take back the knowledge gained and disseminate it among his students and across the airwaves to the Greensboro community.[55] At the same time, Jones was arranging a spectacular lineup for the upcoming Negro History Week festivities. From Jones's perspective, Negro History Week presented an opportunity to lay out a blueprint for liberation, infused with racial pride and imbued with marching orders from luminaries within the field. Indeed the Black lecture circuit was a prominent fixture on almost every Black college campus and featured heavy hitters in the area of civil rights, academics, and entertainment. As a virtual who's-who of the Black experience streamed through campus, students could rest assured that they were being exposed to speakers who were highly accomplished experts in their fields who shared the same freedom dreams that fueled the collective imaginations and desires of Bennett women. The *Banner* reported that John Hope Franklin was returning to campus to deliver a timely lecture titled "The Negro Soldier—A Century of Gallant Fighting." But it was the climax of that week's celebration that ultimately stood out and fully exhibited the type of communitas that David Dallas Jones was constructing in Greensboro.

• • • • • •

Bennett's Contemporary Affairs Committee brought a representative of the NAACP to campus they believed could effectively communicate with students. Activist and community organizer Ella Baker had only been with the NAACP for two years when she arrived on Bennett's campus to address the student body. As a 1927 graduate of nearby historically Black Shaw University, she was well aware of the vital space that she occupied at Bennett, and at various times, her own matriculation at Shaw had been punctuated by both a charge to serve and a hint of militancy that sharpened her commitment to get involved with the struggle for African American liberation. As she took to the podium, Baker not only promoted the work of the NAACP, but she also rallied the young women to envision themselves as change agents. Jones had first encountered Baker as he traveled the professional circuit in New York in the late 1920s, and according to Baker, the two had met on more than one occasion. Impressed, Jones offered Baker a teaching appointment at Bennett, which the young activist turned down in order to pursue hands-on opportunities in community organizing that more closely aligned with her interest in stoking direct action protests against Jim Crow. By the time Baker took a job with the NAACP, her reputation as a firebrand for justice and unconventional womanhood most likely drew Jones to her once again, as he approved her invitation to speak on campus. Baker's critical thinking, tenacity, and knack for finding calm amid the storm would become endearing qualities that continued to draw young revolutionaries to her in the fateful years to come.[56]

Black America continued to denounce the United States for its hypocritical embrace of Jim Crow and white supremacy while it fought a war to uphold the principles of democracy. Yet they also held fast to dreams that patient activism, litigation, and broad pressure on the federal government would soon usher in equal opportunities and first-class citizenship. Several developments after the war heightened African Americans' expectations and sense of urgency. Under pressure from labor leader A. Philip Randolph, President Franklin Roosevelt capitulated to the demands for fair hiring in the defense industries, and the *Pittsburgh Courier*'s Double V Campaign was widely promoted ad embraced. Much like the burden borne by Jackie Robinson, the first African American to break the color line in major league baseball, Black youth attending Black colleges were drilled in a dress rehearsal for the fruits of democracy. According to their instructors, there were rules to the game, expectations that Blacks must adhere to, and a grave responsibility to be paragons of virtue, respect, and excellence as they prepared for the personal and professional opportunities that awaited them in a post-segregated world. For those who administered this message, it was clear that the future success of Black America hinged on how well the first wave of youths who broke the color line would do in proving that they were as sharp and talented as any of their white competitors. Like athletes such as Robinson, those first entrants into professional positions usually reserved for whites carried a special burden to represent the race. At Bennett, this ritual of self-preparedness manifested itself in the "Hold Your Job" campaign.

Founded in 1943 by the National Council of Negro Women (NCNW), the "Hold Your Job" campaign was half instruction and half pep talk. As African American women increasingly entered various industries during World War II, the NCNW saw an opportunity to help advance the careers of Black women. In her study on African American women and wartime industries in Richmond and Detroit, Megan Taylor Shockley largely frames the "Hold Your Job" campaign as a top-down exercise tantamount to Negro clubwomen lecturing working-class Black women on how to keep their jobs without exposing their cultural deficiencies, such as not being "clean, courteous, punctual, and affable."[57] At Bennett, the campaign was interpreted differently. The stories published by the *Banner* dispensed with classism, instead voicing solidarity among Black women. One editorial confronted attacks against *all* "Negro women," and not just those from a specific class, as the writer pointed out that the real enemy of Black female progress in the workplace was prejudice based on "misconceptions"—that is, the stereotypical and racist images of Blacks as lazy, unskilled, and worthless. The editorial read in part, "Negro women . . . have proven themselves capable of competing with women of other races whether the task be a skilled or unskilled one. In many instances they have proved themselves superior."[58] As these college students appeared to already understand, the Urban League's old mantra, "Last Hired, First Fired," was ultimately a result of racist policies and that white supervisors would continue to punish them in the workplace regardless of their contributions on the job or their class status within the Black community.[59]

Bennett women also wielded the pen to assess and protest gender roles during the war. While the Home Making Institute on campus promoted virtues of domesticity, it also fostered an environment in which Bennett students studied the most pressing social issues of their time. The Home Making Institute in 1944 held a seminar called "Health and Nutrition, Child Care and Problems of Youth, and the Employment of Women."[60] The latter subject triggered a passionate response from student reporter Alice Holloway. "There are those who claim that it is the patriotic duty of women to relinquish these jobs to our returning service men," wrote Holloway in an editorial published in the *Banner*. "No one wants to be unpatriotic; this is equally true for men as for women. But patriotism ceases to be a virtue when defined in such an undemocratic term as economic enslavement."[61] Holloway's powerful prose illustrates that Bennett women were acutely aware of sexist ideals that marginalized their lives, and they pushed back against the idea of vacating advancements made by African American women during the war effort. As women like Holloway exited institutions such as Bennett, they were prepared to shatter the historic barriers erected by race, class, and gender. After graduating from Bennett, Holloway moved to Rochester, New York, where she became a pioneering leader in the field of education, serving as the city's first African American vice principal and principal of elementary schools. She was later "recognized as an energetic champion for the school children of New York State," helped to oversee the integration of the school system in Rochester, and played a vital role establishing Monroe Community College, founded in 1961 and located in downtown Rochester.[62] Holloway's life is indicative of how Bennett prepared its students to excel in the face of prodigious challenges, transforming the various communities that they served.

While Holloway used her pen to criticize restrictions against women in the workplace, other Belles sought practical ways to protest the color line. In the fall semester of 1944, Bennett hosted a Student Interracial Ministry conference that welcomed thirty-four different colleges to campus to address "religion, race, brotherhood, and constructive action." Cosponsored by Greensboro College, the three-day conference brought in Atlanta

University–based sociologist Ira Reid as one of its principal speakers. Reid, who took over the editorial duties of DuBois's new journal *Phylon* after DuBois stepped down, was influential in pushing the students to think critically about how they could protest the color line. Students broke out into separate workshops and seminars and as the energy of the conference rose, they resolved to continue their efforts in interracial fellowship. Moreover, although students did not immediately engage in large-scale protests, the conference laid the groundwork for future integrated coalitions that would be far more productive in inspiring students to speak out against injustice.[63] The *Banner* reported that the "climax of the meeting was reached when a resolution was presented stating that this conference would go on record as resolved to work conscientiously to eliminate segregation in the transportation system of North Carolina."[64] The conference also revealed the shortcomings and deep divide in how students attending predominantly white colleges were taught to think about the future of race relations. While liberal white youth were open to the idea of temporary fellowship, they were less optimistic about the postwar world. Durham's Black newspaper the *Carolinian* polled a group of white students who attended the conference on the question, "Do you think the Negro will ever achieve a status equal to that of the white man in America?" Students attending Woman's College, which was later renamed the University of North Carolina at Greensboro, responded overwhelmingly in the negative, with ten-to-three odds that it would never happen. *Bennett Banner* reporter Orial Ann Banks curtly retorted, "What do you think about those Bennett girls?"[65]

Bennett students continued to make overtures toward white college students even though many were pessimistic about racial progress. William and Mary College suspended its campus newspaper and promptly removed its student editor, Marilyn Kaemmerle, because she had argued that African Americans should be recognized as equals and admitted to the private Virginia college. The staff of the *Bennett Banner* responded by extending an invitation to Kaemmerle to join the *Banner* as a guest writer. "Miss Kaemmerle's editorial expressing a belief in racial assimilation as a future possibility violates no superior interest in a democracy," wrote *Banner* staff reporter Betty Powers. "If Miss Kaemmerle's editorial is in violation of State interests, all writings on the issue, whether pro or con, should be in violation."[66] Editorials such as Power's demonstrate that Bennett students were observing racial commentary across the country and building high hopes for a postwar America that would usher in true democracy.

It was the vesper speaker in March 1945 who best illustrated how vitally important Black colleges such as Bennett were in providing a forum for dissenting voices. Described as an eccentric, an iconoclast, a prophet, and the father of the modern civil rights movement, Rev. Vernon Johns arrived on campus with a growing reputation among southerners looking to break through the color line. Johns broke the mold of the conventional southern Black preacher and was known just as much for his photographic memory of the Bible and classic literature as he was for entering pulpits with muddy boots "and mix match socks." At various times, Johns was an itinerant minister, traveling the countryside proclaiming God's word and unabashedly discussing the evils of white supremacy to those bold enough to extend him an invitation to preach. He simultaneously inspired awe in his listeners and kept conservatives of all races on edge as they had no clue what the radical clergyman would say or do next. Historian Taylor Branch notes that as Johns traveled the college lecture circuit, "university officials would answer a summons to his 'office' only to find him at a phone booth in the bus station." It is unclear whether Jones was ever invited to one of Johns's famous summits at the bus depot, but his arrival on campus was surely a grand experience for the Belles of Bennett College. While there is no text record of the speech he delivered at Bennett, less than two months before his arrival he gave a speech at an Emancipation Day celebration in Charlottesville, Virginia, that sheds light on the rhetorical tendencies of the eccentric spiritual revolutionary who was making waves throughout the South. "For almost a century now we have been celebrating our Emancipation when, in reality, our Emancipation has not been won," asserted Johns. "A Negro who calls these conditions in which we live freedom does not deserve to be free. He has disqualified himself for freedom in one of two ways: either by not desiring freedom or else by not knowing what freedom is." Such speeches were indicative of Johns's brand of politics, and his teachings were in lockstep with Jones's own militant views and his career work as a race man at Bennett. Two years later, Johns was invited to become the pastor of Dexter Avenue Baptist Church in Montgomery, Alabama, and would remain in that position until a newly minted PhD recipient out of Boston University named Martin Luther King Jr. replaced him.[67]

As the war ended, campus visitors such as Johns helped make the women of Bennett even more conscious of the burdens and social responsibility that awaited them. With victory achieved abroad through the aggressive push of a newly integrated military and the use of a horrific weapon the likes of which the world had never seen, the pressing question remained, Would America uphold the democracy that thousands of GIs supposedly gave their lives to defend? The answer came quickly. News stories emerged of Black soldiers being lynched, bludgeoned, and castrated, often while still in their uniforms. The country exploded in race riots as defiant Blacks, who were determined to challenge Jim Crow, competed with whites. As the war drew to a close, the women of Bennett closed ranks with African Americans across the country who looked toward new government initiatives to narrow the employment gap that for years had been exacerbated by race-baiting southern politicians who perfected the bigoted undertones of "states' rights" in order to funnel job opportunities and beneficial New Deal policies away from Black Americans. Acknowledging this reality, they supported both the NAACP and the Fair Employment Practice Committee (FEPC), an office established by the federal government in 1941 to ameliorate racism and injustice in the workplace.[68]

Toward the end of 1944, numerous southern politicians worked feverishly to dismantle the FEPC, preparing for the returning Black veterans who joined their fellow laborers in demanding fair treatment and access to the numerous postwar jobs and emerging boom-time industries. During its brief life, the FEPC had achieved modest gains on behalf of African Americans, but by 1945 its fate was all but sealed. Through the nefarious work of powerful southern congressmen such as John Rankin, James Eastland, and the infamous Theodore Bilbo, the House Appropriations Committee decided to choke off funding for the FEPC, branding those who supported the waning program as "Communists, pinks, Reds, and other offbrands of American citizenship."[69] Indeed support to eliminate the FEPC was broad among southern conservatives, leading historian John Egerton to conclude "Practically every Southerner in congress except the maverick Floridian, Claude Pepper, detested the very idea of the FEPC."[70] In both houses, senators and representatives alike filibustered, undercut, and worked aggressively to defund most initiatives associated with eliminating the color line in postwar employment. Nevertheless, the FEPC did not go without a fight. The Black press launched a last-minute effort to salvage the committee, and Jones's good friend Mary McLeod Bethune and NAACP head Walter White personally lobbied President Roosevelt in an effort to rescue the FEPC. The latter development may have directly drafted Bennett's campus into the fight.

The editorial staff of the *Bennett Banner* canvassed the university to determine campus opinion on the question, "What should Negroes do to crystalize gains made in employment during the war?" Responses flooded into the *Banner* office that reflected the militancy of Bennett women and their desire to help the cause. Student Dorothy Walker urged African Americans to "exert power" through the unions, while student Cassandra Moore, in addition to supporting labor unions, also called for "support of pressure groups such as the F.E.P.C., N.A.A.C.P, and other groups whose aim is to secure economic freedom for all regardless of race, color, or creed." Student Doris Newland echoed that sentiment by arguing that unwavering support for the FEPC "will make Negro dreams in this war a reality after the war." In all, the April 1945 edition of the *Banner* contained the testimonies of eight Belles who wrote in to express their support of the FEPC.[71]

While southern legislators worked tirelessly to eliminate all postwar benefits for African Americans, their action had a twofold effect. First, their commitment to bigotry galvanized a new generation of youths who were increasingly emboldened to confront the racist policies that enveloped the nation. Second, they mocked the notion that the war had been fought in part to make democracy a reality for all of humanity. As America settled into a postatomic world fraught with glaring contradictions, these two developments dovetailed perfectly into the formation of an insurgency that was brewing on Black college campuses such as Bennett. Historian Merl Reed appropriately concludes, "It appears that though the FEPC lost ground in the summer of 1945, the civil rights movement may have strengthened."[72]

Solidarity against Jim Crow intensified at Bennett during the fall of 1945. Another campus survey found widespread and enthusiastic support for the establishment of an official NAACP chapter on campus, with one being formed shortly thereafter. Bennett women concretely understood that whatever barriers that impeded Black progress would only be breached or shattered by steady pressure from the disinherited masses. Warning shots in the Bennett press signaled a growing radicalism. In an editorial entitled "Where Do We Go from Here?," one Bennett Belle asked the pressing question about America's future that millions of Black folks wanted to know the answer to. "Will [America] remember that the true road to peace is paved with actions rather than sentiment, and that before she can set herself up as an example of true democracy, there must be peace in her own land among all races and creed of her own people?" And, as always, Bennett continued to host a steady stream of activists and noted leaders who stoked the fires of militancy among the students. Max Yergan, a far-left-leaning activist who cofounded the Council on African Affairs alongside well-known activist and entertainer Paul Robeson, addressed the student body in November 1945 and boldly denounced imperialism. He also informed the women of

Bennett about the coming wars of independence throughout the African diaspora that would catalyze the modern civil rights movement. Yergan declared that, "The people of Africa and the rest of the colonial world are restless, refusing to continue to accept circumstances imposed upon them." In that same month, the students also heard from renowned educator President Benjamin E. Mays of Morehouse College. "Perhaps the atomic bomb may frighten man to his senses, rid races of their arrogance and false pride, and develop integrity among nations, doing for humanity what the gospel of Jesus Christ has not done for nineteen hundred years," declared the renowned educator as he confronted the postwar world. Bennett students reported his comments as "startling," but they soon had their own run-in with churchgoing southerners that reinforced Mays's bold claims.[73]

At the war's end, Bennett students were not only mocking America's feigned embrace and hollow proclamations of democracy; they also began to question its claims as a Christian nation. When several students responded to an invitation to attend service at the West Market Street Baptist Church in November 1945, they were disgusted as the ushers roped them off in a segregated section away from the white congregation. According to one student, embracing segregation in a house of worship revealed "the existing inconsistency and discrepancy in religion which seems to be no more than a 'spoken' practice." Editorials in the *Banner* sharply condemned the West Market Street Baptist Church congregation and a cartoon satirized and ridiculed the idea of segregation in a church that proselytized Christian brotherhood and love for all mankind. However, no students left the church in protest. It is unclear whether the Bennett women who attended church that day yielded to the pressure to uphold decorum and grace in a public place of worship or whether they, like so many others, were not yet ready to display a collective show of force against Jim Crow policies. However, what is certain is that the *Bennett Banner* afforded them a vitally important space to express their angst and frustration with white supremacy—a cathartic alternative and a mild yet significant form of protest that numerous Bennett Belles had taken advantage of over the years.[74]

World War II unquestionably shook the entire nation to its core. Not only did Black veterans return home maimed by the scars of war, but many of them were also deeply disturbed by the intractable nature of white supremacy. The New Negro militancy of the 1920s and 1930s and calls for a "double victory" following World War II created scores of race men and race women who unapologetically embraced their heritage, which America had attempted to undermine. Moreover, the youths of that generation immersed

Bennett student Betty Ann Artis used the pages of the *Bennett Banner* to satirize a racist encounter that she and other students had at a local Greensboro church in November 1945. Black college students increasingly pointed out the hypocrisies of American life following World War II. Image courtesy of the Bennett College Archives at Thomas F. Holgate Library.

themselves in carefully planned instruction that resulted in well-trained constitutionalists who were prepared to stand on the broken promises of a government that failed to uphold their civil and human rights. Black colleges such as Bennett drilled young women in a daily ritual of idealism, cultural nationalism, and race consciousness, and the results of such training produced considerable fruit for the liberation movement. As 1945 drew to a close, one Bennett student offered this profound warning: "In conclusion, of this one thing I am certain—the problem will never be solved until it is attacked directly and without fear. Democracy can never be a full-pledged practice until America uses her national strength to denounce 'tyrannical idealists' and publically abide by a 'democratic way of life.' Unless men become united in one accord, strive to build on a foundation of just equality, and use intelligent foresight to encompass the breach of segregation and discrimination, America's future is doubtful."[75]

The race women of Bennett College unquestionably share a role as forerunners of the modern civil rights movement, and David Dallas Jones played a large role in their politicization. Jones channeled the activists' energies from the New Negro era directly into Bennett, and for the next twenty-five years he molded young women who were vital change agents in the struggle for Black liberation. Bennett students became more emboldened with the shifting political currents, resulting in peaceful public protests and personal acts of defiance. The relatively progressive culture of Greensboro provided space for more aggressive forms of social disobedience—a fact that would result in the Gate City's serving as the epicenter of the student-led protests that would galvanize the movement in 1960 by channeling the collective protest energies of Black colleges throughout the Deep South. It seems unlikely that incidents such as the theater boycott of the late 1930s or endeavors such as the Bennett College radio program could have succeeded in the more hostile portions of Dixie. Furthermore, the communitas/ racialized space that enveloped Bennett College heightened the political consciousness of scores of women and sharpened their abilities to articulate their goals for achieving freedom and democracy for all African Americans. Jones and his students certainly made their mark on the early freedom movement and cultivated a space that became a focal point for local activism during the struggles that lay ahead. Jones encountered health problems and stepped down from the presidency of Bennett in 1955, passing the torch of leadership to Willa Player, the first African American woman to serve as president of the institution. Player continued to cultivate Bennett as a seedbed for activism and played a prominent role in the iconic civil rights protests that emerged just five years later. Ironically, the transition from Jones to Player coincided with a momentous sea change in the national struggle for Black freedom, and this time, a historically Black college located deeper in the heart of the South would play a pivotal role in its development.

4 Our Aims Are High and Our Determinations Deep

Alabama State University and the Dissolution of Fear,
1930–1960

••

We are going to enjoy all privileges that are due first class citizens, and
we are going to do it in a first class manner. We have the constitution
before us and the Supreme Court behind us. We cannot go astray.
Our aims are high and our determinations are deep.

—Loretta Jean Thomas, freshman, *Fresh-More*, December 1955

Of all of the forces drawing the civil rights movement together, music proved one of the most enduring and empowering. The "blues people" that poet LeRoi Jones (Amiri Baraka) wrote of in 1963 helped bind together those who routinely faced the terrors associated with white supremacy. Such was the case in 1955 as the world's focus turned to Alabama's seat of power—Montgomery. The bus boycott famously launched by Rosa Parks sparked the local community in Montgomery to action. Writing for the *Montgomery Advertiser*, journalist Joe Azbell reported on the first mass meeting held in support of Parks and the boycott. "The passion that fired the meeting," he wrote, "was seen as the thousands of voices joined in singing *Onward, Christian Soldier*. Another hymn followed. The voices thundered through the church."[1] While anthems and Negro spirituals lifted troubled spirits, the freedom songs of the movement were most often creative hybrids of traditional musical standards. Popular gospel songs such as "We Shall Not Be Moved" and "This Little Light of Mine" were refitted with lyrics and themes of resistance, stoking a sense of courage and unity in the face of racial violence. One courageous member of the faculty at Alabama State University (ASU) played a key role in this movement that should not be forgotten.

Professor Laurence Hayes was a faculty member at ASU in the Music Department and director of the school's marching band.[2] One of the attendees of the laboratory school at ASU was an eleven-year-old girl named Jamila Jones. Not only was Jones blessed with a gifted voice, she and her feisty older sister Doris were members of the local National Association for the Advancement of Colored People (NAACP) youth group, where they would often learn of the importance of voting rights from Rosa Parks. Jamila and her friends sang songs focused on the burgeoning movement and began calling themselves the Montgomery Gospel Trio.[3] Hayes quickly arranged a tune for the trio called "Ain't Gonna Ride No Bus No More," a song that would become a staple of the Montgomery movement as the young girls traveled to churches, regional tea parties for Black socialites and sororities, and the Highlander Folk School to raise funds and awareness for their cause. They reached a pinnacle in their career when they were showcased at New York's Carnegie Hall in 1961.

To come up with his edgy tune, Hayes reworked the lyrics of a traditional southern folk song called "Ain't Gonna Rain No More" and even left in the word "hell," which was found in a stanza of the original song. The verse read, "How in the hell do the old folk know it ain't gonna rain no more?" which Hayes revised to the more controversial, "How in the hell don't the white folk know we ain't gonna ride them buses no more?" The song became so popular that Hayes would often strike up the Mighty Marching Hornets during ASU football games and lead the students in singing the new anthem that captured the determination and defiance flourishing among local Blacks.[4] Hayes arrived on campus four years before the bus boycott, but he had already captured the respect of both his colleagues and his students, who affectionately referred to him as either Prof. Hayes or Doc. Known for being tough but fair, Hayes went on to train hundreds of musicians in their craft for the next thirty-seven years at ASU.[5]

High-stakes, overt activism was a serious gamble for any person of color in Alabama. Whether they were blue-collar workers, domestics, sharecroppers, or college professors, many breadwinners were silenced by fear of losing their jobs and thus their ability to sustain their families. Yet Hayes stood at the crossroads of history with so many others and determined that the reward of dignity was far greater than the risk of jeopardizing their livelihoods. "A number of them would attend the mass meetings," recalled Jones. "I say 'a number of them' because some were afraid to go at this time, but then you had the people who did."[6] While Hayes counted himself among those bold enough to challenge Jim Crow, the space in which he worked also drew the wrath of the white power structure. Indeed, the rising tide of activism was connected directly with ASU.

· · · · · ·

By the time the bus boycott emerged in Montgomery, a thriving communitas had existed at ASU for almost ninety years. Founded in 1867, ASU underwent growth and development in the Cradle of the Confederacy that was arduous, to say the least. Early principals of the school were forced to defend both their lives and the very existence of the institution with shotguns.[7] Dixie was awash in the blood of outspoken leaders of newly freed slave communities, and the construction of institutions to serve exclusively Black folks brought some of the fiercest opposition. In the midst of Reconstruction, the lingering questions and concerns regarding the white power structure centered on the issue of what type of education Blacks would receive, who would administer that education, and how they could maintain control and influence over the institutions tasked with delivering that education in order to prevent the rise of Blacks who questioned their subordinate position in society. That problem had already beset the town of Huntsville, where William Hooper Councill, the first principal and founder of what would later become Alabama A&M University, caused quite a stir by defiantly attempting to board a railroad car reserved for whites. Councill, a former slave, retreated to conservatism following the outcry of local whites, but his radical actions raised serious concerns about the future of Black colleges and the influence of those who were employed by them. In the summer of 1887, Lincoln Normal School (later renamed Alabama State University) was in the process of moving from the small town of Marion to the capital city of Montgomery. This led a cautious white citizen of Montgomery to pen an editorial for the local paper asking, "Might not the president of this same university march his school into the cars reserved for white people, leaving the colored coach empty, thus reenacting at our own depot the scenes of Saturday at Huntsville?"[8] Despite the paper's attempt to stoke fears among local whites, ASU eventually completed its move to Montgomery and created a pipeline between Alabama A&M that fortuitously brought one of the state's most important race leaders to campus.

Both John William Beverly and George Washington Trenholm took the helm of leadership at ASU after the school's founder, William B. Paterson, died in 1915. Beverly was a dignified educator, widely recognized as the state's first African American historian. He served the institution well but relinquished control to Trenholm after five years, stepping down to serve as dean of the institution and professor of history.[9] Trenholm had a reputation as a determined and capable young man. In 1896 he graduated as the valedictorian of his class at Alabama A&M, where he studied under Councill, and for the next twenty years he served as the principal of the City High School in Tuscumbia, Alabama, a small town tucked away in the northwest corner of the state. Popular on the lecture circuit, Trenholm often recited educator and author Marvin Summers Pittman's book *Successful Teaching in Rural Schools* and repeatedly highlighted the passage, "He must believe in the future."[10] Setting his sights on better days, he accepted the call to come to ASU, and it was not long before he inherited the full duties of leadership during the summer of 1920. His tenure at ASU would be brief, as his health worsened and he died in 1925, yet the greatest addition that he made to the campus was the inclusion of his son as one of his chief administrators.

Harper Councill Trenholm reflected his father through and through. He was the namesake of William Hooper Councill, the man who took G. W. Trenholm under his wing at Alabama A&M. He shared his father's insatiable appetite for education but differed in his politics. As a product of the Nadir and as a man tasked with preserving a place of education for Black youths in the Deep South, G. W. Trenholm took careful steps not to incur the wrath of white stakeholders who kept Black educators under a watchful eye.[11] Straight away, Harper Councill Trenholm was exposed to some of his father's more conservative friends who embraced the paternalism of whites. A letter from Frank Caffey, a boxing promoter and trainer, greeted him upon his assumption of the presidency of the institution. The letter stated in part, "If things get going wrong there, let me know and if a colored man is in your way, my white friends there will soon bring him around your way of thinking."[12] Trenholm did not need Caffey's services. He embraced the New Negro movement that was sweeping the nation, joining the ranks of numerous African Americans who began to gradually shed their fear of speaking out against white supremacy. The alliances that he made and the partnerships that he crafted laid the foundation for ASU's transformation into a seedbed of radicalism in the coming years.

Trenholm was only twenty-five years old when he took the helm at ASU. He was a Morehouse man, graduating with a bachelor's degree in 1920 and earning a baccalaureate in philosophy in 1921 from the University of Chicago. He assumed the interim duties as G. W. Trenholm battled severe illness during his last days in office. When the time came, he had a clear vision for how he would lead the university. His chief innovation was the introduction of a second curriculum that emphasized idealism and encouraged race consciousness undergirded by history.[13]

In one of his very first speeches, Trenholm spoke at an event in Huntsville commemorating the anniversary of the Emancipation Proclamation. Examining the "career" of African Americans since the end of slavery, Trenholm boldly spoke of the "dark side" of race relations in an era in which few Black men in the Deep South dared to acknowledge the realities of the color line. "I would find only too many instances of wholesale disfranchisement by clever laws and by violence," declared Trenholm. "Of peonage and other labor difficulties; of proscription, segregation, lynching and mob violence which made the lot of the Negro precarious and disheartening; and of vicious propaganda through tongue and pen designed to discredit the possibilities of the Negro and to brand the aspirations of his supporters as visionary and a total failure when measured by the first twenty years of freedom."[14] In earlier years, Black men in the South were run out of town for speaking publicly about the harsh social conditions that defined their lives. As a New Negro, Trenholm boldly pushed the envelope.

The ability to practice self-determination while maintaining an autonomous space proved difficult to secure in Alabama's closed society. Nevertheless, Trenholm transformed ASU into an oasis of race consciousness even as it was simultaneously enveloped by hostility and racial violence. From the start, he worked to eradicate any semblance of self-doubt his students may have possessed as a result of being exposed to years of white supremacy. "Unfortunately, our whole problem has been beclouded by misrepresentation," observed Trenholm. "And this prejudice and misinformation must be dispelled."[15] The process of reconditioning the minds of Black youths called for the recruitment of teachers committed to the task, and Trenholm assembled a spectacular team. From institutions such as Morehouse, Spelman, Talladega, Cheyney, Howard, and Fisk, Trenholm gathered young Black idealists who had already been fashioned and impacted by the second curriculum administered at their alma maters.[16] They readily embraced Negro History Week, created by Carter G. Woodson in 1926, and started organizations on campus such as the Delver's Literary Club, which made Woodson's book *The Negro in Our History* the featured book for the entire 1925–26 school year. The club held meetings on campus and often in the homes of faculty and alumni, where professors and students would review, discuss, and recite passages of Woodson's book aloud.[17]

Woodson's campaign to launch Negro History Week provided Trenholm a platform from which to install Black history in the pedagogical strategy of the entire campus. Moreover, Woodson's push to acknowledge the historical contributions of African Americans helped to legitimize the narrative of Black folks in the academy and paved the way for an increase in scholarship about the achievements of Black America. As a bibliophile, Trenholm had a desire to amass scholarship on African Americans that would be accessible for his students, which dovetailed with Woodson's vision for bringing Black history to every home, school, and library. "We want to build up a good reference library on the Negro," reported the campus paper. "And all students, alumni and friends are requested to make their Founder's Day Contribution for that purpose this year. Our slogan is '100 new volumes on the Negro.'" The expansion of race consciousness as a critical component of the second curriculum was not limited to scholarship. Visual reminders also aided in removing psychological barriers to success. Campus faculty planned to "commemorate the day and the week by placing framed pictures of Negro leaders in each classroom."[18]

For Trenholm and those who worked hands-on with Black youths, the unveiling of Negro History Week was a golden opportunity. The campus paper reported, "The whole movement is deserving of emphasis and encouragement. Our students need to know about Negro history. Racial respect is to be developed as we know and receive inspiration from our racial heritage. . . . Let us in our school help to push the cause."[19] Serving as a laboratory of race consciousness, ASU offered classes in rhetoric where students fleshed out their thoughts on the stress and strife caused by white supremacy. On February 11, 1927, in front of a school assembly, young Jule Clayton recited Ephraim David Tyler's poem entitled "The Black Man's Plea for Justice."[20] The opportunities for Clayton to publicly recite a relatively radical poem in almost any other space in the state were limited, to say the least. But surrounded by her peers, encouraged by her faculty, and under the watchful eye of Trenholm, Clayton boldly voiced the freedom dreams of Black folks everywhere.

Implementing the second curriculum served a pragmatic goal. Crafting visions of liberation was a necessity if ASU was to provide direction for students who were tasked with cutting through the seemingly impenetrable layers of intolerance that enveloped life in Alabama. Since the end of slavery, formalizing a plan of action in the hinterlands of the Deep South had been nearly unthinkable, given the violent consequences. But planting the seeds of activism within the enclave is what Black college faculty did best.

In 1929 a special student arrived at ASU. For Solomon Seay Sr., the dawning of racial responsibility did not occur until he enrolled at the university. An itinerant preacher with the African Methodist Episcopal Zion Church, Seay enrolled in colleges when he could, picking up a course or two along the way. "About all that I can remember from that experience," wrote Seay of ASU, "is two courses that did something special to me." To judge from their formal titles, those two classes, Rural Sociology and Human Geography, did not broadcast their militancy. Such was the magic of the second curriculum. Seay's professors had the opportunity to close their doors, begin their instruction, and relate the coursework to the oppressive social, political, and economic conditions Blacks suffered. In doing so, they hoped that the outcome would be conscientious citizens at least—even freedom fighters. They hit the jackpot with Seay. "Both courses helped to awaken me far more than either of those teachers could imagine," he recalled. "This was an additional motivation for my whole civil rights thrust in the years to come." As the movement came to life in Montgomery during the 1950s, Martin Luther King Jr. described Seay as "one of the few clerical voices that, in the years preceding the protest, had lashed out against the injustices heaped on the Negro, and urged his people to a greater appreciation of their own worth." Seay entered the ASU communitas as a young minister and was immediately grounded in the struggle experienced by both the working-class and professional members of his future congregations. If Trenholm was looking for a way to make the daily work on campus central to the freedom dreams of Black folks, he was off to a good start.[21]

Trenholm was by no means reckless in adopting programs that challenged white supremacy. He was no accomodationist, but as the leader of a school in the heart of the Black Belt that was dependent on state funds, he practiced conservatism when it was personally and professionally expedient. One such moment arrived when the law firm of Fort, Beddow and Ray of Birmingham positioned itself to take up the defense of the Scottsboro Boys in the famous case that captured the world's attention in the summer of 1931. They sought the blessing of the Commission on Interracial Cooperation, a nationally organized biracial group of moderates to which Trenholm belonged.[22] In a letter from E. T. Belsaw, a prominent Black dentist from Mobile and the secretary of the Alabama chapter, Trenholm was apprised that "these noted attorneys feel that their case will be prejudiced against them if it is known that they are representing the N.A.A.C.P., which is a very unpopular organization with southern white men of the lower and middle class." They knew that gaining the support of Trenholm would bolster their standing in the Black community, thus aiding them in their attempt to put the Commission on Interracial Cooperation at the head of the case. They also granted him anonymity. "I have been requested to secure your vote as to whether you are willing to have these attorneys make the statement that they are representing the Inter-Racial Commission in attempting to see that these Negro boys receive justice," Belsaw wrote. "Your name will not be known personally in this matter. Only the organization will be known."[23] Trenholm voted in the affirmative.[24] It was all for naught, as the case was litigated by the legal defense wing of the American Communist Party, the International Labor Defense. It is unclear whether Trenholm was trying to distance himself from the radicalized reputation of the NAACP or whether he genuinely believed he was facilitating the most expedient and surest means of finding justice for the Scottsboro Boys. His other political affiliations were far less ambiguous. In the same year that the Scottsboro Boys suffered under the crushing weight of institutionalized white supremacy, Trenholm carved out space for two of his ASU students, J. S. Abrams and Benjamin Davie, to attend the Kings Mountain Student Conference in North Carolina. The retreat, hosted annually since 1912 by the YMCA, brought together Black males with religious leaders, educators, and activists from across the country. Historian Randal Maurice Jelks notes, "The Kings Mountain Conferences provided Black southern men leadership training that they might not receive elsewhere."[25] A closer examination of the individual conference seminars reveals why that was the case. In 1931 Trenholm funded the travel of Abrams and Davie to the conference, where they met with notables such as E. Franklin Frazier, Charles S. Johnson, Marion Cuthbert, Howard Thurman, and Arthur A. Schomburg, to name a few. They also ironically fellowshipped with a young man named Lawrence Dunbar Reddick, who was appointed a special delegate to the conference. Reddick, a student from Fisk University, would play a much larger role in the Montgomery movement in the years to come. The theme for that year's conference was "Life's Deeper Meaning as Revealed Through: Religion, Education, and Race Relations." In the "Seminar on Education," two questions arose for attendees to contemplate: "First should our college help people to adjust themselves to the status quo; or, second, should they help people develop the ability to properly appraise the status quo and, if necessary, to change it?"[26] One can only imagine the robust conversation and debate that such a weighty question unearthed. The inquiry was destined to take center stage once again as political militants and radical thought increasingly found their way onto Black college campuses.

In the years before the upheaval of the 1950s and 1960s, Trenholm was fully committed to lifting up education as a means by which to improve the condition of the race. He served on the Executive Council of the Association for the Study of Negro Life and History (ASNLH), further developing his relationship with Woodson. Trenholm provided space for his professors on campus to deliver instruction on the history of the Black experience, and Woodson's campaign to celebrate Negro history resonated from the campus to the community. Woodson arrived at ASU on March 29, 1936, one of several visits he made to Montgomery on behalf of his friend Trenholm. On that day, he held open forums with students and addressed a campus-wide assembly.[27] He continued to work with Trenholm to ensure Black teachers across the state maintained a supply of resources that stimulated the youths in their care. When Woodson published his *Negro History Bulletin* in May 1937, Trenholm wrote, "I think that it will be very serviceable and will be started at a very opportune time because there is a mounting enthusiasm now for this approach to Negro history."[28] As the Great Depression wreaked havoc across the country and threatened the economic stability and longevity of the ASNLH, Trenholm worked diligently to raise funds for the organization on campus and throughout Alabama.[29]

Woodson was one of many influential friends that Trenholm drew support from to establish the communitas at ASU. His commitment to Black youths stretched to the national level, where he served on the National Advisory Committee on the Education of Negroes, a branch of the Office of Education that was run by Franklin Delano Roosevelt's go-to man on issues related to Black education, Ambrose Caliver. The two like-minded educators were both interested in broadening America's claim as the champion of democracy, an angle that supported the protest agendas of activists that were soon to come. "The proper guidance of Negro youth," wrote Caliver to Trenholm, "is becoming a subject of real concern to a number of persons who are endeavoring better to relate the education of these youth to the lives which they are likely to live."[30] Caliver unknowingly channeled the spirit of the discussion students were having during their sequestration in the mountains of North Carolina. From Caliver's perspective, it was quite clear that it was morally wrong to inundate Black youths with a curriculum that failed to address and question the deep divide between the promises of American democracy and the bitter realities of Black life. It is no coincidence that Trenholm began to advocate more forcefully for promoting the second curriculum within a short time of developing a working relationship with Caliver.

As Caliver oversaw issues related to Black education in the New Deal, administrators of Black colleges increasingly convened to develop strategies at their respective colleges. During a gathering in 1937, Trenholm delivered a speech to fellow educators entitled "The Socio-economic Factor as a Determinant in the Program of the Negro College," where he laid out the necessity of the second curriculum. Trenholm declared, "There is the question, however, as to whether or not there are adaptations and differences in emphasis in the various courses of the college that could be made to the decided advantage of the Negro college student." He proceeded to re-lay the petition of fellow historically Black college and university (HBCU) president Robert Prentiss Daniel of Shaw University, who earlier proposed teaching courses that dealt with "racial psychology, race relations, Negro history and literature, labor problems, vocational occupations and other problems relating to aspects of the problem of racial differentiation into which the Negro college graduate is inevitably thrown."[31] In the immediate future, ASU offered variations of these courses and more, thus encouraging Black students to express their doubts and concerns about America's failed promises of democracy and justice for all. Unlike his father, who years before was silenced by the pressures of white supremacy, Harper Councill Trenholm was fully acknowledging the legacy of Jim Crow and, more importantly, prescribing remedies to be administered in Black schools.

Yet another aspect of ASU's communitas that bolstered race consciousness and primed the atmosphere for increased student activism was the endless cavalcade of Black literati that toured through campus at Trenholm's invitation. At any moment, students were exposed to the top scholars, activists, poets, and entertainers of their day, many of whom brimmed with radical tendencies of their own. In her memoirs, retired ASU professor Leila Mae Barlow, who in 1925 helped to promote Black history through the Delver's Literary Club on campus, recalled the plethora of visitors, some of whom came on several occasions. The list included Langston Hughes, Margaret Walker Alexander, Cheyney State president Leslie Pinckney Hill, Melvin Tolson, Arna Bontemps, Gwendolyn Brooks, W. E. B. DuBois, Charles Wesley, Zora Neale Hurston, Mary McLeod Bethune, Benjamin E. Mays, Marian Anderson, and John Hope Franklin. The great American poet Carl Sandburg visited with Barlow's American Literature class, encouraged the students to join him in sitting on the floor, and then read them poetry that included his epic and lyrical *The People, Yes.*[32] One can only imagine how deeply the line, "The people have come far and can look back and say, 'We will go farther yet,'" resonated with Black youths yearning to break free from the grips of Jim Crow.[33]

Trenholm's most effective work on behalf of the emerging freedom movement was in recruiting many of the outstanding teachers to join the growing communitas of students and faculty at ASU. He was elected president of the National Association of Teachers in Colored Schools in 1931 as the country experienced its greatest economic downturn in history. The association represented the interests of fifty thousand African American teachers across the country who were denied entry into the all-white National Edu-

ASU president Harper Councill Trenholm (*center*) addresses the community
through the local Black-owned radio station WAPX (ca. 1950s). ASU professors
flank Trenholm, with ASU students in the background. Courtesy of Alabama
Department of Archives and History.

cation Association. As it was in need of a stable home and strong leadership, Trenholm convinced the National Association of Teachers in Colored
Schools to relocate to the campus of ASU while the Depression raged on—
often providing resources out of his own pocket to sustain the group.[34]
Trenholm sensed the despair that consumed many of his constituents, and
in one of his first letters to the organization, he sought to revive their spirits. "It is for the teacher to continue to serve nobly and neither to desert
the ranks nor to lessen her enthusiasm and efficiency because of the trials
of our times," he wrote. "A better day must be in store for our interests and
our schools."[35] It is unclear whether Trenholm's correspondence was only
meant to convey hope in the midst of unprecedented financial ruin or
whether it also alluded to the daily stress and strain of the Jim Crow South.

Regardless of his intentions, his optimism for the future made him extremely popular among them. Those same educators, many of whom were beginning to join him on campus, played a large role in the movement that was about to unfold.

· · · · · ·

Jo Ann Gibson Robinson was fascinated by sin and righteousness. Her master's thesis, submitted in August 1948 to the Department of English at Atlanta University, examined the literary works of Victorian novelist George Eliot and her treatment of sin, retribution, and virtue. Entitled "George Eliot's Treatment of Sin," Robinson's thesis combed through eight of the author's novels, analyzing Eliot's portrayal of the "disturbing conditions which existed in England" and with great detail examining her depiction of "the evils of England" as they were manifested "through people of her time." In the last chapter of her study, Robinson focused on the theme of retribution against evil and "the role of virtuous characters."[36] The broader themes found in Eliot's work resembled the backdrop of Robinson's own life. Born in 1912 and raised in rural Georgia, Robinson was all too familiar with the sins of racism in America. Exactly one week after she was born, a local activist named Henry Etheridge was brutally lynched in Robinson's home county of Monroe. One paper reported that he was lynched for "securing recruits for a proposed African colony," and another referred to him as "a trouble maker in his community."[37] His body was found by local authorities just days after the lynching, bound at the hands, riddled with bullets, and dumped in the nearby Towaliga River. One wonders whether stories concerning Etheridge's murder or the countless other lynchings that occurred throughout Georgia ever were topics of conversation in the Robinson home.[38] Robinson was the youngest of twelve children, so her family may have attempted to spare her from the frightening details of white terrorism. However, much like Etheridge, Robinson was on her way to becoming a "trouble maker" who would shake the foundations of the Jim Crow South.

After graduating at the top of her class from Fort Valley Normal and Industrial School in 1938, she taught in local schools before registering for college, located at her old high school, which became Fort Valley State College just one year after she finished there. It is tantalizing to believe that Robinson was present on Wednesday morning in May 1941 when Fort Valley State had a special commencement speaker. The college, still in its infancy, invited Harper Councill Trenholm to deliver the address to a throng of eager parents and well-wishers. It was a time-honored tradition for alumni to return to their beloved alma mater to witness graduation, mingle with old friends, and hear renowned orators speak to the next generation of educators. This raises the possibility that Robinson, a teacher in the local schools, made her way out to hear Trenholm speak that morning. Whether or not she was among the audience the morning of Trenholm's speech, it is clear that Robinson greatly admired the work being done at ASU. The feeling was apparently mutual. She accepted Trenholm's invitation to join ASU's faculty in 1949.

As for Trenholm's commencement speech, it was titled "The Negro Teacher Faces the Problems of the Present World Crisis." Although Trenholm concluded his talk by focusing on the growing military crisis in Europe, his core message revolved around an issue that harked back to conversations he shared with his old friend Ambrose Caliver: the teacher's subversive role in unveiling the failures of a false democracy. "The Negro teacher," declared Trenholm to the crowd, "has the problem of making the most of these untoward instructional circumstances and of developing a resourcefulness which will capitalize upon these seeming handicaps to the advantage of the pupils and their parents."[39] How to handle the "handicap" of white supremacy was a perplexing dilemma for teachers and the professors who trained them. By using their pedagogy to call attention to the paradoxical nature of U.S. democracy, teachers stirred the consciousness of many Black youths who questioned the barriers they found at every turn. After failing to resolve the enigma of Jim Crow in their minds, many students expressed their frustrations through acts of personal defiance that later evolved into bolder forms of collective direct action.

Helping to facilitate that development were women like Mary Fair Burks, who joined the ASU faculty in 1935 and later founded the critically important Women's Political Council (WPC), which spearheaded the bus boycott in 1955. Burks helped to create mock governments called Youth City that allowed students to run for various political positions for a day, and in doing so, she realized the dreams of Caliver, Trenholm, and countless others, who fought for educational relevancy that emboldened the civil rights generation. "In addition to electing counterparts to government officials," Burks recalled, "we also taught Negro students what democracy could and should mean. On the surface we were merely imitating, but in reality we were using subversive tactics to serve our own ends. . . . The age of the swim-ins and sit-ins unfortunately had not yet arrived. However we paved the way for them."[40] If "resourcefulness" to combat white supremacy was what

Trenholm was looking for, he certainly found it in the impressive roster of professors he was recruiting at ASU.

While Lawrence Dunbar Reddick would not join that roster until 1954, he had already made a name for himself in the field of African American history. In 1936 Reddick delivered a paper during the twenty-first annual meeting of ASNLH in which he challenged his peers to confront the contemporary issues of their day. Reddick chided those Black historians who seemingly hid behind the cloak of objectivity, failing to tackle contemporary social problems that suffocated Black life. "We are concerned, at least we should be, that those writing today, especially the younger men, shall not fall into the errors of their literary fathers," wrote Reddick. "Since point-of-view is inescapable, it is, therefore, essential that the frame of reference should be large, generous, and socially intelligent; that the developments in Negro life be seen in connection with those of the general pattern, of other racial, minority and laboring groups."[41] Reddick was clearly angling for the second curriculum to be repositioned as the first, as it related to the instruction and documentation of African American history.[42] Such candor and forthrightness must have excited Trenholm, then serving on the executive council of ASNLH. A disciple of Arthur A. Schomburg and E. Franklin Frazier, Reddick became Martin Luther King's first biographer and one of his principal speechwriters as the movement unfolded in Montgomery. Reddick and Trenholm were destined for a showdown that tested the limits of Black colleges as enclaves for scholar-activists.

What Reddick was ultimately pushing for was a curriculum that was responsive to growing issues in the avant-garde of the liberation struggle.[43] From the New Negro era through World War II, Black Americans sensed a stirring that could break open the floodgates of freedom if properly harnessed. Black militancy began to reach a boiling point with the return of troops from World War II, as rebellious soldiers and Black college students found that they shared a growing sense of idealism and race consciousness. Black soldiers proudly carried with them their commitment to uplift the race, even before they embarked for the various theaters of war across the world. ASU professor Leila Mae Barlow recalled the telegram her students sent to one of their drafted classmates, whose sudden removal left a hole in the cast of a play they were performing. The telegram read in part, "Dear, Leo—The show goes on. Today we celebrate Negro History, today you make Negro History. Play well your part there as we will play ours here."[44]

The veterans who returned to Montgomery looking to put the *Pittsburgh Courier's* Double V campaign into action were often sent off to find the football coach at ASU.[45] Rufus Lewis moonlighted as ASU's football coach and the assistant librarian, but he was a full-time activist and one of the most well-known men in the city. Described by ASU professor Thelma Glass as "one of the hardest workers in voter registration that I've ever met in my life," Lewis was an ardent supporter of returning veterans and saw them as the opening wave that could weaken, if not topple, the walls of injustice.[46] He helped to train Black veterans in job skills through a program that was made available through the United States Veterans Administration. But providing them with career assistance was not his primary interest. Taking a cue from his fraternity, Alpha Phi Alpha, Lewis told the young men returning from war, "A Voteless People Is a Hopeless People."[47] He organized the citizens' coordinating committee that drilled students and veterans on the steps necessary to joining the voter rolls. J. Mills Thornton's voluminous study on the civil rights movement in Alabama describes Lewis's work with veterans as indispensable in priming the early struggle for liberation. "Through the committee, the classes, and the fellowship," writes Thornton, "he encouraged their sense . . . that they were entitled to full citizenship in Montgomery."[48]

The majority population of Montgomery must have viewed entitled Black men as an affront to the well-oiled white supremacist machine.[49] Yet times were clearly changing. And in 1950, the entitled Black men, also known as war veterans, made up almost 25 percent of the student body at ASU, thus setting the stage for increased levels of militancy on campus.[50]

· · · · · ·

Movement activity did not unfold overnight. For all of the accumulated seeds of insurgency, the germination process was fairly slow in the Cold War era. The Red Scare stifled the political climate of America in the 1950s, and fearmongering about the rise of communism tempered student activism across the country, a fact that southern segregationists relied on to muffle the rumblings emerging from Black America. The scholar activists who engaged with Black youths trumpeted democracy as a tool to intrigue students for years—hoping that their inquisitive and idealistic minds developed the questions and tactics that would shame America's love affair with segregation. However, African Americans worked cautiously as southern reactionaries and certain white policy makers created a parallel between the civil rights movement and the Red Menace.[51] As a result, numerous Black and white activists toned down their liberal rhetoric. "The Cold War pressure cooker," writes historian Glenda Elizabeth Gilmore, "trapped rising

African American expectations in a heated, oppressive political environment."[52] Beyond the red-baiting tactics and fear of the political stigma that came along with being branded a Communist, people were paralyzed by a fear that they had known all of their lives—white terrorism.

Nevertheless, issues such as sexual violence against Black women, habitual abuse from city bus drivers, police brutality, and the day-to-day degradation associated with life under Jim Crow pushed Black folks in Montgomery to the boiling point.[53] As the 1950s unfolded, ASU boasted a collection of faculty that any administrator would be proud of. Professors such as band leader Laurence Hayes, English professors Mary Fair Burks and Jo Ann Gibson Robinson, history professors Thelma Glass and Lawrence Dunbar Reddick, and football coach Rufus Lewis were just a few of those well trained in their academic fields. By the first part of the decade, their influence helped lay the groundwork for the student activism in the decade that would follow. The "trapped expectations" that Gilmore speaks of were preparing to break free in a very dramatic way.

In 1950 Sam Green, a white grocer who operated an establishment in the ASU neighborhood frequented almost exclusively by Blacks, raped his family's Black babysitter, fifteen-year-old Flossie Hardman. This particular violation may have touched a nerve because it happened so close to the ASU community; or maybe it was the swelling currents of postwar righteous indignation. Regardless of the cause, African Americans in Montgomery sprang into action, with Lewis and the ASU campus leading the way. With the WPC and his small army of World War II veterans at his side, the football coach at ASU set out to tackle Green economically. They organized a boycott against Green and quickly ran him out of business, providing a small victory for those sickened by the failure to secure justice after years of such abuses. Though Green was brought to trial for his actions, he was acquitted after an all-white jury deliberated for only five minutes.[54] Nevertheless, the Hardman case showed that Black faculty at ASU were prepared to assume a leadership role in future campaigns against white supremacy. The boldness of ASU faculty was rubbing off on their students, while Trenholm observed it all without interfering—at least not in the early stages of the movement.

The students at ASU carried within them the hope of shattering barriers that had successfully marginalized generations of African Americans. How best to extract that potential fell into the hands of scholar-activists like Robinson to determine. The degree of space afforded to Robinson in Montgomery was enough to support a surge in confidence, but not enough to ward off fears of terrorist attacks. During the bus boycott, she slept with a loaded gun by her side every night in an effort to provide security and peace of mind.[55] Added to the fear of physical violence was that of the loss of livelihood. In Alabama, it was inconceivable to the white establishment that state employees would openly dare to bite the hand that fed them, especially when that same hand sponsored and subsidized acts of violence and intimidation that further buttressed Jim Crow. In his masterful study of the Mississippi movement, historian John Dittmer notes that Black institutions supported by state funds were most often devoid of overt protests and voices of dissent.[56] In the civil rights era, groups like the White Citizens Council perfected the use of economic power against activists, often subduing or completely silencing their efforts.[57] ASU professor Thelma Glass confirmed the precipitous drop-off of membership that the WPC (which was composed mostly of ASU faculty) experienced as the threat of the bus boycott loomed. "We began to lose members," recalled Glass. "They got threats if they stayed in the council, their teaching jobs, people had children to feed and all that . . . so gradually membership just dropped and dropped."[58] As working adults increasingly felt the pressure bearing down on them, students—with no jobs, no mortgages, and no children—felt their reins slowly releasing.

Robinson took over the leadership of the WPC from fellow ASU professor Mary Fair Burks in 1950 and was well on her way to becoming one of the principal catalysts in the Montgomery civil rights movement. She also became heavily involved in overseeing the student newspaper on campus. As an English professor, Robinson believed mightily in the power of the pen. Invoking the spirit of Paul Laurence Dunbar's poem "We Wear the Mask," Robinson recalled, "Many white people thought Blacks were a 'happy go lucky' people. Although Blacks felt they were being deprived of their rights, they endured nevertheless, complacent and tolerant, though dreading every occasion on which they had to accept the treatment they received."[59] Segregation naturally created an insular world where Black folks released their pent-up frustrations with white supremacy. On Black college campuses, students enjoyed the freedom of dialogue in their classrooms or while engaging in dorm-room banter with their friends. During her tenure at ASU, Robinson made sure that one of the most useful outlets for students' expressions of angst and anger at segregation was the student paper. At the age of thirty-seven, Robinson directed and heavily influenced the young scribes of the *Hornet* (1950–53) and the *Fresh-More* (1949–60). She molded student writers of both papers in her own activist likeness. Her task in advising the writers of the *Fresh-More* was a special one indeed. All of the staff writers were either freshmen or sophomores. It did not take long for Robinson to find out what kind of students she had and environment she was in. The student paper reported that in December 1949, the ASU Drama Club took their production of *On Whitman Avenue* on the road to Florida A&M University, a Black college in Tallahassee. The play, written in 1946 by Maxine Wood, focuses on the postwar struggles of a Black veteran returning home to confront the color line. Starring in the role of Gramp was a chubby-faced senior named Ralph Abernathy.[60]

The *Fresh-More* in particular offers spectacular insight into the communitas of ASU. Its staff were students who were newcomers to the campus scene, highly impressionable, and eager to make their mark in their new environment. It seems improbable that such students would express views that were not in harmony with their faculty advisers' or that would make them unpopular with their peers. Found within the pages of both the *Hornet* and the *Fresh-More* were searing editorials condemning segregation, concerted efforts to document the fight for liberation throughout the African diaspora, and a profusion of news stories highlighting the heritage of African Americans. Moreover, the newspapers bear the unmistakable influence of faculty who used the enclave of ASU as a crossroads between their job teaching students and the growing struggle for freedom. Montgomery was on the brink of a historic upheaval as the 1950s approached their midway point. In 1952 the *Hornet* reported the growth of activism on campus. A campus chapter of the NAACP started recruiting high school students and announced that its goal was "to further the fight for justice."[61] The campaign to add more youths to the campus chapter came on the heels of the boycott against local grocer Sam Green led by Coach Lewis and his team of veterans in 1951. The students, faculty, and Black community were in lockstep as the political intensity in Montgomery grew.

Almost two years before Rosa Parks's defiant act, and only three months before the historic *Brown v. Board of Education* ruling, the legitimacy of white supremacy was under attack from Robinson's students. In an article describing an on-campus meeting of citizens concerned about local segregation laws, one underclassman declared, "We as citizens of America should do all that we can to help bring about integration among the two races. So far as superiority is concerned one race is no better than another. . . . We do not want the other race particularly to do anything for us. On the other hand, we don't want it to do anything to us—to hurt us, that is."[62] The students' themes were undergirded by self-sufficiency and determination—a fixture in the second curriculum at ASU. Not surprisingly, in that same edition of the *Fresh-More*, students reported an on-campus visit and lecture from Herbert Philbrick, the famous Communist infiltrator who published a wildly popular memoir, *I Led Three Lives: Citizen, "Communist," Counterspy*. With the national movement for civil rights gaining steam and flashes of local discontent on the rise, the white power structure did its best to stem the tide of revolution, hoping that branding any nonconformist activity as communist would do the trick.

Accompanying Philbrick to campus that day was Leland Childs, a Birmingham radio legend who later became an informant with the Alabama Sovereignty Commission, an intrastate surveillance agency that was notorious for gathering information on participants in the movement.[63] That Trenholm could not keep men like Philbrick or Childs away from campus underscores the challenge faced by Black college administrators. Government officials had unfettered access to the campus if they so chose. When leaned on, administrators like Trenholm had little choice but to do the bidding of white legislators. Such a circumstance seems odd in light of the fact that ASU continued to fly under the radar throughout the 1950s, encouraging students in their radical expressions. It also suggests that white legislators who controlled campus purse strings were only interested in and concerned about public manifestations of dissent. It appears that they thus completely overlooked and neglected the seeds of radicalism that were glaringly obvious for anyone who bothered to examine the student newspaper in the post–World War II era or observe the litany of campus speakers who often stoked the fires of militancy among ASU students. The negligence and aloofness on the part of the state created the perfect cover for ASU faculty and administrators to craft a springboard from which students would launch their public crusade for justice.

The expansion of Black consciousness was not limited to the newspaper staff. Strong evidence exists that students in various courses across campus were also engaged in debating and embracing the changes taking place in their community. When Spring Hill College, a Catholic institution in Mobile, integrated in 1954, the social studies class of Mr. Evans, a professor at ASU, invited some of Spring Hill's students to campus to discuss the phenomenon and to share their experiences. When a white male student shared his thoughts on the impact of integration at his school, the *Fresh-More* reported that the following exchange took place: "He emphasized that the Negro seems to be afraid to push out first. If he does push out he will at once forget he is a Negro. (There were many sneers and keen looks carried on among Social Studies members, as a result of the latter remark.)"[64] Due to the tutelage and guidance of faculty like Evans, Robinson, and others, students at ASU were beginning to reject "their place," or at least the place that whites believed they should occupy. By 1954, they were raising poignant rhetorical questions that revealed the pregnant potential of Black political power. "Do you know that Negroes are thinking more than ever before? There are more registered voters in Alabama than ever among our group," one student reporter noted, going on to declare prophetically, "One thing is certain: More still will get registered."[65]

The December 1955 issue of the *Fresh-More* was perhaps the most politically charged yet. The newspaper put forth a scathing indictment of white supremacy and boldly called for the complete dismantling of segregation. Even the cartoon staff took part in lampooning Jim Crow. A comic strip depicting the changing of athletic seasons caricatured football (segregation) on its way out and basketball (full citizenship and equal rights) on its way in. Any idea that President Trenholm was disconnected from the messages disseminated by the campus newspaper was wholly dismissed; the editorial board, composed solely of freshmen and sophomores, stated, "Dr. H. Councill Trenholm, the president, is in harmonious accord with our effort."[66] It is therefore extremely revealing that freshman Loretta Jean Thomas was unequivocally supported, and likely encouraged, by faculty and administration when she submitted her editorial entitled "Is White Supremacy Faltering?" In her article, Thomas wove together a rather detailed historical account of the African American struggle while building her way to a defiant declaration. "We are going to enjoy all privileges that are due first class citizens, and we are going to do it in a first class manner," said Thomas boldly. "We have the constitution before us and the Supreme Court behind us. We cannot go astray. Our aims are high and our determinations are deep."[67] She went on to invoke the tragedy of Emmett Till, and like so many students before her, she lucidly and powerfully composed her thoughts concerning the broken promises of American democracy. It was as though her college instructors had drilled her in it. The evidence strongly suggests they did.

What is not certain, however, is when the news stories for the December 1955 edition were actually submitted for publication. The December issue has no specific dateline, nor does it contain any references to the explosive changes that took place locally in Montgomery after December 5. It is highly likely that submissions to the paper underwent an editing process by faculty who made sure that every i was dotted and every t crossed. One must also factor in the time it took to get a finished product to press; stories for publication must then have been submitted at least a few weeks in ad-

The ASU newspaper the *Fresh-More* was among the most radical student-run papers in the postwar era. This satire depicting the end of segregation and the rise of first-class citizenship was drawn by a student for the December 1955 edition of the *Fresh-More* before the advent of the Montgomery bus boycott. Courtesy of Alabama State University Archives.

vance and perhaps even earlier. The overwhelming evidence that points to earlier article submissions is the fact that many of the news stories reference events that took place in early November. This would suggest that the boldest commentaries of students were antecedents to the Montgomery bus boycott, launched on December 5, 1955. Students, therefore, were not merely reacting to the local movement that captured the attention of the world; rather, they were forerunners of that movement who adamantly believed that a startling transformation was just around the corner and that they could and should play a critical role in that growing struggle.

Evidence points to the presence of just as many internal factors molding students as other external forces. The white establishment, who for years had falsely assumed that the Black college environment was sanitizing and nonthreatening, must have been unnerved, infuriated, and confused by what was coming out of ASU. On November 3, 1955, almost a month before the bus boycott, the controversial firebrand and Harlem congressman Adam Clayton Powell Jr. became the next orator in a long line of prominent Black politicians, scholars, activists, and entertainers to visit campus. In a crowded gymnasium filled with both local Black citizens and students, Powell gave a speech titled, "Living between Two Worlds." He further corroborated what writers in the *Fresh-More* had been writing and, more importantly, what many faculty members had been saying for years. The paper reported that Powell asserted "that the old world was gone and now we are facing a new world, a world of new ideas, new reasoning, free from segregation. He said that segregation had quit being our problem and was now America's problem."[68]

The Montgomery bus boycott was the perfect tonic for a Black community seeking to break free. Members of the community, without regard for class or status, pulled together their energy and resources to challenge years of abuse and degradation. The boycott was a major epoch in the civil rights movement's timeline. Although it was nearly five more years before Black college students finally advanced a national movement of bolder direct-action tactics, such as sit-ins, their participation and, most importantly, their preparation were essential to the growing liberation struggle.

The ASU communitas continued to thrive in the years that followed the boycott. On February 10, 1958, James Jones was the Founders' Day speaker. As an alumnus of the class of 1912, Jones was a bridge between the old and the new. Jones gave the fledgling agitators a compliment before ending on a more ominous note. After saluting the students for the victory won in their fight against local forces, Jones warned, "We have come a long ways but the way is yet still filled with perils that are yet to befall us."[69] In that same month, students celebrated Negro History Week by taking in the movie *Lydia Bailey,* which was shown on campus. The core plot of the film is a romance story involving the main protagonist, who follows a woman to the ends of the earth to discover love. However, it was the backdrop of the film that caught most students' attention. The film was one of the first on-screen depictions of the Haitian Revolution, and it touched such a nerve on campus that it "was shown three times by popular demand."[70] Coming on the heels of their own local revolution, it is certain that many students found the backdrop of the film intoxicating and perhaps slightly provocative.

· · · · · ·

On March 28, 1958, the State of Alabama sent over two thousand volts of electricity through the body of twenty-one-year-old Jeremiah Reeves, who at the age of sixteen was convicted of raping a white woman. The two had been involved in an affair, which caught the attention of her neighbors.

When one neighbor was curious enough to investigate Reeves's presence in the home of a white woman, Reeve's lover played the rape card that was historically used against southern Black men. Reeves vehemently denied the charge, and the local NAACP took up his case, but to no avail. His plea of innocence reached the Supreme Court, which dismissed the case, thus sealing his fate.[71] The editors of the *Fresh-More* published a response to Reeves's execution. Echoing one of Robinson's favorite poems, they noted a shift in their attitudes. "Negroes have learned that 'wearing a mask' to hide their true feelings does not pay off," they wrote. "For a hundred years the Black man has grinned and appeared happy-go-lucky, when his heart broke inside. The years of oppression, deprivation of human rights and subjugation have forced him to cry out publicly against continual abuse. . . . It is proof that 'we don't wear masks anymore.'"[72] Violence against Blacks in Montgomery escalated in the years following their victory over segregated buses. Local leaders like Robinson had acid poured on their cars, snipers shot at Black bus riders, bombs exploded at the houses of those who spearheaded the movement, and random assaults occurred more frequently.[73] But the slow dissolution of fear kept Black hands on the freedom plow. Although no one knew what the next move would be, Jim Crow was far from dead. Desegregating city buses was a major victory. However, Black students at ASU were committed to sealing the casket.

ASU's communitas continued to churn out race consciousness and idealism as the decade slowly drew to a close. The November 1958 edition of the *Fresh-More* reported the on-campus visit of Violaine Junad, a singer from South Africa. It appears that the students were more interested in her politics than her musical talents. In the fairly short article, the paper informed its readers that Junad's interests were in "labor, Negro suffrage, politics, mass movements, and other circumstances that tend to keep minority groups from enjoying first-class citizenship." In that same edition, it was noted that Daisy Bates, one of the champions of school integration in Little Rock, visited King's congregation at Dexter Avenue Baptist Church, where "she talked with several enthusiastic students of the college." If there was one word to describe ASU students' feelings on the emerging movement, "enthusiastic" was it. The space that was carved out years ago for them and preceding generations was essential in the flowering of idealism that was now overflowing since Montgomery's explosive arrival onto the national stage. Although Negro History Week was four months away, student Joseph Laster wanted to "alert the students in due time of the conversations that will be going on in the class rooms and dormitories on the campus."[74]

English professor Jo Ann Gibson Robinson was a powerful force for change on the campus of ASU. In addition to heading up the WPC, which initiated the idea of a bus boycott, Robinson also molded the political consciousness of students on campus by serving as the faculty adviser for the campus newspaper. She is shown in this photo after being arrested for her involvement in the boycott. Courtesy of Montgomery County Archives.

Laster's eagerness to jump-start the conversation on the importance of Black heritage must have made Trenholm proud. He always envisioned education as the force that would move the seemingly intractable mountains of ignorance and intolerance in America. But the enlightenment of both ignorant Blacks and whites on the heritage and contributions of Black folks in America slowly leaked into and informed new assertions of bravado and boldness unlike anything Trenholm and his generation could have ever imagined. This assuredly made him slightly uncomfortable to be so closely aligned with the perpetrators of the public insurrection that brought an end to Jim Crow bus laws. When King joined the Alabama Council on Human Relations, formerly the Commission on Inter-racial Cooperation which Trenholm was a member of, he left many activists in the movement confused. There were distinct degrees of militancy, and many of his supporters believed that King's affiliation with the council watered down his militant credentials. "Many Negroes felt that integration could come only through legislation and court action—the chief emphases of the NAACP," wrote King.[75] Conversely, Trenholm and the members of the biracial committee believed education and enlightenment would bring about a more genteel and tolerant South. While King's rationale accounted for legislation and court action on one hand and education and intellectual suasion on the other, it failed to factor in what students had in mind—direct-action protest.

Black colleges were primed for revolt by the time the sit-in movement took off on February 1, 1960. Students at ASU readily emulated the radical actions of their fellow HBCU students and launched protests of their own in Montgomery. Yet it was the instructors of Black students who laid the groundwork for their entrance into the pantheon of American protests. Black youths did not mystically appear on the scene at the beginning of America's most notorious decade. After years of being exposed to a curriculum laced with race consciousness, enlightened regarding the struggles of Black folks across the country and across the world, and fitted with a mission of service and uplift, a new generation of students were ready to strike out in pursuit of what they believed were their God-given birthrights. While not all faculty played a direct role in training students to press forward, the ones who did must be given significant credit for shouldering such a personal risk in exchange for a chance at liberation.

At ASU, the *Hornet* and the *Fresh-More* served as barometers for political consciousness on campus and the mouthpieces for student dissent. Their stories accurately portray an environment that encouraged students to understand and appreciate their heritage and to use it as a platform to demand better for themselves and for their people. And nestled within the printed word was the acknowledgment of the woman who inconspicuously had her hand in it all: Jo Ann Gibson Robinson. Her influence is felt throughout the student publications of ASU, and students fully acknowledged that her guidance and inspiration helped to hone their radical voices. With gratitude, freshman editor Annie Lee Alexander proclaimed, "The members of the newspaper staff wish to express our appreciation to our adviser, Mrs. Jo Ann Robinson, for her ceaseless effort in helping to make our newspaper a success, for without her aid, we doubt that the newspaper would have been what we wanted it to be."[76] Young Alexander's comments recognizing the proverbial anchor of the newspaper staff also reveal the natural and inherent desires of Black students shaped by their personal experiences and granted a certain element of independence. The paper was indeed what they "wanted it to be."

Students of course wrote about the latest fashion trends, heated sports rivalries, and campus gossip, but it is also true that many of them entered college seeking the mentorship and affirmation that could help them arrive at their own conclusions about the pressing social problems awaiting them when their college experience ended. Their articles and columns in the newspaper undoubtedly acted as a catharsis and provided students with clarity and direction. Even when Black college faculty were bridled in their efforts to speak out publicly against Jim Crow, adopting a second curriculum afforded them space to maneuver lesson plans and inject racial commentary into their classrooms. But the dawning of the new decade rapidly moved those on the front lines of Black colleges from dress rehearsal to live action, thus testing the resolve of movement participants.

Even King felt the impact of these changes. In his brilliant three-part study, King biographer Taylor Branch writes, "King embraced the students for taking the step he had been toying with for the past three years—of seeking out a nonviolent confrontation with the segregation laws. . . . With a simple schoolboyish deed, the students cut through all the complex knots he had been trying to untie at the erudite Institutes on Nonviolence."[77] The movement milestones through the 1950s, combined with the preparation and instruction that they received in the HBCU communitas, gave students enough confidence to seize their moment of opportunity. Story after story was passed down through the generations about the harsh and often violent consequences of challenging the social order, particularly in the Deep South. To slightly revise Branch's description, crossing that deep river of fear was neither "simple" nor "schoolboyish."

The year 1960 permanently restructured the political landscape of America. Black colleges such as ASU proved yet again to be a change agent in the struggle for liberation. However, this new, brash technique sent the old guard scrambling.[78] In a letter to ASU alumnus Rev. Solomon Seay Sr., veteran activist Septima Clark of the Highlander Folk School noted, "The Sit-In demonstrations by Negroes have proved to be very challenging. . . . It's rather startling but revealing to note that neither Negro adults nor white Southerners were considered. The young Negro students revolted against the Southern way of life and started an action program which has spread like a prairie fire."[79] The truth is that the Black college sit-ins that were launched from the communitas of HBCUs throughout the South scared the hell out of those who had done the most to cultivate the levels of militancy that students were now brashly displaying. Nobody more than older Black southerners knew of the real consequences that accompanied overt and public demonstrations against white supremacy. Yet the brazen hubris of youth and the ethos of the second curriculum that HBCU students had been exposed to paired well with the moment. The dawning of the new decade delivered a revolution that had been years in the making, and the fear that had effectively marginalized generations of Black southerners quickly dissolved as ASU students pounced at the opportunity to make history.

The inferno of student activism reached Montgomery on Thursday morning, February 25, 1960. Thirty-nine students from ASU entered the Montgomery County Courthouse and initiated a sit-in. In the days and months that followed, city and state officials placed greater pressure on the man who was responsible for bringing all of these activist synergies together on campus, Harper Councill Trenholm. Mayor Earl James of Montgomery alluded to what many members of the white establishment were thinking when he urged "any responsible Negro leaders to counsel their race to discontinue this harassment." James's search for a shepherd to herd the Black sheep was futile. Much like Clark, the older generation of Montgomery's Black community was confused and nervous about what the students' actions would mean, but no one was prepared to corral the suddenly courageous students of ASU—not even Trenholm. In the students' first public statement concerning the protest, they echoed concepts that they had learned over and over again at ASU, and principles that Trenholm had aggressively promoted beginning in his early days partnering with Ambrose Caliver. The resolute youths declared, "We only wish to gain our rights as guaranteed to us by the Federal Constitution and the Bill of Rights." Ironically, when word was passed down that Governor John Patterson was pressuring Trenholm to expel the students responsible for the demonstration, Rev. Uriah J. Fields, a local Black minister and activist, was reported as saying, "It is regrettable that the governor has attempted to make [Trenholm] responsible for student behavior." The truth was, in the larger picture, he absolutely was the "responsible" party.[80]

Although Trenholm did not take any steps to physically stop the students from continuing the protests, he ultimately broke under the state's pressure to expel the student leaders who rallied the troops back on campus. The reality was that Governor Patterson set up a shadow presidency, swiftly delivering orders to the embattled administrator, who faced a personal and moral dilemma of the highest order: comply with Patterson's directives, or risk the financial future of the school and endanger the livelihoods of all those employed under his watch. The initial sit-in participants were not arrested on the day of their protest, but as the identities of the core leaders were leaked, nine students (Bernard Lee, St. John Dixon, Edward Jones, Leon Rice, Howard Shipman, Elroy Emory, James McFadden, Joseph Patterson, and Marzette Watts) were ultimately targeted and ordered expelled from the university, with twenty others placed on academic probation. Immediately recognizing that it was a mandate from the governor, the students directly petitioned Patterson and once again revealed the residual effects of the second curriculum embedded within them: "We, a united group of students of said college, humbly request that you reconsider your order to President Trenholm." Addressing the paradox of segregation, a topic that they continuously discussed in the communitas that enveloped them, they continued, "It is a flagrant contradiction of the Christian and Democratic ideals of our nation." One can only imagine how startled Patterson must have been. Black students, attending a school that he and generations of southern whites had attempted to cripple through decades of underfunding, were taking *him* to school on the topic of ethics and American government. Their final retort may have caused Patterson even more consternation. Without flinching, the students declared, "Our behavior was in line with what we have been taught."[81]

If the white establishment thought the expulsions would stem the tide of student rebellion, they were far off the mark. Nevertheless, the communitas showed signs of buckling. A campus that had once hosted radical speakers from around the African diaspora no longer provided quarter for students seeking space to plot their next move, relegating them to sanctuaries in the immediate vicinity like Beulah Baptist Church. However, it is highly probable that students moved their meetings off campus in respect for Trenholm and the faculty who nurtured them. If Montgomery authorities unleashed their anger, at least it would not be on the grounds of the place they called home.[82]

That day of reckoning soon arrived. The response to the expulsion of the students in the days following ranged from boycotts of classes to prayer vigils. On March 8, 1960, over one thousand students, more than half of the student population, poured out on the streets adjacent to the campus, several of them carrying signs that read, "Alabama vs. Constitution," "We Want Justice," and "Nine Down and 2,000 to Go." The tension quickly escalated as local law enforcement arrived on the scene. Thirty-seven protesters were jailed, including two members of the faculty, Orlean Underwood, who was booked at the scene, and her husband, Jefferson Underwood, who was arrested when he arrived at the jail seeking to see his wife.[83] Not since the days of the bus boycott had Montgomery experienced such upheaval; and much as in those days, the students received widespread support.

Fearing mounting legal costs associated with filing appeals, the students who were arrested pleaded guilty to failing to obey an officer and disorderly conduct. Adhering to the advice of their legal counsel, which included Fred Gray and Seay, the students then issued a statement on why they pleaded guilty in an effort to inform their supporters of their tactical move and deflect the possibility of dishonor in the court of public opinion. While they certainly had a healthy number of detractors among intransigent segregationists, they also received large doses of support from across the country. Several Black citizens in Gadsden, Alabama, were so inspired by the efforts of the students that they formed an organization called the East Gadsden Brotherhood, which was committed to carrying out the fight for equality locally in the town just outside Birmingham. The brotherhood, along with numerous others, delivered donations to Seay and Ralph Abernathy on behalf of the arrested students.[84] A few years later, Gadsden became infamous in civil rights movement history when cattle prods were used to control Black protesters.[85] With hardline resistance, the employment of sadistic methods to repress protest objectives, and rampant violations of civil and human rights showing no signs of abating, the Alabama model became the textbook approach for those hoping to uphold Jim Crow throughout the South. Although Montgomery remained a citadel of white supremacy, it was still much less violent than other parts of the state, thus prompting segregationists like Governor Patterson to seek out less combative ways to mitigate the student insurgency.[86]

City leaders soon discovered that the impetus behind the activism all along had been the teachers. They were the ones who prodded Black students to think more critically about America's broken democracy, inundated them with themes of cultural nationalism through their lectures and campus-sponsored programs, and provided them platforms such as their student newspapers, campus dorm rooms, and classrooms to formalize in their own minds the ways and means by which African Americans could achieve social, political, and economic liberation. Shortly after the massive student protests in March, Patterson summoned Trenholm to a meeting of the state board of education, where he received explicit orders to fire any and all members of the faculty of Alabama State who were "not loyal to the College in all matters of discipline and of rules and regulations pertaining to the proper functioning of the College at all times."[87] In order to justify the order, Patterson pulled out the familiar red-baiting playbook. First up for removal was Lawrence Dunbar Reddick, King's chief speechwriter and collaborator, and chairman of the history department. The news must have caught Reddick a little off guard. He had only been in town five years—much less time than scholar-activists like Robinson, Mary Fair Burks, or Rufus Lewis. However, Reddick and King became kindred spirits and quickly gravitated toward each other as they fleshed out ideas concerning the demise of Jim Crow. He was a soft target for the white establishment, and their discovery that several years before the sit-ins he spoke at a gathering of writers who embraced leftist politics appeared to seal the deal. Also entered as evidence against Reddick was the fact that he belonged to ASNLH, described by a New York police officer as an organization "affiliated with a Communist dominated teachers union."[88] If they had checked Trenholm's file closer, they would have discovered that Trenholm himself had been an active member and served on the executive board for decades. Trenholm was far from being cleared of wrongdoing. The governor, in fact, had pushed the state board for his removal as well, asking that they give the matter "serious consideration."[89]

Reddick's fall was cushioned by the fact that he was received as a hero on the national and international landscape. Kwame Nkrumah, the president of newly independent Ghana and one of the principal architects behind the movement for African liberation, welcomed him to the West African nation as his guest for a weeklong celebration of the nation's founding.[90] Reddick quickly secured another job at Coppin State University in Baltimore and fielded offers to teach abroad as well.

Trenholm, on the other hand, confronted his own professional tragedy. He rebuffed the state's attempts to access Reddick's employment file. Despite all the uproar in the city and the state concerning his students who demanded recognition of their civil and human rights, he refused to undermine the actions of the youths in his charge publicly.[91] One could easily conclude that given his track record, his established principles, his professional affiliations, and his service on behalf of Black educators and students across the state, the embattled president silently rooted for his students' success. While their tactics may have created a problem, the ends that his students sought were the same ones that he worked for throughout his life.

Nevertheless, his silence drew mixed reviews. Summarizing the case a year and a half later, the American Association of University Professors derided Trenholm, suggesting that he should have "spent some of the accumulated good will and his personal prestige in an effort to blunt the attack of the governor and the state board."[92] King got in on the act as well, describing the actions of the man who formerly served as his deacon at Dexter Avenue Baptist Church as "cowardly."[93] The *Pittsburgh Courier* wrote an editorial entitled "Lo, the Poor College Presidents" that sympathized with the numerous Black college presidents across the country who were placed in the hot seat by governing boards over the student activism that had opened the decade. "It does appear," the editorial read, "that our people are too quick to destroy men and women who have given a lifetime of service. . . . It is the easiest thing in the world to tear down and destroy; it is infinitely more difficult to construct and preserve."[94] By the time the smoke cleared at the end of 1960, it appeared that there was very little left of ASU's radical communitas to preserve.

The stress began to show on Trenholm. "There had been mental strain on the administration, the faculty, and the student body," Robinson recalls. "Dr. Trenholm had suffered as a result of the boycott, though he had not been directly involved. Many of the teachers, including myself, were weary."[95] That weariness led Robinson and twenty other faculty members to tender their resignations by the end of the summer—a move that delighted state authorities. Trenholm continued to soldier through the public defamation of ASU, displaying his battle scars only in his most personal correspondence. In a letter to a family member, he confided, "Although this year of 1960 has been very 'trying' for me, I am grateful for the outcome. I now look forward to a better year professionally as well as personally in 1961."[96] Trenholm was forced into early retirement in 1961 by the white establishment, who felt betrayed that the seasoned educator failed to make his students yield to the expectations of Jim Crow. It was largely due to his influence that they did not. He departed life just two years later at the age of sixty-three.

· · · · · ·

The social discord that unraveled in the Cradle of the Confederacy has become the source of countless dissertations and monographs, and it is a portrait of intolerance in one of America's most turbulent eras. Whatever may be written about the freedom movement in Alabama, one component of that story is undeniable: in order to build momentum, it was essential that African Americans dissolve their fears of racial violence, economic repression, and the day-to-day indignities that they suffered at the hands of intolerant whites. A critical step in that development was the presence of enclaves such as Alabama State where students came under the guidance of race men like

Trenholm. Through his efforts to expose students to race consciousness, cultural nationalism, and idealism, Alabama State transformed into the type of space where students felt free to sing along to band director Laurence Hayes's requiem for white supremacy in 1955. The student-led insurgency of the 1960s therefore was not a failure, as historian Martin Oppenheimer contends.[97] It was the continuation of a long movement for dignity, freedom, and justice. Without the Montgomery sit-ins and the courage that they manifested, there would have been no movement for freedom in the small Alabama town of Gadsden. The dissolution of fear in Montgomery has a direct line to Birmingham, Selma, and Lowndes and to the passage of the Voting Rights Act in 1965. The small steps that were taken by the Alabama State communitas and indeed by the Black community throughout Montgomery are all inextricably linked to a movement that emerged across the heart of Dixie—a movement that forever altered the social and political landscape of America.

With the exception of students' own peers, Black college faculty had the most intimate contact with the generation of insurgency that defined America's most turbulent decade. These were the eyewitnesses on the front lines as students discussed current events in their classes, dorms, and hallways. Ironically, the architects of an empowering curriculum were often left isolated by the results of their own handiwork. Many of them wrestled with the fear that their counsel to students could jeopardize their own positions as faculty members at state institutions. Many wondered whether they were on the wrong side or right side of history. However, most shared the same conclusion that young ASU student Loretta Jean Thomas boldly arrived at when inspired in the very classes that they taught. With high aims and deep determination, Thomas declared, "My readers can see and readily understand, that the white man's claim to 'white supremacy' is faltering and crumbling."[98]

5 Trouble in My Way

Curriculum, Conflict, and Confrontation at Jackson State University, 1945–1963

. . . .

In the larger town, few Negroes vote, but in the thickly settled rural areas, particularly in the counties in the delta, very few, if any Negroes vote. Why? Is it true that Negroes in Mississippi are satisfied with segregation, as Coleman and Eastland repeatedly tell the nation on TV programs? Why don't we challenge them? Why don't we speak out? Why are we so cowardly? No one wants to admit that we are living under a blanket of fear, with constant threats and undertones of violence. . . . What if we open our mouths? We are threatened with our jobs, our homes, our lives, we can not stay here and speak out. We must be silent or leave Mississippi. A revolution is surely taking place, will we win the peace or lose as always in the past to the reactionaries?

—Margaret Walker Alexander, August 12, 1957[1]

In the fall of 1951, a *Time* magazine cover story declared, "Youth today is waiting for the hand of fate to fall on its shoulders, meanwhile working fairly hard and saying almost nothing. The most startling fact about the younger generation is its silence. . . . It does not issue manifestoes, make speeches or carry posters. It has been called the 'Silent Generation.'"[2]

Yet the students at Black colleges, even those remembered as conservative, were far from quiescent. In October 1947 one thousand students from Black colleges and secondary schools gathered in Columbia, South Carolina, to declare war against the stranglehold of white supremacy. One of the attendees of that meeting, a student at Jackson State University named George Swan, described a generation that was far from silent. "The Southern Youth met in solemn session," Swan said. "Militant, courageous, Negro youth of the South. Youth—which must and will be served. Youth—dedicated to the struggle for freedom. Youth—determined to achieve that freedom in its lifetime."[3] Swan and Estemore A. Wolfe, another conference attendee, returned to campus to share these new declarations with their professors and peers as they recounted the conference proceedings in the student newspaper.[4]

After serving as the first president of the Jackson State chapter of the Southern Negro Youth Congress, Swan graduated, married his college sweetheart Herene Wolfe, and started his career in Detroit. Like many other Black college graduates, Swan found it difficult to secure a job that matched his talents and training but he eventually landed a position at the Chrysler Detroit Tank Arsenal. As George and Henrene settled into the Detroit community, they never relinquished the activist roots that they had embraced as young students at Jackson State. They became members of the National Negro Citizens Alliance and worshipped at Detroit's Hartford Baptist Church under the guidance of Rev. Dr. Charles Hill, a local minister who was an outspoken advocate for civil rights and whose church was a hub for social activism. George played an integral role in bringing the historian Lerone Bennett and activist Medgar Evers to the church (both of whom were his former schoolmates in Mississippi), and as president of the local chapter of the Jackson State Alumni Association, George welcomed to Detroit a young man who was formerly enrolled at Jackson State but who now sought bravely to challenge the restraints of Jim Crow by registering at Ole Miss—James Meredith.

Though some have argued that historically Black colleges and universities (HBCUs) were ineffective in fostering radicalization and dissent among students during the nascent stages of the civil rights movement, there is evidence linking Black colleges to the politicization and mobilization of scores of students from one generation to the next. The most overlooked of these generations is composed of those who immediately preceded the classic years of the civil rights movement. These were difficult years for administrators, faculty, and students working within the enclaves of HBCUs, yet the constructive and redemptive work of racial uplift continued. The second curriculum endured, bestowing racial consciousness, political drive, and a blueprint for action on its students. Far from being silent or conservative, these Black college students, educated in the southern Black Belt during World War II and the Cold War, formed a critical nexus between the New Negro of the 1920s and 1930s and the college militant of the 1960s, and their ascent and the challenges that confronted them can be seen clearly at Jackson State.

· · · · · ·

In September 1947 a young marine sergeant stepped off a bus in Jackson, Mississippi, returning from war abroad to fight a new battle at home. As it did for countless other returning Black veterans, military experience had hardened the sergeant's resolve that things could never be the same again. Raised in Starkville, Mississippi, and the only son of working-class parents, John Peoples never imagined that twenty years after his discharge he would assume the presidency of his alma mater. Influenced by war, by military training, and by the experiences he had as a student of the very school that he would later oversee, the administration of Peoples became the axis on which change presented itself to the students, faculty, and staff of Jackson State in the late 1960s.[5]

Peoples immediately demonstrated his commitment to justice by taking bold steps in claiming a role in the democracy that he had fought for abroad. Peoples recalled, "I decided when I came back to Mississippi that I was going to have a certain conduct. That I was not going to accept any old discrimination or racism. In the city of Jackson, there was no movement necessarily for civil rights, but we veterans took advantage of the fact that Mississippi had passed a law which said that veterans would be exempted from the poll tax. . . . So those of us went down to challenge that and we did register to vote. I registered to vote in 1948."[6] Veterans were not alone in this fight. The diverse faculty of Black colleges worked diligently and often under great duress to enlighten and embolden Black collegians to believe in their own potential to act as agents for the betterment of society.[7]

Needless to say, there was variation in how direct faculty could be in delivering messages of resistance. Particularly in a state like Mississippi, administrators and instructors had to reckon with the possibility that violent repercussions might result from open calls for Black liberation. What ensued was a delicate balancing act between self-preservation and the dogged, at times creative, pursuit of equality and full citizenship.

Many of those Black community institutions that had previously challenged the policies of Jim Crow suffered extreme reprisals. These included the firebombing of radical churches, the persecution of civil rights organizations, and the brazen execution of countless organizers and activists. Black colleges nevertheless worked steadily to stamp idealism and agency onto impressionable young minds. Scholar Joy Ann Williamson sums up these invaluable spaces' importance to the freedom struggle in Mississippi by suggesting, "Their conversion into movement centers actively plotting against white supremacy was made possible by constituents determined to use any and all means for their cause."[8]

Professors taught lessons that included both thinly veiled and often blunt critiques of American society, highlighting the inherent contradictions of a country that professed democracy but sanctioned discrimination and violence against its own. In an interview, longtime Jackson State professor Margaret Walker Alexander described her strategy in simple terms. "I personally believe that Black people need to preach in their work, but to preach so subtly that you don't think of it as preaching," noted Walker. "The greatest art is the greatest propaganda. The greatest propaganda is not necessarily the greatest art."[9]

For insight into how students absorbed and reacted to such instruction, we might look to the self-described "true voice of Jackson College," the Jackson State student newspaper, the *Blue and White Flash*. Published on a monthly basis, its stories and editorials index a race consciousness on the rise.

The professional Black press was engaged in a campaign to challenge African Americans to achieve victory at home and abroad. In the *Blue and White Flash*, it becomes clear that the student press was publishing similar calls to arms. In 1942 a student named Susie Baughns challenged her peers to defy the boundaries of the closed society and to unite in solidarity for freedom. Her article declared, "This is the time for plain speaking. The Negro's vital stake in victory, his unexcelled record of patriotism give him the right to be concerned about his civil liberties. In an hour of crisis, broad social problems come into sharp focus. . . . Here on campus we have an organization, the Youth Council, which uses psychological and constitutional procedures to help Negroes in their struggle for full emancipation and to secure this ideal. . . . Help solve the problem of segregation and racial discrimination."[10] In that same month, student representatives attended the fourth annual student conference of the National Association for the Advancement of Colored People (NAACP), which was held at Clark College in Atlanta. The conference's theme that year was "War and Post War Problems for Negro Youth."[11]

The students at Jackson State did not sit idly by as more radical and militant forms of protests were emerging. Open protest would have surely stirred trouble on campus, potentially putting students in harm's way. Nevertheless, campus organizations, conferences, and articles written in the campus paper were all forms of dissent that could be shielded from the state in some reasonable way. The thin veneer the walls of the campus provided was just enough protection to plant seeds of insurgency that would develop in due time.[12] Furthermore, no one appeared to prevent them from joining in the struggle as it flowered in its early stages.

Mississippi's violence proved all too real when the time came to leave campus behind. No longer protected by the shelter of the Black college environment, many graduates opted to subvert oppression through education. Given Jackson State's long-standing reputation as one of the leading producers of African American teachers, alumni were able to preserve and pass along the same second curriculum training that they had received as young students. Some students, like Onezimae Clark, were already preparing themselves for this challenge before graduation. Clark recorded her petition to God in the *Blue and White Flash* and dedicated it to her graduating class: "Grant us O' God the ability as prospective teachers to inspire instead of discourage, to give light, where there is darkness. To help where it is needed, and to fight for justice for all. Unless O' God we are able to do these things there will be so few leaders and great men and women of tomorrow that the progress of our race will be impeded. Today we launch, O' God, teach us how to sail and where to anchor."[13] While articulating the race consciousness so crucial to the second curriculum, Clark's prayer suggests that a pedagogy that inspired both activism and dissent could offer respite and hope in an environment consumed by fear.

For the *Blue and White Flash*, the accomplishments and efforts of activist Black students were often front-page stories. The fact that reports chronicling the budding movement were not buried in back pages or censored altogether is informative in its own right. It suggests that the paper's editors and advisers were not censored, even when they supported highly politicized messages. If Jackson State had been a completely repressive environment, the probability of students' displaying political consciousness or movement connections so publicly would have been quite low. Such was not the case.

In the 1940s and 1950s students consistently demonstrated that the instruction they received conveyed a distinct requirement to pursue the full citizenship that had escaped previous generations of African Americans. "We are moving forward to serve humanity," wrote student Johnny Edwards, "and we have been thoroughly oriented in how to solve our own problems; for our teacher training has been directed toward social ends, that is, toward the perpetuation, progress and welfare of all men. . . . We realize that the educational objectives that we now possess should become consciously integrated with all social organization to the end that the educational objectives may determine the direction of social change, whereby all men would reap the benefits of our democratic society."[14]

In 1949, the year those words appeared, the American political landscape was still years away from making a significant shift. Students attending Black colleges throughout the South would ultimately prove to be one of the major catalysts for that transformation. The collegians who raised these informed critiques were student leaders. They were editors of newspapers; presidents of fraternities, sororities, and campus organizations; and officers in the student government association. Even in the seemingly conformist prelude to the 1960s, student voices were not silenced, a telling sign that the dreams and desires of an emerging civil rights generation found a measure of freedom, even if only on campus.

The pendulum between hope and doubt swung freely in the 1950s. Students would become emboldened by achievements through the judicial branch and conversely shattered by the lynching of Emmett Till. The shared experiences and concerns of students bound them together as more difficult days rapidly approached. Encouraging his fellow students to press on, Jackson State student Earl Gooden wrote, "To find self-contentment one must be satisfied with his or her responses to the forces encountered; the most successful way that this may be achieved is to set up a definite set of values and on these to stand at all times, not succumbing to doubt, peril, or any subduing forces. On these I stand: democracy, self realization, faith, and love of and respect for all mankind."[15] Navigating their way through the conservative climate of Mississippi, students found supporters of such messages wherever they could. In January 1951 a valuable ally and student advocate arrived in the person of Jane McAllister.

· · · · · ·

McAllister was born in 1899 in Vicksburg, Mississippi. She was a 1919 graduate of Talladega College, a small Black liberal arts college in Alabama. McAllister received her graduate training at the University of Michigan, and in 1929 she became the first Black woman to earn a PhD in education as a student at Columbia University. She returned to Mississippi in 1951 to serve first as a consultant and later as full-time faculty in the Department of Education at Jackson State. Her tour of duty as an educator had taken her to Black colleges throughout the South, but she returned to Mississippi to be closer to her mother in Vicksburg. Her arrival on campus earned a lead story in the campus newspaper. When asked about her feelings on arriving at Jackson State, McAllister gave a sense of the ideals that underpinned her own teaching as she praised the school's faculty, where "each individual [is] aware of the tragedy of wasting the human resources of the college by not understanding (1) the cultural patterns of the students and (2) the rural scene from which they come."[16]

· · · · · ·

A dogged promoter of free thought, McAllister never hesitated to advocate for freedom and equality to her students at Jackson State, regardless of the political climate. "In my own opinion, and I am a native Mississippian," she said, "nothing can do more for the South than breaking down its isolation of ideas."[17] Almost immediately upon returning to Mississippi, she set out to do just that.

McAllister's arrival at Jackson State coincided with the celebration of the college's seventy-fifth anniversary. The theme that year was "Education for a Free Nation." Black students, faculty, and even administrators clearly understood the irony of using the word "free" in such a context. As organizers planned various lectures and symposiums in honor of the anniversary, McAllister hinted at the promotion of the second curriculum. She suggested that such forums "point the regular college curriculum experiences more directly toward the goal of making students effective citizens in the free nation."[18]

Unlike the majority of Black college faculty, McAllister had a reputation for not mincing her words when discussing Mississippi's state of affairs. Former student Ouida Kinnard recalled, "She spoke her mind about everything. She was not afraid, and she talked about the people here in Mississippi. About how they were so prejudiced and all."[19] Serving as a drill sergeant for justice, McAllister converted her classroom into a training ground and openly urged students to take bold strides against white supremacy. She used to say, "Only evil will triumph if the good do nothing," recalled activist and former student Dorie Ladner. "She told us that we had to take a stand, and to sit and do nothing we wouldn't triumph."[20]

McAllister's political interests also played an important role in broadening the worldview of her students, connecting them with struggles for freedom unfolding on an international stage. Independence for Africa became one of her most important concerns. In her work outside Jackson State, McAllister served on several boards, most notably the board of trustees of her alma mater, Talladega College. She was very influential in the initiation of the Teacher Training Program at Talladega, even proposing an exchange program between Ghana and Talladega in 1958. The purpose of this program was not to re-create the old missionary relationships that had characterized previous contact with Africa. McAllister and the board envisioned Talladega students becoming active builders in a new Ghana by serving as civil servants and teachers. In a letter to the president of Talladega, McAllister wrote, "I know you and Dean Simpson will laugh at the wildness of my dreams but it seems to me that Talladega is well fitted to take the lead in seizing this opportunity to help in African education."[21] Hardly a week had passed between Ghana's declaration of independence and McAllister's petition for an exchange program with the newly sovereign nation. The country's independence was interpreted as an important step in a worldwide freedom movement for which McAllister continued to prepare her students.

The vision and idealism of McAllister kept afloat the promise of dissent on Jackson State's campus in the 1950s. Her outward support of political insurgency made her an anomaly among most professors employed there. Many Black faculty members at Jackson State either felt constrained from fully and openly supporting student activism or were not inclined to support radical thought at all. McAllister was one of a handful of instructors who were candidly supportive of students engaging in conflicts with white supremacy head on.

Most instructors at Jackson State were native southerners and, like much of the Black adult population of the South, were hesitant to cross that psychological river of fear that contributed to the longevity of Jim Crow policies. Economic reprisal and physical harm were still looming threats for those bold enough to voice publicly their displeasure with white society. Nowhere was this threat more pronounced than in the state of Mississippi. Most of Jackson State's all-Black faculty had to choose between livelihood and liberation. No Jackson State professor represented this conflict more than the legendary literary giant Margaret Walker Alexander.

Born in Birmingham, Alabama, in 1915 to a Jamaican-born Methodist minister and a mother who worked as a musician and teacher, Walker soon developed a love for the written word. At the age of ten, her family moved to the colorful town of New Orleans, where she honed her poetry skills. As a young woman, she moved to New York and took residence in Harlem, befriending fellow artists and scribes like Richard Wright, Arna Bontemps, Langston Hughes, and Elizabeth Catlett. In 1937 she published her most well-known volume of poetry, *For My People*. She became indoctrinated with Marxism, and the militant tone of the New Negro movement and the Harlem Renaissance intrigued and inspired her. She married Firnist Alexander in 1943 and accepted a teaching position at Jackson State in 1949.

Walker was a mystic and a self-professed God-fearing woman, and her religious beliefs were essential to both her teaching and her writing. She wrote, "As a Negro woman, my religion is necessary to my integrity, to help me build a ground, moral and spiritualistic life, and I find it necessary often in order to maintain anything like emotional stability and equilibrium."[22] She often struggled with depression and health setbacks, explored astrology and prophecy, and composed in her journals what can best be described as psalms of praise and contrition. Yet she was also deeply conflicted. The repressive climate of Mississippi and the harsh work environment of Jackson State gnawed at her, silencing and sidelining one of the great writers of the twentieth century.

Like countless other African Americans in Mississippi, Walker observed world events with a hopeful heart. If the struggle for Black liberation continued to expand, then perhaps it would soon make its way to the state most notorious for the marginalization of Black freedom rights. In 1949 Walker foresaw future events that soon consumed the Magnolia State. She prophetically declared, "Prejudice, segregation and Jim Crow are in for a death struggle and I hope they will die. Our schools will no longer be separated, neither our churches and acts of prejudice in the commercial place like stores and hotels, places of amusement, etc. will be punished as crimes against the people. I think it will take only a mere ten years for that change to take place."[23]

Although her writing served as an important outlet, Walker had limited space to practice the activism that had defined her life as a young radical in New York. She continued to prophesy, however, that liberation was within reach. "Eisenhower will station troops in the south because of serious trouble and unrest over Jim Crow law in Dixie," she wrote in 1950, seven years before Little Rock. "All of this is due to happen while Uranus is in Cancer and it does not leave for good until 1956 . . . and a great new era for art and religion and all forms of culture will be ushered in."[24] Such visions did little to prepare her for the frustration she was about to endure as a professor at Jackson State.

· · · · · ·

A storm was gathering in Mississippi. The forces of white supremacy became even more deeply entrenched as threats from a growing Black insurgency increased. Anyone aligned against the de facto and de jure traditions that had anchored the Magnolia State since the end of the Civil War was declared an enemy of the state. Over the years, fear had effectively frozen many African Americans in silence as their thoughts turned toward protection of their families and loved ones and toward self-preservation. However, this fear was slowly beginning to thaw as resistance efforts increased and a world movement against oppressive forces took flight. In 1955, after earning her graduate degree, Walker noted that ever since the *Brown v. Board of Education* decision, "Mississippi has been in a worse state than the world had been over the atomic bomb. I came back to tension and fear which has steadily increased; incidents of violence, intimidation, reprisal, indignity and gross injustices fill a huge volume."[25]

Cutting through the fear of reprisals was a herculean task for Black Mississippians. Whites were more than prepared to employ terrorist tactics to defend their way of life against those who dared challenge the white power structure. "The war of nerves and harassments have [*sic*] included real bullets to back up threats," wrote Walker. "We on our job at Jackson College have been told that if we make any frontal attack on segregation we will not get our checks. Very few of the faculty members dare belong to the NAACP."[26]

As a politically aware and racially conscious writer, Walker mulled over her options. Obtaining a job outside Mississippi would not be a problem. Her husband and family wanted out of Mississippi, but as she was the breadwinner for the household, the decision ultimately resided with her. She decided to stay. Although she would question that decision quite frequently in her writings, her reasoning was not unlike that of millions of other African Americans who felt a vested interest in the land of their mothers and fathers.[27] In Mississippi, flustered and temporarily neutralized on the sidelines of the war against Jim Crow, Walker captured the struggle that many African Americans across the country dealt with as they contended with their human frailties in the midst of a brewing confrontation for civil rights. "Why don't we challenge them? Why don't we speak out? Why are we so cowardly?" She openly opined, "No one wants to admit that we are living under a blanket of fear, with constant threats and undertones of violence. . . . What if we open our mouths? We are threatened with our jobs, our homes, our lives, we can not stay here and speak out. We must be silent or leave Mississippi. A revolution is surely taking place, will we win the peace or lose as always in the past to the reactionaries?"[28]

Much like numerous other professors working on the front lines of a growing Black student revolt, Walker chose to confront her obstacles by dedicating herself to her students and her work. Former students recalled that she was passionate about teaching and was capable of entrancing her students with vivid images of slavery from the pages of her work. "There were so many memories about her book *Jubilee* that she told in her class," recalled former student Gloria Douglas. "Her expressions and how she told the story were very inspirational."[29] Her classes often intertwined discussions of

Margaret Walker Alexander used her extensive connections within the literary world to bring numerous scholar-activists to Jackson State University in her thirty years teaching at the institution. Such relationships and exposure nurtured students and further stoked militancy on campus. In this photo, she is featured seated as former honoree and recipient of the Langston Hughes Award at City College New York in March 1986. Front row standing (*left to right*): unidentified, Bernard Harleston (president, City College New York), Paule Marshall, Ossie Davis, Toni Morrison, Toni Cade Bambara, James Baldwin, and Ruby Dee. Back row standing (*left to right*): Michael Harper, Raymond Patterson, and Roscoe Lee Browne. Courtesy of Philip J. Carvalho.

literature with innuendos of racial liberation, a clever way to alleviate fears of reprisal from the administration or the state. One class in particular, Bible as Literature, allowed her to combine her profound knowledge of the Bible with her understanding of Black liberation theology, a staple of the Black church. "She knew that Bible and she could just make it come alive; you would just sit there in awe," recalled former student Ouida Kinnard. "She would discuss the Bible as literature. . . . If she was really talking about the Bible she would somehow inject that [race] into her discussion of the Bible."[30] All the while, Walker worked continuously on what would become her signature work, *Jubilee*, which would be published in 1966.

Amid the repression of Mississippi in the 1950s, professors such as Walker, McAllister, Lee Williams, and Willie Dobbs Blackburn touched the lives of their students in a very real and significant way. Douglas noted, "I knew I wanted to be a teacher or a nurse. And then at Jackson State I learned that you could be a writer if you wanted to or do other things besides become a teacher or nurse. And I remember that Margaret [Walker] was a college professor and she was a writer."[31] A likely explanation of what occurred at Jackson State was that Black professors represented what was possible for their students; conversely, students represented what was possible for the future of Black America. Walker had one final prophetic vision before the close of the decade, foreshadowing what was to come. She wrote, "There are going to be cataclysmic changes in my job in the next three calendar years, 1959, 1960, 1961. Only God knows what those years will bring. Change is inevitable and the greatest change obviously is going to take place in 1960."[32]

· · · · · ·

To come to grips with the sudden outbreak of Black student activism, the white power structure of Mississippi put increasing pressure on Black college administrators. Though classes and instructors' office hours remained sanctuaries for professors and their students, Black college presidents were called into the chambers of legislators frequently in the 1960s.[33] While there were a few university presidents who resisted legislators' efforts to enlist them as the chief subordinators of student protests, most complied, and some went above and beyond.

Few Black college presidents represented the politics of confrontation as well as Jacob L. Reddix. Reddix was a native son of Mississippi, born in Jackson County, and as president of Jackson State from 1940 to 1967, he had the longest tenure of any president there. He had left Mississippi to earn his college degree from the Illinois Institute of Technology and completed his graduate work at the University of Chicago. As a young man, Reddix's professional work reflected the words and sounds of Black resistance and uplift that defined the 1920s and 1930s. Reddix was fascinated with the concepts of self-dependency and collective economics, the very doctrines that served as the ideological foundations for leaders such as Booker T. Washington and Marcus Garvey. Shortly after the completion of his graduate work, Reddix published numerous works on the merit and worth of cooperatives for African Americans. These publications were well received in devitalized communities seeking to pull together their limited economic resources, and they won Reddix the support of W. E. B DuBois and John

Hope II, the latter of whom was a past president of Morehouse College and former professor of economics at Atlanta University. DuBois touted Reddix's research on cooperatives in the renowned Black newspaper the *Pittsburgh Courier*, causing Reddix to receive numerous written inquiries about his work.[34] Writing in 1939, Hope conveyed to Reddix that "the story of your courageous trail-blazing effort and that of others like you in pointing the way to economic and social betterment through mutual self-help needs to be told to our youth who will shortly step forward to be a liability or an asset to the group."[35]

Reddix's message of self-sufficiency and determination resonated with young people as well. Those inspired by his research on cooperatives did not hesitate to reach out to the young educator, often writing to him for research advice. One student from Tougaloo College wrote, "I've read your pamphlet, 'The Negro Seeks Economic Freedom Through Cooperation,' and I am asking you to send me the latest statistics or reports of your cooperative store."[36] An inspired student from Hampton sought his help, noting, "I am interested in the Cooperative movement among the Negro, and have selected 'Cooperation, The Hope of the Negro' as a topic for a thesis which I am about to write. I am also preparing an address for Negro History Week on the same subject."[37] As Reddix's message of empowerment and economic resourcefulness spread, his opportunities for advancement increased. In 1940 he was awarded the position of "advisor on cooperatives" with the Farm Security Administration but stayed only briefly. Just ninety days later, he was selected as the fifth president of Jackson State.[38]

It is difficult to imagine what Reddix might have been thinking as he returned south to begin his work. Surely he understood that he was venturing into territory where polemics on race would be unwelcome. There would be little room to conduct any research that may unsettle white supporters or deliberately embolden African Americans. An all-white board had selected him with the understanding that his guidance of Jackson State would be consistent with Mississippi's long-standing traditions and culture. That culture had zero tolerance for educated Blacks who sought to break stride with the expectations of local custom or law.

In the end, Reddix embraced the conservative nature that defined Mississippi's Black leadership. In his memoirs he wrote, "I have never personally participated in an organized protest. Undoubtedly, I have been criticized for not doing so. For more than fifty years, I have devoted my life to the education and enlightenment of young people. . . . I believe this contribution is as important as participating in organized protests."[39]

Reddix became the prototypical Black college administrator during an era when the Black Left boldly and increasingly critiqued the policies of Jim Crow. The activities of determined World War II veterans and the relatively conservative yet steadfast efforts of organizations such as the NAACP and the Congress of Racial Equality did not reflect the agenda that most Black college presidents were prepared to adopt. Caught between the necessities of economic survival and political posturing to please state legislators or white benefactors, many Black college presidents displayed a vainglorious machismo that was implicitly and often forthrightly wielded on their respective campuses in an effort to ensure that faculty, staff, and students toed the line that the white power structure expected. While several Black college presidents skillfully chose to navigate that line in an effort to preserve the interstitial space that defined the Black college communitas and shield faculty-student relationships, others refused to risk their jobs or, as many saw it, the very existence of institutions that had served Black communities for years.

As prominent and respected leaders in the Black community, college presidents were the supreme custodians of college-bound Black youths and were often venerated as such. Yet many presidents struggled to connect the idea of subservience to white "supporters" with the charge of uplift, a concept that drove Black institutions and their students since their inception. This personal and sociopolitical battle with the power structure took its toll on Mississippi's Black educators, who relinquished the challenge of openly confronting white supremacy to the next generation. Peoples recalled one confrontation that Reddix faced in 1965:

> He got a call from the governor's office, wanting him to check the
> roll of all his teachers and workers, and they wanted to know if there
> were any of them in that march [the Selma to Montgomery March].
> If they are not present, they want to know where they are. He
> covered and said they're all here . . . but he was so angry that they
> would do that you know. So I saw what he had to go through. I sat
> there by his desk and he was angry that they were going to call and
> tell him to check the roll of his teachers and make sure that nobody
> was in that march with Martin Luther King and if they were he
> wanted them fired right now. He didn't even check, but he said he
> did. He would say things like "Things are going to change, and
> you're the young man who can probably do it." He said, "These
> people, they're all racists but it's going to change."[40]

This incident took place during the twilight of Reddix's administration. During the twenty-five years that preceded it, Reddix guided Jackson State with little or no compromise for those who were not on board with his agenda. But the actions and direction of the national student sit-in movement, which, in a domino effect across southern Black colleges, arrived in Mississippi on March 27, 1961, increasingly influenced Reddix's agenda. In early spring, the flowering of activism that took generations to cultivate burst forth in downtown Jackson; nine students from nearby Tougaloo College challenged public accommodation laws at the local library.[41] Any boundaries that gave previous generations of Jackson State students space to express radical opinions or create militant organizations on campus were now erased. Reddix moved quickly to save the university and perhaps himself from the spectacle that would surely be generated. Jackson State students had other ideas, as they prepared to assume their own places in the insurgent movement now consuming Black colleges.

Dorie and Joyce Ladner were enrolled as freshmen at Jackson State when the student movement first arrived in Mississippi. The two sisters shared a close relationship all of their lives. Growing up in the small community of Palmers Court, located in Hattiesburg, both sisters were exposed to the ravaging effects of white supremacy. Legendary Hattiesburg activists Vernon Dahmer and Clyde Kennard mentored Dorie and Joyce during their formative years.[42] Commenting on their relationship with Kennard and Dahmer, Dorie remembered, "He [Kennard] also helped to develop the NAACP youth chapter, which we were members and we were also exposed to Vernon Dahmer and his sister Ilene Beard. They would take us to NAACP meetings here in Jackson."[43]

The Ladner sisters arrived on Jackson State's campus in the fall of 1960 just as HBCUs throughout the Deep South were embroiled in an open struggle to topple Jim Crow. The Tougaloo students demonstrated both their political savvy and their healthy fear of southern violence in determining their point of attack. By choosing a public setting rather than a private establishment, they circumvented the classic segregationist argument over the right to regulate their own private property. The Tougaloo students had notified the press before their arrival and were prepared to face whatever hardships awaited them. As word floated over to Jackson State, hundreds of students, the Ladner sisters included, moved quickly to show their solidarity with their cross-town companions, and students urgently bolted from their dormitories in an effort to seize the moment. Later that afternoon, throngs of students began to gather in front of the campus library, "where they sang hymns, prayed, and chanted, 'We Want Freedom.'"[44]

Reddix was disturbed at home by reports of student protests. Visions of harsh reprimands from state officials and perhaps even a decision to close the school must have entered into his nervous mind. He later explained to the media, "I don't know what happened. This is more trouble than we have had here in 20 years."[45] Gripped with fear and rage, Reddix lashed out. Dorie Ladner recalled that "Emmett Burns was president of the student government and he was attacked by the president. The president came running out from his home . . . like a wild man. He was just flailing his arms, and just trying to strike me out too. Because I guess he saw his whole world crumbling being a state employee."[46]

Reddix's fears were not without merit: the Jackson police department was already on the scene. Reddix linked forces with local authorities to order a cease and desist for the students' "illegal" rally. The crowd soon disbanded, the threat of expulsion initially doing its work. But they still gathered in smaller groups along the edge of Lynch Street, the busy thoroughfare that ran through the middle of campus. Protesters could be heard proclaiming, "They haven't seen anything yet. This will go on until we have freedom."[47] It was later reported that Reddix had assaulted two students, striking one female in addition to pushing another student to the ground. Such tactics were not surprising; keeping Black students prostrate in the face of Jim Crow was implicit in his job description.

Reddix remained cooperative with the state in the days that followed. The Mississippi State Sovereignty Commission (MSSC) had previously identified at least forty-five Jackson State students as possible threats to the status quo and corresponded with Reddix to request the name, class rank, and home address of each student "whose name appears on the propaganda list."[48] The MSSC's propaganda list included the names of Dorie and Joyce Ladner. Both sisters were eventually expelled from Jackson State. They then enrolled at Tougaloo. Dorie remembered, "We had been told we weren't going to be allowed to come back, plus we didn't want to come back."[49] Reddix did not fail to provide the information that was requested of him, relinquishing all names and home addresses, regardless of the harm that students and their families might have faced as a result.

Jackson State's student body was buzzing with excitement. In dormitories across campus, students discussed the events that had transpired on March 27. Many of them had serious reservations about staging protests and standing up to authority figures who acted in loco parentis. For those students, it was enough fear and reservation to prevent many of them from taking a role in the movement. But hundreds more decided that the struggle presented a defining moment. Perhaps it was their youthful exuberance and innocence that convinced many of them to participate. It is not quite clear why students "acted out" against the establishment when they did, nor is it certain what prompted such a collective show of force. When they did so, however, Black colleges were the universal launching point for the Black student movement in America. On March 28, Jackson State students continued their defiance of authority and their show of solidarity with Tougaloo by launching a boycott of classes.

Word of an impromptu rally spread quickly as students gathered on the campus lawn. A small band of students thought it prudent to march downtown to the city jail, where the Tougaloo students were being held. Advancing on the local white power structure in this way was sure to heighten the wrath of campus administration. Such a suggestion was undoubtedly enough to give even the boldest of campus activists considerable pause. When the call for marchers went out, only fifty students joined the ranks of those willing to make the short trek downtown.

Among those was Dorie Ladner. Both Ladner sisters were struggling in their adjustment to college life. Chief among their dislikes at Jackson State were the numerous social restrictions administrators placed on the student body. Students were expected to observe curfews and attend mandatory vespers on campus. When students did gain free time, it was allotted in small doses and was under the sharp observation of dorm mothers and chaperones. Like many college students, the Ladner sisters expected the excitement of freedom from home and the relaxation, if not removal, of the strict rules that stifled the social aspirations of young men and women ready to discover themselves—and each other. Most students coped with the social limitations found at Jackson State. If not, they certainly found sly ways to subvert the rules to make their environment more palatable. Social stimulation was not, however, the only thing important to the Ladner sisters; and if Jackson State offered anything to them, it was the close proximity of the local NAACP headquarters located on Lynch Street.

It was there that the two sisters formed a close relationship with a man who inspired many of Jackson State's politically frustrated students. In his small, second-story office, Medgar Evers spent numerous hours counseling Mississippi's Black youths and speaking to them about a freedom that he envisioned for the future and the distinct role they would play in helping to usher in that new era. Perhaps it was those moments conversing with

Evers that convinced the Ladner sisters and others to march into downtown Jackson in support of the Tougaloo students.

The local power structure, too, had strong convictions: it wished to send a clear message to Jackson State and Tougaloo students that Mississippi would not become the next staging ground for the student movement. The day before the students' decision to march downtown, Jackson's local law enforcement invaded Jackson State's campus, bringing with them police attack dogs to dissuade students from future campus rallies. "Within two hours they brought dogs in," recalled Dorie Ladner. "They had dogs running up and down the dorm on Jackson State's campus."[50] As students entered downtown Jackson, they were greeted by the same attack dogs. In addition, police were armed with clubs and tear gas to disperse the students when they refused to turn back.

Even when the students faced toxic fumes and attack dogs, they found protection with those who were most invested in their success: the Black community. The histories of Black colleges bear out the fact that any separation between town and gown was superficial at best. Black colleges were beacons of hope to the impoverished communities that often surrounded them. Even those who could never muster the time or money to attend realized that within the "shelter" of Black colleges, an important component of the future of the race was being formed. As the Black student movement descended on Jackson, Black conservatives and the working class would not refuse the needs of even the "rowdy" students.

As Black youths ran throughout the streets of Jackson seeking refuge, kind and familiar voices began to call out to them. "And I now know how strange people felt, because we were running and trying to hide," recalled Dorie Ladner. "And one Black woman said, 'Come into my house,' and she cleaned my face off and she said 'Come out and sit on the porch.'" Dorie's rescuer opened her home to her as if she was one of her own, and together they watched the terror unfold before them. As evening fell, both Dorie and her anonymous Good Samaritan realized they had witnessed the dawning of the civil rights movement in Jackson. "I sat on the porch and saw folks running up and down the alley and all around with the dogs," Dorie recalled. "I sat there like I lived there, and by nightfall I went back to campus."[51]

As the smoke literally settled on the streets of Jackson, those who had witnessed the events of the last few days realized that the collision of different worlds and interests had set in motion an irreversible chain of events. The Tougaloo Nine were given suspended jail sentences, and the case was

later thrown out on appeal. They returned to campus as heroes of the movement. Local whites' frustration with Tougaloo and its seemingly renegade
students was rapidly increasing. Restraining the protests at Tougaloo would
require more imaginative and clandestine approaches; however, suppres-
sion at Jackson State would prove much easier. President Reddix's ego was
severely bruised by this defiance. The buck stopped with him, a fact that
he was all too aware of. If the state came calling or questioned whether
Jackson State was biting the hand that fed it, then it was he who would be
subject to immediate reprisal. This pressure led him to crack down on faculty and lash out at students and professors alike. As Walker remembered,

> He cracks the whip and rattles his saber and struts across the stage
> a pompous and tyrannical jackass. The faculty meetings at Jackson
> College have deteriorated into ludicrous puppet shows where the
> president performs in a ridiculous manner. The trustee board
> downtown calls him in to lay down the law of how to keep his
> Negras "in line." And he comes down the freight elevator with the
> garbage and slips out at the back door for fear some of us have seen
> that he has been to see the governor and that he swells up on the
> campus and knocks the student to the ground. And then intimidates
> the mother of the girl, with the threat of expulsion so that she will
> deny he struck her down, despite the obvious accounts of students,
> teachers and of average citizens in town.[52]

For a brief moment, Jackson State students broke away from their conservative bonds and the expectations of their enraged president and allowed
the second curriculum to breathe free. They helped to set the tone of activism in the state by rallying to Tougaloo's side. After all, Tougaloo's cause
was theirs also.

When students returned to Jackson State from the sultry Mississippi summer, they found that they had less room than ever to articulate their concerns on campus. Reddix dissolved the Student Government Association at
the start of the fall semester. "I just had to put my foot down," he declared.
Likely, he caved to local and state government pressures. His decision caused
a backlash among the student body of Jackson State. Four hundred students
boycotted classes in protest. Later, the students gathered at the college sta-
dium and "paraded around the campus."[53]

Despite the outcry and decision to boycott classes, the atmosphere at
Jackson State was simply not conducive for sustaining overt protest, particularly as the state ultimately decided whether the doors of the institution

should remain open. In addition, the background of many Jackson State students was much different from their counterparts' at Tougaloo—a private institution that had developed a relative elitist reputation by the mid twentieth century. Many of Tougaloo's students came from educated parents, and the student body was composed of students who represented, in many cases, the aspirations and expectations of the privileged Black middle class. The typical Jackson State student was more than often the first of his or her family to attend college. They represented the hopes of sharecroppers and domestic laborers who saved all that they could just to enable their son or daughter to have an opportunity to attend college. For generations, African Americans invested heavily in the concept that education was a passageway that would lead to the collective uplift of the race. The apparent decision of many of these youths to fling this opportunity to the wind was risky, even if those actions were motivated by desires to achieve Black liberation. Abandoning that dream and risking expulsion was a sacrifice that many of Jackson State's students were not yet willing to make.[54]

Reddix would later suggest that his major contribution to the Black struggle was the granting of over five thousand degrees during his tenure as president. Unknown to Reddix, one of his best and brightest students had already put in motion a series of events that would serve as a litmus test for democracy and rock the very foundation of the state.

In January 1961 James Howard Meredith was in his first year as a student at Jackson State when he wrote to the University of Mississippi to inquire about admission. A native of Kosciusko, Mississippi, Meredith clearly understood the rules and boundaries of Jim Crow. Yet by the time he made his first contact with Ole Miss, the dawning of a Black student movement was in full swing and Black youths across the country were increasingly questioning the restrictions white supremacy forced on them. Fewer Black students were heeding the prescriptive observations of men like Jimmy Ward, columnist and editor of the *Jackson Daily News*, who noted, "It would appear by now that prudent people will not wantonly toy with traditions or tamper with the soul of a civilized society."[55] Meredith's lone struggle would spark a fierce and hateful backlash, the likes of which Mississippi had never seen.

In 1961 Governor Ross Barnett appeared in a movie produced by the MSSC entitled *Message from Mississippi*, where he declared, "No student can get a better education than is offered the Negro children in Mississippi."[56] Both Meredith and Barnett knew this to be false. Black colleges had successfully produced generations of local and national leaders, activists, professionals, and a talented working class that waited patiently for America to live up to what it professed in its founding documents. Yet a stigma of inferiority hung over Black education that was caused by segregation and was further reinforced by the paucity of resources made available to Black educators.

After numerous creative attempts on behalf of the Ole Miss Board of Trustees to bar Meredith from enrolling, the federal courts finally upheld Meredith's constitutional right to become the first African American student at the state's most elite institution of higher learning.

Meredith confronted both solitude and hostility, and his tormented nights at Ole Miss were not without the constant reassurance and encouragement of a familiar voice he knew well at Jackson State, that of McAllister. McAllister remained in contact with Meredith during his ordeal and gave him the tutoring, advice, and nurturing to which he was accustomed at Jackson State. Indeed, she kept in contact with most of her former students, signing her correspondence with them as their "teacher and friend." More than anything, Meredith needed a friend in the moments when he felt most abandoned, and in his most desolate and darkest hours at Ole Miss, he reached out to his "teacher and friend." McAllister wrote to a colleague, "Your letter came soon after I had a telephone conversation with James Meredith who was one of our students. He asked me if I could hear the noises of the cherry bombs as he was trying to study. When students act in mobs, I almost lose my faith in the power of education."[57]

But McAllister never truly lost faith in education. Behind the closed doors of her classroom, in her private office hours, or through her correspondence with current and former students, she never stopped investing in those she believed capable of changing the world. In a letter to a troubled former student, she wrote, "Keep in mind that only when a man's fight begins with himself is he worth anything. Begin your fight with yourself and begin now."[58]

McAllister knew that the personal was—and had to be, for Blacks—political. Indeed, as the battle for America's soul spilled over into Jackson, young men and women were forced to come face to face with racialized demons that had perplexed the souls and consciousness of generations before them. Meredith began this fight with himself and concluded that the time was right to trouble the waters of segregation. When the smoke settled in Oxford and the long road to healing began, McAllister wrote to J. D. Williams, the president of the University of Mississippi, to convey her support for Williams, who attempted literally to rebuild Ole Miss in the wake of the riots. McAllister lent her support to Williams: "In the 42 years of my teaching in Mississippi and Louisiana colleges and in travel in various countries; students, faculty and I, regardless of race, color, or creed have met on the common ground of ideas. . . . May I congratulate those students to whom you pay tribute, for it is upon such as they—and again I say regardless of race, creed, or color—on whom will depend the salvation of our state."[59]

· · · · · ·

As members of the Student Nonviolent Coordinating Committee began entering Mississippi in the early 1960s, many ventured into the impoverished rural communities of the state. Yet even as late as 1963, and even in the biggest cities, access to public accommodations was still unthinkable for Black Mississippians. In more progressive and politically moderate southern cities, such as Greensboro, Nashville, and even Montgomery, public accommodation laws had either changed or were in the process of being altered. Mississippi, once again, represented one of the last bastions of segregation.

Jackson was a logical target for direct action, as Mississippi's largest urban setting. Most white southerners were astonished and appalled by the audacity of Black youths who swarmed lunch counters, crammed into jails, and defied customs and traditions, usually facing severe retribution as a result. They worked quickly and vigorously to patch any holes that student activism may have caused in their fortress of intolerance. Activists' most visible foes were federal, state, and local authorities who governed without visible compassion or sympathy for movement participants, who were viewed as nothing more than political troublemakers. In Mississippi, the MSSC stepped up its surveillance of suspected subversives, even making a call to a new hire that Jackson State had made during the fall of 1962.

That autumn, Professor George Lee Robinson, with his wife, Delores, and their newborn infant, moved to Jackson from Baton Rouge, Louisiana. George Robinson had just been fired from the faculty of Southern University for vehemently objecting to the way in which President Felton Grandison Clark handled student protesters on his campus.[60] His new place of employment was even more inhospitable to student activism than his former one. As Robinson settled into his new home and got acclimated to his new position, neither he nor Jackson State's administrators, including Reddix, knew that he was under the watchful eye of the MSSC.

When the phone rang at the Robinson residence on the morning of April 16, 1963, Delores Robinson was unprepared for the hostile interrogation she received. The menacing call unsettled her as she tended to her newborn. The director of the MSSC, Erle Johnston Jr., instructed investigator Andy Hopkins to telephone the Robinson home to inquire about their intentions as employees of Jackson State. Major W. R. Jones, chief of the Investigative and Identification Division, "especially requested that the President of Jackson State College not be informed that their department has requested an investigation into the background of these subjects."[61] Hopkins questioned Delores about her place of employment and her decision to apply for her driver's license under her maiden name. Ironically, in his report, Hopkins noted that Delores was rude, despite the fact that *he* was the stranger calling her home and asking personal questions, which under normal circumstances should not have concerned him. But to the lead investigators of the MSSC, nothing (outside of white supremacy) was normal in Mississippi anymore, and the Robinsons' activist past, including their decision to apply to vote in Jackson, stirred the investigators' deepest concerns and suspicions. Perhaps most unsettling to the MSSC was the venue in which George Robinson now worked, which was proving to be a thorn in the side of white supremacy throughout the South: historically Black colleges.

The fear of violence was a major factor for Black Mississippians, perhaps more so than for residents of any other place in the country. Nevertheless, the enclaves that most white southerners never expected to produce streams of agitation were now churning out a steady flow of students undaunted in their efforts to take the steps that their parents had yet to take. Older generations were molded by a spirit of conservatism, informed by decades of violence and hostility. Assigned to compile a study on what both high school and college students thought of the unfolding civil rights struggle, McAllister wrote, "Some of the principals were afraid for me to ask students some very simple questions. Fear is something you can touch here in Jackson."[62] Hesitation was noticeable among most of Mississippi's older Black generation. They hesitated out of concern for their jobs. They hesitated because many were the sole providers for their families. They hesitated for fear that some injury or death may come to their children. And perhaps most importantly, they hesitated because they, like most others, were not yet ready to die.

By 1963, the riddling of homes with bullets, hospital visitations, and untimely funerals were frequent occurrences. Agitating and provoking local whites by deliberately breaking social codes made many elders of the Black community uncomfortable. They knew the capacity for violence among white Mississippians and were victims of it more times than they cared to remember. The fact that this violence now openly targeted Black youths made them even more uncomfortable.[63] Black students had ascended to positions of leadership within the movement, and along with that came the anguishing reality that some decisions could result in bloodshed. More and more student activists shouldered this physical and psychological burden. Former student activist David Dennis painfully recalled what life on the front lines was like: "I was very responsible for sending people to go do jobs, and assigning people [to jobs] that didn't come back. So you don't forget that, you don't forget the last time you saw them. You don't forget the last words they said to you. You don't forget the expression on their face."[64]

Hard as it was for students to cross a deep river of fear and engage in direct-action protest, convincing an older Black generation of the necessity of doing so proved a chore unto itself. Dorie Ladner recalled her confrontation with the parent of a former classmate at Jackson State who was shot in the head after she became involved in voter registration activities in the Delta. She noted, "After being informed about Marylene [Burk] being shot, I went to visit her at a local hospital in Jackson and her mother started screaming at me and accusing me of her daughter getting shot, saying if it hadn't been for me, her daughter wouldn't have gotten shot. I had never been so hurt and I was overcome with grief."[65]

This generational divide posed a serious problem for movement organizers seeking a unified front in the struggle against white supremacy. However, in a culture where deference to one's elders still mattered, the relationship between Black youths and the adults who cared for their well-being never withered. Dennis recalled,

> But underground that is, there was really the adult and elders who gave support to the movement, who provided all kinds of stuff. Made everybody food, food came out of nowhere. . . . I mean they [students] were housed in private homes, they were our hotels. . . . You had kids out there because they were trying to keep their jobs. . . . And a lot of the meeting places we had was in churches you see, and even when the ministers couldn't come out front, they would turn their back, because the deacons would take over the church, you know and say you gone meet at the church. . . . So you had this, but none of that could have happened without adult participation.[66]

The strong presence of an elder Black community that quietly supported the actions of Black youths was a strong component of the movement. They fed the hungry, they gave guidance to those venturing down dangerous pathways, and they too provided shelter in a time of storm. Nevertheless, student activists' questioning the authority figures who appeared to be in lockstep with the white power structure was an increasingly common theme within the movement. Although many found support among members of the older generation, others progressively raised serious doubts about the policies, programs, and actions of the Black conservative establishment.

Jackson mayor Allen Thompson was skilled in evading the immediate concerns of local Black activists. In addition to avoiding the demands of movement participants, Thompson was also an expert in manipulating the power struggle among local Black leadership. In the mass meetings that occurred before students took to the streets in 1963, Thompson worked frantically to restructure the movement in his favor. He hoped that he could cool the tempers of disgruntled activists scheduled to meet with him by carefully placing conservative puppets such as Reddix and Percy Greene, editor of the local Black newspaper the *Jackson Advocate*, on the delegation.[67] Actions such as these caused students to become increasingly disenchanted with the established Black leadership, creating a deeper generation gap, which ultimately factored into the movement's splintering after 1966.

Throughout the controversial mass protests of 1963, Medgar Evers remained untainted in the minds of Black students. Despite his professional allegiance to the NAACP, symbolically and spiritually he was intrinsically linked to the Black youths of Jackson who felt betrayed by the actions of the Black establishment.[68] Although he knew that an uncompromised union with students would set him on a collision course with his employers, years of soul searching brought him closer to the interests and goals of students.[69] At a mass meeting in Greenwood, Mississippi, Evers applauded a group of student activists and local citizens, stating, "You've given us inspiration in Jackson."[70] With his conscience torn and his political outlook shifting toward a more radical and militant form of protest, Evers was constructing a vision that aligned him with the marginalized masses of Black folks, a fact that brought great stress to a man who spent years devoutly and faithfully serving an organization that demanded of him a more conservative and nonconfrontational course of action.

The embattled civil rights hero to countless Black youths was murdered by Byron De La Beckwith on June 11, 1963. While Evers lay dying in his own driveway, so too did the local civil rights movement in Jackson. In the days following his assassination, activists experienced a range of emotions that included rage, sadness, and doubt about building a local insurgency. Although students served as the majority of protesters involved in the

Jackson protests, they received much of their inspiration and encouragement from the man whose life was snatched from them by the forces of white supremacy.

On Jackson State's campus, most students were stiffened by the murder of Evers. Their reaction, or lack thereof, did not stop organizers from attempting a coup. Tougaloo students Anne Moody and Dorie Ladner immediately went on campus to rouse the emotions of students, to no avail. The majority of Jackson State's students were unready to take to the streets in defiance of their campus administration, let alone white authorities who could place them even more severely under the thumb of white supremacy. Frustrations and tension ran high as Moody and Ladner paced the hallways of Jackson State seeking anyone possessing the courage to step out in the spirit of rebellion. Their actions had little effect on students frozen by fear. Moody reacted with disgust: "I felt sick, I got so mad with them. How could Negroes be so pitiful? How could they just sit by and take all this shit without any emotions at all? I just didn't understand."[71]

As they prepared to leave campus, Ladner and Moody encountered President Reddix. It was only two years earlier that the Ladner sisters and other Jackson State students had butted heads with campus authorities over the student body's decision to show support for the Tougaloo Nine. That confrontation led to Dorie and Joyce Ladner's transfer to Tougaloo. In that span of two years, both the Ladners' and Reddix's worlds had undergone transformation. The Ladners found a space at Tougaloo where they could actively participate in movement activity and engage other likeminded activists who longed for liberation and the overthrow of southern apartheid. Conversely, Reddix faced mounting pressure from state authorities following the campus protests of 1961 and constricted his students' sphere of political expression.

As Reddix ushered the young ladies from the hallway and off campus, a rumor circulated through the school that Reddix struck Dorie, who had fallen to the floor in bitter disappointment at Reddix's unwillingness to recognize Evers's slaying. Even so, at the rallying point for protesters who planned to participate in the march, Ladner and Moody ran into Jackson State students who were there to join in the demonstration. Moody noted, "We noticed a couple of girls from Jackson State. . . . They told us a lot of students planned to demonstrate because of what Reddix had done. 'Good enough,' Dorie said, 'Reddix better watch himself, or we'll turn that school out.'"[72]

No mass demonstration occurred following Reddix's run-in with Ladner and Moody, but it was impossible for Jackson State students to remain totally removed either mentally or physically from the movement. By the spring of 1963, small examples of the shifting political consciousness could be found on campus. That spring, as the mass protests were building throughout the city and Jackson became the center of the largest civil rights movement demonstrations in the state, Jackson State student and editor of the *Blue and White Flash* Cleve McDowell took out his frustrations with his peers who dared to sit passively on the sidelines as events unfolded around them. After taking a seminar at Jackson State where students were allowed to trace the historical steps of social progression, McDowell wrote an article entitled "One Hundred Years of Progress?" "After one hundred years of legal freedom, have we as students done as much as we could have to aid the procession?" asked McDowell. "The answer is obviously no! Our dedication to education, perpetually weak, has perpetuated weak leaders who have impeded the progress of the procession. . . . Education is more than theory, it is application. For example, as a student in political science, I cannot understand how students can walk around on campus and call themselves majors in this field and not apply this knowledge of political theory to the campus political situation as well as to an evaluation of the state and national political scene."[73]

Although Jackson State was the largest Black college in Mississippi, very few of its students seemed to be reacting in a heated moment when their leadership was needed the most. McDowell found himself among only a handful of Jackson State students who were prepared to approach that threshold. Despite the conservative nature of the institution, Jackson State was still operating as a shelter in the midst of political chaos and social anarchy. McDowell himself was granted the safe space to ponder such critical questions and even given a public forum to express his views in writing. His reference to "weak leadership" could even be interpreted as an underhand swipe at the administration of President Reddix and the lack of leadership among Jackson State's adult community.

For the handful of Jackson State students who were taking notice and playing more active roles in the local movement, their ability to engage openly with students and faculty who were pondering the same questions was extremely significant and important in the development of their political consciousness. From the shelter of Black colleges such as Jackson State, they were free to explore and express their doubts, feelings, and pent-up frustrations with the political structure that sought to mute their latent hatred of the system. In reference to an incident that took place in her classroom, McAllister noted, "Students found the Rebel Antigone quotation which had so intrigued them; only they changed 'king' to governor. (I know [Ross] Barnett would never appreciate that.) The quotation was: 'The Rebel Antigone, who defied a king rather than betray her own conscience.'"[74] Such subtle forms of protest suggest students were comfortable enough to engage these ideas in the campus setting but still too hesitant to lay their dissatisfaction with white supremacy at the feet of the governor himself.

• • • • • •

The struggle for Black liberation would soon begin to take different directions both in the state of Mississippi and across the nation. But throughout the 1960s, Black colleges proved themselves as the most radical incubators of insurgency. Young activists who demanded equal access to political accommodations in the first half of the decade began to question the lack of economic empowerment in the Black community, the absence of Black elected officials, and the historical shortcomings in the housing industry. Black colleges provided a forum in some shape or form at every turn.

By 1967, Reddix was ready for retirement. Indeed, the tone of his administration during the turbulent decade caused former governor Barnett to thank Reddix in a personal letter for cooperating in "every way."[75] Unquestionably, Reddix, like numerous other Black college presidents, resented the pull and tug of the puppet strings, as those who have no personal control or voice so often do. Their emasculation resulted in a professional atmosphere that was paternalistic and domineering in fashion. Nevertheless, he must be credited for supporting an environment that put wind in the sails of budding activists and strengthened their resolve in the first twenty years of his tenure. As the world changed around them, the second curriculum fostered a multitude of tactics to confront mounting troubles.

From the shelter of Black colleges, students entered society as teachers, ministers, doctors, insurance agents, lawyers, and law-abiding citizens yearning and fighting for the day when the laws would shift to favor all Americans. They had been trained in this for years at Black colleges, and in spite of the trouble in their way, alumni, students, and common Black folks continued to press toward the realization of their freedom rights.

6 We Can! We Will! We Must!

The Radicalization and Transformation of Southern University, 1930–1966

· ·

It is common knowledge that democracy is not only on trial, but
very near conviction, unless new evidence is produced to liberate it.
The adequate defense of democracy is a knowledge of democracy.
Totalitarianism survives and flourishes under the veil of ignorance.
The university must set the standards of individual freedom, national
development and world citizenship. Adequate education of its youth
is the life blood of democratic society.

—Rodney Higgins, Southern University professor, 1948

Felton Grandison Clark had a flair for the dramatic. Not long after his father
and predecessor at the helm of Southern University passed in 1944, the
young and confident college administrator began marking the anniversary
of the school's founding by staging annual marches to his father's gravesite
across campus with full faculty and student body in tow. According to a former professor at the university, Clark headed the annual procession—and
wept every year.[1]

Clark held the post of president of Southern University with a viselike grip
for thirty years, starting in 1938. The arrival of the civil rights movement
prompted a transformation of sorts. Clark became the very archetype of an
unyielding, ruthless, and tyrannical Black college president. He infamously
expelled student protesters, terminated employees, and lorded over the campus as though it were a family inheritance bequeathed to him alone.[2] Over
the course of the turbulent 1960s, he became a lightning rod for controversy
and a reminder of the limitations Black colleges placed on the movement.

Yet for all the drama of Clark's antics during the turbulent 1960s, the
twenty-two years of Clark's administration that preceded the outbreak of
direct-action protests tell a different story. In an article he wrote for the
Journal of Negro Education in 1934, Clark got it partially correct when he
suggested, "The greatest contribution of these colleges is to be seen on
the more strictly psychological side."[3] He went on to argue that Black colleges

stood to transform white sentiment toward Blacks. The truth was just the opposite. In fact, Black colleges altered how Black students perceived their place in an oppressive white world. Clark presided over an extremely active communitas in Baton Rouge that at various times flowed with militancy and radicalism that primed the atmosphere for the charge that students would take against white supremacy in 1960. As at other institutions, the energy of radicalism would ebb and flow over the years, often mirroring the Black protest currents nationally. Nevertheless, expressions of dissent abounded during Clark's administration in the postwar era that led up to the 1960s. The historical evidence contradicts former student activist D'Army Bailey's assertion that "there was essentially no political climate at all" on Southern's campus.[4] By the time Bailey arrived in Baton Rouge in 1959, Southern University had exposed several generations of youths to subversive and progressive idealism, thus setting the stage for one of the largest mass movements on a Black college campus.

· · · · · ·

Founded in New Orleans in 1880, Southern University entered a local political climate that was in flux. Compared to other cities below the Mason-Dixon Line, the political culture and public sentiment concerning segregation were fairly relaxed in the Crescent City. For a brief period in the late nineteenth century, the color line was still somewhat blurred. Within the city's social realm, the races mixed and mingled, often sharing classroom space, points of leisure, and various modes of transportation.[5] This spirit of moderation was short lived.

In 1896 Louisiana was the epicenter of the Supreme Court's *Plessy v. Ferguson* decision, setting the precedent for de jure segregation nationwide. From the bayous and sugarcane fields in the South to the cotton plantations of the North and all parts in between, white supremacy held full sway over Louisiana. As the Nadir of race relations slowly crystallized, African Americans confronted a new and bitter reality of degradation and abuse at the hands of white Louisianans. In historian Roger A. Fischer's telling, "The proud Black people of Louisiana found it necessary to submit to these humiliations . . . because every possible alternative to submission had been taken from them."[6] Paralyzed by political impotency, racial violence, and the wholesale denial of human rights, Black folks across the state responded by constructing spaces that affirmed their humanity and delivered a counternarrative that not only outlined the contributions of the race but also offered a blueprint for social, political, and economic uplift.

To defend against oppression, Black Louisianans had to be subtle and creative.[7] Brazen and overt resistance was a rarity. By the time Southern University relocated to the state capital of Baton Rouge in 1914, there were few places where Blacks could find cover from the policies of Jim Crow. Even creoles, previously afforded a distinct racial classification, were now subjected to the brand of second-class citizenship applied to all Blacks.[8] The emergence of chapters of the National Association for the Advancement of Colored People (NAACP) throughout the state provided a rare glimmer of hope. The Baton Rouge branch opened in 1919, the same year that race riots gripped the country and thousands of exasperated Blacks left the southland in droves. The NAACP's strategy to expand south hardly made a dent in the segregationists' armor, yet for many Black Louisianans, the NAACP's presence provided a shot of much needed optimism.

As the Roaring Twenties came to a close, there was little change in race relations in Louisiana. The accommodationist tactics put forward by Booker T. Washington loomed large. While NAACP activists like James Weldon Johnson and W. E. B. DuBois rejected these ideas, southern race leaders such as Joseph Samuel Clark embraced the Washington formula as a necessary and pragmatic tool when negotiating the color line. As the first president of Southern University upon its move to Baton Rouge, the elder Clark almost recited Washington word for word before a crowd of thousands at the South Louisiana State Fair on October 13, 1929. "Give the Negro a chance and he will have no need to leave the South," declared Clark. He later emphasized that "the Negroes are very good friends to their white neighbors and will do anything within their power to make them happy and comfortable." Yet just as the Wizard of Tuskegee subversively harbored ulterior motives for the advancement of the race, so too did Clark. He concluded his address with a mild suggestion. If whites hoped to stem the tide of Blacks migrating north, they might consider constructing new schools, improving housing, and increasing wages for plantation workers. It is unclear who the dominant audience was among the fairgoers that afternoon, but the student paper reported that he received "generous applause."[9]

Modern sensibilities may chafe against Clark's approach to race in public forums. His depiction of the loyal Black servant was passé even in the 1920s and 1930s, particularly among the New Negro types. However, outside of politically moderate New Orleans (and, to a lesser extent, Baton Rouge), there were virtually no safe havens where Black leaders could publicly oppose white supremacy without fear of repercussions. This was especially true of northern Louisiana, where during the summer of 1930, Clark once again toed the fine line between pragmatism and emasculation. Known as one of the most violent places in the state and throughout the South, northern Louisiana was home to numerous plantations, lumber yards, oil refineries, and schools. Selected to deliver a commencement address at a local college in the town of Ruston, Clark faced another diverse audience that included the city judge, sheriff, president of the Polytechnical School (later renamed Louisiana Tech), and president of the First National Bank. Clark chose his words carefully, again castigating Blacks in the audience for their shortcomings. "The negro has a great friend in many of the best white people and great is the loyalty of the Negro to the white man," declared Clark. "Pray that there shall never spring forth one who could be so thoughtless as to cut his bond of friendship asunder." The student paper reported that at the end of his address, "most" of the white city fathers "gave him a hardy hand shake."[10]

It is difficult to believe that any African American who survived the atrocities endemic to the region could believe in the "bond of friendship" Clark evoked. Just a few years after Clark's address in Ruston, the "best white people" in town facilitated the brutal lynching of W. C. Williams, a nineteen-year-old wrongfully accused of the murder of a local white man and the rape of his white lover. Lincoln Parish sheriff Bryan Thigpen, whose father was among the men who greeted Clark when he spoke in Ruston earlier in the decade, tortured Williams with a searing hot screwdriver and handed him over to a murderous mob. Thousands turned out to participate in the beating, stabbing, shooting, and hanging of this innocent man.[11]

In such a culture, college administrators' negotiations with the "best" men were precarious indeed. Yet any idea of a more confrontational strategy was checked by memories of the violence of the recent past. Enough mangled bodies had been cut down out of trees, enough charred remains had been collected, and enough loved ones had been fished out of rivers and bayous to give effective pause to the idea of a frontal assault on white supremacy. In light of this reality, men like Joseph Samuel Clark retreated to the relatively safe confines of campus. It was there that seeds of insurgency were planted for future generations.

With direct action against racial violence and Jim Crow off the table, the Southern University communitas excelled at championing Black Louisianans and their causes. During the economic destruction of the Great Depression, Southern rallied to the aid of Black farmers, providing training and seminars on best practices and advocating for their concerns. Clark addressed agricultural conferences in Monroe and Tuskegee, and Southern

University annually hosted the largest agricultural conference in the state, offering free meals and room and board to any farmer who attended the event. Farmers were welcomed as industry leaders and encouraged to share their knowledge with campus and state officials. Moreover, conferences provided a safe forum for Black farmers to discuss the inequities they experienced as intermediaries collected valuable data illustrating the collective hardships Black farmers endured as a result of the color line. Speaking before the National Advisory Committee on Education at the Department of the Interior, Charles Mann, president of the American Council on Education, testified in 1930 that there were six demonstration farms in Alabama for white farmers, but none for the critical mass of Black farmers throughout the state. Mann pointed out that federal intervention would perhaps be necessary to correct the problem, a development that would be used in later years to advance numerous issues related to the freedom movement.[12]

Concern and advocacy for Blacks in the rural farm communities of Louisiana were not the only issues percolating within the Southern University communitas. As a student of Booker T. Washington's ideas, Clark embraced the concept of separatism. The student paper reported an exchange he had as a guest speaker of Louisiana State University's chapter of the YMCA. Clark outlined for his white audience the need and desire among Black Louisianans to "remain distinct," an idea he apparently expressed in "a very diplomatic, yet authentic fashion."[13] By advocating for distance between the races, Clark was able to maintain a racialized space where students could steadily gain exposure to the militant ideas that were circulating throughout Black America during the Depression era.

The fruits of that exposure were already beginning to show. As early as 1929, the young editor of the campus paper mocked the country's failed notions of "liberty and justice for all." In an article entitled "How Do We Think?," the student declared, "We also talk about democracy and I'm wondering whether we know just what democracy means, and if we realize that it is an ideal and really does not exist."[14] From the Depression through the postwar era, militant expressions such as these would continue to emanate from the campus.

Clark continued to ply his strategy of offering conciliatory gestures toward southern whites while advocating for institutions that would serve African American needs. Clark spoke at a cornerstone-laying ceremony for Dillard University in New Orleans, making a rare public appeal for the recognition of civil and human rights for Blacks: "Everybody knows what the Black people want . . . freedom from economic exploitation . . . freedom from political domination. . . . We want the stigma of inferiority lifted from us; we want to be able to walk down the streets of the world and into the common gathering places of mankind free from contempt."[15] Clark did not outline how Blacks should go about securing those freedoms in the face of overt and widespread racism. Such a conclusion would have called for him to openly critique the social forces at work against African Americans, a step he clearly was not prepared to take. Nevertheless, he did foster the proliferation of self-consciousness, race pride, and idealism on Southern's campus, paralleling the awakening of progressive sentiments nationwide.

The pillar of the Southern University communitas was race consciousness. Throughout the administrations of both Joseph Samuel Clark and his son Felton, professors, guest speakers, and the campus paper all exalted Black history and cultural nationalism. An editorial from the student newspaper used a clever metaphor of a scribe who was tasked with preparing the room for other scribes, a tedious and backbreaking chore that caused the student to slumber while those who benefited from his having prepared the room enjoyed a head start in their work. Arising from his slumber, it was now imperative that the scribe catch up with his fellow scholars of the world, a task that would be greatly aided by those who were knowledgeable about their heritage. The editorial stated, "To the young Negro who is blessed with the opportunity of having within his grasp the effulgent fountain of educational opportunities, this history of his predecessors, the handicaps of whom were an hundred-fold in comparison with those of today, should serve as an inspiration and impetus which shall forever keep this invincible race in one steady ascend."[16]

Joseph Samuel Clark was not just an innocent bystander in the promotion of race pride on campus. At the onset of the Depression, he extoled the contributions of Black working-class men and women during a local Labor Day radio broadcast, and on March 15, 1930, he brought the activist and poet Alice Dunbar-Nelson to campus. According to a campus reporter, "her main object, it seemed was to try to interest the young people to do their best everyday between the races." Yet Clark shied away from addressing the racism and prejudice that was rampant throughout the American workforce, just as the passionate Dunbar-Nelson deflected the opportunity to address openly the conditions that millions of Blacks endured.[17]

Nevertheless, even these muted public discussions of race benefited students. At the very least, they were granted the space and opportunity to discuss these matters with their professors and friends, and to map out their own path in dealing with segregation and racial violence. Students were destined to enter a world that devalued their humanity regardless of their pedigree, training, or mental aptitude. Southern provided them a space to prepare for the white aggression they would someday face. One such student, Sherman Briscoe, was a founding officer of the College Men's Forum, an organization that, among other things, sought to "enable young men to argue more intelligently and diligently." Upon graduating, he ventured into the harsh climate of northern Louisiana, teaching at the local Black high school in Monroe and coaching the young men of the school in football. The power of persuasion that he perfected as a student at Southern called him into the journalism profession, and Briscoe founded the first Black newspaper in Monroe. The *Southern Broadcast* had an effective but relatively short life of seven years, counterbalancing the negative portrayal that Blacks received in the white press. Briscoe soon left Louisiana to become the national news editor and director of public relations for the *Chicago Defender*, one of the most prominent Black newspapers in the country. He moved on once again to serve as an information specialist in the Department of Agriculture in Washington, D.C., an unsung soldier of the movement. An article memorializing his passing in 1979 referred to him as a civil servant, leader, and pioneer in the long battle against Jim Crow in the nation's capital—a career arc that began when he was emboldened and empowered along with his peers at Southern.[18]

Southern served as a main wellspring for the cadre of teachers who fanned across the state in the 1930s, transferring racial consciousness to their pupils in the same way in which it was imparted to them.[19] Black teachers did not embrace the necessity of racial heritage through some casual observation; they were oriented to this mission as part of their college training. Students on campus readily embraced the founding of Negro History Week, flocking to hear Carter G. Woodson speak before a "packed house" on campus in February 1933. A month before Woodson's visit, a student published an article on the importance of Liberia, a commentary that illustrated the student's worldview and interests in the diaspora. One student even went so far as to denounce and discredit Abraham Lincoln's role as the "great emancipator" in an editorial—a claim that was especially sacrosanct in the Black community. And while the very thought of establishing Black studies as an academic field was still decades away, for a brief moment in time, Southern offered an actual class in "Negro history" that developed a play on "Negro life" in 1933.[20]

Overt activism was still far away, but Depression-era Southernites demonstrated that the key ingredients necessary to nurture it were not only present, they were largely provided by the administration of Joseph Samuel Clark, the faculty he employed, and the communitas they helped to create. By the time that his son Felton Clark took over as president in 1938, the school was well on its way to becoming a seedbed for radicals. The organization of a youth branch of the NAACP in Baton Rouge in 1938 proved a harbinger of things to come.

Such chapters tended to be sporadic in nature, often going defunct only a few years after their creation.[21] An activist cohort might come together on campus and then naturally disband upon graduation, which could lead to a chapter's becoming dormant if a new crop of campus leaders failed in their duty to keep the torch of radicalism lit. In this way, the chapters' development resembled the ebb and flow of normal social movement activity, both then and through the dawning of the turbulent 1960s.

Yet the NAACP's youth chapter in Baton Rouge transcended these limitations. Not only did it mount important campaigns against white supremacy on the eve of World War II, it emerged from a sizable flourish of campus activity representing the leading edge of a burgeoning movement for liberation. Under the guidance of Delphine "D. J." Dupuy, herself a seasoned activist and officer within the local senior branch, the youths of Baton Rouge enlisted "in a fight to secure for Negroes the maximum benefits of democracy."[22] To achieve that, the students explored a topic close to the heart of traditional race leaders: economic solidarity laced with Black Nationalism.

Young Emmett Bashful carried none of the characteristics of his surname. A campus leader at Southern, he was elected president of the NAACP youth chapter. His immersion in the study of mathematics and the social sciences proved valuable in his leadership of the chapter. In 1938 the group of students launched a "Buy Negro campaign" after surveying both the economic plight and the potential of the Black community. Undoubtedly the students' drive to increase the patronage of Black enterprises was motivated by the daily disrespect they endured from white business owners who accepted their money but refused to accept their humanity. However, their appeal to their fellow students struck another tone that was consistent with the racial pride and cultural nationalism engrained within them through their training. In reaching out to their fellow Southernites and local members of their community, the students declared, "We believe that you love your race and would like to see it progress in business. You can do much toward bringing this about. Simply spend your money where it will do the most good for you and your race. Spend it where your boy or girl will be able to obtain jobs of trust and be paid decent wages." This cut to the heart of the matter and raised a very important question: How could Black institutions best be utilized in the liberation of African Americans? For Bashful and his peers, it was clear that at least a portion of the solution lay in strengthening the financial core of the Black community. However, the support of banks and businesses could not accomplish that alone. It was necessary to have institutions in place to both crystallize this vision of Black solidarity and spread it to others, so as to perpetuate a cycle of service to the race. In short, Bashful got some help on the inside of Southern's communitas.[23]

Southern's faculty members gave the young militants a sense of determination, dignity, and purpose—vital values for crafting new freedom dreams. Bashful became the student assistant to William Fontaine, a philosopher on campus who, according to the findings of his biographer Bruce Kuklick, served as a constant inspiration to student groups. Kuklick also notes Fontaine's fascination with the absurdity of segregation, a perspective he passed on to many of his students. There was also Leroy Posey, a mathematician whose instruction so stimulated Bashful that he signed up for every math course available. This training was surely of use in planning the Buy Negro campaign. Last, but certainly not least, there was Elsie Lewis. A historian by training, Lewis rejected the notion of Black inferiority in every way and proceeded to cultivate the freedom dreams of the youths in her charge. She initiated mock campus-wide elections where students ran not for campus president but for the governorship of Louisiana itself. According to the campus paper, the election "created much interest in the entire student body which was shown by their full cooperation in every instance." These exercises in democracy expanded the idea of what politics could offer Black youths, even in a closed and segregated society. Perhaps they could one day transform the political landscape and with it the fates of millions of previously disenfranchised people. Bashful tried his hand at running for the top office but fell short. He eventually made up for it by being appointed as the first chancellor of Southern University at New Orleans in 1959, a post he would hold for twenty-eight years.[24]

· · · · · ·

In the coming war years, students continued to mull over proper responses to a nation that fought for democracy and victory overseas but ignored bigotry and racial violence on the domestic front. There were campaigns to initiate a chapter of the NAACP on campus, and it is unclear whether attempts to establish the chapter were stalled by Felton Clark or local NAACP leadership. What Clark surely did not stop was the proliferation of radical thought at Southern. Student columnist A. J. Scott provided a rather scorching condemnation of Blacks who aimed to close their ranks in the name of patriotism and hope for postwar acceptance. Pointing to the widespread racial violence and rampant intolerance that followed World War I, Scott encouraged his readers to ignore any new calls for Black support. "I do not even think white America wants another war," wrote Scott. "But should they catapult into this conflict, let them fight without Black America. We want no part of this or any other war. What would we fight for anyway?"[25]

Other students theorized a radical transformation that would only come about from Black participation. Scott's classmate Cedric Jackson proposed a more militant approach. "There is a crying need for a purer, more forceful form of democracy in America," argued Jackson. "The American Negro must rebel against the increasing ills of a rottening economic and political order." Jackson continued to argue for the participation of youths in that rebellion and looked to his fellow Southernites to serve as the shock troops of the transforming social order. So too did DuBois. The world-renowned race scholar made his first visit to Southern University as the decade began, and he primed the atmosphere for an explosive decade, twenty years to the day before Black colleges across the South would launch a social revolution.[26]

The insurgency that would finally tear down Jim Crow was still years in the making. That did not stop Elsie Lewis from practicing the second curriculum and deliberately sowing seeds of idealism and resistance in her students, a campus-wide practice that made Southern a viable threat to the established order of things in Baton Rouge. She put together a quarterly campus bulletin called the *Observer*. Tellingly, at least half of the articles concerned voting rights and the political process. Seeing suffrage as a pathway forward, students increasingly flocked to the campaign to secure the vote. Felton Clark himself led a penny fund-raiser to send student representatives to the Southern Negro Youth Congress convention in New Orleans in April 1940. In spite of that modest effort, a large body of students objected to the idea of sending just a chosen few. The campus newspaper reported that several students from Southern "took it upon themselves to attend this important meeting." Armed with the vote, students believed they could reverse the tide of injustice in American courts, elect representatives to fight in the best interests of beleaguered and forgotten communities, and bring equitable funding to impoverished Black schools. The slow and uphill road to securing those rights continued to be a source of contention and frustration that fashioned the doorway for the massive protests that lay ahead.[27]

Radicalism emerged across campus as the global conflict grew nearer. Students and faculty assaulted white supremacy through the campus paper, the local airwaves, and sponsored programs. When a group of Louisiana State University graduate students were invited to campus in April to hold a discussion on race relations with Southern faculty and students, both Felton Clark and his father, Joseph Samuel Clark, attended, perhaps in an effort to ensure the exchange did not get too testy. A month later, students were treated to a town hall meeting entitled "Is the Negro in the South Ready for the Ballot?" Its official conclusion was, "The Negro in the South IS ready for the ballot—especially in comparison with other enfranchised groups."[28]

As the rhetoric on campus heated up, the local mood followed suit. A spate of incidents involving local law enforcement disrupted the summer of 1941. Pursuing two men who got into an altercation at a Black-owned theater, a small platoon of police ran roughshod through the Black community, causing George Butler, a local Black physician, to create a petition denouncing police brutality. The petition generated enough buzz that a grand jury was formed to look into claims of rampant and ongoing abuse by the Baton Rouge police. Though no sanctions against the police emerged from this effort, it demonstrated that African Americans were speaking out in new ways.

Though the fall semester began quietly, by its conclusion, the communitas stirred students to action. In early December, Howard University professor and historian Rayford Logan delivered an address at the general chapel assembly, invoking the spirit of protest on campus. "The Negro should wake up and find himself if he expects to have any place in the world after the war," argued Logan, "or he will be in the same position as after the last world war." Himself a veteran of the armed forces, Logan was also a veteran of the long struggle for Black equality. He urged the young troops into battle, declaring, "The Negro should begin to fight now before it's too late, for those things which he feels that he should possess." Yet even if they followed Logan's urgings, how these students would confront the traditional obstacles faced by all Black Louisianans remained an open question.[29]

At the dawn of World War II, students seized the opportunity to embrace the wartime political rhetoric by promoting it on campus, enlisting in the armed forces in large numbers, and revving up local protest energies that would soon be harnessed for an unprecedented frontal assault. Indeed, the war was a boon for Southern in many ways. As one of the largest Black universities in the country, Southern was designated as a regional training center for defense, instructing both soldiers and citizens who made valuable contributions to the war effort. The war brought federal dollars to Southern that helped its rapid increase in both student population and popularity among Blacks as one of the premier sources for higher education in the Deep South. As the war teased out patriotism in Baton Rouge and on campus, it also squarely brought into focus the stinging hypocrisy of America's domestic policies.[30]

To vent their resentment against the absurdities of the color line, students turned once again to the campus paper. Free from the stringent politics that loomed ahead, the student paper became the safest place for student expression outside of classroom exchanges and dorm-room banter. In a section entitled "Jottings," campus writers poked fun at Jim Crow policies such as the establishment of segregated bomb-proof shelters throughout Baton Rouge, with one student humorously pondering what would happen if that tragic moment struck and a white person "was caught in a Negro district." Campus reporter Oby Jefferson wrote a revealing piece entitled "Our Town," where he described the contributions Southern was making in radicalizing and politicizing youths. "Our beloved Southern University may not be permitted to organize groups to go down to the polls en masse and demand the right to vote," Jefferson opined. "But Southern does teach courses in social sciences that enlighten one as just how to vote. In addition to that we have studied history and learned that any people who were not permitted to govern themselves were exploited, shamed, and reduced to slaves of the worst type."[31] Jefferson's disclosure of how Southern professors engaged in instructing youths in the tools of liberation demonstrates exactly how charged the political atmosphere was for students matriculating at what was now the South's largest historically Black university for African Americans. Additionally, Jefferson's tantalizing comment that Southern students were not "permitted to organize groups" en masse to "demand the right to vote" suggests that perhaps the idea of mass protests had at least been broached by those within the Southern communitas.

When they were not being politicized in class, students were exposed to activist energies through sponsored campus events. The town hall forum, mandatory for students, was particularly notable. "Town Hall, in my estimation attempts to bring to us questions and problems of immediate importance to us," wrote Jefferson. While featuring figures from the Black lecture circuit, many of whom made their own cases against white

Southern University students designed their class photos in 1942 to show their solidarity with the *Pittsburg Courier*'s Double V campaign. African Americans declared a desire to achieve victory against America's foreign enemies during World War II but also pledged to defeat the forces of segregation and white supremacy at home. From *Southern Digest* 15, no. 12 (June 1, 1942), © The Archives Department/John B. Cade Library/Southern University and A&M College/ Baton Rouge, Louisiana.

supremacy, some of the most interesting exchanges were produced by students themselves. In one extremely provocative town hall on August 3, 1943, students debated the question, "Is the present Global war an indication of the failure of Christianity?" Perhaps most interesting is that the efficacy of Christianity was being debated at all, a topic not often broached in the American Bible Belt. Nevertheless, much as they did with America's paradoxical professions of democracy, students had a tough time digesting the empty rhetoric of brotherhood and redemption streaming from white, racist Christians. After another round of police brutality swept the Black community earlier in the year, resulting in the arrest of sixty-nine African Americans, the debate of "what would Jesus do" ensued. The speakers taking up the affirmative position of Christianity's shortcomings in the town hall debate concluded "that Christianity has failed to bring about a better relationship between the races. The tension, hatred, and exploitation existing are not things evolving from the success of Christianity but rather from its failure. Even now, the races are so high and deep that race riots have caused death and injury."[32]

Even Felton Clark did his part to advance the cause of democracy at home and abroad. When Louisiana adopted a statewide course titled Louisiana Civic Problems in 1943, Clark petitioned state authorities to promote positive and realistic images of Blacks, hoping that such a move would ameliorate misunderstandings and negate the perpetuation of falsehoods and stereotypes. "If all children can see the true pictures of people of all races during the impressionate years," Clark argued, "they will live more harmoniously in later life." The state kept Clark's request in a holding pattern. Later in the year, Clark made an appearance at the Istrouma Methodist Church, where, speaking before "an almost capacity white audience," he laid out a call for racial equality. "Out of one blood, God created all men equal which refutes the old belief of a superior race," declared Clark. Methodist churches were known for being more politically progressive than the racially volatile Southern Baptist denominations, but it was nevertheless a remarkable feat for any race leader in that time and place to stand before a predominantly white audience and essentially repudiate the tenets of white supremacy.

At least for a brief period of time, Southern's chief administrator bolstered campus militancy, facilitated youth politicization, and stood boldly and publicly against bigotry and intolerance. When "Pelican" Hill Jr., a Southern student serving overseas, wrote Clark a personal, and politically edgy letter, Clark decided to publish it in the student newspaper. Not only did the student make a plea for his fellow Southernites to join the NAACP, but he told a joke about the devil's Christmas present from God. According to Hill, God had gifted Mississippi, Georgia, Alabama, and several other southern states to the devil, which led Hill to joke that "it has been hell there since then." He concluded by encouraging Clark and his peers to pray for God to reclaim the South, noting that only "then you will see a hell-of-a change."[33]

There was no civil rights organization more widely embraced in Louisiana than the NAACP. The organization of the nation's oldest lobbyists on behalf of Blacks' freedom rights grew exponentially during the war years, becoming the go-to group on all race matters in the state. When Southern's on-campus chapter debuted, its promotion of both education and voting rights as pathways toward Black liberation fit the second curriculum at Southern perfectly. So enthusiastic were students about merely attending a student conference held by the NAACP at Lincoln University in Pennsylvania in 1943 that an election was held just to see who would be the campus representative. Rosalie Allen, a senior secondary education major, won the contest over eight competitors. By the time the campus branch finally received its charter in 1944, it was already recognized as the largest school-based chapter in the country.[34]

Southern was also a major site for the training of teachers, a key constituency of the NAACP and a significant portion of Black Louisiana's professional class. It was not just the political current found within national Black newspapers but also the continuous tide of militancy and idealism they were exposed to as college students that shaped them to view themselves not merely as teachers but rather as liberators. When the NAACP took up the issue of equalizing Louisiana teacher salaries in 1943, a strong base of politically conscious teachers stood ready to embrace the strategy—at least in theory. They were less prepared for the long, drawn-out, public battle with segregation that could cost them their jobs in Baton Rouge and get them effectively locked out of other positions throughout the state. After an uphill battle with several defeats, salaries were finally equalized in 1948. Aside from those teachers who participated, the majority of Black Louisianans still appeared frozen, willing to embrace the rhetoric of confrontation but wary of action. Across the state and in other industries and occupations, the policies that reinforced discrimination went undisturbed.[35]

This did not stop the rhetoric from flowing at Southern. In April 1944 Reid Jackson, professor of education and adviser to the campus chapter of the NAACP, published an article entitled "A Negro Looks at the South" in the *New Republic*. The scholar registered a powerful and loaded opinion when he wrote that the southern Black was being "steadily driven to the point where he will die for liberty at home." By war's end, there were no willing martyrs. Not yet. What did tragically exist were numerous cases of racial violence across the country. Both the protests that often touched off the upheavals and small acts of defiance across the country were reported in the *Southern University Digest*, a fact that within itself was a small leap forward. The campus paper picked up Associated Negro Press (ANP) stories covering the arrest of student protesters in Evansville, Indiana. Two young white girls were arrested for deliberately breaking the color barrier in a Greyhound Bus station restaurant. That same edition of the *Digest* contained an ANP story detailing an FBI investigation into voting irregularities in Mobile, Alabama, that followed the Supreme Court's ruling in *Smith v. Allwright* that the South's all-white democratic primaries were unconstitutional. And on December 7, 1944, the *Digest* published its first article that documented racial violence against Black Louisianans.[36]

Students clearly knew about the effects of white terrorism across the state, and it is not a stretch to assume that nearly all of them had some experience with the physical brutality associated with Jim Crow, either personally or through friends and family. Previous incidents, as numerous as they were, simply did not appear in the pages of the *Digest*, and the fact that this one did demonstrated courage among *Digest* staff and perhaps even school administrators. Earlier that summer, J. Leo Hardy, a NAACP organizer in the southern Louisiana town of New Iberia, was savagely beaten by local law enforcement and forced to leave town along with other NAACP supporters who sought to open a welding school in the area for young Black men. The student paper at Southern described the perpetrators of the assault as part of a "white fascist uprising." The *Digest*'s knowledgeable readers would have been well aware of Europe's fascist regimes, regarded as enemies of freedom and democracy during the war. With an increased NAACP membership on campus, it is possible that the staff resorted to this rhetoric in response to an assault against one of their own. However, it may be that mounting frustrations with white supremacy and racial violence had simply reached a breaking point. The edition that followed the week after the Hardy story was printed contained another ominous headline. When the paper reported that Charles Wesley, president of Wilberforce University, spoke in Chicago, the *Digest* paraphrased the subject of his talk with the headline, "White Attitude toward Negro Must Change, for Peace."[37]

· · · · · ·

As the nation's foremost Black labor organizer and a preeminent civil rights leader, A. Philip Randolph was famous for successfully and aggressively compelling Franklin Delano Roosevelt to ban discrimination in the defense industries by signing Executive Order 8802 into law in 1941. To accomplish this, Randolph threatened to flood the streets of Washington, D.C., with thousands of labor activists and working-class Black folks from across the nation. Roosevelt yielded, giving future Black organizers a new entry in the activist playbook—the threat of mass protest.

Randolph brought his fervor for justice to Southern's campus in the spring of 1945, attempting to push Black students ever closer to the tipping point. Speaking to a packed house in the school auditorium, Randolph made a global connection to the struggle that Black Louisianans confronted on a daily basis. "Two-thirds of the world population is of color," declared Randolph. "These people crave freedom and independence: these 130,000,000 people want freedom." As one of the principle architects of the mass action strategy, Randolph was acutely aware of the courage that was summoned when oppressed individuals knew that they were not alone. Like so many other orators who made their way through the Southern University communitas, Randolph urged the students on by proclaiming, "The colored people of America are moving. There is a doctrine of the Master Race theory . . . but the peoples of the minority group are not contented to remain under the domination of others." The *Digest* reported that Randolph's challenge to the students was interrupted several times by thunderous applause.[38]

Randolph's message appeared to reverberate for some time through the Southern community, although not everyone saw the future through rose-colored glasses. A rare summer edition of the *Digest* noted that Professor Adrian Pertee's Negro History class was "now looking in wild-eyed anticipatory skepticism toward the post-war world." Students at the school had discussed global events before in their classes and in other special forums, but the postwar outbreak of independence movements in countries previously dominated by Europeans received special attention. As one student wrote concerning the rash of global developments, "All have important bearing on the future welfare of Negroes, including Southern University students." The increased political consciousness among Southernites coincided with the return of numerous male students from battlefields across the globe. The returning GIs had rubbed shoulders with African Americans from all over the country and had fraternized with people from every corner of the earth, and they had done so while in a position of authority. As their return coincided with the global winds of change, the *Digest* staff started a new column entitled "Which Way World?" that featured news stories reporting on the latest international developments. Echoing Randolph's call for a new massive front against white supremacy, student reporter Willie J. Hodge wrote, "I am only one person and can do very little. But there are millions like me. Together we can literally move mountains. The answer to 'Which Way World?' depends on us."[39]

The NAACP's indirect tactics represented another source of resentment for Louisiana's would-be radicals and activists. The organization's legal maneuvers and compromises proceeded at a glacial pace, as Louisiana's racial politics remained in stasis. The classism, sexism, factionalism, and internal bureaucracy of the organization further isolated membership. As the dominant civil rights organization throughout the state, the NAACP left activists without alternatives in their fight against racial tension. Dupuy Anderson, a well-known local activist, described the city's civil rights leaders as easily pacified, a characteristic that trickled down to the Black denizens of Baton Rouge. "Those of us that wanted the whole pie, or half of the pie, was rabble-rousers," recalled Anderson.[40]

In 1947 Southern University opened its Law School, the origin of which was rooted in a NAACP case that sought to desegregate Louisiana State University's Law School. Rather than hearing the rationale and legal precedence for integration, the presiding judge dismissed the case and ordered the state to open a school to serve African Americans at Southern. Naturally, the underfunded school never even lived up to the idea of separate but equal—the very concept that the NAACP was working to overturn. Accepting the ruling as a temporary stopgap measure, the NAACP moved forward anew with its efforts to desegregate Louisiana State University's Law School five years later.

Native Louisianan Alexander P. Tureaud was a soldier in the NAACP's litigation brigade that tackled cases such as these from state to state. Trained at Howard University by Charles Hamilton Houston, the dean of civil rights law, Tureaud was the lead lawyer in the Louisiana State University case, and he basked in the idea that his work led to the opening of Southern's Law School. According to Tureaud, it was a watershed moment that opened the floodgates for Black lawyers throughout the state. Although Southern's Law

School appeared to be a shrine to appeasement, or just a sliver of pie, it too was enveloped in the campus communitas, churning out foot soldiers in the fight to bring justice for Black Louisianans. In the year before its opening, attorney Louis Berry, who served on the NAACP's team of lawyers, visited a business law class on Southern's campus, informing the students "that an assault is now being made in the South to break down segregation and discrimination." Berry continued by declaring that the work to desegregate Louisiana State University's Law School was "only the beginning and definitely not the ending here in Louisiana." While Berry and the NAACP's slow negotiations with the Louisiana judicial system were not the type of action some radicals hoped for, his prognostication about the future of the movement was spot on.[41]

Four days after Berry spoke on campus, two Southern professors, Marie Davis Cochrane and Montgomery King, boarded a local city bus headed home. The bus quickly filled, and when Cochrane and King were ordered to give up their seats, they refused. The two were arrested, held in jail for over an hour, and released. Cochrane and King solicited the services of Tureaud, Berry, and the NAACP and filed suit to collect $12,000 in damages as opposed to engaging in direct-action protest against the bus company. That the NAACP chose that route was no surprise, nor was it a surprise that the case was dismissed in February of the following year without fanfare. However, one can only imagine the buzz the pair of professors made on campus. Students likely peppered them with questions about the experience both in and out of class. No professors had taken the steps to match the rhetoric of the communitas with action against the white supremacist machine. So popular was Cochrane that she was invited to Louisiana State University's campus as guests of Horne Huggins and his wife, who ran the Episcopal Student Center on campus. Huggins asked Cochrane to share a few words concerning their bold stand against Jim Crow, which she described as "an illogical race pattern stemming from the caste system of slavery." King's and Cochrane's targeting of the Baton Rouge buses was a harbinger of things to come.[42]

Southern received an unexpected visitor at the beginning of 1950. Students at Southern were used to white Louisianans visiting campus for an obligatory checkup or campus tour, but liberal white scholars were somewhat of a rarity in the campus lecture circuit. Arnold Rose, a young sociology professor at the University of Minnesota, arrived at the Negro History Week Convocation to deliver a talk entitled "Distortion in the History of American Race Relations." He focused on the importance of correcting

Faculty NAACP Drive Successful

A record number of faculty and staff members joined the National Association for the advancement of Colored People in the recent membership drive on Southern's campus. According to Mr. Horace Dawson, English Instructor who headed the drive, 57 members of the summer faculty and staff paid membership dues.

The majority of persons paid the regular membership fee of $2.00. Many others, however, subscribed to the Crisis Magazine in addition to paying the membership ($3.50), and still others paid the sponsoring fee of $5.00.

The following persons became members of the NAACP during the recent campaign: J. L. Hunt, Mrs. M. D. McLeod, Dr. Charles E. Harrington, B. V. Lacour, Mrs. V. J. Tellis, G. Leon Netterville, Jr., Dr. Mildred McK. Satterwhite, Dr. L. R. Posey, Louis E. Puryear, H. J. Thomas, E. R. Brantley, Mrs. Ida S. Sisk, J. W. McLeod, Mrs. Rebecca F. Netterville, Mr. J. W. Fisher, Dr. J. Warren Lee, Horace G. Dawson, Jr., Benjamin F. Kraft, I. S. Graham, Mrs. Louise H. Talton, Russell M. Ampey, Miss A. A. Boley, S. W. Austin, Miss P. E. Thrift, H. L. group, and Miss Villian Kennedy, Director of Materials Bureau of East Baton Rouge Parish, was consultant for the upper elementary.

Mrs. Camille Shade, university librarian, was director of the workshop conference.

Dozens of Southern University faculty members joined the NAACP in 1951. Black students became the direct beneficiaries of the increased militancy of professors who raised the political consciousness of the students they instructed. These relationships nurtured the massive overt protests that took over Southern's campus in the early 1960s. From *Southern Digest* 22, no. 19 (July 21, 1951), © The Archives Department/John B. Cade Library/Southern University and A&M College/Baton Rouge, Louisiana.

pseudoscientific myths that enforced the ideas of white supremacy and Black subservience. Rose also examined the long arc of history and the role that students should play in creating a new narrative for justice and democracy in America. The time for creating a new arc of history in Baton Rouge was quickly approaching.[43]

While a culture of appeasement and timidity lingered in Baton Rouge, it did not stop Southern students from exporting the idealism and militancy that they picked up on campus. In 1951, Southernites Jewell Prestage, a junior, and George Pitts, a freshman, returned to their hometown of Alexandria, Louisiana, to initiate a rare display of direct action. For years, the embattled and outspoken leader of the local NAACP, Georgia Johnson, had slogged it out with both segregationists and the head brass of the NAACP, who tried to rein in her more aggressive strategies. Further influencing the climate in Alexandria were teachers in the local schools who practiced the second curriculum and instilled race pride among the local youths. When Prestage and Pitts heard that the Rapides Parish School Board worked in conjunction with local planters to shut down the Black school in order to send the students into the cotton fields, the two sprang into action. Leaving Southern, they traveled two hours back to their central Louisiana hometown and led students on a march to the office of the local newspaper, the court-house, and eventually the school board's office itself. They carried protest signs that read, "What Color Is Cotton," and "Let the Hand That Takes the Change Pick the Cotton." The board immediately reopened the school. The bold actions of Prestage and Pitts must have shocked both local whites and the Black community in Alexandria, including Johnson, who, as militant as she was, still adhered to the strategy of pursuing freedom rights by se-curing the ballot and legal redress. Prestage and Pitts gave Alexandria its first taste of overt protest, and how traumatizing it must have been to see young, determined Blacks defiantly marching through the streets of town, picketing the offices of the white establishment.[44]

Yet a drastic change in the political culture soon undermined Southern's thriving communitas. Beginning in the 1950s, there was a noticeable change to the tone of the *Digest*. Cold War–era politics were on the rise, and as the Red Scare worked its way through campus, the radical entries that had defined the paper soon withered away. Many columns proposed questions such as, "Should teachers be fired for refusing to testify about Communist affiliation?" and, "Should teachers be required to take Loyalty Oaths?" Cam-pus militancy had taken a hit just as a mass movement was about to be unleashed in Baton Rouge.[45]

• • • • • •

The seeds of the 1953 movement were planted in soil familiar to Southern students. The Baton Rouge city council passed an ordinance in 1949 that monopolized the local busing system to the advantage of the Baton Rouge Bus Company, a white-owned and white-operated business. This effectively cut out the minority-operated buses that primarily served the Black side of town, and it subjected African Americans to the cruelties of white bus drivers who enforced the color line with extreme prejudice. The indepen-dent buses were taking a large number of customers away from the Baton Rouge Bus Company and severely undercutting its profit margin. The self-sufficiency and self-determination embodied in the community's patronage of the local Black-owned buses harked back to the cultural nationalist leanings of Southern's first president, Joseph Samuel Clark, and echoed the Buy Negro campaign—the very first program initiated by the newly chartered campus chapter of the NAACP back in 1938. The Baton Rouge city council was determined to negate the economic solidarity of the Black community that sheltered them from white hostility, and in doing so, it set the stage for a showdown.[46]

At the center of the 1953 ordeal was Theodore Judson Jemison, an Alabama State University grad who arrived in town in 1949 as the new pastor of Mount Zion First Baptist Church. Before Jemison's arrival, Rev. Gardner Taylor had served as the pastor of Mount Zion and, through his leadership, had established the church as a hub of civil rights activity. Jemison's relocation to Baton Rouge in 1949 coincided with the adoption of the city ordinance that eliminated the Black-owned buses that acted as a buffer against Jim Crow policies. With that safeguard no longer in place, Jemison fielded numerous complaints from exasperated parishioners and community members. In the spring of 1953, community leaders successfully negotiated Ordinance 222, which made segregation aboard city buses more pliable. Blacks could now board the bus from the back to the front and were no longer essentially roped off from "white only" sections. Considering that the overwhelming majority of bus riders were Black, the ordinance was a welcome change to weary riders looking to rest themselves after a hard day's work. This move offended the racist sensibilities of white bus drivers, who immediately went on strike and demanded that Ordinance 222 be overturned. When the drivers' demands were met through a new court ruling on June 18 that defended the overarching system of segregation, Jemison and the leadership of the newly organized United Defense League called for a boycott.[47]

The boycott lasted only eight days, and after the dust settled, it was fairly conclusive that in spite of some concessions, segregation remained the winner. The white establishment amended their policy to reserve the first two bus rows for whites, with the rest of the seats being filled on a first come, first served basis. Many Blacks were upset that the leadership of the movement accepted the city's offer, with many of them favoring a prolonged boycott until there was full capitulation with Black demands to end segregation unequivocally and without reservations. Nevertheless, the abbreviated struggle served as a template for the boycotts in Montgomery and Tallahassee that soon followed. The students' efforts to create a foothold for the NAACP (both on campus and throughout the city), increase voter registration and political literacy, and enter the local workforce as conscientious citizens played a critical role in making Baton Rouge what sociologist Aldon Morris refers to as a "movement center." Geographically, Southern was not well suited to serve as a host for boycott-related events. The boycott was centered downtown and utilized venues closer to the target area, such as Mount Zion First Baptist Church and McKinley High School, as central meeting places. It is likewise unlikely that Felton Clark would have embraced a boycott against the white establishment—a high-stakes game of overt protest that Clark was clearly not prepared to play.[48]

Southern did, however, make contributions in other ways. One of the unsung heroes of the boycott was Horatio Thompson, a 1937 graduate of Southern. A self-made man who owned numerous gas stations in Baton Rouge, Thompson was the founder of the Negro Chamber of Commerce and supported the growth of Black businesses throughout the city. One of the jobs he had held down while he was matriculating at school was chauffeuring for President Joseph Samuel Clark, who likely gave him an earful on the topic of Black economic solidarity as Thompson whisked him around town and throughout the state. Feeling an obligation to the movement and his people, when the boycott commenced, he provided gas at cost for the fleet of cars that were volunteered to transport the protesters, becoming a financer of the boycott. Nor was he the only one. Southern alumni were unquestionably among the thousands of Blacks in the city who supported the boycott. Moreover, the highly politicized students and alumni were certainly among the multitude of people who contributed their meager earnings to a cause drawing the attention of the entire South.[49] Yet for all the impact the boycott had on the national stage, the *Digest* ran no stories or columns reporting on the incident.

Southern was an institution whose communitas remained among the most vibrant throughout the world of historically Black colleges and universities (HBCUs). Steeped in the teachings of cultural nationalism, its students served as couriers of militancy, traveling and participating in student conferences, serving the NAACP, and entering the professional ranks as racially and politically informed teachers, ministers, and soldiers. That they were now either asked or ordered to keep silent about the tumultuous social events capturing the nation's attention marked a betrayal of the second curriculum that had served them well in years past. Not until the beginning of 1954 did any radical utterings appear in the *Digest*, when a student reporter remarked, as if in code, "We pay tribute to leaders who are only interested in conserving their own golden calves. They give lip service to liberty; lip homage to peace and harmony and kick at the true spirit of winning equality and equal justice and rights for all people of the world." Whether the message was targeted at Clark, Jemison, or someone else completely, it bespoke how Black folks in Baton Rouge felt about a movement that fizzled out far too quickly in their minds.[50]

The sea change that people were expecting was still years away, and negotiating minute victories while bartering away the demands of the masses did nothing to accelerate the freedom dreams of African Americans. The monumental decision in *Brown v. Board of Education* was mitigated by a subsequent and infamous ruling, *Brown II*, which allowed segregationists to move at "all deliberate speed." The decision did not make a major splash until three years later in Little Rock, Arkansas. The NAACP's hand-picked group of nine kids endured physical, verbal, and mental abuse on a daily basis, and even after the intense and historic developments in Little Rock, the local school system shut down for the academic year, providing enough time and space for the rise of a white, independent school movement that ducked the issues of justice and morality and barred Black youths from the best educational opportunities available. All of these events, including the Baton Rouge boycott, shared one common characteristic. They were dependent on and trusted in the systemic removal of historic inequities.

All of their lives, numerous Blacks maintained faith in the idea that the system would eventually bend toward the arc of justice, and so they decided to work within that framework. However, postwar anxieties firmly convinced African Americans that they were entitled to a level of democracy, opportunity, and justice that should not be measured out in small doses but rather should be justly and immediately granted to them as American citizens and as children of God. The fact that the establishment, undergirded by white supremacy, chose to ration out justice step by fragile step did not mesh with the lessons in American civics in which Black youths were consistently drilled.

Southern's student enrollment was just under three thousand by the middle of the decade, making it unquestionably the largest HBCU in the country. In the fall semester of 1955, the critical mass of Black youths matriculating at the institution witnessed an increase in the second curriculum that further stimulated militant views of Jim Crow. The Law School welcomed to the faculty attorney Vanue Lacour, who believed that one of his greatest achievements was his "success in fighting for Negroes to vote in the St. Landry Parish." In the English Department, Blyden Jackson introduced a course in Negro literature, and Earl Thorpe, a member of the radical Social Science Department, developed a Negro History course to be offered in the spring of 1956. In addition to the course on Black history, the Social Science Department held yet another popular dress rehearsal for voting rights. No longer were students running for governor, as they had in 1938; this time the top prize was the office of president of the United States. Felton Clark himself presided over a convention that got so testy and realistic, the "delegation" from Georgia and Mississippi walked off the floor in a dispute over the adopted platform. Across Southern's communitas there was talk about initiating a voter registration drive in the neighboring community of Scotlandville, and the campus NAACP chapter rebooted itself after falling dormant for a few years—but yet again, there were no reports in the *Digest* covering the launch of the Montgomery bus boycott in December 1955, a trend that followed the curious omission of the Baton Rouge struggle that inspired it.[51]

While the rhetoric for radicalism was thick at Southern, the institution's leaders appeared to shrink in the face of challenges to the very culture of intolerance that students, staff, and faculty critiqued on a daily basis. With the country entangled in McCarthyism, it is not altogether impossible that the staff of the *Digest*, along with the administration, sought to keep headlines capturing current controversial events out of the paper. While the paper did not alert students to the Montgomery movement in real time, it did announce Rev. Martin Luther King Jr.'s arrival in Baton Rouge to speak at Jemison's Mount Zion First Baptist Church—almost a year after the boycott in Montgomery was initiated.[52]

The sudden silence of the *Digest* may have been linked to Clark's emerging autocratic tendencies. In a September 1955 *Digest* entry written by Clark, he hinted that the staff should avoid making the *Digest* "a 'type' paper." The issue that followed a month later carried a news story from the Baton Rouge *News Leader* that praised Clark as the type of administrator who "will get rid of any faculty member in a minute if such person does not 'fit' in to the Southern way of doing things." When the American Friends Service Committee, a Quaker-affiliated civil rights organization, set up shop in Baton Rouge in 1955, they sought Clark's blessing in recruiting top Southern students who could test the limits of racial discrimination in the Baton Rouge workforce. Clark recoiled from the idea, fearing that if word got out detailing his involvement, "segregationists in the state legislature would destroy the university." Clark's defensiveness and aggression emerged more frequently in the coming years as students and faculty raised a pertinent question framed by the explosive events unfolding around them: What exactly was the "Southern way," and what did it mean for the social, political, and economic strivings of a people who increasingly demanded freedom now?[53]

While Clark may have evaded public confrontation with white supremacy, his students were still taking it on within the pages of the *Digest*. In 1957 an English major at Southern by the name of Alvin Aubert reached his breaking point. As a veteran of the Korean War, Aubert recalled an incident in South Korea in which he observed insurgent students of that country bravely confronting the government and risking their lives in the process. Aubert described them as a "great human mass moving in one direction—toward one goal: Freedom." He then juxtaposed the youths of Korea with students at Southern and challenged his peers to make a bold stand against Jim Crow. "Students, you are the leaders of the world!—not tomorrow, or the day after, but now!" declared Aubert. "You are not the 'future' leaders, as you are so often typed, but leaders of today. What are you waiting for?" Aubert did not have to tarry long for an answer.[54]

The *Digest* reported that Hampton University students were boycotting local movie theaters in Virginia during the fall semester of 1956. That same year witnessed Alabama State University students playing a distinct role in the escalating Montgomery movement. Down in Tallahassee, students at Florida A&M played a critical role in launching a boycott of local buses there. And in Greensboro, North Carolina, the students at North Carolina A&T publicly booed Governor Luther Hodges when he spoke at their Founders' Day ceremony in 1955. The poor governor for some reason just could not pronounce the word *Negro* correctly, opting instead for the highly offensive "Nigra." The militant reaction from A&T's students startled and befuddled school president Ferdinand Bluford so badly that he had a heart attack two days later, dying within a month. By the mid-1950s, Black college students across the South were stirring, with many of them looking to pick a public fight with Jim Crow. Alongside the social and political transformations of the mid-twentieth century, students were fed a steady diet of the second curriculum and experienced a rising confidence that was developed within the HBCU communitas. The early movement witnessed an increase in students who were itching to jump-start a revolution that had been considerably delayed by the slow methods and soft pressure applied by an older generation.[55]

Things were no different in Louisiana. Jemison later recalled a relatively clandestine operation emerging in Baton Rouge in the late 1950s. According to Jemison, students at Southern began to meet at Mount Zion to draw up a plan of attack. The proposal was to initiate sit-ins at the local Kress and Piccadilly Cafeteria. However, the strategy was flawed from the start. It involved tipping off the police ahead of time and negotiating with the white waitress on duty so that she would duck out before the students arrived, leaving only a Black staff member who refused to break the Jim Crow policy of not serving African Americans at the counter. Lacking the dramatic punch of unannounced civil disobedience, these efforts failed. The project was shelved—but not for long.[56]

• • • • • •

Interest in the liberation movement in Africa spiked on Southern's campus in 1959. With the continent embroiled in decolonization efforts in several countries, the *Digest* ran three separate news stories in the spring semester that highlighted the numerical advantage Africans had over their colonizers. In a story covering the brewing turmoil in Nyasaland (later renamed Malawi), a headline read, "Spark Struck May Soon Set African Continent Ablaze." Stateside events ran parallel, as Black students with their eyes trained on freedom struggles throughout the world were about to bypass the fear that had paralyzed them for so long. Previous movement activity had largely been defined by individual, localized efforts. Black youths were about to coalesce into a massive bloc of united insurgency emanating from the country's Black colleges.

When the sit-ins of 1960 arrived in Baton Rouge, they had the potential to serve as one of the most dramatic and effective mass movements for freedom that the country had ever seen. As in the liberation struggle in Africa, Southern's critical mass of Black students was unmatched by the population of any other HBCU in 1960, presenting a powerful strategic tool to be used in an assault against Jim Crow. Beyond the mere numbers, the communitas at Southern had primed students for this event—for decades. It was foolhardy for administrators or faculty to think that the constant rhetoric of militancy and radicalism and the dress rehearsals to exercise their access to democracy would not eventually influence students to take action. Felton Clark turned out to be one of the fools.[57]

Former Southern student Mack Jones was one of the thousands of students at Southern who took Clark at his word. Jones recalled the tough talk against segregation that characterized Clark's speeches to students and faculty during campus events. "Felton Clark used to give these speeches indicating that Black people had to stand up and fight and do all these good things," remembered Jones. "And we thought when Felton Clark came back to town that we would have somebody to really defend and support us. That turned out not to have been the case."[58]

It began when the Southern University student body received what was essentially a dare to follow in the footsteps of other Black college activists. The all-white state board of education warned the Black youths of Louisiana that any students attempting to bring the sit-ins to the state would face "stern disciplinary action." As one student declared, "When the Board spoke, it became a challenge to us and we could not ignore it."[59] The die was cast on March 28 when seven students from Southern entered the Kress (this time unannounced) and were promptly arrested. The bond that students had with the Black community was put to the test and the community responded, raising $10,500 to bail all seven students out. The very next day, nine other students staged sit-ins, two at the Greyhound bus station and seven at the appropriately named Sitman's drugstore. They too were arrested and were released on bond after spending six days in jail.

The second arrest unleashed the pent-up energy of the student body. A total of 3,500 Southernites clogged the streets of Baton Rouge and made their way to the state capitol. The massive show of force must have been unnerving for local citizens, and not just whites. Clark was apoplectic. He gathered a core group of faculty he knew would back him, and after initially suspending seventeen students, he finally settled on expelling them. Campus life ground to a halt as thousands of students were left in limbo over the fate of their friends and the direction of the school.[60]

The arrival of the sit-ins demonstrated the power of the Southern University communitas. A few hundred demonstrating students would have been powerful enough in displaying the spirit of dissidence on campus. But when over three thousand students collectively threw the gauntlet down and called into question the legitimacy of white supremacy in Baton Rouge, the sit-in movement received a crucial boost during its nascent stage.

It is unclear why all of the students participated in the protest. Each one surely had individual and varied reasons. But what is certain is that Southern's culture of idealism, which challenged them to think critically about the validity of Jim Crow, bolstered their sense of righteousness and aided in uniting them under one common goal that day. Over the years, their Social Sciences Department contributed to planting seeds of insurgency by sponsoring a range of programs that stoked their militancy. Students spent both their classroom and leisure time discussing and debating the Black liberation movement as it unfolded across the world. Indeed, the space provided at Southern had been dedicated in part to cultivating a powerful culture of radical thought. Without it, it seems almost impossible that over three thousand students would suddenly strike in unison to upend the social order. The movement on Southern's campus could not be characterized as the fringe faction of a radical few, either. It was a product of the core of student life, which was demonstrated when Marvin Robinson, the Student Government Association president in 1960, made the call to initiate the sit-in and was one of the first to be arrested and subsequently expelled.[61]

In their account of the Baton Rouge movement, expelled student leaders Major Johns and Ronnie Moore write that Clark "received several hundred letters and wires from all over the world—not one of them complimentary." While it is certain that Clark had numerous detractors, he did receive at least one interesting piece of correspondence from a supporter attempting to steer him in a different direction. Warmouth T. Gibbs was serving as president of North Carolina A&T when the sit-ins exploded on the scene in Greensboro. Gibbs was among the handful of Black college presidents who refused to reprimand or punish their students for engaging in overt protests. Gibbs, who was eleven years older than Clark, a friend of the family, and also a native Louisianan, reached out to the embattled but hardened administrator. Endeavoring to influence Clark to adopt the model of engagement that he employed at A&T, Gibbs recalled, "I wrote Felton and told him, but somehow he didn't feel as though he could do anything. . . . That's the way it happened. This young man lost favor with the students, the teachers, and the community . . . he caused all of that." Clark was unmoved by Gibbs's appeal. Gibbs was no "outside agitator" seeking to destroy Southern, as Clark believed so many naysayers were. He was Clark's peer, and unlike him, Gibbs had the foresight and conviction to stand with the students in their historic assault on Jim Crow.[62]

In the days that immediately followed the sit-ins, Clark completely unraveled any trust he had built up with the students over the years. White lawmakers demanded that Clark align his campus and his students with the expectations of the white establishment, and in the name of preserving Southern, Clark obliged. Stealing a page out of the segregationists' playbook, he even labeled the student protesters as Communists.

Clark may have hoped to preserve the system and the conservative method of tactfully reshaping it through litigation and moral suasion, but what the sit-ins of 1960 illustrated was that Black college students were concluding that the social and political structure needed a jumpstart of epic proportions. In the frustrated years that followed the sit-ins, many Black students concluded that the system itself was due for a complete overhaul, if not a complete replacement. One of Southern's more famous student protesters of the 1960s, H. Rap Brown, frames it this way: "When the people cannot find a redress of their grievances within a system, they have no choice but to destroy the system which is responsible in the first place for their grievances." This placed students directly at odds with school leaders like Clark who had played a significant role in heightening their levels of race consciousness and idealism in the first place. While the older generation maintained strong desires for a radical shift in American race relations, many were still unable to free themselves of the mental conditioning they received growing up in the shadow of white supremacy. Push too hard, push too fast, step out of line once, and fierce reprisal was sure to follow. Clark's response to the sit-ins was a demonstration of that age-old ritual in motion.[63]

When students finally returned to campus in the fall of 1960, the climate was noticeably different. The sit-ins elevated a critical question surrounding the movement: What exactly was the function of the Black college, and how did its mission align with the advancement of the movement? Administrators and scholars of HBCUs, frozen in the fear of the moment, appeared blind to the linear progression of the communitas, which traced a path from enlightenment to critical thought, assessment, and finally action. In suddenly and anxiously reversing their positions, Black college administrators abdicated the roles they had played in producing the massive insurgency.

The fluidity of radicalism that defined Southern's campus diminished under pressures from the state. In the name of preserving Southern and protecting careers, administrators and teachers alike collapsed the spaces previously reserved for drilling youths in militant rhetoric. In the years following the *Southern University Digest*'s temporary suspension between March 9 and October 15, 1960, its editorials, once laced with sharp condemnations of the South's closed society, dropped off significantly. The *Digest* staff managed to maintain some of its old luster by opting to pick up news feeds from the ANP, as well as carrying articles that were contributed by students at other universities. However, an outside evaluation of the *Digest* conducted by the National Scholastic Press Association revealed that the paper was indeed under censorship and had "an editorial policy that tended to present only one side of the University image." Some criticism of the eroding political culture on campus made its way into print. In October 1961 the *Digest* carried an editorial written by a student from Oklahoma State University that denounced press censorship on college campuses across the country. D'Army Bailey, a junior on campus, was bold enough to produce a critique of Southern's own in loco parentis culture in an article he submitted to the *Digest*. In another article the following month, he criticized the administration of Jackson State College for dissolving the student government in the wake of campus protests. Lacking internal support for the new protest maneuvers, students sought direction from outside the communitas. This stark reality dovetailed with the arrival of the Congress of Racial Equality (CORE) in Baton Rouge.[64]

The north-based organization arrived in Baton Rouge with a long track record of supporting, organizing, and leading direct-action protests. Championing civil disobedience and nonviolent resistance, CORE's members saw the developments in Baton Rouge as a perfect setting to implement their strategies. Assisting CORE's programmatic launch in Baton Rouge was twenty-year-old David Dennis, who was no stranger to the city or to Southern. Dennis attended Southern's laboratory school, graduating there in the same class with H. Rap Brown in 1960. In fact, it was Southern's massive demonstrations during the first round of sit-ins that ultimately politicized Dennis and swept him up into the leadership ranks of CORE. "My greatest influence is when I came to high school in Baton Rouge," recalled Dennis. "That had a lot of impact on me because it was the beginning of the real efforts . . . in the country among college students. And so that was my senior year there at the high school, that was the year that Southern University had its first big demonstration . . . and so we at the high school did the same thing."[65]

CORE saw serious potential at Southern University. After sending James McCain, one of the architects of the organization's southern campaign, to the first round of protests in 1960, the following year CORE attempted to tap into activist energies still lingering on campus. Felton Clark deployed a range of efforts to nip the protest in the bud. Among them was enlisting the campus registrar to issue a warning through the *Digest* to out-of-state students, further evidence that points to Clark's paranoia over possible external influences in the local movement. According to registrar J. J. Hedgemon, not only were students' academic records up for review, but so too were their citizenship records. According to Hedgemon, the onus was on out-of-state students to "make a good name for the University on and off campus." The news story's final paragraph revealed the real interest of Hedgemon and Clark. There was deep concern that tarnished citizenship records would deprive Southern of "praise from the Board and the State Department of Education where they must be based upon new regulations of the Board of Education." In short, students engaged in activism were giving Southern a bad name among legislators who held the purse strings in the state capital.[66]

Nevertheless, students linked up with CORE ambassadors to launch one more strike against Jim Crow in 1961. Student leaders solicited support from adults and leaders in the local community in advance of the protest, a benefit they lacked the first time around. Yet the ally they needed most desperately remained implacably opposed to them, as Clark once again positioned himself to carry out the bidding of the Louisiana legislature.

Twenty-three students, including Dennis, were arrested on December 14 for picketing downtown stores. Once again students employed themes of cultural nationalism that had long been promoted in the communitas of Southern University. Pickett signs read, "Have money, will buy elsewhere," and, "Don't buy here, this store discriminates." Following the arrest of the protesters, former Southern student Ronnie Moore, who was a leader during the 1960 sit-ins, addressed a crowd of three thousand students on campus, and the next day, four thousand students marched to the prison in downtown Baton Rouge in support of their arrested comrades. The swarm of determined and defiant students invoking both God and the Constitution was the last straw for the white establishment. Local law enforcement rained tear gas canisters into the crowd, unleashed police dogs, and bullied and bruised numerous students before rounding up forty-nine of them to arrest. Clark once again became the fulcrum on which the movement turned.[67]

The State of Louisiana was unmistakably clear about its expectations for both students and administrators. Defying the United States Constitution, the state board of education and a U.S. district judge banned student demonstrations, and the state board gave Clark marching orders to expel any student who failed to comply. The primary question confronting Clark was whether he would go so far as to block the protest efforts of his students. A small portion of other Black college presidents either stepped down from their positions or silently endorsed their students' actions by refusing to rule against them—defying the white establishment in such a way would not have isolated Clark as some lone rebel. Yet after originally informing students that he would "submit his resignation before he would suspend any of the student demonstrators," he made a reversal that stunned and saddened the thousands of Southernites who expected him to hold to his promise. Southern student Frank White attempted to rally the troops one last time in a letter to the *Digest*. "Broadly speaking, we have endorsed the doctrine that we will be given freedom, justice, and equality in due time," wrote White. "I firmly believe that such a proposal is null and void. No human being will give us these things. Unless we are prepared to fight. . . . This is the 'proposed' reason for our being here—to prepare to meet more efficiently the challenges that arise in our future lives." White's words failed to reverberate through the administration. On January 17, Clark expelled seven student protesters, and when a group of one thousand students showed up on Clark's doorstep, he left them in the cold for twelve hours, refusing to even acknowledge their presence.[68]

Student leaders tried to muster support for a boycott of classes. However, by this point, Southern's campus was swarming with local law enforcement, campus security, and informers, who effectively weakened the morale of would-be protesters. In addition to the seven who were initially expelled, Clark froze the registration of an additional forty students from the university. Clark then moved to placate the faculty during a convocation held on January 18. He viciously berated the students who committed themselves to civil disobedience, which was more than many faculty members could stand. Almost half of Southern's three-hundred-member faculty signed a petition that declared, "We regret the action which has been taken against Southern University students for their demonstrations. We feel there is a need for constructive reappraisal of the present policy regarding student participation in such protest." Political science professor Adolph Reed took it a step further by sending Clark a ten-page letter that likened him to a war criminal. Reed then resigned from his post, along with several other faculty members. In the wake of the 1961–62 movement, the deeply wounded and fractured Southern communitas was left to pick up the pieces.[69]

With the recent insurgency still fresh in their minds, students and faculty came together to push for healing and reconciliation. A group of student senators drafted eight proposals for the improvement of campus life. Among them were attempts to reinstate their dismissed peers, a meeting with Clark to address the recent events, several measures that pushed for greater student autonomy and voice, and a request for the university to drop charges against "persons defined as 'trespassers on private property.'"[70] An editorial was submitted to the *Digest* that cleverly juxtaposed the explosion of student protest to the mission found in the *Southern University Catalog Bulletin*. Framing it as a "misinterpretation," the writer claimed that Southern was misleading its students by declaring one of its missions as "making students individually sensitive to community problems" and promising to equip students with "fundamental facts which must be used in carrying out worthwhile human relationships, while attempting at all times, to improve the immediate society."[71] Armed with their school's own bylaws, thousands of students could argue that the direct-action protests initiated by Southernites achieved exactly what the university had trained them to do. Nevertheless, Clark's willingness to carry out the bidding of the state legislature left students bitterly frustrated and pondering the future of the campus movement.

Students had much to be proud of. They had pioneered direct-action protests in Louisiana. Numerous Southern University activists, like Major Johns and Ronnie Moore, continued to serve in CORE and advance the freedom struggle throughout the South. As one Southernite framed it, "As long as this world of ours is not a Utopia, there will be unrest and it will, for the most part, stem from the activities of young people."[72] Yet, for all their achievements, white supremacy in Louisiana seemed intractable.

The nation's top power brokers remained complacent, and the patience of activists wore thin—particularly among the students who fought in the trenches. In early 1962, even Dr. King became frustrated with the deferment of Black folks freedom dreams. The *Digest* informed its readers that King "criticized" the Kennedy administration for "'piecemeal' attacks on a problem which [King] said 'requires massive social mobilization, uniting the strength of individuals, organizations, government, press and schools.'" Such fumbling and apathy over the nation's most pressing domestic issue wore a hole into the patience of activists. Dennis was among the Black youths of Louisiana who were firmly entrenched in movement activity. After his stint in Baton Rouge, he became embroiled in the struggle in Mississippi and later grappled with America's failures to institute meaningful change. Dennis later recalled, "I think that the problem was that most of the people who were involved at that time . . . really believed that this country was going to do this stuff you know. . . . And so there was a lot of dissolution when that happened." Baton Rouge was not Student Nonviolent Coordinating Committee territory; however, the student activists at Southern experienced identical barriers and stall tactics that caused the nation's premier student organization to make a dramatic shift in its protest objectives. As Black colleges served as an epicenter for the early stages of the movement, so too would HBCU campuses become the sites on which new phases and transitions in the freedom struggle played out.[73]

As Southernites were beckoned to the forefront of the movement, they desperately desired that their beloved institution would become aligned with the urgency of the times. For many students, it seemed unthinkable that Black colleges could betray the mission and the message that resonated within the communitas. The *Digest* reminded its readers that not every HBCU buckled under the threats of segregationists, running an ANP story that highlighted the determination of Alfonso Elder, president of North Carolina College (later renamed North Carolina Central University). Speaking at the National Student Association conference, Elder reminded youths that it was the constitutional right of both students and teachers to engage in protests. Elder declared, "When such actions are taken by students, the school can 'only hope that a good job of teaching has been done.'"[74]

Yet for all of the setbacks and resistance, change was unquestionably in the air. In late November 1962 students from Southern who returned from a football game against Tennessee State University noted the joy of triumph over Jim Crow laws in the bus terminal. Fresh on the heels of a victory against a college rival, *Digest* contributor Arthur Thompson declared that the small victory over white supremacy was much greater than the outcome of the game because of the elation and dignity it brought to all African Americans. Thompson's clear metaphor was not intended to cheapen the freedom struggle by comparing it to a football game. Instead, what he conveyed were the emotions that countless Black southerners felt as the signs that mocked their humanity and degraded them all of their lives slowly came tumbling down. It was indeed a rare victory that was long in the making and one that was greatly aided by the massive protests generated by students at Southern. In Louisiana, it was the insurgency of youths that served as the fundamental catalyst for generating the grit and resolve that Blacks desperately needed to pursue their freedom rights in the face of constant threats. In spite of the recent repression on campus, the spirit of idealism and race consciousness that created the social revolt in the early 1960s was far from being depleted. With the freedom struggle now venturing into new territories, the Southern University communitas resumed its routine of priming Black youths in idealism and race consciousness. During the spring semester of 1963, the Political Science Department sponsored bimonthly seminars with titles such as "Twentieth Century Political Theory," "Commentary on Contemporary American Society," and "Problems in Race Relations." The *Digest* reported that the seminars prompted "spirited discussions." Among the notable faculty of the department was Jewell Prestage, the Southern University alumna who, in 1951, helped to lead her own direct-action protests in Alexandria that reopened schools for Black youths.[75]

Southern's mission of cultivating race consciousness remained strong. Students were kept abreast of the decolonization efforts in Africa through the library's subscription to *Africa Today*; the student senate sponsored a delegation to a human rights conference in Washington, D.C., and the Deep South Human Relationships Conference; and there were a number of stories that ran on the 1964 Civil Rights Act, including an editorial urging Southern students to "write their congressmen" in support of the groundbreaking legislation. And when two churches in the paper mill town of Jonesboro, Louisiana, were set ablaze and destroyed by arsonists in the early part of 1965, Southern students were among the volunteers who bravely traveled to the northern Louisiana town to clean up and rebuild. Nevertheless, in the years that led up to the Black Power movement, the overt radicalism that characterized student life at the outset of the decade tapered off considerably. The movement outside Southern's racialized space barely registered a pulse in the greater Baton Rouge community, with the NAACP proclaiming that its Baton Rouge chapter was virtually defunct by 1966.[76]

As the summer of 1965 approached, all signs pointed to a major shift on Southern's campus. Following the end of the Student Nonviolent Coordinating Committee (SNCC) campaign known as Freedom Summer in 1964, young Black activists throughout the country were ready for a change. Tension grew with every movement setback, and students were primed and ready to feed their frustrations into something new. In April, the *Digest* ran its first story on Malcolm X who had been assassinated two months earlier. Malcolm's fiery rhetoric of resistance had captured the attention and imagination of youth across the country and helped to fuel a growing generational divide. The campus speaker for the university's convocation that year, Howard University president James Nabrit, symbolized the complexities surrounding the growing chasm between the old and the young perhaps better than anyone. Nabrit had dedicated a lifetime of work to taking on Jim Crow policies and trained an army of lawyers to follow in his footsteps as a former professor and dean of the Howard Law School. The comments he offered at the convocation were relatively bold. "When Negroes are blocked from their voting rights and beaten back when they demonstrate, it weakens the leadership of democracy in this country," he declared.[77] However, in just two years, Nabrit found himself ensnarled in controversy as he expelled several students and faculty members in the midst of campus protests—a move that suggested he was cut from the same autocratic cloth as Clark. Students grew increasingly weary of an older generation that failed to embrace the sense of urgency that defined the actions and new direction of the movement. One month later, Southern's Alpha Tau chapter of Delta Sigma Theta hosted an all-day civil rights workshop on campus that discussed a move-ment that was in flux while also deliberating the development of anti-poverty programs throughout the country.[78]

Although Clark did the bidding of the state legislators by aggressively snuffing out overt direct-action protests in the early part of the decade, the student body of Southern University once again stood at the beginning of a watershed moment in the struggle for Black liberation. Once again the com-munitas was surging with race consciousness and cultural nationalism. New campus organizations emerged, such as the Democratic Youth Movement, the Negro Liberation Coordinating Committee, and the W. E. B. DuBois Club. And in the August 1965 edition of the *Digest*, the first critiques of the Vietnam War appeared that outlined the troubling paradox of fighting against communism abroad but not dealing with racial injustice at home.

But for all of the militant posturing that occurred during the nascent stages of the Black Power movement, Southern also illustrated some of the inherent weaknesses that made HBCUs susceptible to critiques. One of the emerging voices within the campus press was Jacob Bouie Jr., who first enrolled at Southern in 1958. Bouie was drafted to fight in Vietnam in 1961 and served for three years before returning to campus in 1964. He became a political columnist for the *Digest*, and his thoughts reflected the counter-view held by conservatives on campus. Bouie attempted to persuade stu-dents to be wary of radicalism and the outgrowth of militant groups at Southern. As the United States attempted to close ranks around Vietnam at the onset of the conflict, Cold War inclinations kicked in and students like Bouie hedged their bets against rhetoric that espoused anticolonialism, com-munism, or other left-wing brands of politics. Labeling such organizations as nefarious fit right in line with the broader policies of the American mili-tary and certainly gained the approval of conservative campus leaders like Clark. Nevertheless, Bouie's opinions took a back seat to the surge of mili-tancy that prepared to take Southern into a new chapter of activism that would have a long-ranging impact on the culture of campus in the years to come.[79]

When the Political Science Department held a "Black Power" seminar in October 1966, a standing-room-only crowd of three hundred students in the auditorium listened to Southern faculty member Alex Willingham outline and address the latest phase of the liberation struggle. But the concepts of Black Power had never been far from the rhetoric that flourished within Southern's communitas—a point that several students actually brought up at the event. The ideals that made Joseph Samuel Clark a follower of Booker T. Washington included self-sufficiency, economic empowerment, and cultural nationalism. Black students for generations had been taught to embrace and celebrate their history and had been deliberately exposed to racialized spaces that uplifted their heritage. This curriculum was not hidden but rather thrived as a core initiative of the educative process at Southern. And while elitism certainly played a critical role in developing sharp class divisions within the Black community, those divisions were never so impermeable that Black youths forgot the humble beginnings from which the vast majority of them directly came or had roots in.[80]

Southern was a hub of activity for *all* of Black Baton Rouge. Homecomings, social and sporting events, and adult education and training sessions for local farmers all illustrated the vital role that the state's flagship Black college played in enhancing and enriching the lives of Black folks across the state, regardless of their class status. And while the Black Power movement certainly raised powerful and valid critiques concerning the effectiveness of institutions that ultimately existed at the pleasure and whim of the white power structure, generations of Blacks, young and old, continued to fight to change but save Southern University as the institution's fiscal lifeblood was consistently choked off by state legislators who saw Southern as both inferior to neighboring Louisiana State University and a threat to the perseverance of Jim Crow and white supremacy.

The Black Power movement at Southern created new community-based initiatives that targeted issues such as systemic poverty and built new bridges and inroads into the surrounding neighborhood of Scotlandville. Furthermore, the new phase of the movement tapped into the sense of cultural nationalism that had undergirded the institution for years. Students in afros and dashikis, proudly flying the Black Nationalist flag, felt perfectly at home at an institution that strongly encouraged its students to be proud and unapologetic about their Blackness. With the most explosive and violent chapter of student activism at Southern yet to come, the historical evidence points toward a generation of insurgency that ebbed and flowed throughout the turbulent decade of the 1960s. Before that decade, which witnessed an intense crackdown from the state legislature, students, faculty, and even controversial administrators such as Felton Clark contributed to crafting a space that challenged the tenets of white supremacy and ultimately aided in reshaping American democracy. Without those developments, it would have been impossible for thousands of students to respond instantaneously to the calls for direct action that emerged at the beginning of the student movement. That clarion call for overt resistance to Jim Crow resonated with the student body because they were already immersed in a culture that encouraged principles of defiance and dissent.[81]

The scrutiny that fell on the campus administration from Jim Crow legislators, coupled with the hard-line demands to cease and desist with overt direct-action protests, transformed what was once an oasis of Black radical thought in the early to mid-twentieth century into an institution that embodied the classic conservative image of universities that stymied the militancy of Black youths. Southern's legacy as a seedbed for activism reveals the complexities and paradoxes of institutions that were central to the struggle for Black freedom.

7 Their Rhetoric Is That of Revolution

North Carolina A&T and the Rise and Fall of the Student Organization for Black Unity, 1966–1974

· ·

We do not say that Black institutions should be preserved merely to be preserved. But they represent the most logical potential at this point in our history to provide the educational process that is most relevant to the masses of Black people.

—Nelson Johnson, 1971

During the fall of 1969, students at North Carolina A&T State University crowded into a gymnasium to hear Howard Fuller, a nationally known community activist, speak on the shortcomings of a movement that appeared to be splintering. "We . . . should get the feeling that seemingly exists at A&T," Fuller exclaimed. "Students here not only talk, but act. Their rhetoric is that of revolution . . . a rhetoric of action."[1]

Historically Black colleges and universities (HBCUs), the epicenters of the insurgency that had defined the decade, continued to serve as flashpoints for confrontations with the white power structure as the 1960s drew to a close. Colleges across the country experienced a surge in mobilization, violent exchanges with local and federal authorities, and a robust ideological debate that probed the varying and often conflicting theories regarding the liberation of Black people. Greensboro, North Carolina, was like many other American cities in the throes of the civil rights movement. While visible barriers to equality were slowly receding, institutionalized white supremacy was becoming more deeply entrenched, a fact that did not go unrecognized by a growing number of student activists. Issues such as systemic poverty, America's foreign policy in Vietnam, and the failure to deliver basic resources to historically marginalized communities became frontline problems as the decade drew to a close.

As the Black Power movement unfolded in Greensboro, it was clear that A&T was the engine that churned local activist energies. The institution produced most of the local leadership, served as a rallying point for insurgents, frequently hosted nationally known dissidents, and served as a beacon of pride for the local Black community. A&T's history as a source of activism in fact reached back into the beginning of the twentieth century.[2] By the time February 1, 1960, arrived, the student body of North Carolina A&T was primed by a tradition of resistance that the sit-in movement took to unprecedented levels. Generations of students at A&T had successfully transmitted a message and mission of service underpinned by race consciousness. One of the pioneers of the sit-in movement, Jibrell Khazan (Ezell Blair), described that message and that linked sense of fate as having been "taught to us by the time we were in grade school. . . . Our teachers in the segregated school system told us they were preparing us for the day that we would be free and that we were going to be the leaders of that freedom. This is before Martin Luther King and Rosa Parks came along. This is what I was taught in my school system in Greensboro."[3]

By 1960 many of the students who engaged in the crusade to dismantle Jim Crow had been empowered by their interactions with teachers, mentors, and community leaders, many of whom were trained at Black colleges. This relationship proved critical as the decade unfolded. Unlike in other settings of the civil rights movement, the struggle for liberation in Greensboro received support from a diverse cross section of the Black community.[4] This broad coalition, inspired by new tactics from the Congress of Racial Equality, led to the mass jail-ins of 1962 and 1963.[5] Greensboro native Claude Barnes recalled that during this stage, "we had masses of people. Ordinary people. Maids like my mother. Store clerks like my aunt. Teachers, janitors, young people like myself. Across the gamut and across class lines. . . . They were attracted to the strength of this movement."[6] The town-gown relations between the Black denizens of Greensboro and the state's largest HBCU had never been stronger. Most A&T students had come from families employed in local mill and factory jobs or the numerous agrarian jobs worked by thousands of Blacks across the state. And while there were a decent number who arrived from middle-class homes, A&T students never had the elite or privileged reputation of Howard, Fisk, Hampton, Spelman, or Morehouse students. Class cleavages that could have created divisions in the midst of the movement were virtually nonexistent. The struggle for liberation that emerged from the campus of A&T was a movement by and for the people—a fact that would define the struggle in Greensboro and play out in the various campus protests to come.[7]

Despite the growing number of rank-and-file citizens enticed to join the struggle, it was the resolve of the local white power structure that set the tone for future protests.[8] While "white only" signs had been mostly removed

Jackie Robinson arrives on campus in 1966 to recognize A&T for its role in launching the sit-ins six years earlier (*from left to right*: Jackie Robinson, President Lewis Dowdy, and two A&T students). By the end of that year, the Black Power movement would be in full swing, bringing tension between many activists of the old guard and a new generation of Black radicals. Courtesy of Ayantee '66 Collection, Ferdinand Bluford Library Archives, North Carolina Agricultural and Technical State University.

throughout Gate City by 1965, the policies that defined the day-to-day struggles of common Black folks were largely unaffected. Poor and inadequate housing, indecent health care, wealth disparities, and police brutality were issues that universally affected impoverished communities from the rural shanties to the urban slums. Across the country, local and federal officials fortified their positions under the banner of "all deliberate speed" while remaining ambivalent regarding the needs of people marginalized by the color line. Greensboro was no different. In the words of historian William Chafe, "The failure of white leaders to initiate more substantive programs toward racial equality carried a dual message: not only would renewed direct-action protest be necessary for further change; the next time such protests would be fueled by the anger that came from knowing how little past rhetoric had accomplished."[9]

The definitive conditions that led to the creation of the Student Organization for Black Unity (SOBU) at A&T were thus well in place by 1968.

The most prominent factor that led to the creation of this organization was the desire to recapture the potential of militant youths as instruments for substantive change. The Student Nonviolent Coordinating Committee (SNCC) was crumbling. Despite attempts to continue what sociologist Charles Payne refers to as the "organizing tradition," the majority of field projects sponsored by the organization had all but ceased by 1968. As the various projects of SNCC were coming to a close, the activist energies of Greensboro were still simmering, as they had been since the launch of the sit-ins at the beginning of the decade. Greensboro was not SNCC territory, nor was it characterized by the rising class divisions that many SNCC organizers were finding in the field. These realities and the continued discriminatory practices of the Greensboro power structure provided the foundation for an organization that was directly connected to A&T and the early rise of SOBU: the Greensboro Association of Poor People (GAPP).

• • • • • •

In 1964 President Lyndon Baines Johnson officially declared a "War on Poverty." As LBJ set out to break the cycle of poverty with government programs, local Black neighborhoods still struggled against discriminatory housing, the denial of key resources, and the obstinacy of white community leaders insensitive to Black concerns. The united response to Jim Crow policies in Greensboro during the first half of the decade all but ensured that as the focus of the movement shifted to more institutionalized issues after 1965, a concerted effort from the Black community would follow. "We will no longer be intimidated by 'gun toting' landlords, and non-acting city officials," exclaimed Lula M. Pennix, a local community leader. "We are demanding immediate actions be taken."[10] With explosive days still ahead, many students at A&T remained conscious of its surrounding environment and the social and economic vices that concerned women like Pennix. The members of the Black community, and particularly of the community that surrounded A&T, were victims of long-standing and institutionalized policies that choked off the economic lifeblood in working-class and poor neighborhoods. East Market Street, the main corridor that fronted the campus, was full of meagerly supplied shops, substandard housing, and the sense of economic deprivation. In short, as in most cities across the country, one undoubtedly knew when you had entered into the Black part of town that enveloped A&T. For most Aggies and the residents who lived in the campus area, Jim Crow was still very much alive.

For all the Greensboro white power structure's failure to address racial inequality, it was an incident in Orangeburg, South Carolina, that regalvanized the spirit of dissent within the communitas of A&T. On February 8, 1968, after an attempt to desegregate a local bowling alley, three students from South Carolina State University were murdered and thirty-four were wounded by South Carolina highway patrolmen. South Carolina State University was one of A&T's closest rivals in football, and there were numerous students attending A&T who either were from South Carolina or had family ties to the state. When word of the Orangeburg Massacre reached A&T, students immediately reacted in anger and protest. A group of students obtained a casket from a local mortician to symbolize the death of their fallen comrades at South Carolina State University and hung the governor of South Carolina in effigy. Students then marched to downtown Greensboro. Whatever commitment students held to a nonviolent philosophy that had characterized earlier demonstrations at the start of the decade had clearly been exhausted.[11] Further exacerbating the racial tension, two months after the Orangeburg Massacre, Martin Luther King Jr. was assassinated in Memphis, Tennessee, while standing in solidarity with striking sanitation workers. Floyd McKissick, a prominent civil rights figure with the Congress of Racial Equality during the sit-in movement, voiced the feelings of many Black folks when he stated, "Nonviolence is a dead philosophy and it was not Black people that killed it."[12]

In the wake of the assassination, A&T students marched once again through the heart of downtown Greensboro. However, upon their return to campus, students unleashed a torrent of bricks and bottles on white drivers as they passed through the economically starved side of town. The National Guard was called in, marking the beginning of a yearlong struggle between the students of A&T and federal and local law enforcement. The shattered glass and broken bricks that lined the streets of campus were apt symbols for the fragile state of Black emotions across the country. Numerous Black communities were on edge, angry at the glacial pace of change, and ready to unleash their pent-up frustrations with the white power structure. And as had been the case for the entire decade, the events that enveloped A&T and the Black residents of Greensboro during the late 1960s exhibited both the power and limitations of Black colleges as nerve centers for the movement.

Following King's assassination, the spirit of self-determination that defined the rising Black Power objectives of city and student activists was embodied in the creation of GAPP. Building on the collective experiences of Greensboro's impoverished communities and the failure of local agencies to address their concerns, GAPP launched in the summer of 1968 with the merger of several interests and previously existing organizations. Residents of the city's public housing had formed the United Neighborhood Improvement Team to focus on inequities in housing and created an intern program by partnering with twelve professional Black men within the city and the Foundation for Community Development in Durham. The goal was to channel the energy of the earlier student movement directly into a new initiative by offering six community organizing internships to students.[13] By the end of the summer, all involved parties decided to continue their collective efforts, thus launching GAPP. However, GAPP quickly expanded its agenda beyond issues of fair housing and tenants' rights to include labor concerns, police brutality, public schools, and cooperative economics within the Black community. The GAPP paradigm was "designed to organize black people around their immediate problems and material concerns in such a way as to create a sense of power and determination sufficient to effect change on the policy level."[14] GAPP's presence within the Black community now set the stage for a vital support network ready to sustain the activism of militant youths as A&T continued to serve as a rallying point.

For many A&T students, Black Power was an idea whose time had come. Cutting against the slowness exhibited by the political landscape of Greensboro and the nation in embracing change, the ideologies that informed and directed the Black liberation struggle promised to move much more quickly—or at least activists hoped that they would. Black Power ideology flowed through the halls and dormitories of Black colleges. Capturing the growing social, political, and economic frustration of marginalized communities, Black Power was an alluring concept. For the young, it possessed a boldness and bravado that nonviolent rhetoric lacked. It offered the opportunity to "stick it to the man," something that many Black youths had secretly desired to do all their lives. Most importantly, it prescribed aggressive solutions to white supremacist policies and made the political climate of campus conducive to mass mobilization. Former student activist Claude Barnes recalled, "During that time, I can remember the SGA [Student Government Association] would call a meeting. I don't care if they called it at 2:00 A.M., Harrison Auditorium would be filled up. People would come out of their dormitories with rollers in their hair. It was that kind of attention. It was that kind of concern among the student body at that time about what's going on in this community and what role could A&T play."[15]

The synergy that existed between A&T and GAPP was displayed in numerous ways, and unlike at public HBCUs in the Deep South, the administration at A&T was fully on board with pushing the new agenda. While GAPP was still settling in and forming objectives, A&T's president was lining up ideas that complemented GAPP's platform and reflected the cultural nationalist leanings that had thrived within the communitas of various Black colleges for years. Lewis Carnegie Dowdy took over as president of the university in an interim capacity from 1962 to 1963 and became the fully installed president and, eventually, chancellor from 1964 to 1980. As interim president, Dowdy was at the helm during the mass jail-ins where A&T and Bennett students stood shoulder to shoulder with the Black residents of the city, marching through the streets and packing the city jails in an effort to topple Jim Crow policies throughout the city. During the mass jail-in campaign, the state legislature had forced Dowdy to direct his students to cease and desist with their protests. However, as the Black Power era dawned, A&T's headman underwent a critical philosophical shift. After meeting with numerous student and campus leaders, Dowdy proposed the construction of "an all-black grocery store." Had Dowdy's proposal for a store where Blacks had "sole ownership and control" been submitted anonymously, one would have easily thought it was the product of a Black Power militant. "The white man has trained us not to trust each other," declared Dowdy. "And this could be, and is in fact today a hang up in the unification of black people. Blacks should first believe in themselves."[16]

In spite of Dowdy's radical rhetoric, the progressive administrator struggled to keep up with the rapid pace of the Black Power era. Sensitive toward the failures of the early movement and increasingly critical of the trappings of capitalism, students found targets at every turn. When over five hundred people (mostly A&T students) gathered at the Greensboro courthouse for a "teach-in," campus leader Willie Avon Drake concluded the demonstration by informing the students and teachers that they "have a job to do." As fate would have it, the upcoming spring semester of 1969 would test the strength and will of the A&T communitas in unprecedented ways. For Dowdy, the pressures of the movement would land at his doorstep—literally and figuratively.[17]

Nothing illustrated the bonds across class lines that Aggie students shared with the community better than a strike of cafeteria workers on A&T's campus during the spring of 1969. The growth of Black colleges throughout the twentieth century had made HBCUs viable workspaces for numerous working-class Blacks. Members of the community worked as janitors, groundskeepers, physical plant operators, and canteen and lunchroom attendants, often forming bonds with the students they worked among. A&T's

cafeteria workers demanded better wages and working conditions, issues that resonated with the student body. The strike lasted three days and, according to the campus newspaper, received support from 90 percent of the student body. Students formed an ad hoc committee that helped to organize efforts to eat off campus while the cafeteria was closed. Three days into the strike, the administration of A&T reached a settlement with the cafeteria workers, bringing quick resolution to the matter. However, without the pressure and support of the student body, it is uncertain how successful the workers' efforts would have been. Student leader Vincent McCullough exclaimed, "The will of black people can never be suppressed."[18] McCullough not only reflected the sentiment of his fellow Aggies but additionally conveyed the communal support that made the Greensboro model a standout among other "movement centers."[19]

A violent exchange with local law enforcement defined the end of the academic year. In the midst of the three-day strike, 2,500 students decided to show their support for the cafeteria workers by marching to the home of President Dowdy. Tensions increased when the predominantly white police force arrived on the scene to disperse the crowd. "The students then marched to East Market Street where cars were stoned, traffic was held up, and windows were broken," reported A&T student Cohen N. Greene. "The rock-throwing crowd concentrated at Sid's Curb Market until the police arrived later. George Bain, owner of the curb market, was confronted earlier on Wednesday and asked to contribute food during the strike, but refused. . . . This curb market was probably singled out because 'it is the only white owned business in that area and most students feel it shouldn't be there.'"[20] The local grocer refused to support the social and political agenda of student activists who were also his primary consumers, further highlighting the need for Dowdy's "all-black" grocery store. With the launch of the cafeteria strike and the way it played out in the local community, the fissures between A&T students and the white power structure in Greensboro were only beginning and promised to become even wider.

The tenets that served as the underpinning of Black Power manifested in the streets of Greensboro during the 1969 strike. Students who believed that their rights had been marginalized lashed out at anything they regarded as symbolic of white authority. A state-run institution that exploited its workers, police who harassed and abused students and local citizens, and white-owned businesses that were not supportive of student causes and exploited student's dollars were the focal points of the student's wrath. In the aftermath of the A&T cafeteria strike, two students suffered gunshot wounds, and several more were injured when local law enforcement opened fire on the crowd. In the days following the riot, many students called for retaliation and revenge.[21] The police violence in Greensboro was part of a national trend, as gun-wielding National Guard soldiers and police were called in to suppress inner-city rebellions—wounding and killing African Americans in the name of law and order. Rather than deal with long-standing Black grievances, conservative white politicians built and rode a backlash against Black militancy by acting as though unruly and lawless youngsters, who needed to be brought to heel, were the source of chaos and confusion. In doing so, the white power structure overlooked the adverse effects of years of segregation and the white supremacist ideals that permeated throughout various institutions.

In the absence of specific programs and concerted efforts to eradicate such barriers, many African Americans felt lost, forgotten, and frustrated, thus triggering the latest wave of protests toward the end of the decade, which adopted a far angrier and more determined tone. The *A&T Register* proclaimed, "The business community of Greensboro must pay for police brutality. The simulated battleground, for which police used A&T's campus, should be responded to by the Aggie family with redress and insurrection."[22] Tensions were building in Greensboro. In A&T students' recent exchanges with the white power structure, the students' controlled anger, coupled with an intensive effort from city officials to extinguish all signs of overt militancy, produced a war zone within Greensboro, with actual tanks and even military spy planes being used to keep watch over the campus that served as the catalyst for a social revolution that defined the decade.[23] With the nation still reeling from the King riots and Vietnam War protests still gripping colleges across the country, local, state, and federal officials kept their sights trained on the students from A&T. Such developments did not go unnoticed in the local community and beyond. The city's Black high school youths, adult community activists, and young radicals across the country were mindful of the developments taking place at A&T as well. Just two months after the fallout from the cafeteria strike, all of them would converge on the institution to create SOBU, elevate the call for Black Power, and witness one of the most violent campus exchanges in student movement history.

· · · · · ·

They called themselves the Syndicate. Calvin Matthews, Leander Forbes, Vincent McCullough, Willie Avon Drake, and Robert "Tazz" Anderson made up a small, informal fellowship of young, cool, and conscious "brothers" who arrived on A&T's campus as freshmen in 1965. By the time they became upperclassmen, the young men had developed leadership skills as student government officials. McCullough, who later become SGA president, jokingly carried a folder marked TOP SECRET just to give the impression that he and his comrades were "in the know." But student life on A&T's campus in the latter half of the decade was no laughing matter as the young men entered the burgeoning movement.

College students across North Carolina were becoming more involved in activism, but the movement was in flux. By 1968 SNCC had lost its campus presence and there was no mass-based national Black student organization. In January 1969 A&T students sent a delegation to the North Carolina Student Legislature, a statewide forum for college youths, with the hope of assuming a greater leadership role in the organization. John Tabb, an A&T student, was selected as the delegate to the National Student Association meeting later in February. Members of the Syndicate accompanied Tabb to the meeting and prepared themselves to address the concerns of Black college students nationally.

Before an audience of intent Black students, Greensboro representatives advocated pulling out of the National Student Association altogether and forming their own organization. This act of disassociation drew from the same ideology that members of SNCC had adopted three years earlier when white members of the renowned organization were asked to leave and focus on organizing and mobilizing like-minded members of their own race. "Before the discussion progressed further, Drake told the gathering that we already had an organization started at A&T and were planning a conference in the spring," recalled Syndicate member Forbes. "When asked what was the organization's name, without hesitation, he blurted out, 'SOBU—Student Organization for Black Unity.' Though no such organization existed at the time, Drake asked Tazz, Vincent, and myself to go back to A&T and try to set things in place for the first meeting."[24]

This impromptu attempt of the Syndicate to make A&T the launching point for a new national organization could have backfired, had it not been for A&T's tradition of radicalizing and organizing youths. The conference was scheduled for May, and a number of Aggies were eager to welcome this new cadre of militants to campus. Chief among them was Nelson Johnson, a young but experienced activist who served as a "master organizer" with GAPP and was the vice president of A&T's SGA during the 68–69 school year. Johnson had started at A&T in 1965, the same year that the young men of the Syndicate first arrived on campus, but as an Air Force veteran, he possessed a higher level of maturity and political savoir faire than most campus activists. "What we need is a Black university to serve the needs of Black people," declared Johnson. "Such should be the goal and destiny of A&T State University."[25] With Johnson helping to lead the charge, youths and community activists were funneled into one of the most racially and politically charged spaces in the country. Designed to recapture and reimagine the fractured remains of SNCC, SOBU gathered on A&T's campus on May 8, 1969.

Arriving from both predominantly white and historically Black colleges, sixty Black students arrived to develop a platform infused with the tenets of Black Power. SOBU moved quickly beyond the ideological debates surrounding purpose and membership that had so limited SNCC's campus presence in the mid-1960s. Student correspondent David Lee Brown reported that "SOBU was founded because there has been a growing desire and need on the part of students of Afro-American heritage to form a student organization that would be solely Black—physically, mentally and spiritually."[26] Brown's comment underscored the prevailing sentiment shared by frustrated students who were more than ready to define the future of the race without the involvement or input of white liberals, whom the Black community had lost its trust in due to past failures of the larger civil rights movement. Greensboro, and A&T specifically, was clearly an ideal setting, a fact that was not lost on the conference's students. It turned out to be both ironic and precipitous that as students began sorting out the organization's future path, the city teetered on the verge of its most explosive racial violence yet.

Dudley High School was among the jewels of Greensboro's Black community. The oldest Black high school in the city was less than two miles from A&T. Its close proximity to A&T allowed college students to serve as tutors, mentors, and role models for the high school students. Generations of Dudley students had gone on to attend A&T, and the linkage between the two institutions and with the surrounding Black community could hardly have been stronger. When students at Dudley launched a protest of the student government election results that year, they found a sympathetic ear on campus. At issue had been the election of Claude Barnes, one of Dudley's young militants. Though Barnes had received enough write-in votes to win the election, officials barred him from assuming the presidency. Not only did a number of older Blacks fail to embrace the aggressive political stance adopted by youths, but a great many had trouble warming up to the era's new cultural styles emanating from this younger generation. Historian

William Chafe describes how just four months before the election, "a male student had been suspended for wearing bib overalls to school. Before that the same punishment had been meted out to girls who wore 'Afros.'"[27]

What should have been a mere cultural impasse between older high school administrators and young people arising from changing styles of dress had smoldered during the opening weeks of May. Compounding the issue was the fact that Owen Lewis, the white public relations director of the Greensboro School Department, was ordered to subvert the authority of Principal Franklin Brown, a well-respected Black man who had served on the faculty since 1937 before being promoted to principal in 1965. Whatever sympathies Brown may have possessed for the students' concerns took a back seat once Lewis, in a power play, demanded that students cease and desist with their calls for restitution.[28] Beginning with Barnes's suspension on May 7, students staged a walkout. When the report of tension and trouble at Dudley arrived in the midst of the founding SOBU meeting, students reacted swiftly. Johnson shuttled a group of the SOBU conference attendees down to Dudley in an attempt to cool off what was becoming an increasingly tense setting. By May 1969, Johnson had become the face of the movement in Greensboro and public enemy number one to the local white power structure. He had led the coordination for GAPP, was a key player in the creation of SOBU, and had been elected vice president of student government at A&T. The blame for the Dudley uprising quickly shifted to Johnson, leading to his arrest on trespassing charges. In assessing the direction of the liberation movement in the days after his trial, Johnson wrote, "To the degree that our analyses and interpretations are incorrect, we hope that our motives exonerate us to the generations that have gone before and those which must follow. To the degree that we are forced to use means that we would not rather use, may God forgive us. The torch of liberation burns on for our people."[29] The commotion over Barnes's election was only the opening salvo. In the coming days, SOBU attendees, citizens of Greensboro, and the entire nation would witness a town under siege and a university in the crosshairs of the white establishment.

Ed Whitfield had been a student at Cornell University before he arrived at the SOBU conference. Like many others, he left politically stimulated by what he had witnessed. As president of the Black Student Organization at Cornell, Whitfield had helped to pioneer the Africana studies program on campus, but Greensboro offered a laboratory for Whitfield to turn theory into practice, a fact that would soon draw him back to the city. As SOBU participants returned to their respective campuses, they received the startling news of how violently Greensboro authorities had reacted to the escalating Dudley-A&T revolt. Whitfield recalled, "When I went back to school a few days later I looked in the newspaper, and on the front page of the *New York Times* here I see a picture of North Carolina A&T State University, Scott Hall with some National Guardsmen crouched down behind some barricades and I was telling people, you know I was just there a couple of days ago."[30]

Whitfield was describing the state's tactics to force the dissidents from A&T into line. On May 23, two weeks after the initial melee at Dudley, A&T came under attack. Governor Bob Scott ordered National Guard soldiers to sweep the university, thus "routing hundreds of students with gunfire and tear gas."[31] Targeting A&T seemed to be the logical strategy for state officials, since the institution had been an enclave for young activists, a dominant source of insurgency in the city, and an influential locus for movement activity throughout the state. Steady protests at Dudley High School in the first weeks of May were fueled by activist energies from the nearby university. Scott set out to extinguish those energies with the full resources of the state.

Storming the male dormitories of Cooper and Scott Halls, National Guard soldiers attempted to confiscate weapons that had allegedly been used by snipers. George Simpkins, former president of the local chapter of the National Association for the Advancement of Colored People, recalled, "You could hear the tanks coming up the street at 5:00 in the morning to move on to the campus."[32] University president Dowdy had already ordered students to leave by six o'clock that evening due to the brewing conflict. However, male students awoke that morning to the sound of gunfire as shells penetrated the walls of the dormitory. Vernice Wright, a student writer for the *A&T Register*, reported, "Dowdy made it quite clear that no authority, referring to Mayor Elam and Police Chief Paul Calhoun, notified him of the intended 'sweep' of Cooper and Scott Halls. . . . Consequently, male students there were subjected to tear gas and were marched from their living quarters in towels thrown around the waist and in pajamas. . . . Dowdy added that upon completing the search of the two male dormitories, only two operable weapons were found by the guards."[33]

In the wake of the attack, students were stunned to discover that Willie Grimes, a freshman from Greenville, North Carolina, had been shot and killed by unknown assailants; several more were injured. The federal government called for congressional hearings, thus providing a national forum to expose the root cause of the revolt. The North Carolina Advisory Committee to the U.S. Commission on Civil Rights issued a report entitled *Trou-*

ble in Greensboro, which concluded, "Law and order must be accompanied by justice. . . . The State of North Carolina and the city of Greensboro must show to all, but especially to black students, that the law is neutral and race plays no part in its enforcement. The North Carolina National Guard cannot take pride in its actions at A&T State University."[34] Despite these findings, the state did virtually nothing to make amends for its assault on A&T, and the murder of Grimes has gone unsolved to this very day.

The violent end to the academic year at A&T left physical and emotional scars on campus. In its fledgling state, SOBU remained dedicated to organizing students across the country to embrace its Black Nationalist platform. However, the organization continued to look toward Greensboro and North Carolina more broadly as a foundation for its new efforts. The group's first conference had hosted sixty students on A&T's campus and, during its inception, fittingly witnessed and took part in a civil insurrection centered on the rights of Black youths. Members returned to North Carolina in November 1969 for their second conference, this time converging in Durham. Their numbers had increased tenfold. Six hundred students attended from across the country and appointed Nelson Johnson as their national convener. In their second meeting, students further outlined their goals and vision. A correspondent from A&T reported, "As a result of the SOBU conference, a better communication between Black campuses is being developed. A SOBU newspaper will be started with plans for bi-monthly publication."[35]

By this point SOBU had become a national organization, even though it remained linked to the Greensboro community and institution from which it first sprang. This was due in large part to the continued presence of Johnson, who now assumed leadership roles on campus, in GAPP, and in SOBU. Within activist circles, A&T was becoming a proving ground for a more radical form of protests, a fact applauded by many of its students. Some students even interpreted the standoff with law enforcement as a victory. In a gathering of students on campus, Johnson addressed the issue. "The image of A&T is an all-time high as far as blacks are concerned," the *A&T Register* reported. "If the enrollment is down . . . the students at A&T are not to blame. If whites are afraid to attend sports events on this campus, that too was unfortunate. But the blood Willie E. Grimes shed was noble blood and he died in this country for his people.' At this time the audience again interrupted Johnson with applause."[36]

Tension in the city remained elevated as students returned to campus. Much to the chagrin of Greensboro's city leaders, SOBU dropped a permanent anchor in the city, preparing to carry on the organizing tradition that had made SNCC legendary in civil rights circles. Unlike in many other major southern cities, such as Birmingham or Nashville, by the end of the decade the movement in Greensboro was still escalating. This crucial element drew even more proponents of Black Power to the city. Thanks to the efforts of Howard Fuller, a new and innovative African American educational institution was born, further raising the city's profile among Black Power proponents.

Founded in the wake of Black student protests at Duke University in 1969, Malcolm X Liberation University (MXLU) was the radical outgrowth of a surging argument for independent schools that advanced a curriculum designed to liberate the minds and communities of Black people. In its second year of operation, its founder, Fuller, relocated MXLU to Greensboro and staffed the school with community volunteers and members of SOBU. Among them was Ed Whitfield. Whitfield represented the type of young, idealistic Black Nationalist who was committed to the work of SOBU. "All I knew for sure was that I was dedicated to spending my life trying to improve the condition of the community of which I was a part," Whitfield recalled, "and to be a part of the struggle that had been part of my consciousness since childhood. And that's what brought me to Greensboro."[37]

With GAPP, MXLU, and SOBU all maintaining a heavy presence in the city, it was clear that, by 1971, Greensboro had become, in Chafe's phrase, "the center of Black Power in the South."[38] The mobilization and organizing that characterized the Black political landscape of Greensboro was punctuated by the ideology of Black Nationalism. As A&T alumnus Jesse Jackson reminded a hall full of activists and organizers at the 1972 National Black Political Convention in Gary, Indiana, it was "nation time."[39] Fuller's effort to launch MXLU was being duplicated through other channels in Greensboro. GAPP and SOBU also supported the efforts of MXLU staffers and disenchanted Dudley High School students in developing the Willie Ernest Grimes Freedom School for secondary and primary training, whose goal was to establish "authentic independent Black education institutions for themselves."[40] In a 1970 *Ebony* magazine article, leading Black scholar Vincent Harding captured the evolution of these new educational endeavors: "Although the movement towards a Black University has often been misunderstood, misinterpreted, and sometimes misguided, it has touched every one of the traditionally black campuses, and in some cases has pressed faculties, administrations, and trustees into black oriented directions which were unforeseen a few years earlier."[41] Harding's characterization of reform efforts as "misunderstood, misinterpreted, and sometimes misguided" was not reserved for Black education alone. The Black Power era suffered from external and internal factors that threatened its longevity. These factors would soon arrest the development of the movement and create major problems for both GAPP and SOBU.

· · · · · ·

For young activists committed to Black Nationalism, Pan-Africanism represented the next logical ideological step. If the concept of nation building began as an effort to go block by block and school by school in an attempt to construct self-determination and empowerment, then the decision to cast a wider net across the diaspora seemed a rational transition. In discussing the objectives of SOBU, Whitfield recalled, "Before there was an African Liberation Support Committee and African Liberation Day, we organized at the United Nations in the spring of 1970 in commemoration of the Sharpeville massacre."[42] SOBU's decision to sharpen its focus on worldwide struggles against white supremacy was the beginning of an increasingly divisive debate over the proper path to liberation.

From pool halls to dorm rooms, Black youths debated and discussed the ideas of Marxism, cultural nationalism, and Pan-Africanism, all the while fixated on the overarching theme of liberation. What developed in the midst of these discussions was what Nelson Johnson would later refer to as a "blacker than thou" mentality.[43] A&T offered itself as an ideal forum for these competing beliefs, as young intellectuals matched wits, arguing into the wee hours of the morning. Stokely Carmichael arrived on campus in 1971 (one of several visits he made to A&T) and outlined the problem that would continue to afflict the movement for years to come. "Now from South Africa to Nova Scotia, the Black world finds itself in political chaos," Carmichael declared to the overflowing gymnasium. "We are in political chaos simply because we do not have a common ideology which represents our common interests. . . . Thus, it is necessary for us to seek an ideology around which we can be unified."[44] Although Carmichael was a committed Pan-Africanist, it remained to be seen what theory, if any, would unite and guide the development of Black empowerment in Greensboro and beyond.

This debate was not new. The struggle for Black liberation in America is replete with philosophical disunity. The inability to coordinate the efforts of competing organizations had in many ways impeded Black progress in the past, and it threatened to do so again in Greensboro during the Black Power era. Whitfield's journey to Greensboro as an activist with MXLU and

SOBU was a rocky one. He came to realize that in a growing number of political circles, diverging points of view and competing theories were not welcome. A growing critique of classism garnered the attention of many radical youths who sought to broaden the civil rights movement beyond its concerns with the color line, as defined by W. E. B. DuBois in his earlier career as a scholar. Whitfield wrote a controversial editorial in SOBU's national newspaper, the *African World*, declaring that the civil rights movement "was dead." He argued instead for a sea change in the struggle for liberation that would embrace broader proletarian concerns. His peers were not supportive. Whitfield recalled, "I remember people looked at it and got angry because they thought I was saying everything was okay. I was one of the people that was struggling a lot inside of SOBU for . . . trying to look at how the workers' movement was developing, and the extent that that's going to begin to address . . . economic issues."[45] Whitfield's position was emblematic of the ideological struggles that lay ahead for the movement as student activists wrestled with their place within the movement and debated the most effective ways to tackle institutionalized white supremacy.

As a new decade dawned, GAPP and SOBU confronted the same issues that multitudes of civil rights groups were struggling with. Co-optation, surveillance, and repression by government officials and local authorities presented a litany of problems for committed Black radicals, but several organizations and institutions were additionally burdened with a leadership crisis stemming from distrust of a seemingly growing field of opportunists. Limited access to the financial resources needed to keep their agendas afloat and their doors open presented yet another challenge, undermining the effectiveness and longevity of grassroots efforts. However, the flames of internal discord were most often fanned by the controversy over the direction of the movement.

But before this decline occurred, GAPP and SOBU made an impact on Greensboro. With former students from A&T at the helm, GAPP successfully organized strikes among public school cafeteria workers, sanitation workers, blind workers employed by Industries of the Blind, and exploited tenants in public housing. For people living in condemned homes and renting substandard property in Greensboro, GAPP's protest for immediate reform and restitution resonated far more strongly than ideas of Black nationhood. The tenants of Greensboro's public housing might be able to relate to the struggles of people in the slums of Soweto and the shanty towns of Brazil or the dreams of complete Black autonomy as expressed within the tenets of Black Nationalism, but the more pressing matter was pragmatism. Organizers needed feasible and accessible methods of protest that would deliver basic services and human rights to their constituents. In their estimation, Marxism increasingly became a more attractive philosophy than the Pan-Africanist theories embraced sometimes by SOBU and exclusively by the leadership of MXLU. As SOBU leader Nelson Johnson recalled, "Community people in Greensboro also criticized pan-Africanists for doing nothing but talk. They told us that waiting for African revolution is no solution for everyday folks."[46]

While Marxism failed to attract aspiring middle-class students, Pan-Africanism and cultural nationalism most certainly did. Several students on A&T's campus relished intimidating older professors with the aggressive rhetoric of Black Power and in their youthful brazenness vowed to defend the Black community against the imperialist forces of America. Their language was bold and brash, attracting both students who were committed to the rhetoric and those who were simply curious to see what defiant move they would take next. Although there was no credible threat of Black Panther Party organizing within Greensboro, a handful of students gravitated toward the idea of self-defense.[47] Calling themselves the Black Liberation Front, a group of A&T students promoted a more aggressive stance on campus by stashing weapons and declaring their intention to use them against white aggressors, echoing Black Panther rhetoric and tactics. One student characterized them as "walking around with their tams and black shirts and pants—everything was black—urging students to join the Panthers."[48] While the Black Liberation Front's violent tone attracted the curiosity of its members' fellow students, it failed to resonate en masse, rendering it a spectacle and not a mass-based campus movement. What the organization did accomplish was establishing itself as a touchstone for defiant Black manhood and womanhood, an important ideological current and counternarrative that was well represented in various elements of the Black Power era. However, there was method to what many conservatives perceived to be the madness of Black Power.

The spirit of nation building and Pan-Africanism blossomed on A&T's campus. Pressure was mounting against HBCUs to move from veiled expressions of their racial identity to explicit endorsement of all things Black, and SOBU activists on campus provided that thrust. SOBU created significant inroads that linked them with the global struggle for Black liberation. Historian Anthony James Ratcliff notes, "Just as SNCC activists had developed the Pan-African Skills Project and Drum and Spear Bookstore, which built direct links with progressive African governments, SOBU established a

Pan-African Medical Program providing Southern African liberation movements, as well as community health centers in the U.S., with vitally needed medical supplies, tools, and money."[49] In addition to the Pan-African Medical Program, SOBU adopted several more initiatives that were framed by the concepts of Black Nationalism. Among them were the Save and Change Black Schools Program and the National Community Work Program, and the group also participated in the formation of the African Liberation Support Committee. Their main source of pride also operated as their main source of communication: the *African World*, a newspaper that clearly modeled itself after Marcus Garvey's *Negro World*. By 1974, they boasted circulation in forty-nine states and thirty countries.[50] Moreover, the SOBU agenda tapped into the spirit of cultural nationalism that had permeated throughout Black colleges for years.

SOBU's expansion on a national level was due in no small part to intense organizing by a cadre of dedicated student activists. Black students exchanged ideas through the *African World* and campus newsletters. But they also fragmented with considerable speed, as various leaders and ideologies jockeyed for position. Many inspired by the spirit and idea of SOBU quickly split into new Black Power cells. The National Association of Black Students, the Pan African Students Organization in the Americas, and the Congress of African Students soon joined SOBU. These new outgrowths engaged in robust ideological debates, with the National Association of Black Students and the Congress of African Students soon adopting the same Marxist paradigm that SOBU eventually embraced, a transformation that did not go untested.

Battling for ideological hegemony did not immediately impede SOBU's early growth or influence. Like most other civil rights organizations, SOBU found its strength in coordinating local people and dispatched a number of student activists into the field to draw new youths to its cause. Ed Whitfield, who served as the northeast regional coordinator, mobilized students from the New York area before dedicating his full energies to MXLU after 1970. Gene Locke, a dedicated student activist from Houston, directed organizing efforts in Texas. Tim Thomas coordinated SOBU efforts in Washington, D.C., and Ron "Slim" Washington, a standout basketball player turned fulltime activist, led a group of Black radicals who organized students in Colorado, in Kansas, and throughout the Midwest.

But the heart of SOBU was in Greensboro. Even as the organization cast a wide net throughout the country and the diaspora, the work and mobilization taking place in North Carolina directed SOBU's agenda. SOBU's working relationship with MXLU and GAPP and close proximity to A&T gave it direction.[51]

With students serving as the main foot soldiers of a movement that had rocked the foundations of America and captured the attention of the world, the epicenter of the insurgency was still playing an active role in stoking the fires of revolution. When Howard Fuller (who by the beginning of the 1970s was going by the name Owusu Sadaukai) promoted the idea of African Liberation Day in 1972, he requested that SOBU members Nelson Johnson and Jerry Walker serve as the North Carolina state coordinators of the national effort. Johnson and Walker recruited campus leaders from Shaw University, Bennett College, North Carolina Central, Winston Salem State, and the University of North Carolina at Charlotte to support the new initiative.[52] The efforts of SOBU and other nationally prominent civil rights organizations resulted in the convergence of over sixty thousand demonstrators in San Francisco, Toronto, and Washington, D.C., on May 27 who defiantly called for an end to Africa's occupation by foreign powers. In doing so, activists orchestrated a powerful connection with freedom fighters across the global diaspora who were also engaged in a struggle against imperialism and white supremacy. Back in Greensboro, students at A&T kept a watchful eye on the proceedings in the nation's capital. They were not alone. Over the years, A&T's faculty proved to be a vital ally in the emergence of radical activity on campus and throughout the community. As the Black Power era ushered in a new phase of the movement, the support and involvement of A&T's faculty would be essential in maintaining the spirit of insurgency on campus.

· · · · · ·

In May 1970, the crowd that poured in to hear John Marshall Stevenson address students attending the University of North Carolina at Greensboro were eager to learn about the rapidly shifting issues and events that had transformed a once-moderate southern city into a major hub of the Black Power movement. They could not have selected a better speaker. Stevenson was the quintessential image of a man in flux. The explosive era and his proximity to the heart of the local revolution gave him a bird's-eye view of a community in struggle with itself. Born in Little Rock, Arkansas, in 1930, Stevenson joined the faculty of North Carolina A&T in 1962, shortly after students there had placed the school and the city on the modern civil rights map. Stevenson watched the struggle for Black liberation unfold with a keen eye, and it was not long before the eccentric professor of theater made himself available for students seeking direction and advice in the movement. In 1967 Stevenson created and published his own local newspaper, which became popular throughout the Black community. The name of the paper illustrated Stevenson's broader concerns and hopes for a society in turmoil—the *Carolina Peacemaker*. Stevenson was also evolving from an ideological and spiritual standpoint. He, like so many other older members of the Black community, struggled to grasp the aggressive tone of the Black Power era. But Stevenson was younger than many of his colleagues at A&T (he was thirty-two when he joined the faculty), and his conversion to Judaism in the latter half of the decade identified him as a man in search of his cultural and spiritual self. Commenting on the former, Stevenson informed the University of North Carolina at Greensboro crowd, "I'm talking about a revolution in thinking. I'm referring to the difference between 'Black' and 'Negro.' . . . Any black man who accepts the term Negro is willing to compromise his rights."[53] Changing his name to John Marshall Kilimanjaro, he guided his newspaper to become an essential voice for the Black community in Greensboro, proving the power of the HBCU communitas all over again. In an era in which the popular mantra was "Trust no one over thirty," students attending A&T found critically important allies throughout the faculty who helped to shape their sense of self and provide them direction as the movement swirled around them.

The legacy of Black protests in the city was firmly rooted in the local Black institutions and the communities that depended on them. This reality greatly shaped the mind-set of numerous faculty and administrators at the state's flagship HBCU. Without their input, guidance, and support, the student-led revolution that would go on to rock the nation would likely have dissipated with little fanfare. Looking back to the late 1940s, former student and local activist Randolph Blackwell recalled, "I know of my own knowledge that there was a kind of yearning inside the leadership of that school for the same kinds of things that would have been called publically radical." The functionality of A&T's thriving communitas was on full display as the movement gained momentum. Professors and administrators provided shelter for students to work out their angst concerning white supremacy, distribute leaflets, and hold campus-wide meetings concerning the movement, and as the mass jail-ins hit the city in 1963, professors visited the prisons, providing students emotional support and passing out quizzes and exams to keep students on top of their academic responsibilities. Indeed, the "open society" that defined Victor Turner's communitas and granted Black college students the social mobility for maturation and politicization was readily visible on A&T's campus. As the Black Power era dawned, even the most militant students found tacit and explicit support from mentors within.[54]

Several of Kilimanjaro's colleagues joined him in supporting the sharp political and ideological transitions taking place in the latter half of the decade. Dean of Students Ernest McCoy, a member of A&T's administration since 1958, publicly called for shared governance and student autonomy on campus during a "teach-in" held by students and faculty in downtown Greensboro. By declaring that students should have a say in policy making, McCoy aligned himself with young folks who sought an end to the paternalistic in loco parentis atmosphere that prevailed on college campuses across the country, but particularly at HBCUs.[55] Frederick A. Williams was a stalwart of the movement for years. A 1931 graduate of A&T, he arrived on campus to teach in 1950 after spending several years working under Felton Grandison Clark at Southern University. Williams played a critical role in organizing local "political issues" forums throughout the 1960s to keep African Americans abreast of the changing political currents, and he exposed numerous students to news from within the African diaspora as a former visiting professor at the University of Khartoum in Sudan from 1961 to 1963. It was Williams—who by the late 1960s had become an administrator as the director of planning and development—who pushed through the founding of a Black studies program on campus in the months just before the Dudley-A&T Revolt.[56] While fledgling programs that emphasized African American culture and heritage were at the top of students' concerns for campus improvements, their arrival also meant radical changes for the future of Black faculty. Scholars such as Tendai Mutunhu represented the growing conflict.

As a newly appointed instructor of African American history, Mutunhu became a popular professor on campus in the latter half of the decade. A native of Zimbabwe, Mutunhu relished the opportunity to further connect students to the liberation struggles emerging throughout the diaspora. In a fall meeting of student leaders in 1969, sponsored by the Mu Psi Chapter of Omega Psi Phi, Mutunhu illustrated the nexus between Black youth movements across the globe and the empowerment of students through race consciousness. "A man or woman needs something to look back on . . . his own heritage," declared Mutunhu. "When you begin to learn something about yourself as a Black people . . . you become proud of yourself." Mutunhu's rhetoric was well received—and not only at A&T. Mutunhu became one of the first Black academics to be courted by neighboring Guilford

College, and he received a full-time job at the institution in 1977. Scholars like Mutunhu were becoming more visible in the Black Power era as Black student bodies at predominantly white institutions demanded access to Black faculty mentors. To fill the void, white institutions began to seduce faculty away from HBCUs with the promise of more pay, greater resources for research, and fewer teaching demands. Developments and losses such as these hit A&T hard, and probably no departure was more significant than that of Darwin Turner.[57]

Turner arrived at A&T in the fall of 1959, just before the sit-ins were launched at the start of the spring semester. A journeyman of several HBCUs, Turner settled in at A&T, anchoring the English Department until 1966, when he accepted a position as head of the graduate school. Aggies of that era considered Turner young, hip, and politically conscious. In addition to his duties as the dean of the graduate school, Turner had also been tapped to direct the new Afro American Center on campus. As a delegation of A&T SGA members returned from Howard University's "Toward a Black University" conference that fall, they knew that pushing A&T toward an academic curriculum that more forthrightly embraced the liberation of Black people would garner Turner's support. Those beliefs were confirmed when it was Turner who helped to facilitate and arrange Stokely Carmichael's first visit to campus in December 1968.[58]

Not only was Turner talented at navigating the relationship between the student body and the older generation of faculty and administrators, he was also accomplished in his field. As a faculty member and administrator at A&T, Turner edited two books on Black American literature focusing on fiction and poetry, published extensively in academic journals, served in various professional organizations within his discipline, and was appointed to a four-year term on the Graduate Record Examination's board in Princeton, New Jersey. Much like Mutunhu, Turner had impeccable credentials that caught the eye of predominantly white colleges that began scouring the country for capable scholars who could teach and interpret the Black experience within the ivory tower of the academy. In the spring of 1969, the University of Wisconsin at Madison was so impressed with Turner that they arranged for him to commute two days every other week to teach a course entitled Afro-American Writers in Modern Literature—a round trip of 1,773 miles. "I don't really know why I accepted the opportunity of teaching at Wisconsin," stated Turner. "I guess I wanted a different kind of experience. It is really a novelty." "Novelty" was an understatement. The campus community in Madison was so enamored by the idea of a Black professor lecturing on the Black experience that a local CBS television affiliate came in to tape the event. For the Black students at A&T and other Black colleges who had become used to scholars of Turner's caliber teaching their courses, nurturing their freedom dreams, and serving as powerful allies in the struggle for Black liberation, time was running short. By the following semester, Turner had left A&T and began a full-time stint as a professor of African American literature at the University of Michigan.[59]

Turner did not leave the cupboard completely bare at A&T. Former activists recalled several faculty members as key partners during the Black Power era: Walt Sullivan, who served as chair of the Chemistry Department; Reginald Armory of the Engineering Department; Sylvester Broderick, an instructor in the Foreign Language Department; James Johnson in the Department of Sociology; and Mattye Reed, whose growing collection of African art gathered from her foreign travels led to the creation of the African/Afro-American House, now known as the Mattye Reed African Heritage Center. In the absence of an official Black studies department, collections such as Reed's helped to feed the growing interest that Black students had in the celebration of African culture. Furthermore, Black faculty were able to transcend disciplines and inspire students to embrace their lingering doubts about America's commitment to justice while simultaneously remaining steadfast in their belief that they could transform and reshape American democracy.

Two professors who particularly excelled in channeling the energy of the movement were Frank White and Wayman McLaughlin of the History Department. McLaughlin, who was trained as a philosopher, was a classmate and friend of Martin Luther King Jr. when they both were in graduate school at Boston University, and he was described as the only one of King's peers who was "considered closest to King in scholarship ability." Danville, Virginia, native Joyce Glaise recalled White's and McLaughlin's expertise in "challenging those brilliant minds of students . . . who had lots of experiences, and questioned the Constitution, the history books for the lack of inclusion of Blacks, and also the lack of opportunities and privileges still denied people of color." Concerning McLaughlin, Glaise particularly noted that "he made you want to read and achieve." Such attributes formed the essence of the second curriculum being espoused at A&T. The A&T model defied the prevailing notion that a generational divide rendered Black college faculty powerless and ineffective during the Black Power era. Thus it was no surprise when all of the aforementioned professors turned out to welcome Fuller's MXLU as it relocated to Greensboro from Durham in order to build on the activist energies still emanating from A&T as the explosive 1960s came to a close.[60]

. . . . . .

The long history of the movement for Black liberation contains various moments when the flourishing of cultural nationalism undergirded the transformative zeitgeist of the era. Black Power activists concretely understood that positive self-imagery, the establishment of counternarratives, and the strengthening of Black institutions were essential to the concept of nation building. On college campuses throughout the country, Black youths donned all of the accoutrements of Black Power and celebrated a powerful Black Arts movement whose roots were intertwined with the heart of the Black college communitas. Scholars such as Margaret Walker Alexander at Jackson State, Sterling Brown and Toni Morrison at Howard University, and Darwin Turner at North Carolina A&T not only shaped the discourse surrounding Black literature and artistic expression but also shaped the minds of youths who occupied the front lines of the Black student movement. Stokely Carmichael recalled Morrison as "a challenging teacher who was really down with black literature and our people's culture." Such personal exchanges informed the cultural nationalist leanings of scores of Black youths—a relationship that became much more pronounced in the Black Power era.[61]

The rising tide of social and political consciousness could also be seen in fashion, art, and music. Black artists formed a bond with Black students at HBCUs and drew inspiration from the struggle they found on campus. Recalling such a moment he experienced as a student at A&T, former activist Claude Barnes noted, "It was a hell of a thing to watch Nina Simone come on stage in her combat boots and talk about how she had heard so much about A&T. And this was not just an act, she had heard about the students at A&T and they had a reputation that was well deserved because again anytime there was any issue that the Black community was concerned about, the A&T students were there." In September 1972, A&T students crammed Harrison Auditorium to see legendary soul singer Joe Tex take to the stage, not to do "the bump" or sing his smash hit "I Gotcha" but to discuss his conversion to the Nation of Islam. His tour that year was dedicated to raising funds to "build a hospital in Chicago for Blacks."[62]

Joe Tex (or Minister Joseph X, as he introduced himself) had picked the right crowd. Not only were students at A&T sympathetic to such causes, the university's administration openly embraced the concept of nation building through economic empowerment and the creation of infrastructure that could transform the lives of local Black folks. The presence of organizations such as GAPP, SOBU, and MXLU, which were staffed with a number of students and alumni of A&T, only served to further strengthen the objectives of the A&T communitas during this era. The thrust to close the wealth gap and to improve the lives of countless African Americans (who, because of discriminatory practices, had never tasted the fruits of New Deal policies or the middle-class boom that accompanied the end of World War II) became a prominent focus of local Black Power activists and campus leaders. At the beginning of 1970, A&T developed a project to train "leaders of low-income areas," bringing to campus once a month fifty community leaders to "discuss community problems and plan for solutions to these problems." President Dowdy stated, "We are happy that this training is not at the doctor-lawyer level, but lower than that—where the problems are." By creating programs to empower the grass roots as opposed to the Black elite, A&T officials aligned themselves with the concerns and objectives of the movement that sought representation among the most often overlooked and forgotten members of the Black community.[63]

The effort to empower impoverished members of the community complemented the activist energies that swirled about A&T's campus. In the spirit of nation building, students flocked to seize various opportunities to do their part for the struggle. The *Carolina Peacemaker* reported, "A&T students have initiated several outstanding programs of community service on their own. They run a tutorial program for low-income children lagging behind in their school studies. Student volunteers also work with the Youth Education Service in the city and with the city's redevelopment office. During the recent General Elections in North Carolina, more than 50 cars of students and faculty members were used to transport voters to the poll." Beginning with the sit-ins at the start of the 1960s, A&T students excelled in understanding the complex game of how to apply local political pressure, and both the A&T administration and the local white power structure recognized the threat that the student body collectively posed and responded accordingly. Hal Seiber, the public relations director of the Greensboro Chamber of Commerce, declared, "Once we became aware of the injustices and these were brought to our attention, we tried to move ahead as a whole and A&T has been very conspicuous in our community leadership." By 1972, the effort to link the power of the A&T communitas with the surrounding community crystallized into the establishment of a distinguished professorship of urban affairs in order to assist the university in becoming "more actively involved in identifying and finding solutions to urban problems." The position was named in memory of Frederick A. Williams, the long-serving administrator who established deep connections with local Black folks throughout Greensboro, who had passed away just two years earlier.[64]

Even A&T alumni took up the mantle of Black Power in an effort to transform their communities positively. In 1970 six A&T alumni and two others founded the Greensboro National Bank and opened up their doors to the public in 1971. Among the Aggie founders were James Burnett, Ernest Canada, W. Edward Jenkins, A. N. McCoy, Durel Long, and Henry E. Frye. Although Frye and his cohorts were older than most of the Black Power activists who were still on campus, they were deeply in tune with the tenets and value of cultural nationalism. A native of Ellerbe, North Carolina, Frye recalled with great clarity the impulse that drove them to jump-start this new economic initiative. "The only way that I know how to explain this is that every building I went into, I saw white people," he declared. "The only blacks I saw were people who were operating the elevators or sweeping the floors or coming in to buy something if it was a regular store or something like that."[65] Frye's consternation over the absence of Black faces in positions of power or influence became a driving force of the Black Power movement, spawning wave after wave of Black elected officials in major American cities and fueling local movements that sought agency and empowerment for local Black people—from increased opportunities for civic service to thriving Black-owned businesses with access to wealth and capital for improvements to decaying infrastructure.

"One day I went into [the] North Carolina Mutual Life Insurance Company building in Durham and I saw all of these black folks in there with suits on and women dressed up and everything and working. I said, 'Boy, this is really something,'" continued Frye. "Then I came back to Greensboro and I didn't see that. I didn't see any of that." While Frye and his partners were unlikely to encounter examples of Black wealth in Greensboro on the scale that existed in Durham, they did have access to examples of Black excellence as it existed within the communitas of A&T. In their administrators, professors, and steady stream of accomplished Black visitors, scores of Black college students saw models of how to break free from white expectations that placed limitations on what Black people ought to be and do. Indeed, one of the greatest legacies of Black colleges such as A&T was the fact that generations of students were encouraged to push far beyond what they *could* do and instead envision what they *should* do in order to serve the freedom dreams of their people. In 1968 Frye became the first African

American to be elected to the state general assembly in the twentieth century and in 1983 he was appointed to the North Carolina Supreme Court.[66]

The Greensboro National Bank stalled right out of the gate, never reaching the full potential that its Aggie founders intended. In spite of its broad support within the Black community, a number of internal and external factors (including bad loans and a weak 1980s economy) brought about its demise within two decades of its opening. In many respects, it was a microcosm of the Black Power movement as it unfolded. The rally to accelerate the spirit of cultural nationalism reached its apex in the early 1970s. The pledge to create, support, and protect Black institutions initiated an interesting paradox that struck at the heart of the ideological battles unfolding within the movement. Could Black-owned banks solve the problems associated with dilapidated and historically neglected Black neighborhoods, or was this exercise in pluralism and capitalism infected with the same toxicity that many Black Power activists pledge to deconstruct through the embrace of Marxism? Could Black colleges, lampooned by so many civil rights activists as "plantations" where Black youths "pretended to be white," be salvaged, or should they be scrapped and replaced with new institutions such as MXLU and the growing number of independent Black schools throughout the country? For SOBU, the national organization that had been conceived, launched, and essentially run under the auspices of several individuals connected to A&T, it did not take long to develop a position on the matter.[67]

What many Black Power activists were concerned with was the power, efficacy, and position of the second curriculum. Indeed, race consciousness had been at the heart of most Black colleges' founding principles—but why should it be *second* at all? Instead of coursework overwhelmingly saturated with European history, culture, and ideals, why not advance a curriculum uniquely centered on Africanity? With racial violence, systemic poverty, neocolonialism, and the entrenchment of white supremacy still widespread throughout Black communities, a number of activists demanded that the second curriculum become the first priority and objective in training Black youths. Following the murder of two students on Jackson State University's campus by police gunfire, the administration, faculty, and students at Atlanta University drafted a position paper that captured the anger and passion that many HBCUs developed as they increasingly became staging grounds for violent attacks by law enforcement in the late 1960s and early 1970s. The paper also assessed the purpose and potential for Black colleges.

"A university should never give its attention to scholarly interests and divorce itself from the problems of the larger community," declared the body politic of Atlanta University. "This university recognizes its responsibility in helping the nation understand the implications of racism and in encouraging men of reason and goodwill to marshal their resources in defense of human dignity." In response to the reinvigorated interest in the potential impact of Black colleges, SOBU spearheaded its Save and Change Black Schools (SCBS) program and began walking back the tone and rhetoric of the late 1960s militants who undercut the value of HBCUs. With an emphasis on both changing and saving Black colleges, youth activists acknowledged the intrinsic value of these historic institutions and their tremendous contributions to the struggles of the past, as well as the pregnant possibilities of what they could contribute in the freedom struggle that lay ahead.[68]

The SCBS program was also a direct response to efforts by state legislatures to undermine Black colleges that had served as vital recruiting grounds for movement activists. Black colleges, already suffering under the weight of historic underfunding and neglect, became targets for budget cuts or mergers, as state legislators considered combining North Carolina A&T with its neighbor, the University of North Carolina at Greensboro. For all of the criticism that Black Power activists lodged against HBCUs, the vital institutions were still widely embraced throughout Black America as the primary source for educating Black youths. Attempts by white legislatures to weaken and damage Black colleges were interpreted as direct attacks on one of Black America's greatest treasures. The *A&T Register* reported that it "was SOBU's belief that such moves were designed not only to destroy the potential for acquiring positive Black education at these schools, but also a direct act of political repression against certain campuses where growing Black consciousness was beginning to threaten the traditional white control of Black education." Not only was SOBU perceived as a threat, but the Black colleges that supplied many of its members and leadership were perceived as seedbeds for activism that threatened the stability of the white power structure. SOBU organizer Ron "Slim" Washington also noted that the SCBS program helped to revitalize dormant protest energies at HBCUs, stating that it "solidified our presence and influence in black colleges all throughout the South." Students rallied to the cause by the thousands, and the A&T communitas was once again well suited to embrace and promote the campaign.[69]

SOBU unveiled its latest initiative in the spring of 1970 at a conference held at Spelman College. To build on that energy, SOBU organizers selected the perfect candidate to headline a banquet in December that would be hosted at A&T in order to highlight and raise money to support the new SCBS program. Julian Bond was not only a newly elected representative to the Georgia State Legislature but also Black college royalty. His father, Horace Mann Bond, was a titan among HBCU administrators and scholars, having served as the president of both Fort Valley State University, in Georgia, and Lincoln University, located just outside Philadelphia. At prestigious Morehouse College, Julian was among several students who helped to launch the sit-in movement in Atlanta and later became a prominent figure within SNCC. Bond was tied to the traditionalists who were often portrayed as the overseers of the so-called Negro college plantations, and he was also deeply embedded in the radicalism of the Black Power era. Indeed, his campaign for state representative had been seen as a model of Black Power politics. Bond reminded his audience at A&T that the struggle to preserve Black colleges was rooted in a long history of institutions perilously close to financial disaster, operating on shoestring budgets, and teetering on the edge of constant closure. Yet it was A&T alumnus and SOBU headman Nelson Johnson who best assessed both the present crisis and the meaningful future of Black colleges: "It is of the utmost importance that Black institutions continue to crystallize and institutionalize the changes in educational philosophy and process that are geared to the needs of Black people."[70]

SOBU's campaign to draw attention to preserving Black colleges proved effective. The looming threat to the financial and cultural survival of HBCUs remained a constant fixture on the agenda of A&T's SGA in the years ahead. The SCBS movement was at the top of the itinerary during the opening meeting of the SGA in the fall of 1971. SGA president Ronald Ivey declared, "I am hoping for a year of seriousness as Black students are still waging an intense struggle for the survival of our colleges." With the serious threat of scores of militant A&T students ready to swarm the state capitol in protests or even bring back the overt insurgency that violently marked the spring of 1969, Aggies effectively kept the simmering ideas about legislating a merger between A&T and the University of North Carolina at Greensboro at bay. However, as is the case for many HBCUs, the fight for equity in funding carries on to this day, with profound effects on the growth and potential of a number of state-controlled Black colleges.[71]

The spirit of preserving Black institutions and refitting them with an agenda to more directly address the derivatives of white supremacy that continued to marginalize Black communities became a prevailing undercurrent of the Black Power era. Those objectives created an interesting, if shaky, alignment between A&T activists, the Greensboro community, and the newly relocated MXLU that quickly developed a reputation as one of the preeminent models for the union between Pan-Africanism, cultural nationalism, and education during the movement. The existence of MXLU was heavily dependent on previously existing institutions that were deeply rooted in the Black community. The fledgling institution tapped into the communitas of A&T and, in doing so, helped to create a template for Black studies that included the creation of inroads into the communities that its students studied and served. But MXLU's headman, Fuller, pulled no punches in his critique of Black institutions, an assessment that was echoed by a number of Black militants who sought aggressive change. In a position paper he delivered at MXLU, Fuller wrote, "We find that the educational system of America is set up to support America—so it develops and pursues programs that are consistent with that objective. We have discovered that even Black Studies programs are being structured to be consistent with that objective. This then is the problem for the black student today—How can we gain ideology, get the skill, develop allegiance within the confines of institutions set up to destroy us?" Fuller's hardline stance, rooted in Black Nationalism, broadly took American colleges to task, including the one that, up to that point, had played the most central role in the development of the Black Power movement throughout the state and the one that he would eventually lean on the most to recruit students, volunteers, and activists— North Carolina A&T.[72]

Fuller and other young Black militants took a principled stand against what they viewed as the ineffectiveness of the old guard. But such intractable positions undercut the usefulness of people and organizations that provided blueprints for community organizing and institution building. The failures of both sides to create mutual understanding and dialogue became a hallmark of the era. In an unpublished interview he gave in 1980, Fuller contemplated some of these early missteps. On the topic of unifying grassroots support, Fuller tipped his cap to the Black establishment for the successful inroads they made into the community: "You could talk all the shit you want about the Urban League and the NAACP, but when they have conferences, they pull people," stated Fuller. "They got some continuing local base in some continued relationship to whoever their constituency is and I really think that those of us who are more progressive or see ourselves as revolutionary have got to do that. I mean we have got to be rooted in something that is real beyond just our rhetoric and beyond just a few of us who get together and reaffirm whatever we say. I still think that's a fundamental weakness we have."[73]

To understand the nuances of relationship building and to create inroads with the Black community in Greensboro, Fuller increasingly relied on people like Nelson Johnson, who could move seamlessly through the circles of young militant radicals on A&T's campus, as well as the Black elite and professional class, a skill that Fuller still did not possess. As historian Devin Fergus notes, "More than any other single factor, the coalition-building talent of Johnson was the reason MXLU moved to Greensboro."[74]

With A&T at the center of the burgeoning Black Nationalist movement in North Carolina and Greensboro perfectly situated to serve yet again as a critical springboard in the struggle for liberation, Fuller understood that his window was narrow. One wrong step could alienate MXLU from the support base it so desperately needed. For Fuller, his ill-fated move came with his attempt to expand into an area of the surrounding community that many folks within the old guard revered. When the school attempted to acquire the defunct Palmer Memorial Institute, a historically Black school located just outside Greensboro that was founded by educator Charlotte Hawkins Brown in 1902, the Black community was less than enthused. Fuller stated, "The Palmer thing showed me there was a certain kind of isolation surrounding the school." The disastrous and failed attempt to acquire Palmer was a microcosm of Fuller's difficulties with understanding nuance and the deft touch that was required in courting relationships with local Black folks.[75]

For Fuller and MXLU, it seemed simple—they needed space, and the property had gone relatively unused for years. Yet another complex layer lay in the historical dichotomy between the two institutions. MXLU unapologetically trained young freedom fighters in Pan-Africanism, technical trades, and, at times, the value of armed struggle against neocolonialism. Conversely, Brown was submerged in the respectability politics that defined her era. The Palmer Institute operated much like a finishing school for Black youths, teaching various academic disciplines, manners, and social etiquette. The two educators possessed philosophies on Black education that were not only situated in different time periods but were also polarized by two completely different visions about how Black folks should go about improving their conditions. None of that mattered to the African American community of Greensboro. Brown, who passed away in 1961, was still held in high esteem, and many saw her and the Palmer Institute as a cultural treasure to be preserved, not converted into an enclave for Black radicals who seemingly devalued Brown's importance to the long struggle for Black liberation in North Carolina. MXLU was secluded from the larger Greensboro Black community and not nearly as entrenched in the city as A&T, Bennett, or GAPP, thus making its position and its future far more precarious.

Assessing the unraveling of MXLU, Fuller denied that financial problems had ruined the school, instead suggesting that it was ideological differences that were the root cause of the school's collapse. While both issues created complex problems and weakened the school's chances for survival, another major oversight by Fuller was the miscalculation of the value of previously existing Black institutions and organizations. Black student activists in Greensboro had no need to turn to MXLU as a source of rhetoric or action. Both Bennett and A&T shaped and molded activists such as Nelson Johnson and supplied MXLU with a steady stream of volunteers and organizers during the school's brief duration. Black colleges had opened their doors to Fuller for on-campus solicitation, speeches, and organizing in the same way that they had done for other militants over the years. Indeed, Black students' desire to preserve and value HBCUs through SOBU's SCBS program as opposed to abandoning them for a new wave of independent schools such as MXLU was a telling sign of where their allegiances lay. Young activists still sought much of the change that Fuller had dedicated his life to. However, they were unwilling to jettison completely the institutions that had historically served the Black community. In the minds of many students, the schools they attended were unquestionably Black, a position that ran counter to that of individuals who questioned HBCUs' commitment to advancing the struggle for Black liberation. The dilemma lay in how to transform and enhance the agenda and mission of Black colleges in an effort to maximize their potential and generate social, political, and economic change for Black folks throughout the diaspora. However, as these ideas were debated on campuses such as A&T, the movement itself was fraying in ways that would threaten its longevity.[76]

· · · · · ·

The creation of the North Carolina Black Assembly in 1972 demonstrated the hard lessons Fuller and other activists were learning. The assembly was the outcome of the North Carolina delegation's attendance at the National Black Political Convention in Gary, Indiana, where they witnessed firsthand how strife and disunity could derail organizing efforts. North Carolina activists now sought to coordinate their efforts and unify their fight against institutionalized white supremacy. Presiding over the Black assembly's first meeting in October 1972, Fuller addressed the rift between integrationists and nationalists: "We call for the development of working unity among democrats, republicans and independents, among integrationists and nationalists, among youth and aged, and among working people and professional people who form our communities." The diminished opportunity to exchange freely in healthy debate over common goals steadily choked the intellectual lifeblood out of the movement. A number of activists surrendered to divisions that were both political and personal in nature. Disagreements over the proper path to liberation were most often accompanied by a harsh tone and bravado that isolated and destroyed opportunities for constructive discourse. In recalling the growing division between committed Pan-Africanists and an emerging cadre of Marxists, Fuller recalled, "I think the critical error that was made was when those of us began to take up the study of Marxism and tried to just come in there and change everything. And instead of really trying to figure out a way to broaden we really were pushing people out, which was a real mistake. . . . In reality you can understand why people would get a goddamn attitude."[77]

With external factors steadily mounting against the movement, internal divisions frustrated activists committed to the struggle. Infighting, splinter groups, and disaffection muffled intellectual exchange and damaged opportunities to achieve mutual understanding. Debates over Marxism, cultural nationalism, and Pan-Africanism created ideological discord that fueled animosity between friends and warring factions both on campus and in the broader community. On a national scale, the Black Panther Party provided the best illustration of the disharmony that was consuming various outlets for Black Power politics. "In the end, neither side scored a victory and the biggest loser turned out to be the party itself," writes Panther historian Curtis Austin in documenting the split between the Huey P. Newton and Eldridge Cleaver camps. Austin provides an excellent analysis of the division that existed between Newton and Cleaver—one that was manipulated by the FBI. The former vowed to bring the Panthers above ground and fight discrimination through more traditional means, while the latter favored the armed self-defense strategies broadly associated with early Panther tactics. Austin notes, "The open warfare compelled members to leave the organization in droves." Complete denunciation and repudiation of diverging theories kept many organizations in static positions, unable to find common ground with those who professed a desire to advance the freedom movement.[78]

Within the student movement, nothing illustrated those widening ideological fissures better than the split between Pan-Africanism and Marxism. Militants influenced and persuaded by the grassroots antipoverty campaigns of the late 1960s debated the efficiency of movements predicated on race-based analysis. For a growing number of activists, the mantra of "Power to the people" now expanded beyond race to incorporate the struggles of all individuals caught within the web of capitalism. This new alteration of the discourse did not exclude poor whites victimized by the class line, nor did it focus exclusively on the cultural roots of African people, a fact that was unsettling to many Black Nationalists. Reflecting this shift, in 1972 SOBU shed its singular identification with students and renamed itself the Youth Organization for Black Unity, a move that signaled a broader concern with capitalism, political economy, and class analysis, as well as a wholesale rejection of the Black elitism that many believed characterized HBCU students studying and striving to break through and establish themselves in corporate America. Activists across the country boldly articulated their position in the pages of SOBU's *African World*, with one particular essay drawing a discernible line of demarcation that was damning to the so-called Black college elite. "The revolutionary intelligentsia and other parts of the middle-class must in fact commit suicide as a class and join the making of a totally revolutionary society," argued SOBU editor Milton Coleman. In spite of Coleman's incendiary advice, the overwhelming majority of Black student activists had no intention of jettisoning the dreams of their parents, who believed that their daughters and sons would go on to be successful in the American workforce and, in doing so, not only make their families proud but also perhaps break open new opportunities for those who did not have the same advantage of attending college. Coleman, himself a graduate of the University of Wisconsin–Milwaukee, failed to adhere to his own counsel for "middle-class suicide." He went on to take a position at the *Washington Post* in 1976 and sustained a long and distinguished career fighting for Black folks and championing diversity—from within the system.[79]

In Greensboro, there were still A&T students who aligned themselves with GAPP's agenda by serving as volunteers, registering the concerns and complaints of Greensboro citizens regarding slumlords and police brutality, and canvassing the community for support for the organization. However, Marxist principles that promoted scientific socialism and declaimed the class contradictions inherent in a capitalistic society fell abruptly short of explaining the racism that disproportionately funneled Black people into overcrowded and underresourced ghettoes or placed them in front of a police officer's gun. And while Marxists and Black Nationalists argued back and forth in an attempt to achieve ideological hegemony, another phenomenon proceeded to undercut them both. Beginning in the mid-1960s, an increasing amount of federal and corporate money flooded Black college campuses. In the same way that the academy came calling for professors of color, various companies and firms raided Black colleges, recruiting people of color to provide a mirage of progressivism within corporate America. And HBCUs, long ignored in fields such as engineering and technology, became the surprising beneficiary of grants and research dollars that created a hard shift from the humanities, social sciences, and teacher training that the schools had largely been known for. The *A&T Register* reported that corporate recruiters were so bold as to "offer suggestions on what course to take." In 1963 A&T had only "$3,000 worth of research." By 1973, yearly research dollars topped out at $1.4 million—an astonishing increase of 466.6 percent. Developments such as these created crucial questions concerning the future strength and radical potential of the A&T communitas.[80]

As waves of Black college students readied themselves to break new barriers in the corporate world, the rapid transitions taking place within and around the movement raised questions and dilemmas that African Americans had never confronted. "The initial perspective of the young student activists was that of militant reformers," writes sociologist Rod Bush. "They wanted to make a place for themselves in the system." Yet student desires had never been purely selfish. They were indeed "the dream and the hope of the slave." Their place within "the system" was a result that millions of Black folks had prayed for and applauded. Nevertheless, the co-optation of Black college students and the communitas that produced them transformed what was once a formidable group of foot soldiers for the liberation movement into a cadre of eager recruits waiting to taste the new fruits of corporate America. The lingering question concerning their viability for the freedom struggle would be, Would Black college students use their newfound opportunities for their own material gain and thus confirm the fears of Black Marxists concerning the inherent weakness of the academy and the products of elitism and the bourgeoisie? Or would they channel the lessons of race consciousness, idealism, and cultural nationalism instilled in them through the A&T communitas into their new positions of influence and, in doing so, create new platforms of social, political, and economic power for *all* Black folks?[81]

While A&T students enjoyed their newfound fortunes, the organizations they were most closely associated with began on a slow track to implosion.

The divisions within SOBU over ideological direction led many of the officers who resided in Greensboro to direct their time and energy toward local organizing as spearheaded by GAPP, thus leaving SOBU with little direction from the national headquarters. However, the organization whose efforts had transformed Greensboro into a stronghold of the Black Power movement and served as a springboard for SOBU was on its last legs by 1974. Composed of a broad cross section of the Black community, GAPP faced struggles that demonstrated how the movement was dissipating on all fronts. Many youths were becoming disenchanted, committed adult activists clung to limited resources, and the white power structure strengthened its efforts to suppress the demands of the once-formidable organization. "GAPP is at a low point: we have no money; there is no program; the board is confused, disorganized and weak; the staff is virtually non-existent," wrote Nelson Johnson. "We have reached a point where a clear decision must be made. We must declare whether we are going to close shop and go home or whether we are going to reorganize, reconstruct, and, indeed rebuild." GAPP's legacy is one that deserves greater study. Despite its brief life, GAPP not only was one of the most effective local organizations but also left a strong national imprint. SOBU and its offshoots could all trace their developmental roots back to the mobilization that was the direct result of the North Carolina nationalists chiefly residing in Greensboro and in the shadows of North Carolina A&T.[82]

The A&T model illustrates the formidable strength of HBCUs as a source for agency during the height of the civil rights movement. Black colleges were just as central to the flowering of the Black Power movement as they were to the wave of overt activism that first unfolded on college campuses in 1960. Students at A&T were profoundly shaped by their peers, their professors, and the messages of defiance they received from campus visitors who promoted the rhetoric of revolution that was already found on campus. It is no surprise, therefore, that Black Power organizations like SOBU and GAPP were directly linked to educational institutions such as A&T that served as enclaves, producing idealism and ultimately spawning a rebellion that revitalized the concepts of freedom and democracy for all Americans.

Epilogue

It's a Different World: The Rise of the Hip-Hop Generation and the Corruption of the Black College Communitas

••

So what took place was that the Black schools were being raided by the white schools with their own faculty being offered tenured positions and higher salaries. Younger Black scholars who were just coming out of the graduate schools—and there weren't very many of them at the time—would literally have their pick of really good jobs, lots of time for research, light course loads, at predominantly white institutions with usually the promise that their minority recruitment would be stepped up and they would have an active role to play in Black Studies programs.

—John Dittmer, former professor at Tougaloo College

It was one of those seminal moments in my youth when I thought I had arrived. It was January 1988; I was a twelve-year-old Black kid growing up in a middle-class Black neighborhood, enamored with the hip-hop culture that was quickly swallowing every element of pop life in America; and there I sat, glued to my television set, immersed in an episode of *A Different World*. It was a new comedy series that everyone was talking about, a spinoff from *The Cosby Show* set on the campus of Hillman College, a fictional historically Black college (HBCU) in the Hampton Roads area of Virginia. One of the star characters was Dwayne Wayne, a lanky and witty nerd who sported a pair of flip-up sunglasses while pursuing (and being rejected by) all of the beautiful women on campus. But this episode from the first season was different. Not only did Dwayne end the episode by walking into the campus eatery with an incredibly gorgeous woman who most of his peers thought was out of his league, but the scene faded to black while pumping the sounds of Eric B and Rakim's song "I Know You Got Soul," sampling the infectious lead guitar riff of Bobby Byrd's song of the same title. The inclusion of a record from what is widely considered to be one of the greatest albums in hip-hop history was an important crossroads in Black popular culture. Simultaneously, the scene perfectly captured the convergence of Black masculinity and hip-hop and made the idea of attending Black colleges cool, signaling that both hip-hop and Black colleges had arrived in prime time. As the episode's credits rolled, I knew two things moving forward: I wanted to be like Dwayne Wayne, the smart, precocious, and cool nerd who got the girl in the end, and I was most definitely attending a historically Black college.

Indeed, Black colleges experienced something of a renaissance through the late 1980s and early 1990s. During a period when African American students were increasingly exploring their options for enrolling in predominantly white institutions (PWIs), film director Spike Lee placed a powerful yet highly dramatized depiction of the Black college communitas front and center with the theatrical release of his film *School Daze* in 1988. Soon after, a first-time director named John Singleton released *Boyz n the Hood*, a critically acclaimed 1991 hip-hop drama set in South Central Los Angeles at the height of gang warfare and the crack epidemic. A fairy-tale ending allows the main character, Tre, and his love interest, Brandi, to escape their harsh environment and set off for Morehouse and Spelman, two prestigious HBCUs located in Atlanta.

A new fashion company called African American College Alliance (AACA) outfitted hip-hop and pop culture celebrities with sweatshirts and T-shirts emblazoned with the names of Black institutions. Watching these performers don the AACA gear on shows like *Arsenio Hall, In Living Color, Yo!MTV Raps, Rap City, Martin,* and HBO's *Def Comedy Jam,* an entire generation of Black youths rushed out to pick up clothing celebrating institutions that most white Americans had never heard of. I vividly remember my amazement and joy when one of the era's greatest rappers, Redman, sported a sweatshirt displaying the name of my hometown HBCU, Winston-Salem State University, in his "Time 4 Sum Aksion" video.

And then of course there was *A Different World* itself. The popular sitcom ran for six seasons, from 1987 to 1993, boldly taking on a variety of heavy issues while exposing America to its vision of Black college life. Indeed, by the second season, the show's new director, Debbie Allen, revamped the sitcom to illustrate the vital and historic role Black colleges played in nurturing Black youths and effectively politicizing them on various issues. The show explored race consciousness around campus, highlighting topics such as South African apartheid, classism and colorism within the Black community, date rape, the 1992 Los Angeles Riots and police brutality, HIV/AIDS, homelessness, white privilege, and the crisis of survival for Black businesses, just to name a few. The renaissance of HBCUs reached a crowning moment in 1997 when Florida A&M, a Black college located in Tallahassee with its own storied history, was crowned *Time* magazine's and the *Princeton Review*'s "College of the Year."[1]

Yet all was not well with HBCUs. For all of the attention they received from musicians, media, and pop culture, during the very same era, HBCUs' historic ability to foster Black radical thought and deeds was being tested. In the wake of the civil rights movement, Black colleges, like many institutions historically rooted in the Black community, faced a three-pronged assault.

First, these critically important institutions had to reckon with the challenges of integration. They were sapped by a Black "brain-drain" as both talented students and Black faculty left for "greener pastures." With the bulk of talented, race-conscious faculty slowly being siphoned off to PWIs, the historic and nurturing relationship between faculty and the critical mass of Black students that had previously been formed almost exclusively within the environment of Black colleges was severely undercut. Second, the curriculum itself faced serious challenges. The promise of corporate and STEM (science, technology, engineering, and mathematics) jobs, which offered a higher earning potential after graduation caused many to steer clear of the humanities. Potential activists were less and less likely to take the traditional courses that had the potential to politicize them. Last, years of historic underfunding exacerbated these institutions' internal struggles, marring relationships between trustee board members, administrators, faculty, and students, and thus created a public relations nightmare that effectively weakened the brand of HBCUs and prevented a new generation of potential students and faculty from considering matriculation and work on Black college campuses. The vital space that had cultivated and molded generations of Black youths had entered into "a different world" of its own. The resulting corruption of the HBCU communitas still reverberates to this day.

· · · · · ·

As the 1960s drew to a close, a host of developments emerged to pacify and mitigate the militancy of Black youths. Following a decade of effective protests, African Americans integrated into white institutions of power in far greater numbers. Many of them channeled the energies of the civil rights movement into those institutions, forcing corporations, universities, and other private and public industries to adjust. Within higher education, this movement produced Black studies departments and Black student centers on predominantly white college campuses. In the business world, these dynamics supported affirmative action hiring, which brought well-trained Black students into the fold of corporate America for the very first time. Critical as these advances were to Black empowerment, they weakened traditional Black institutions. Black colleges, secondary schools rooted in Black communities, and even neighborhoods themselves were experiencing vast transformations that changed the historic roles these institutions had played in buttressing the advancement of African Americans.

The position of disadvantage from which HBCUs would operate was foreshadowed as early as World War II. Originally referred to as the Servicemen's Readjustment Act, the GI Bill was enacted in the summer of 1944, providing unprecedented access to a college education. This caused enrollment rates at numerous institutions to balloon, allowing trustees and administrators to demand increased funding and improved infrastructure from state legislators and private benefactors alike. The postwar upsurge meant something different for HBCUs. In spite of increased enrollment, systemic racism ensured that Black colleges were cut off from the state and federal resources that PWIs enjoyed. Thousands of Black veterans were reluctantly turned away from institutions that simply could not accommodate them. Historian Ira Katznelson concludes, "Without funds and facilities, there simply was insufficient room. By contrast, 'flagship universities like the University of Wisconsin and the University of Michigan in the North and the University of Texas and the University of Alabama in the South were able to expand rapidly to meet the needs of returning veterans under the G.I. Bill.'"[2]

The upsurge in enrollment and government funding had a snowball effect for PWIs. By enrolling more students, they enlarged their alumni databases, further profiting from the fact that their mostly white graduates could enter a world with few socioeconomic barriers, allowing them to swiftly return generous donations to their alma maters in the name of institutional progress. Many of these institutions thrived in the postwar years, investing in campus infrastructure and bells and whistles that looked particularly attractive when compared to HBCUs still hampered by segregation. Throughout the late 1960s, and into the present day, Black athletes were seduced away from the Black colleges where they had traditionally matriculated with the promise of assuming a position on the "big stage." Their athletic talents further increased the coffers of PWIs, as collegiate sports became a billion-dollar industry in the 1980s and beyond.[3] By the time an influx of Black student applications arrived during the years following the civil rights movement, numerous PWIs basked in the glow of increased funding, swelling endowments, and improved infrastructure, all thanks to postwar, GI Bill–induced largesse from which HBCUs had been systematically excluded. The higher salaries, plethora of full scholarships, and lush resources that PWIs dangled in front of would-be Black faculty and student recruits had come about in large part through the continued marginalization of and systemic discrimination against the nation's historic Black colleges.

The Black college communitas was not completely broken, but the privileging of STEM fields would further undermine the intellectual foundations of Black militancy. The idealism, race consciousness, and cultural nationalism that defined the second curriculum had fed the freedom dreams of Black college students for generations. It was powered by faculty who operated out of departments and programs that stimulated critical thought. Students, in turn, linked those ideas with the messages that they received from visiting speakers, returning alumni, and sometimes administrators themselves. Following the climax of the civil rights movement, however, those departments were increasingly marginalized. Almost every major financial investment coming into HBCUs was being funneled toward the hard sciences. Social science programs and humanities departments languished. After a brief bump at the beginning of the 1970s, enrollment in the humanities suffered a precipitous dip toward the end of the decade and flatlined for almost the next forty years with negligible gains. Black colleges, which had originally been founded to train ministers and teachers, witnessed education majors plummet at the beginning of the 1970s, while STEM fields steadily rose from the mid-1960s and skyrocketed with the dawn of the 1990s. This same period witnessed fairly new fields such as communications, architecture, vocational studies, and social work undergoing exponential growth, ballooning from just a couple hundred majors in 1966 to over ten thousand by 2014.

While this growth clearly reflected the boom in tech fields and the demand for workers in this area, the impact on HBCUs was significant. Black colleges had served as the primary sites where generations of teachers in training became practitioners of the second curriculum. College students embraced Negro History Week with great pride and enthusiasm and went out to serve students of their own, teaching them that Black folks had a past to be proud of and a mission of uplift to fulfill. Without a critical mass of Black teachers receiving this training and with scores of Black youths increasingly being instructed by white teachers who were desensitized to or unaware of the holistic nature of Black education, the partnership between traditionally Black schools, neighborhoods, and community institutions was transformed, leaving in its wake fragments of a broken and only partially successful movement for liberation.

Perhaps one of the oddest blows to HBCUs in the late twentieth century came in the arena of public relations. Whether or not the stigma was deserved, Black colleges developed a reputation for being archaic in their business dealings, indifferent to students' concerns for modernization and better customer service, and unbearable in their workspaces. Professors tended to be saddled with massive teaching loads in paternalistic environments that lacked shared governance and competitive pay. There was not a student throughout the latter half of the twentieth century who did not dread having to deal with financial aid offices, register for classes, or secure campus housing—all three encounters were routinely punctuated by long lines, frustration, and confusion. Limited resources stifled the abilities of many HBCUs to modernize their business practices successfully, thus compounding many of these conditions.

While conveying horror stories to family and friends, many students and alumni vowed to withhold financial support or opted instead to send their children to the relatively flush PWIs rather than their alma maters. Like many public relations issues, the controversy over poor customer service and broken business models contained both elements of truth and large doses of fiction. It did not matter that students attending PWIs also shared many of these experiences; the stigma of inefficiency was almost unshakable for Black colleges and in many ways still haunts them today.

As the hip-hop generation came of age in the 1980s and 1990s, the HBCU communitas was in a state of crisis. Although the Black radical tradition had been nurtured by the racialized spaces of institutions such as Bennett, Alabama State, Southern University, and North Carolina A&T, it was an open question whether Black colleges would hold the same meaning and serve the same purpose for a generation already alive to the spirit of race consciousness thanks to the music of hip-hop artists like Public Enemy, KRS-One, and Ice Cube. Artists such as these forthrightly and unapologetically expressed political militancy through the music that the burgeoning hip-hop generation readily consumed. Fortunately, in spite of the vast challenges that Black colleges faced in the postsegregation era, students attending HBCUs in the 1980s and 1990s found lingering messages of political and social consciousness within the communitas that complimented the overt militancy found within the subgenre known as conscious hip-hop. Black college students targeted issues such as South African apartheid, became

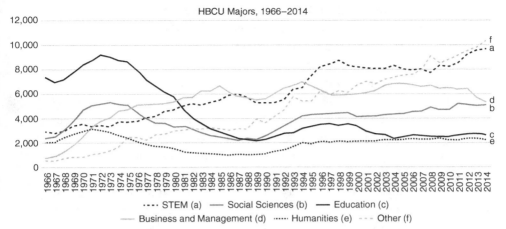

HBCU Majors, 1966–2014

···· STEM (a)   —— Social Sciences (b)   —— Education (c)
—— Business and Management (d)   ······ Humanities (e)   --- Other (f)

As the Black Power era dawned, HBCUs were increasingly courted by corporations and STEM-related industries with research grants and external funding. In large part, students were lured to these new fields due to the promise of higher salaries. The result was an erosion of the importance of majors such as teaching, social sciences, and the humanities, which had effectively politicized generations of students in the past. Table generated by Rhonda V. Sharpe using IPEDS (Integrated Postsecondary Education Data System) Completions Survey, https://ncsesdata.nsf.gov/webcaspar/.

involved in the campaigns of a host of politicians who inserted themselves into local and national politics, and continued to fight for the survival of HBCUs by demanding equitable funding and staving off attempts to close or merge several historic institutions.

However, Black student protest objectives in the 1980s and 1990s come across as markedly reactionary compared to the proactive crusade for social and political justice that had defined student activism in years past. Whether because they were blinded by the hypercapitalism and mass consumption that defined the 1980s or for some other reason, many Black college students en masse appeared to ignore the rampant mass incarceration, environmental racism, and other forms of institutionalized white supremacy that continued to plague the Black experience in America. Furthermore, an intense generational divide created a chasm between the activists of the modern civil rights movement and the new hip-hop generation. Indeed, numerous veterans of the movement have noted that there had been a failure to pass the torch of activism from one group to the next. In response to that development, Hollis Watkins, a well-known veteran of the civil rights movement, declared, "That's part of the reason that I totally promote the intergenerational model. . . . So I think part of what we can do is that, we provide a safe place for young people to intimately be involved in what is going on today with us, those of us that are still attempting to do things."[4] Without the direction and instruction of past generations in how to channel their energies, historic moments such as the Million Man March in 1995 and the Million Woman March in 1997 successfully built new networks of activists but often fizzled with little fruit to bear. While an argument can be made that perhaps new protest models were needed for a new generation, the failure to readily consult and develop working partnerships with veterans of the civil rights movement who could offer counsel on past mistakes and pitfalls can only be interpreted as a missed opportunity.

As we move into the twenty-first century, new voices and scholarship have emerged that challenge us to rethink the critical importance of space. In her most recent book, *Lost in the USA: American Identity from the Promise Keepers to the Million Mom March*, historian Deborah Gray White has forced us to reconsider the surge of mass protest marches that dotted the political landscape of the 1990s. White argues that well-meaning gatherings of various groups with varied political interests represented a generation of Americans in search of something. "It is that identities were in flux during the postmodern 1990s, and the mass gatherings of the decade were therapeutic places where people did not just express their identity but where they sought new identities as well," argues White. "People went to the marches and gatherings because they felt lost and were seeking a more settled place in the country they called home. Some found what they were looking for; others did not."[5]

The generation that produced the largest collection of youth protests the nation had ever seen called the communitas of Black colleges home. "The yard," a euphemism and term of endearment adopted by Black college students to describe the intimate spaces of the HBCU campus, formed a critical enclave for the hip-hop generation too. There was nurturing on the yard. One could be edified and made to believe in oneself on the yard. The yard always welcomed you back. One could simply be Black on the yard without having your place, your intellect, or your humanity called into question. As historian Manning Marable noted, the educational enclaves crafted by generations of Black folks provided a "sense of dignity, and a sense of mission."[6] Even when institutions caved to the pressures of state legislators and expelled numerous students who participated in overt public protests, Black colleges still provided a vital and enriching communitas that utilized its interstitial spaces to pass on messages of resistance and dissent. Indeed, many of the students who were expelled in the early 1960s resurfaced at other HBCUs that took them in.

In essence, during the 1990s, scores of Black youths and would-be activists became disenchanted and unmoored from the traditional spaces that had shaped and molded previous generations. This was coupled with the fact that many of those spaces became corrupted and dislodged from their original purpose and mission. In a 2008 speech delivered at Cornell University, cultural critic Mark Anthony Neal connected the postindustrial economy to the elimination of jobs and corruption of institutions in the Bronx, New York, just as the hip-hop generation arrived on the scene. Neal posited the idea that "recipes were being lost" and traditions eroded in large part due to the destruction of these critical spaces that had once given Black youths a style to model and a vision to run with. According to Neal, not only did the socioeconomic phenomenon known as "white flight" undercut the tax base, but so too did "Black flight," which also threatened the long-term ability for Black youths to be directly nurtured by past generations within meaningful and historical spaces. Neal recalled jazz-funk trumpeter Tom Browne, a Jamaica, Queens, resident, and keyboardist Bernard Wright being mentored and trained in the neighborhood by members of jazz legend Duke Ellington's band when they were not on tour. A vital relationship and apprenticeship took shape in a space that teemed with cultural resonance, one that was directly linked to the freedom dreams of Black folks. "What happens when there is no longer an institutional base in these spaces that allows for an articulation of Black cultural expression to be passed on from one generation to another?" asked Neal. "And it wasn't just about music right, it's about language, it's about certain kinds of moral sensibilities, right, it's a range of stuff that gets lost, right, when there are no longer institutions in our communities that allow for us to reproduce our sense of what it is to be Black and brown in these spaces."[7] In light of such developments, Neal contends that scores of Black youths who came of age in the 1980s and 1990s, including himself, carved out spaces of their own and either politicized themselves or allowed the sounds of hip-hop to inform their visions of Black liberation.

Neal's commentary reminds us that in the high-stakes game of nurturing future generations, space matters. For Black students, the intellectual traditions and training that had previously challenged youths to think critically about racial barriers that affected African Americans, and to serve as the progenitors of change as they encountered those obstructions in their various walks of life, happened almost exclusively under the auspices of the Black college communitas. A new question emerged: With an increasing number of Black college students attending PWIs in the postsegregation era, how would their matriculation in those spaces affect their own personal experiences and change the tone and tenor of Black student protests in the late twentieth century and into the next millennium?

Black student activism both on Black college campuses and at PWIs persisted through the rise of the hip-hop generation. As had been the case in the late 1960s and 1970s, much of the student activism generated on predominantly white campuses targeted the colleges themselves. Inclusion had long been a dominant theme of Black activism, yet what many students sensed at these institutions was an absence of empathy for the Black experience, both on campus and at large. Many students felt threatened and isolated, feelings that were compounded by the failure to address the systemic racism found at various levels across the nation's predominantly white colleges. Historian Richard M. Breaux documents that "between 2002–2009 at least 15 Blackface, twenty six noose, twenty-four neo–Ku Klux Klan, and over 260 racist email, sign-flyer, or graffiti incidents hit the American university with a vengeance." During Black History Month in 2014, a noose was found tied around the neck of the statue of civil rights icon James Meredith on the campus of the University of Mississippi. In 2015 explosive incidents of racial intolerance at the University of Oklahoma and the University of Missouri were brought to national attention through the power of social media. The latter incident led to a boycott by Black football team members who refused to play for the school until the university president resigned. Tragically, hate crimes, acts of intolerance, and attempts to extinguish Black protests have continued to be distinguishing characteristics of the Black student experience on predominantly white campuses.[8]

While the protests by Black students attending PWIs were indeed significant—and, in the case of Missouri, highly effective—the hostility of the space itself remained glaring. As has been the case since Black students began entering PWIs en masse, students and faculty have attempted to reckon with this hostility through the formation of Black culture centers; the reinterpretation and creation of living and learning centers based on race, culture, and ethnicity; and even separate commencements that provide students of color an opportunity to exit the university on their own cultural terms. All of these manifestations on predominantly white college campuses developed as an attempt to provide shelter in a time of racial hostility on campus and provide students with an enriching, welcoming, and supportive environment.

While these phenomena can all be interpreted as supportive measures to help students of color excel, they can also be seen as attempts to re-create the communitas of HBCUs in a space antithetical to racial consciousness.[9] In a 2015 article, *New York Times* columnist Charles Blow empathized with Black protesters in search of a campus enclave by looking back on his own youthful maturation and fondly recalling, "There existed for me a virtual archipelago of racial sanctuaries, places—communities, churches, schools— where I could be insulated from the racial scarring that intimate proximity to racial hostility can produce. That is, I assume, what these students want as well."[10] In contrast, Black students fighting to change PWIs have exhibited symptoms associated with what education professor William A. Smith refers to as "racial battle fatigue." Many Black students from PWIs have come away exhausted, frustrated, and reeling from simply trying to live and operate in a space historically reserved for whites.[11]

The formula for mass protest and sustained insurgency among youth was perfected at HBCUs before the rise of the hip-hop generation. The second curriculum ethos established a mission and delivered a purpose to countless students who worked methodically to counter white supremacy wherever they found it. In her keynote address at Harvard's inaugural 2017 all-Black graduation, newly minted alumna Courtney Woods declared of her alma mater, "Harvard's institutional foundation is in direct conflict with the needs of Black students." She continued, "There is a legacy of slavery, epistemic racism and colonization at Harvard, which was an institution founded to train rising imperialist leaders. This is a history that we are reclaiming."[12] Wood's assessment of Harvard's institutional history and purpose strikes a far different tone from the collective histories of the nation's HBCUs that maintained a commitment to uplift, service, and the dogged pursuit of full liberation for African Americans. Indeed, inscribed on the campus bell that adorns Bennett College are the instructions, "Proclaim liberty to the captives and the opening of the prison to them that are bound," words from the Old Testament that have illuminated a path to protest for generations of Bennett women.

In a nation founded on the principles of white supremacy and exclusivity, and in an era in which people boldly mock the very concepts of "social justice" and "progressive," what can we extrapolate from the history of our nation's HBCUs? American studies professor Roderick A. Ferguson reminds us, "History shows us that the modern Western university was erected as an institution fundamentally antagonistic to every-day people in general and people of color in particular. . . . And so we find ourselves in institutions that—for the most part—have never cared to fully imagine us."[13]

Yet the same cannot be said for HBCUs. The Institute for Colored Youth, first opened in 1837 and now known as Cheyney State University, has dedicated its long history to not only fully imagining the holistic abilities of Black youths but also feeding the freedom dreams of people such as Octavius Catto, Fanny Jackson Coppin, Leslie Pinckney Hill, and countless others who thrived within its communitas. These men and women became freedom fighters in large part due to the communitas that they were exposed to, which helped them develop a sense of linked fate with the masses and embrace forms of dissent that pressed America on its abiding paradox of democracy and citizenship *for all*. It is conceivable to assume that without these institutions, a broad movement for inclusivity and liberation would have never reached the heights and explosive tension that it did in the turbulent 1960s or resulted in legislation that radically transformed American democracy. Space matters.

For these historic institutions and incubators for student activism, the future is uncertain. Due to years of past discrimination and neglect, many of them are beleaguered and struggling to stay afloat. Others are continuing to open their doors to the masses as they have for over a century. Attempts to remedy historic and systemic inequality and chronic underfunding have offered a mixed bag of results. Legal cases in both Mississippi and Maryland have created a precedent for Black colleges to seek equity through litigation, and these strides have been meaningful to students and alumni. Nevertheless, sociologist Melissa Wooten makes the case that HBCUs have not done enough to clearly outline the meaning of race and its role in higher education, a position that is increasingly challenged by those who posit the baseless theory of a postracial America. "Until advocates articulate to the public and policymakers why race still matters and its effect on issues related to higher education," declares Wooten, "then it will not be clear why Black colleges are still a necessary part of the higher education system."[14] The critiques and criticisms of HBCUs' failures to adapt to the quickly shifting landscape of the postsegregation era do not end there. Scores of education scholars have compiled studies that hold Black colleges accountable for rigid social conservatism, low graduation rates, lack of shared governance, and the persistence of a dated in loco parentis atmosphere that smacks of the conservatism of college campuses before the 1960s.[15]

While all of those issues underscore critically important social and cultural problems that need to be addressed, Black colleges must also strive to become more competent guardians and caretakers of their historical legacies. Such goals are undermined when humanities and social science programs that could best flesh out and contextualize those histories are neglected in favor of STEM, business, or other fields. Far too many of these institutions also devalue their archives and place the professionals whose job it is to preserve and catalog those legacies in dismal conditions with little support or appreciation for the work that they do. Indeed, my original plan for this book was to include in the study a specific HBCU in the Deep South that possesses a rich history of activism. This plan was thwarted upon learning that the archivist at that institution, and the archives themselves, would only be available and open to receiving me as a researcher two days a week. Another institution opened its doors to me, only revealing archives in disrepair and suffering from severe neglect—clearly on display when I discovered a letter from W. E. B. DuBois to the college president stuffed and crumbled in an old file cabinet. With numerous institutions sitting on a virtual treasure trove of unprocessed papers that languish in environmental conditions that undermine their preservation, now is the time to act, reclaim, and glean wisdom from those collective histories. Shutting out those who wish to further understand one's legacy, or failing to preserve that legacy adequately, can consign a legacy to be forgotten.

In spite of these limitations, the intensification of hostile rhetoric and hate crimes on PWI campuses has seemingly brought the alternative space offered by Black colleges sharply back in focus for a new generation. Enrollment at HBCUs has been on the rise since 2015. While there have been no scientific studies or surveys yet that definitively explain the recent upsurge, many conclude that the acerbic and vitriolic language of the far right wing that questions and threatens the very presence of minority students at PWIs has led to this recent trend.[16] In post–World War II America, it took a movement emanating in large part from the country's Black colleges to dismantle Jim Crow policies and topple barriers that had marginalized generations of African Americans. Yet those policies never fully deteriorated, instead becoming even more insidious in American institutions as the hip-hop generation came of age. New policies were crafted that trapped scores of youths in underperforming schools, created school-to-prison pipelines, exposed entire neighborhoods to toxic waste and environmental racism, neglected soaring unemployment among African American youths, witnessed the erosion of voting rights gained just fifty years earlier, and birthed a seemingly endless practice of police brutality that has continued to claim the lives of unarmed citizens as it has for decades. If students are returning to HBCUs in the midst of these festering problems afflicting the Black community, will a thriving second curriculum meet them there and arm them with the intellectual tools necessary to tackle these issues as it did for youths in generations past?

Mack Jones, an esteemed scholar of the Black experience who has spent much of his personal and professional life attending, teaching, and researching these vital spaces, offers a point of concern. "It is not clear that Black colleges, or the Black community as a whole, for that matter, have developed useful descriptions of the current reality that besets us as a people and determined the appropriate role of the Black college in the continuing struggle for racial equality," argues Jones. "In my view it is imperative that we do so now because we are at a critical juncture in both the struggle for racial equality and in the history of the Black college as a national and community resource. We need to launch a national effort for the reclamation, transformation and relevance of the Black college."[17] Jones hopes to see HBCUs become vital centers for policy making on the behalf of marginalized Black folks across the world, a concept that has been years in the making. Perhaps the closest that Black colleges came to realizing this dream was the Institute of the Black World (IBW), a national think tank founded in 1970 whose base of operation was in and around the Atlanta University Center, a consortium of HBCUs currently comprising Spelman College, Morehouse College, and Clark Atlanta University. "The IBW recognized, as did [Martin Luther] King, that true equality would require structural changes to political, economic, and cultural institutions," writes IBW historian Derrick White. "The analytical framework of civil rights was less applicable in a post–Jim Crow America, signaling a need for alternative institutions and new ideas."[18] Perhaps the visions of scholars such as Jones, coupled with a history of the success and failures of previous organizations such as the IBW, can provide useful blueprints for action that will invigorate a new generation of students to pick up where their predecessors left off.

Political and activist organizations committed to this type of work have already begun the process of developing new models. Historian and Ella Baker biographer Barbara Ransby published a piece in the *New York Times* on the parallels between Baker's model of activism, followed by SNCC, and the new models being adopted and practiced by Black Lives Matter, pointing to the strengths and the weaknesses of the latter organization. Ransby concludes that Black Lives Matter needs an "easier way for people to get in-

Students at A&T hold a "B'more Proactive Rally" to protest the death of Freddie Gray, a Baltimore man who died while in police custody in 2015. While the political landscape of HBCUs has greatly shifted in the last fifty years, students are still finding and projecting their voices on various issues. Courtesy of *Greensboro News and Record*. Photograph by *News and Record* Staff, © *News & Record*, All Rights Reserved.

volved" and a "space for broader ideological and policy debates."[19] The long history of the Black liberation movement in America illustrates that there is a lot to be said for the benefits of operating out of institutions that are rooted within the community. Black churches, schools, and colleges were the most vital spaces for the cultivation of radicalism, militancy, and action throughout the long arc of the struggle. Black colleges, in particular, primed a critical mass of young minds to reject the corrosive effects of white supremacy, to see themselves as agents for social and political change, and to link that agency to a broader vision of freedom for all marginalized people. Indeed, this development is the most unique attribute of the HBCU legacy, and it distinguishes HBCUs' collective histories from those of the host of other institutions engaged in higher education. As the twenty-first century continues, perhaps Black college campuses will welcome a new generation of youths and once again dedicate their institutional space to the type of work that can connect a critical mass of students directly with solutions that will achieve the freedom dreams of the masses.

It is without question that African Americans have experienced significant progress in the United States, particularly in the last fifty years. It is also true that Black colleges played a critical role as catalysts for politicized youths who in turn made that progress possible. In spite of class divisions, Black youths found a sense of linked fate with the masses that helped them craft visions of freedom and blueprints for action that were aimed at uplifting the race. If current and future generations of Black youths are to reignite that sense of empowerment and once again make Black colleges the epicenter of a social revolution, then they would do well to heed the words of movement veteran Stokely Carmichael. Speaking at North Carolina A&T on March 21, 1971, in honor of the eleventh anniversary of the Sharpeville Massacre in South Africa, Carmichael powerfully declared,

> You are Black students! Your people are in trouble. You have an obligation to your people. Your obligation is as students to use your analytical minds for the development of your people, not for yourselves; that's a nigger concept. It is you who must analyze the problems, you are the students, you have the analytical minds. The farmers, and the peasants, and the sharecroppers cannot do that; the breadwinners of the families cannot do that. But you have the opportunity and you have the tools at your disposal in the terms of the books and the library, it is your duty to study, it is your duty to use your minds for the benefit of your people to analyze the problems that we pose and to give us the correct solution. That is your duty. What other purpose do you serve?[20]

Acknowledgments

Shelter in a Time of Storm gave me new perspective on the term "labor of love." When my graduate adviser first suggested this ambitious task of telling a more thorough and comprehensive story of historically Black colleges, I had no idea where that path would lead me. Indeed, the completion of this manuscript presented me with personal and professional challenges that introduced me to the highest highs, as well as the lowest lows. I can only pray that what lies within is an accurate and honest assessment of invaluable institutions that have shaped the lives of thousands of African Americans and played a critical role in the most important social movement in American history.

While numerous people contributed to the production of this manuscript, I reserve a special acknowledgment for five scholars who directly impacted my life and work in an incredibly meaningful way. I extend a posthumous thank-you to William E. Nelson Jr. Nick, as he was so fondly called, made sure that graduate school was possible for me at the Ohio State University and took me under his wing. My cohort warmly remembered the "Nelsonian question" that Nick would hold over our heads as we discussed scholarship in his seminars. "What does this have to do with the liberation of Black people?" Nick, I hope that I have addressed that question as it pertains to Black colleges with my humble offerings here. To Leslie Alexander, you provided me a model of scholarship, excellence, and compassion as I navigated graduate school, and your constant encouragement let me know that you were deeply invested in our holistic success and matriculation. Indeed our small cohort all aspired to be just like you and we still strive to live up to the example that you set. Our kindred paths and shared life experiences will forever remain special to me. Posthumous and profound gratitude is extended to Srinivas Aravamudan. Srinivas, you invested in my work not once but twice. And without the second investment, this project would have never materialized. Thank you, my friend, for creating one of the most incredible spaces for young scholars to work through their ideas, research, write, and produce. Godspeed as you sojourn with your ancestors. To Taylor Branch, I have no words to express fully what our fateful encounter and your eventual phone call meant to me that day. I am forever indebted to you for your willingness to extend your hand to me at my lowest professional moment and to invite me along for the experience of a lifetime. You blew renewed life into my career, and I humbly thank you for acknowledging me in that way. Additional thanks to the University of Baltimore for carving out the necessary space to make our Citizenship and Freedom class possible.

All I ever wanted to do was to be like my big brother Hasan Kwame Jeffries. Hasan, you pushed and shaped this project more than anyone and molded me into the scholar that I am today. Your arrival at the Ohio State University allowed me to flourish. As Nas would say, you gave me "a style to run with," from your brilliant scholarship to your impeccable dress. I have always sought to make you proud, and I hope that this book certainly does that.

To my editor, Brandon Proia, I cannot adequately describe the feeling that overcame me when I first described this book to you and observed your enthusiasm about this project. As you read through my drafts and welcomed me into the University of North Carolina Press family, I quickly learned why everyone was so excited about the "new guy at UNC." You have been invaluable to me along this journey, and I see why you are a master at your craft. Special thanks to the UNC Press Board of Governors for valuing the manuscript, and additional thanks to my anonymous reviewers, who offered their brilliant insight and suggestions on how to strengthen the work. I am also extremely grateful to the entire editorial and marketing team at the University of North Carolina Press; your professionalism and dedication is par excellence.

· · · · · ·

The intellectual seeds of this manuscript were first planted while I was a graduate student enrolled in a course taught by the incredible Beverly M. Gordon at The Ohio State University. The course was entitled The History of Black Education. Dr. Gordon introduced us to the works of scholars who are titans in this field. I was indelibly impacted by the scholarship of Vanessa Siddle Walker, James Anderson, and V. P. Franklin. They wrote the type of history that I could only aspire to write, but I strove to emulate their prose and tell the type of bold stories that illuminated the critical role that Black educators played in transforming the social and political contours of our country through the instruction of their students. I would be remiss not to acknowledge you all as my academic heroes, and I thank you for lighting my path. I hope that my offering here is an important continuation in the profound work that you all have accomplished.

To my Clayton State University family, I am deeply appreciative for the encouragement that you have provided to me as I have wrapped up this project. Beyond providing what financial resources were available to back my scholarship, you also enthusiastically welcomed me into your community. Thank you to Mari Roberts, Khalilah Ali, Eric Bridges, Shannon Cochran, Erica Dotson, Virginia Bonner, Roberto Gibraltarik, Ebony Gibson, Christina Grange, Barbara Goodman, Joe Johnson, Taralyn Keese, Marko Maunula, Susan Copeland, Rafik Mohamed, Robert Pfeiffer, Leon Prieto, Christopher Ritter, Adam Tate, J. Celeste Walley-Jean, Eckart Werther, Christopher Ward, and LaJuan Simpson Wilkey for being incredibly supportive colleagues. Additional thanks to the College of Arts and Sciences and the Clayton State University Foundation for providing financial support to complete the manuscript.

The act of balancing teaching, scholarship, and service can be incredibly time consuming. Often colleagues are so saddled with various tasks that it becomes impossible or too burdensome for them to break away to accommodate additional work. Therefore, I am extremely grateful to all of those who took time out of their hectic schedules to read portions of my manuscript and offer critiques for improvement or suggest gaps that needed to be filled. I am extremely appreciative to James Anderson, Stefan Bradley, Curtis Austin, Carlton E. Wilson, Martha Biondi, Ibram Kendi, Robert Cohen, John Dittmer, Adam Fairclough, V. P. Franklin, David Garrow, Randall Jelks, Mack Jones, Anne Miller, Ted Ownby, Brett Berliner, and David Snyder for lending your intellectualism to this project. Your firm and sometimes stern corrections hopefully made this project that much stronger. And to my sister and friend Regina Holden Jennings, whose red marks first pushed me to become a better writer several years before this project was even conceived, thank you for always being there when I needed your critical eye and ear.

· · · · · ·

With very few exceptions, most Black college archives are terribly understaffed, woefully underfunded, and criminally underappreciated. Within these invaluable spaces lie records that outline the rich histories of institutions that have played a central role in the shaping of the United States. While their burdens are many, several archivists and librarians went out of their way to make sure that I had access to the materials necessary to piece this narrative together. I owe a great deal to the following people who served as gatekeepers and guardians of the treasured sources used throughout this book. Special thanks to Robert Luckett and Angela Stewart of Jackson State University; Alma Fischer and Minnie Watson of Tougaloo College; Howard Robinson and Jason Trawick of Alabama State University; F. Keith Bingham of Cheyney State University; Paul Baker, Julia Scott, Devin Stokes, and Danisha Baker Whitaker of Bennett College; Angela Proctor of Southern University; and Gail Favors, Edward Lee Love, Gloria Pitts, and James Stewart Jr. of North Carolina A&T. Special thanks to Joellen El Bashir of the Moorland-Spingarn Research Center at Howard University. I am also grateful to the archivists at the Historical Society of Pennsylvania, the Greensboro Historical Museum, the Mississippi Department of Archives and History, the Louisiana State Archives, the Montgomery County Archives, and the Alabama Department of Archives and History. Special thanks also to the former activists who allowed me to peruse and use personal and unprocessed collections. This book is forever indebted to those former students, activists, and community folks who provided me the incredible opportunity to sit down and glean from your wisdom through oral interviews, as well as those who gave the oral interviews that I found previously recorded. Your stories added a richness and depth to the manuscript that is incalculable. Special thanks to my dear friend Dorie Ladner. Much of my work and research on HBCUs began with conversations and inspiration from you. Thank you for validating my work and opening the doors of Mississippi to me as a young researcher.

· · · · · ·

In the state of North Carolina it is often said, "You are born and then you choose." As a native of the state, I grew up a lifelong fan of UNC basketball, which makes it ironically humorous to me that no other institution has supported the production of this book more than Duke University. In 2008 I was offered an opportunity to officially launch my research into historically Black colleges as an inaugural recipient of the Mellon HBCU Fellowship at the John Hope Franklin Humanities Institute. Special thanks to the aforementioned Srinivas Aravamudan, Ian Baucom, Christina Chia, John Orluk, and Mary Williams for making the FHI and Duke a true home away from home. I am also indebted to my incredible fellowship cohort from that year, Fatimah Tuggar and Dana Williams, for their friendship and support. Additionally, I thank the Mellon Foundation for making that year possible. In 2013 Duke welcomed me back once again to continue the writing phase of this project as a Humanities Writ Large Fellow. I am deeply indebted to William "Sandy" Darity for creating space for me in the African and African American Studies Department to serve as visiting faculty. I was fortunate to have a second set of cohort fellows who became very dear to me in 2013. To Jordana Dym, Elizabeth Langridge-Noti, Pierce Salguero, and Yvonne Welbon, I extend a hearty thank-you for welcoming me into your fold, and thanks to Laura Eastwood for looking after all of us. Several Duke faculty members provided mentorship and support for me during my tenures on campus. Special thanks to William Chafe, Lee D. Baker, Paul Berliner, Laurent Dubois, Thavolia Glymph, Karla Holloway, Wahneema Lubiano, Mark Anthony Neal, Rhonda Sharpe, and the late Raymond Gavins for all of your encouragement and advice. I extend an additional special thanks to my dear friend Wesley Hogan. Wes, your support and embrace of me as a scholar and a friend have meant more to me than I could ever put into words.

· · · · · ·

My first foray into Mississippi as a meager graduate student on a limited budget was spent leaning heavily on the good graces of others who were willing to open up their doors to me and provide me with shelter as I worked my way through the Magnolia State. I will never forget the kindness of the Piney Woods School, which provided me with a room as I traveled to and from Jackson. Additionally, the family of Rashida Jeffries embraced me as extended family, and I am deeply grateful to Stan and David Barton and Versie Simmons. I also was welcomed into the home of the Honorable William Truly and Generique Truly Stewart. Generique, friendship truly is "essential to the soul." I thank you, my friends.

I spent nine years of my life in Columbus, and eight of those were spent at The Ohio State University, where I grew exponentially as a scholar and as a human being. My home will always be in the African American and African Studies Department, where I first began. Thank you to Ted McDaniel, Ike Newsum, James Upton, Demetrius Eudell, and Beverly Gordon, with additional thanks extended to Shirley Turner. My matriculation and growth as a scholar were just as fruitful as I continued my education across the street in the History Department. I am forever grateful to Stephanie Shaw, Warren Van Tine, Kevin Boyle, Kenneth Andrien, and Steven Conn, for their investment in me as a young budding scholar.

My time in Columbus was bolstered by one of the greatest communities of friends one could ask for. To my awesome cohort that joined me at Ohio State in 1997 and to those that followed, I say thank you. Without the bonds that we developed, surviving graduate school would have been a challenge. Special thanks to Derrick

White, Javonne Stewart, Risikat Okedeyi, Tyree Ayers, Garrick Farria, Heather Frazier, Erica Taylor, Bayyinah Jeffries, Tonya DeVaughn, Cheria Dial, Cicero Fain, Michael Jackson, Khalilah Brown-Dean, Bo Chilton, Shakeer Abdullah, Monique Armstrong, Chantae Recasner, Robert Bennett, Dionnne Blue, Lakeyta Bonnette, Tanika H. Campbell, Damani Davis, Sarbeth Flemming, Heather Grant, Martine Jean, Esther Jones, Alvin and Zykia Lee, Aleia Long, Rich Milner, Sowande Mustakeem, Luther Palmer, Jason Perkins, Andre Patterson, Zebadiah Daniels, Ernest Perry, Travis Simmons, Larry Williamson, Vincent and Carla Willis, Eric Wilson, Donna Nicol, Tony Gass, and everyone connected with the Black Graduate and Professional Student Caucus between 1997 and 2006. I also developed bonds throughout the broader Columbus community that I leaned on heavily. On an ice-cold day in March 2000, the Alpha Rho Lambda chapter welcomed me into Alpha Phi Alpha Fraternity. Thanks to Issam Khoury, Danny Hoey, Derrick White, Mark Hatcher, Diallo Wilkerson, Dwayne Zimmerman, and Darryl Cobb for supplying a fraternal bond that helped to sustain me while in Columbus and beyond. Special thanks also to Deborah Lipscomb, Catherine Willis, Amanda Downey, Amy Cisrow Peterson, Tamara Staley, Amina Warrick, and Lester Simpson for your support and friendship.

I was Aggie born and Aggie bred. I spent much of my formative years being indoctrinated by my parents with something called Aggie Pride, and that love for North Carolina A&T State University eventually led me to attend the school as student from 1994 to 1997. My time on the yard edified me significantly in various ways. The History Department took me in and taught me how to expand my horizons, think critically, and fill in the missing pages of history. I am extremely grateful to Linda Powell Addo, Claude Barnes, Margaret Dwight Barrett, Olen Cole, Fuabeh Fonge, Peter Meyers, Conchita Ndege, and Sandrea Williamson for stoking the intellectual fires within me. A special posthumous thank-you to Wayman McLaughlin. You taught generations of students to "think outside the box" before the phrase ever became fashionable. To my college crew, thank you for all of the memories that we made then, and the ones that we are still making today. To James Clyburn, Aldea Coleman, Mkeka Copney, Greg Dugan, Melanie Jones Harrison, Greg Johnson, Robert King, DelShana Dene' LeGrant, Japhet LeGrant, Thomasina Lentz, Vondell Richmond, Alfred Shaw, Erika Simon, and Eric Tucker, Aggie Pride forever.

I am proud to share space within academia with an incredible family of scholars. Like so many others, my journey through academe has been treacherous at times, but the bonds that I shared with you all helped me to survive. I am thus forever grateful for your friendship. I am deeply appreciative to Lauren Araiza, Sherwin Bryant, Greg Carr, Daphne Chamberlain, Stephen Hall, Shirletta Kinchen, Derek Musgrove, Deirdre Cooper Owens, Walter Rucker, Jason Tatlock, Akinyele Umoja, Ben Vinson, Michael Vinson Williams, and Darius Young. I extend a special thanks to Maurice Hobson and Talitha Leflouria. Both of you really helped guide me through the final process of preparing the manuscript, and I am grateful to call you my comrades in the struggle. I am also deeply appreciative of the support that I received from my former students, Michael Cobb, Amy Cole, Darlean Conley, Ebonee Davis, Beekaa Jalata, Lasean Robinson, Rahsaan Simon, Asantewa Boakyewa, Vanessa Bowling, Diamond Powell, Gregory Washington, and Versean Truell. Thank you, my friends, for taking the initiative to work on my behalf. Your kindness will never be forgotten.

In the bleakest times of my journey, it was my "village" that saw me through. I have been incredibly blessed with a host of families whose love, prayers, smiles, and jokes ministered to my soul. To the Howell/McMillan families, Ryan and Leslie Palmer, Braxton and Rachel Davis, Ryan and Brie Buchanan, Charles and Rhonda Fischer, my good friend and brother Alvin Conteh, Michael and Kristy Lindsay, Rory and Andi Goodwin, Carlos and Courtney Ingram, Umoja and Jamercina Thomas, Seith and Elyce Mann, Rob and Nicole McCann, and Vic and Tiscia Rasco, may we never run out of jokes to tell and wonderful memories to fall back on. Your friendships have meant more to me than you will ever know.

To my Winston crew, neighborhoods like Reynolds Forest nurtured us; teachers like Madeline Gerald-Mckoy and Fleming El-Amin guided us; programs like Kenan, Project Ensure, and Upward Bound molded us; and the golden age of hip-hop was our soundtrack to it all. You all formed my first extended family, and it is true that iron sharpens iron. While that community both shrank and grew over the years, the love and respect that we have had for each other have never wavered. Special thanks to Tracy Christian, Kalli Pettigrew, Anthony Greene, Kimberly Jones Green, Patrick Douthit, Tia Watlington, Randy Kilgore, Lonnie Rice, Clea Currie, Derrick Gilliam, Joneice Peppers Pledger, Juan Davis, Russell Debnam, Darryl Barr, Lester Smith, Terry Mebane, and Okeyma Young Wright, with a posthumous thank-you to Marcus Spurgeon. Additional thanks to Scarlet Allen Linville, Tiffany Gattling, Monica Holland Lyles, and Kawasak Penn for your support through the years.

My family members have played a distinct role in supporting me through this endeavor. I am forever grateful for your continuous prayers and well wishes as my research took me from state to state. Thank you to the Favors, Goode, Hill, Lampley, Moore, Patterson, Thigpen, and Wallace families. Additional thanks to the Hodge, Phillips, Thompson, and Wheeler families. Special thanks to Tommy Williams. Tommy, your constant support, encouragement, and inquiries about the process and my progress meant a lot to me, especially when the going got rough. Thanks for showing that you cared. To my big brother Sekou Favors, in our formative and adolescent years, you were the standard bearer for excellence in our family. It gave me something to chase after, and I hope that I have made you proud over the years. May God continue to bless you and your wonderful family. Special love and thanks to my nieces, Tasneem and Lena; to my nephews, Umar, Yusef, and Zayd; and to all of the Greaves family.

To my incredible mother, Gail Favors, your warmth, kindness, and godliness have served as my foundation since birth. Thank you for enveloping our family with love, praying for me through my tribulations, and rejoicing in my triumphs. You are everything that an awesome mother should be. I extend a posthumous thank-you to my father, Paris Favors Jr. Dad, I still smile when I read your books with your notes scribbled in the margins, or say things that sound exactly like something you would have said. Although several years have passed since your transition, I think about you every day. Thank you for starting me on this journey. I pray that you are proud of what your hardheaded son has become. Rest in peace.

As this project was continuing to unfold in 2012, I received the most precious gift that any man could ever wish for—a beautiful daughter. Paris, from the moment that I learned of your conception, to the time that I first wrapped you in my arms, and until this very moment, you have brought me an unending stream of happiness. I breathe your smile, I am addicted to your laugh, I suffer to see you in pain, and I am overwhelmed with gratitude that God saw fit to bring you into my life. You are my joy—from now until "dolphins fly and parrots swim the sea."

To my wife, Knachelle, I have been toiling over finding the right words to express my gratitude to you, and I am failing. This book has been just as much a challenge to you as it has been to me. It has tested the limits of our relationship, asked for you to make extreme sacrifices, and stressed us in ways that only you and I will ever know. Perhaps my chief joy in writing this acknowledgment is knowing that these words will live on in perpetuity and that those who pick up this book and peruse its pages will know that none of it would have been possible without Knachelle Favors. Thank you. Thank you. A million times, thank you. For what you have done for me, our family, and this project that has consumed our lives, you are the true MVP of *Shelter in a Time of Storm.* I love you.

Notes

Introduction

1. California Newsreel, "SNCC 50th Reunion," filmed April 2010, YouTube video, 2:43, posted February 18, 2011, https://www.youtube.com/watch?v=aTPbNsAcy9s.

2. Within the last decade, scholars have moved quickly to answer Jacquelyn Dowd Hall's groundbreaking article that raised interest in documenting the "long movement," particularly as it relates to the Black freedom struggle. Her work has spawned critics, as well as new book-length studies that attempt to fill in the gaps of various phases, organizations, and institutions affiliated with the civil rights movement and their evolving role over time. For more on Hall's thesis, see Jacquelyn Dowd Hall, "The Long Civil Rights Movement and the Political Uses of the Past," *Journal of American History* 91, no. 4 (March 2005): 1233–63. As excellent examples for addressing the long movement, see also Nikhil Pal Singh, *Black Is a Country: Race and the Unfinished Struggle for Democracy* (Cambridge, MA: Harvard University Press, 2004); Peter Lau, *Democracy Rising: South Carolina and the Fight for Black Equality since 1865* (Lexington: University Press of Kentucky, 2006); and Hasan Kwame Jeffries, *Bloody Lowndes: Civil Rights and Black Power in Alabama's Black Belt* (New York: New York University Press, 2009). For a strong critique of the long movement theory, see Sunidata Keita Cha-Jua and Clarence Lang, "'The Long Movement' as Vampire: Temporal and Spatial Fallacies in Recent Black Freedom Studies," *Journal of African American History* 92, no. 4 (Fall 2007): 265–88.

3. For more on Brown and his place in the history of Black America, see Benjamin Quarles, *Blacks on John Brown* (Champagne: University of Illinois Press, 1972); Benjamin Quarles, *Allies for Freedom: Blacks and John Brown* (Oxford: Oxford University Press, 1974); Stephen Oates, *To Purge This Land with Blood: A Biography of John Brown* (Amherst: University of Massachusetts Press, 1984); and David S. Reynolds, *John Brown, Abolitionist: The Man Who Killed Slavery, Sparked the Civil War, and Seeded Civil Rights* (New York: Vintage Books, 2006).

4. Although the overwhelming majority of Black colleges never experienced the random acts of violence that so commonly afflicted other Black institutions, these structures at times did come under serious threat. On April 14, 1865, the same day that President Abraham Lincoln was assassinated, Wilberforce College, a Black school founded in 1854, was victimized by arson. The attack on Wilberforce and the rising animosity toward institutions that served African Americans made noncollapsible spaces all that more valuable as Reconstruction dawned. For more on the arson attack on Wilberforce, see Horace Talbert, *The Sons of Allen: Together*

with a Sketch of the Rise and Progress of Wilberforce University (Xenia, OH: Aldine, 1906), 272; and Daniel Payne, *Recollections of Seventy Years* (New York: Arno, 1968), 153–54.

5. William H. Watkins, *The White Architects of Black Education: Ideology and Power in America, 1865–1954* (New York: Teachers College Press, Columbia University, 2001), 181–82.

6. There were a number of broad interests represented within the Niagara Movement. Consequently, whereas there are several studies detailing various individuals, causes, and organizations linked with the movement, there are few that specifically highlight the actual movement that led to the NAACP with particular detail. For those studies that do provide intimate detail, see Elliot M. Rudwick, "The Niagara Movement," *Journal of Negro History* 42, no. 3 (July 1957): 177–200; David Levering Lewis, *W. E. B. Du Bois: Biography of a Race, 1868–1919* (New York: Henry Holt, 1993); Kevin Gaines, *Uplifting the Race: Black Leadership, Politics, and Culture in the Twentieth Century* (Chapel Hill: University of North Carolina Press, 1996); Shawn Leigh Alexander, *An Army of Lions: The Civil Rights Struggle before the NAACP* (Philadelphia: University of Pennsylvania Press, 2011); and Angela Jones, *African American Civil Rights: Early Activism and the Niagara Movement* (Santa Barbara, CA: Praeger, 2011).

7. Ironically, Storer College forever closed its doors in 1955 as a result of the West Virginia legislature's pulling its financial support of the institution in the wake of the *Brown v. Board* decision argued successfully by the NAACP. For more on Storer College and its role in the early struggle for Black liberation, see "Storer College: It Was Here a Century Ago the NAACP Took Its First Steps," *Journal of Blacks in Higher Education*, no. 51 (Spring 2006): 21–22; Vivian Verdell Gordon, "A History of Storer College, Harpers Ferry, West Virginia," *Journal of Negro Education* 30, no. 4 (Autumn 1961): 445–49; Dawne Raines Burke, "Storer College: A Hope for Redemption in the Shadow of Slavery, 1865–1955" (PhD diss., Virginia Polytechnic Institute and State University, 2004); and Dawne Raines Burke, *An American Phoenix: A History of Storer College from Slavery to Desegregation* (Pittsburgh: Geyer, 2006).

8. There has been a paucity of studies that exclusively examine the long history and legacy of Black colleges and their role in producing militancy and dissent. Black education has often been lumped together to tell a collective narrative of primary, secondary, and higher education. Of these book-length treatments, a few have become classics in the field and have greatly informed this study. Among them are Henry Allen Bullock, *A History of Negro Education in the South: From 1619 to the Present* (Cambridge, MA: Harvard University Press, 1970); V. P. Franklin and James Anderson, eds., *New Perspectives on Black Educational History* (Boston: G. K. Hall, 1978); James Anderson, *The Education of Blacks in the South, 1860–1935* (Chapel Hill: University of North Carolina Press, 1988); and Adam Fairclough, *A Class of Their Own: Black Teachers in the Segregated South* (Cambridge, MA: Harvard University Press, 2007). A great deal of studies that examine the spaces of these institutions invariably approach the narrative from a top-down perspective, focusing primarily on the varied funding sources that supported Black college infrastructure,

the relationships that those governing bodies shared with HBCU administrators, and the classic debate between supporters of liberal education and those of vocational educational philosophies in the early twentieth century. While many of those studies have successfully combed through the records and primary sources of philanthropic boards, trustee minutes, and presidential papers, they have rarely examined sources that provide a fresh perspective on exactly how Black students were politicized before the modern civil rights movement. Few book-length treatments have examined the intimate space and relationship shared between faculty and students on campus and how that relationship produced various elements of Black militancy and resistance through successive generations since the founding of the first Black college in 1837. There are, however, a few studies that either apply the long movement theory to analyzing Black college activism or have produced episodic histories that examine these crucial spaces over a certain segment of time or during major events. Among these are Raymond Wolters, *The New Negro on Campus: Black College Rebellions of the 1920s* (Princeton, NJ: Princeton University Press, 1975); Jack Bass and Jack Nelson, *The Orangeburg Massacre* (Macon, GA: Mercer University Press, 1984); Robert J. Norrell, *Reaping the Whirlwind: The Civil Rights Movement in Tuskegee* (Chapel Hill: University of North Carolina Press, 1998); Hoda M. Zaki, *Civil Rights and Politics at Hampton Institute: The Legacy of Alonzo G. Moron* (Urbana: University of Illinois Press, 2007); Joy Ann Williamson, *Radicalizing the Ebony Tower: Black Colleges and the Black Freedom Struggle in Mississippi* (New York: Teachers College Press, 2008); and F. Erik Brooks, *Tigers in the Tempest: Savannah State University and the Struggle for Civil Rights* (Macon, GA: Mercer University Press, 2014). There have been a handful of book-length treatments that cast a much wider net and have produced brilliant analyses of Black student activism at both predominantly white colleges and HBCUs. Among those are Harry Edwards, *Black Students* (New York: Free Press, 1970); Martha Biondi, *The Black Revolution on Campus* (Berkeley: University of California Press, 2012); and Ibram Rogers, *The Black Campus Movement: Black Students and the Racial Reconstitution of Higher Education, 1965–1972* (New York: Palgrave Macmillan, 2012).

9. For more information on the role of philanthropy in the construction and management of Black colleges, see Alfred Perkins, *Edwin Rogers Embree: The Julius Rosenwald Fund, Foundation Philanthropy, and American Race Relations* (Bloomington: Indiana University Press, 2011); Mary Hoffschwelle, *The Rosenwald Schools of the American South* (Gainesville: University Press of Florida, 2006); Horace Mann Bond, *The Education of the Negro in the American Social Order* (New York: Octagon Books, 1966); Raymond Fosdick, *Adventure in Giving: The Story of the General Education Board, a Foundation Established by John D. Rockefeller* (New York: Harper and Row, 1962); Joe M. Richardson, *Christian Reconstruction: The American Missionary Association and Southern Blacks, 1861–1890* (Tuscaloosa: University of Alabama Press, 2009); Kenneth James King, *Pan-Africanism and Education: A Study of Race Philanthropy and Education in the Southern States of America and East Africa* (Oxford: Oxford University Press, 1971); J. L. Curry, *A Brief Sketch of George Peabody, and the History of the Peabody Educational Fund through Thirty Years* (New York: Negro Universities Press, 1969); Augustus F. Beard, *A Crusade of Brotherhood:*

A History of the American Missionary Association (Boston: Pilgrim, 1909); and Merle Curti and Roderick Nash, *Philanthropy in the Shaping of American Higher Education* (New Brunswick, NJ: Rutgers University Press, 1965).

10. I am borrowing this phrase from Chandra Guinn, director of the Mary Lou Williams Center for Black Culture at Duke University. Wesley Hogan, director of Duke's Center for Documentary Studies, first informed me that Chandra used this phrase in a discussion with her.

11. For more on Turner's theories of communitas, see Victor Turner, *The Ritual Process: Structure and Anti-Structure* (Ithaca, NY: Cornell University Press, 1969), 94–165.

12. James Weldon Johnson, *Along This Way: An Autobiography of James Weldon Johnson* (New York: Viking, 1968), 66.

13. Turner, *The Ritual Process*, 112.

14. For more on how educators, sociologists, and feminists have interpreted the "hidden curriculum," see Paulo Freire, *Pedagogy of the Oppressed* (New York: Bloomsbury, 2000); bell hooks, *Teaching to Transgress: Education as the Practice of Freedom* (New York: Routledge, 1994); and David L. Martinson, "'Defeating the Hidden Curriculum': Teaching Political Participation in the Social Studies Classroom," *Clearing House* 76, no. 3 (January–February 2003): 132–35.

15. Various sociologists have attempted to analyze the life span of social movements and pinpoint the key ingredients in their origins and their demise. While many of these sociological models are often flawed in their attempts to reduce activism to one particular formula, two of the more useful studies in this area are Doug McAdam, *Political Process and the Development of Black Insurgency, 1930–1970* (Chicago: University of Chicago Press, 1982); and Aldon Morris, *The Origins of the Civil Rights Movement: Black Communities Organizing for Change* (New York: Free Press, 1984).

16. Benjamin E. Mays, *Born to Rebel: An Autobiography* (Athens: University of Georgia Press, 2003), 41.

17. Howard Thurman, *With Head and Heart: The Autobiography of Howard Thurman* (New York: Harcourt Brace, 1979), 35.

18. For more on the rise of elitism and classism in Black America, see E. Franklin Frazier, *Black Bourgeoisie* (New York: Free Press Paperbacks, 1997); William B. Gatewood Jr., *Aristocrats of Color: The Black Elite, 1880–1920* (Fayetteville: University of Arkansas Press, 2000); David Levering Lewis, *When Harlem Was in Vogue* (Oxford: Oxford University Press, 1989); Lawrence Otis Graham, *Our Kind of People: Inside America's Black Upper Class* (New York: Harper Perennial, 1999); Jacqueline Moore, *Leading the Race: The Transformation of the Black Elite in the Nation's Capital, 1880–1920* (Charlottesville: University of Virginia Press, 1999); Gerri Major and Doris Saunders, *Black Society* (Chicago: Johnson, 1977); and Stephen Birmingham, *Certain People: America's Black Elite* (Boston: Little, Brown, 1977).

19. Maurice J. Hobson, *The Legend of the Black Mecca: Politics and Class in the Making of Modern Atlanta* (Chapel Hill: University of North Carolina Press, 2017), 227, 238.

20. Clarence Fisher, phone interview by the author, August 27, 2018.

21. Kelly Miller, "The Practical Value of Higher Education," in *The Opportunity Reader: Stories, Poetry, and Essays from the Urban League's "Opportunity" Magazine,* ed. Sondra Kathryn Wilson (New York: Random House, 1999), 415.

22. For more on the growing militancy among African Americans during the interwar period, see Glenda Elizabeth Gilmore, *Defying Dixie: The Radical Roots of Civil Rights, 1919–1950* (New York: W. W. Norton, 2008); Penny M. Von Eschen, *Race against Empire: Black Americans and Anticolonialism, 1937–1957* (Ithaca, NY: Cornell University Press, 1997); Pauli Murray, *The Autobiography of a Black Activist, Feminist, Lawyer, Priest, and Poet* (Knoxville: University of Tennessee Press, 1989); Rod Bush, *We Are Not What We Seem: Black Nationalism and Class Struggle in the American Century* (New York: New York University Press, 1999); John Egerton, *Speak Now against the Day: The Generation before the Civil Rights Movement in the South* (New York: Alfred A. Knopf, 1995); Robin D. G. Kelley, *Hammer and Hoe: Alabama Communists during the Great Depression* (Chapel Hill: University of North Carolina Press, 1990); Erik McDuffie, *Sojourning for Freedom: Black Women, American Communism, and the Making of Black Left Feminism* (Durham, NC: Duke University Press, 2011); Carol Boyce Davies, *Left of Karl Marx: The Political Life of Black Communist Claudia Jones* (Durham, NC: Duke University Press, 2008); Dayo F. Gore, *Radicalism at the Crossroad: African American Women Activists in the Cold War* (New York: New York University Press, 2011); Larry Tye, *Rising from the Rails: Pullman Porters and the Making of the Black Middle Class* (New York: Holt Paperbacks, 2005); and Paul Robeson, *Here I Stand* (New York: Beacon, 1998).

23. It is conceivable that a considerable amount of the students Hughes interviewed feigned ignorance of the Scottsboro case because the famous writer may have been considered an outsider whose on-campus agitation may have led to some students' being physically harmed or jeopardizing their academic standing. In light of the fact that numerous Black colleges carried the leading African American newspapers in their libraries and students had access to this information, it is highly unlikely that the students at Tuskegee had no knowledge of such a visible case, which occurred practically in their own backyard. For more on this, see Langston Hughes, "Coward from the Colleges," *Crisis* 41 (August 1934): 226–28.

24. W. E. B. DuBois, "Education and Work," in *The Education of Black People: Ten Critiques, 1906–1960,* ed. Herbert Aptheker (Amherst: University of Massachusetts Press, 1973), 67.

25. Steven Hahn, *A Nation under Our Feet: Black Political Struggles in the Rural South from Slavery to the Great Migration* (Cambridge, MA: Harvard University Press, 2003), 428.

26. Mays, *Born to Rebel,* 26.

27. Richard Wright, *Black Boy: A Record of Childhood and Youth* (New York: Harper and Row, 1937), 276–77.

28. The illegality of educating Blacks during slavery led to a long tradition of subversive tactics being adopted to advance educational initiatives. See Carter G. Woodson, *The Education of the Negro prior to 1861* (New York: Arno, 1968); Henry Bullock, *A History of Negro Education in the South* (New York: Praeger, 1970); Grey Gundaker, *Signs of Diaspora, Diaspora of Signs: Literacies, Creolization,*

and *Vernacular Practice in African America* (New York: Oxford University Press, 1998); Thomas Webber, *Deep like Rivers: Education in the Slave Quarter Community, 1831–1835* (New York: Norton, 1978); Janet Duitsman Cornelius, *When I Can Read My Title Clear: Literacy, Slavery, and Religion in the Antebellum South* (Columbia: University of South Carolina Press, 1991); Ronald Butchart, "'Outthinking and Out-flanking the Owners of the World': A Historiography of the African American Struggle for Education," *History of Education Quarterly* 28, no. 3 (Autumn 1988): 333–66; Janet Duitsman Cornelius, "'We Slipped and Learned to Read': Slave Accounts of the Literacy Process," *Phylon* 44 (3rd qtr., 1983): 171–86; V. P. Franklin, "'They Rose or Fell Together': African American Educators and Community Leadership, 1795–1954," in *The Sage Handbook of African American Education*, ed. Linda Tillman (Thousand Oaks, CA: Sage, 2008); David Freedman, "African-American Schooling in the South prior to 1861," *Journal of Negro History* 84, no. 1 (Winter 1999): 3; and Grey Gundaker, "Hidden Education among African Americans during Slavery," *Teachers College Record* 109, no. 7 (July 2007): 1591–612.

29. James Gregory, *The Southern Diaspora: How the Great Migrations of Black and White Southerners Transformed America* (Chapel Hill: University of North Carolina Press, 2005), 134.

30. For more information on "speech acts" as a form of activism during the Nadir, see Kidada E. Williams, *They Left Great Marks on Me: African American Testimonies of Racial Violence from Emancipation to World War I* (New York: New York University Press, 2012).

Chapter One

1. The ICY was founded in 1837 with the financial backing of Richard Humphreys, a white Quaker who reserved in his will a financial allotment to be used for the creation of an educational institute for "the descendants of the African race." The school moved from Philadelphia to Cheyney, Pennsylvania, in 1903, was renamed the Cheyney Training School for Teachers in 1914, and was renamed the State Teachers College at Cheyney in 1933. The institution is now known as Cheyney State University. Other historically Black colleges have laid claim to the title of first Black college, arguing that Cheyney was founded as a training and normal school and not a four-year, degree-granting institution. Among those institutions that lay claim to the title of first are Lincoln University, founded in 1854 as Ashmun Institute, and Wilberforce University, founded in 1856. The latter was actually the first institution of higher education to be owned and operated by African Americans, as it was a creation of the African Methodist Episcopal Church. I recognize Cheyney State University as the first Black college based on its founding date and its later evolution into a four-year, degree-granting institution. Additionally, the work being assigned to early students at the ICY was on par with that at a number of degree granting, white-only colleges at that time. For more detailed history on the founding of Cheyney and its institutional history, see Charline Howard Conyers, *A Living Legend: The History of Cheyney University, 1837–1951* (Cheyney, PA: Cheyney University Press, 1990).

2. T. Morris Chester, "Negro Self-Respect and Pride of Race," in *Pamphlets of Protest: An Anthology of Early African American Protest Literature, 1790–1860*, ed. Richard Newman, Patrick Rael, and Richard Lapsansky (New York: Routledge, 2001), 308.

3. Roger Lane, *Roots of Violence in Black Philadelphia, 1860–1900* (Cambridge, MA: Harvard University Press, 1986), 9.

4. "City Affairs," *Philadelphia Day*, January 16, 1877.

5. For further details on Kelly's arrest, escape, and criminal activity in Cincinnati, see "How Banning Was Elected," *Philadelphia Press*, January 24, 1877; and Henry H. Griffin, *The Trial of Frank Kelly for the Assassination and Murder of Octavius V. Catto, on October 10, 1871* (Philadelphia: Daily Tribune, 1888).

6. Untitled article, *Philadelphia Press*, January 24, 1877, William Dorsey Scrapbook, No. 22, Roll 2, Cheyney State University Archives.

7. "Kelly's Guilt Undoubted," *Public Record* (Philadelphia), June 28, 1877.

8. Daniel R. Biddle and Murray Dubin, "Who Was O. V. Catto?," *Philadelphia Inquirer Magazine*, July 6, 2003.

9. W. E. B. DuBois, *The Philadelphia Negro: A Social Study* (New York: Shocken Books, 1967), 40.

10. Elizabeth McHenry, *Forgotten Readers: Recovering the Lost History of African American Literary Societies* (Durham, NC: Duke University Press, 2002), 23. The histories of literary societies yield some of the most fascinating evidence of how Blacks made the connections between learning and liberation. It is further testimony of Black education's role in expanding the imagination and articulation for freedom. Studies on these societies include Tony Martin, "The Banneker Literary Institute of Philadelphia: African American Intellectual Activism before the War of the Slaveholders' Rebellion," *Journal of African American History* 87 (Summer 2002): 303–22; Jacqueline Bacon and Glen McClish, "Reinventing the Master's Tools: Nineteenth-Century African-American Literary Societies of Philadelphia and Rhetorical Education," *Rhetoric Society Quarterly* 30, no. 4 (Autumn 2000): 19–47; and Dorothy Porter, "The Organized Educational Activities of Negro Literary Societies, 1828–1846," *Journal of Negro Education* 5, no. 4 (October 1936): 555–76.

11. Minute book, 1855–1859, Banneker Institute, American Negro Historical Society Collection (hereafter ANHS Collection), Roll 1, Frame 720, Historical Society of Pennsylvania.

12. Martin Delany to Frederick Douglass, *North Star*, December 1, 1848, Moorland-Spingarn Research Center, Howard University.

13. Gary Nash, *Forging Freedom: The Formation of Philadelphia's Black Community, 1720–1840* (Cambridge, MA: Harvard University Press, 1999), 202.

14. "Minutes and Proceedings of the Third Annual Convention for the Improvement of the Free People of Colour in These United States, Held by Adjournments in the City of Philadelphia, From the 3d to the 13th of June inclusive, 1833," Leslie Pinckney Hill Papers, Cheyney State University Archives.

15. James Horton and Lois Horton, *In Hope of Liberty: Culture, Community, and Protest among Northern Free Blacks, 1700–1860* (Oxford: Oxford University Press,

1998), 168. For more on Jacksonian-era politics and the entrenchment of white supremacy in the North, see Jonathan H. Earle, *Jacksonian Antislavery and the Politics of Free Soil* (Chapel Hill: University of North Carolina Press, 2003); Leonard Curry, *The Free Black in Urban America, 1800–1850: The Shadow of a Dream* (Chicago: University of Chicago Press, 1981); Harry L. Watson, *Liberty and Power: The Politics of Jacksonian America* (New York: Hill and Wang, 2006); and James Brewer Stewart, "The Emergence of Racial Modernity and the Rise of the White North," *Journal of the Early Republic* 18 (Summer 1998): 181–217.

16. Maria W. Stewart, "What If I Am a Woman?," in *Let Nobody Turn Us Around: Voices of Resistance, Reform, and Renewal*, ed. Manning Marable and Leith Mullings (Lanham, MD: Rowman and Littlefield, 2003), 43.

17. Oliver Johnson, *William Lloyd Garrison and His Times*, in Dorothy Sterling, ed., *Speak Out in Thunder Tones: Letters and Other Writings by Black Northerners, 1787–1865* (New York: Doubleday, 1973), 85.

18. Nash, *Forging Freedom*, 259–60.

19. Horton and Horton, *In Hope of Liberty*, 169. See also Paul Finkelman, "Prelude to the Fourteenth Amendment: Black Legal Rights in the Antebellum North," *Rutgers Law Journal* 17 (Spring/Summer 1986): 415–82.

20. Julie Winch, *Philadelphia's Black Elite: Activism, Accommodation, and the Struggle for Autonomy, 1787–1848* (Philadelphia: Temple University Press, 1988), 137.

21. Martin Delany to Frederick Douglass, *North Star*, February 16, 1849, Moorland-Spingarn Research Center, Howard University.

22. Conyers, *Living Legend*, 16.

23. Conyers, 12.

24. Daniel R. Biddle and Murray Dubin, *Tasting Freedom: Octavius Catto and the Battle for Equality in Civil War America* (Philadelphia: Temple University Press, 2010), 156.

25. Roger Lane, *William Dorsey's Philadelphia and Ours: On the Past and Future of the Black City in America* (New York: Oxford University Press, 1991), 136.

26. Horton and Horton, *In Hope of Liberty*, 216.

27. Joan R. Sherman, ed., *African-American Poetry of the Nineteenth Century: An Anthology* (Urbana: University of Illinois Press, 1992), 49.

28. Benjamin Bacon, *Statistics of the Colored People of Philadelphia* (Philadelphia: Philadelphia Board of Education, 1859), 9.

29. Eric Gardner, *Unexpected Places: Relocating Nineteenth-Century African American Literature* (Jackson: University Press of Mississippi, 2009), 142.

30. Sarah M. Douglass to William Basset, December 1837, in Sterling, *Speak Out in Thunder Tones*, 96.

31. Conyers, *Living Legend*, 60.

32. Lane, *William Dorsey's Philadelphia*, 139–40.

33. Biddle and Dubin, *Tasting Freedom*, 166–67.

34. Benjamin Quarles, *Black Abolitionists* (New York: Oxford University Press, 1969), 76. For more on the free produce movement, see Carol Faulkner, "The Root of the Evil: Free Produce and Radical Antislavery, 1820–1860," *Journal of the Early Republic* 27 (Fall 2007): 377–405.

35. Jacob White Jr., "The Inconsistency of Colored People Using Slave Produce," December 30, 1852, ANHS Collection, Roll 2, Frame 1015, Historical Society of Pennsylvania.

36. Jacob C. White Jr., "Address Made on the Reception of Gov. James Pollock at the Institute for Colored Youth," May 24, 1855, Jacob C. White Papers, Historical Society of Pennsylvania.

37. Historian Harry Silcox provides a somewhat different interpretation of White's formative years. Silcox contends that there was an element of pacification embodied in the teachings of the ICY. According to Silcox, much of this was a result of its Quaker origins and its grounding in Christian doctrine. Silcox argues that Reason believed "white prejudice and abuse could be tolerated by Blacks" and proceeds to point to Reason's (and most other African Americans') belief in and teachings on the hereafter as proof of this. Contrary to Silcox's findings, Reason was an active participant in the Colored Conventions, leading the Colored Convention in Albany in 1840 and attending in Rochester, New York, in 1853, thus adding his voice to those of others who were advancing an agenda pertaining to the liberation of Blacks. This offers strong evidence that Reason brought this activist background with him to Philadelphia and exposed his students to his social and political beliefs. See *Proceedings of the Colored National Convention, Held in Rochester, July 6th, 7th, and 8th, 1853* (Rochester, NY: printed at the office of Frederick Douglass's paper, 1853); and William Pease and Jane Pease, "The Negro Convention Movement," in *Key Issues in the Afro-American Experience*, vol. 1, *To 1877*, ed. Nathan Huggins, Martin Kilson, and Daniel M. Fox (New York: Harcourt Brace Jovanovich, 1971), 191–205. For Silcox's article on White, see Harry Silcox, "Philadelphia Negro Educator: Jacob C. White, Jr., 1837–1902," *Pennsylvania Magazine of History and Biography* 97 (January 1973): 75–98.

38. Biddle and Dubin, *Tasting Freedom*, 168.

39. "Minutes and Proceedings of the Third Annual Convention for the Improvement of the Free People of Colour in These United States, Held by Adjournments in the City of Philadelphia, From the 3d to the 13th of June inclusive, 1833," Leslie Pinckney Hill Papers, Cheyney State University Archives.

40. Christopher Teal, *Hero of Hispaniola: America's First Black Diplomat, Ebenezer Bassett* (Westport, CT: Praeger, 2008), 36.

41. Teal, 42.

42. R. J. M. Blackett, *Beating against the Barriers: Biographical Essays in Nineteenth-Century Afro-American History* (Baton Rouge: Louisiana State University Press, 1986), 139–43.

43. Robert Campbell to Alfred Cope, November 17, 1856, in *The Black Abolitionist Papers*, ed. C. Peter Ripley (Chapel Hill: University of North Carolina Press, 1991), 4:353.

44. The prospect of removing African Americans from the United States was known as colonization and was variously supported, debated, and rebuked by a wide variety of Americans, such as Frederick Douglass, Martin Delany, Thomas Jefferson, and Abraham Lincoln, to name a few. This controversial idea formed the building blocks of Black Nationalism as an ideology and was seriously entertained by scores of African Americans frustrated by the constant enforcement of white

supremacy in both the North and the South. It was also embraced by numerous whites who had designs of eliminating the Black presence altogether in the United States. Nevertheless, the overwhelming majority of Blacks consistently rejected the premise of leaving their loved ones in bondage, or leaving the land that their ancestors built with their blood, sweat, and tears. For more on this topic, see Richard Blackett, "Martin Delany and Robert Campbell: Black Americans in Search of an African Colony," *Journal of Negro History* 62, no. 1 (January 1977): 1–25; Martin R. Delany and Robert Campbell, *Search for Place: Black Separatism and Africa, 1860* (Ann Arbor: University of Michigan Press, 1969); Wilson Jeremiah Moses, ed., *Classical Black Nationalism: From the American Revolution to Marcus Garvey* (New York: New York University Press, 1996); Sterling Stuckey, *The Ideological Origins of Black Nationalism* (Boston: Beacon, 1996); Phillip Magness and Sebastian Page, *Colonization after Emancipation: Lincoln and the Movement for Black Resettlement* (Columbia: University of Missouri Press, 2011); Eric Burin, *Slavery and the Peculiar Solution: A History of the American Colonization Society* (Gainesville: University Press of Florida, 2008); Sheldon Harris, *Paul Cuffe: Black America and the African Return* (New York: Simon and Schuster, 1972); Lamont D. Thomas, *Rise to Be a People: A Biography of Paul Cuffe* (Urbana: University of Illinois Press, 1986); and Charles Dixon, *African America and Haiti: Emigration and Black Nationalism in the Nineteenth Century* (Westport, CT: Greenwood, 2000).

45. R. J. M. Blackett, *Beating against the Barriers*, 150.

46. "Negro Protest over the Dred Scott Decision," *Annals of American History*, accessed July 16, 2018, http://america.eb.com/america/print?articleId=385960.

47. Lane, *William Dorsey's Philadelphia*, 140.

48. Tony Martin, "Banneker Literary Institute," 316.

49. Wendy Ball and Tony Martin, *Rare Afro-Americana: A Reconstruction of the Adger Library* (Ann Arbor: University of Michigan Press, 1981), 4.

50. F. B. Sanborn, ed., *The Life and Letters of John Brown* (New York: New American Library, 1969), 521.

51. Teal, *Hero of Hispaniola*, 44.

52. Ball and Martin, *Rare Afro-Americana*, 4.

53. Benjamin Quarles, *Allies for Freedom: Blacks and John Brown* (New York: Oxford University Press, 1974), 131–32.

54. October 12, 1861, William H. Parham to Jacob C. White Jr., Jacob C. White Collection, Moorland-Spingarn Research Center, Howard University.

55. William H. Parham to Jacob C. White Jr.

56. Harry Silcox, "Nineteenth Century Philadelphia Black Militant: Octavius V. Catto (1839–1871)," *Pennsylvania History* 44, no. 1 (January 1977): 59–60.

57. "Addresses of the Hon. W. D. Kelley, Miss Anna E. Dickinson, and Mr. Frederick Douglass, at a Mass Meeting, Held at National Hall, Philadelphia, July 6, 1863, for the Promotion of Colored Enlistments," 1863, African American Pamphlet Collection, Library of Congress.

58. Octavius Catto, *Our Alma Mater: An Address Delivered at Concert Hall on the Occasion of the Twelfth Annual Commencement of the Institute for Colored Youth, May 5th, 1864* (Philadelphia: C. Sherman, Son, 1864), 4–5.

59. "Proceedings of the National Convention of Colored Men, Held in the City of Syracuse, N.Y., October 4, 5, 6, and 7, 1864; with the Bill of Wrongs and Rights, and the Address to the American People," in *Minutes of the Proceedings of the National Negro Conventions, 1830-1864*, ed. Howard Holman Bell (New York: Arno, 1969), 9.

60. Hugh Davis, *"We Will Be Satisfied with Nothing Less": The African American Struggle for Equal Rights in the North during Reconstruction* (Ithaca, NY: Cornell University Press, 2011), 19.

61. "Proceedings of the National Convention," 18.

62. Preamble and Constitution of the Pennsylvania Equal Rights League, Historical Society of Pennsylvania.

63. For more on the stratification of economic classes and the role of Philadelphia's Black elite in the early civil rights movement, see Julie Winch, *Philadelphia's Black Elite: Activism, Accommodation, and the Struggle for Autonomy, 1787-1848* (Philadelphia: Temple University Press, 1988).

64. Hugh Davis, *"Satisfied with Nothing Less,"* 28-29.

65. Linda M. Perkins, *Fanny Jackson Coppin and the Institute for Colored Youth, 1865-1902* (New York: Garland, 1987), 13-49.

66. Fanny Jackson Coppin, *Reminiscences of School Life, and Hints on Teaching* (Philadelphia: A.M.E. Book Concern, 1913), 14.

67. Biddle and Dubin, *Tasting Freedom*, 242-43.

68. Pennsylvania Equal Rights League, minutes of the executive board, 1864-1868, ANHS Collection, Historical Society of Pennsylvania.

69. W. E. B. DuBois, *The Souls of Black Folks* (New York: Signet Classic, 1995), 55.

70. Biddle and Dubin, *Tasting Freedom*, 326.

71. "A Synopsis of the Proceedings of the Second Annual Meeting of the Pennsylvania State Equal Rights League, at Pittsburg, August 8th, 9th, and 10th, 1866," ANHS Collection, Roll 9, Frame 738, Historical Society of Pennsylvania.

72. "To the Honorable the Senate and House of Representatives of the United States, in Congress Assembled," February 20, 1866, ANHS Collection, Roll 9, Frame 762, Historical Society of Pennsylvania.

73. Hugh Davis, *"Satisfied with Nothing Less,"* 31.

74. "Washington News," *New York Times*, November 27, 1872.

75. William Nesbit, "To the Colored People of Pennsylvania," June 24, 1874, Leon Gardiner Collection, Box 1G, File 4, Historical Society of Pennsylvania.

76. Quoted in Biddle and Dubin, *Tasting Freedom*, 396.

77. "To the Colored People of Pennsylvania," June 25, 1868, ANHS Collection, Roll 9, Frame 769, Historical Society of Pennsylvania.

78. Horace Mann Bond, *Education for Freedom: A History of Lincoln University, Pennsylvania* (Princeton, NJ: Princeton University Press, 1976), 266.

79. Hugh Davis, *"Satisfied with Nothing Less,"* 65.

80. Teal, *Hero of Hispaniola*, 52.

81. Linda M. Perkins, *Fanny Jackson Coppin*, 113-19, Eric Ledell Smith, "To Teach My People: Fanny Jackson Coppin and Philadelphia's Institute for Colored Youth," *Pennsylvania Heritage* 29 (Winter 2003): 10.

82. Coppin, *Reminiscences of School Life*, 24.

83. Linda M. Perkins, *Fanny Jackson Coppin*, 127.

84. Perkins, 128.

85. Coppin, *Reminiscences of School Life*, 35.

86. Leon Litwack, *Been in the Storm So Long: The Aftermath of Slavery* (New York: Random House, 1980), 276.

87. "Yours for the Uplifting," ANHS Collection, Roll 9, Frame 885, Historical Society of Pennsylvania. While this source from the ANHS provides no direct evidence of who the author of the correspondence is, there is a strong possibility that it was the product of ICY graduate Sallie Daffin. Daffin traveled south during Reconstruction and taught in both Virginia and Tennessee. For more on the work and life of Daffin, see Gardner, *Unexpected Places*, 139–51.

88. For more on the wave of educators who went south during Reconstruction, see James D. Anderson, *The Education of Blacks in the South, 1860–1935* (Chapel Hill: University of North Carolina Press, 1988); Robert C. Morris, *Reading, 'Riting, and Reconstruction: The Education of Freedmen in the South, 1861–1870* (Chicago: University of Chicago Press, 2010); and Jacqueline Jones, *Soldiers of Light and Love: Northern Teachers and Georgia Blacks, 1865–1873* (Athens: University of Georgia Press, 2004).

89. Biddle and Dubin, *Tasting Freedom*, 383.

90. Sheryll Cashin, *The Agitator's Daughter: A Memoir of Four Generations of One Extraordinary African American Family* (New York: Perseus Books, 2008), 34.

91. Coppin, *Reminiscences of School Life*, 34.

Chapter Two

1. M. W. Whitt, "Address before the Alumni," *Tougaloo Quarterly* 6, no. 1 (June 1889).

2. See Rayford Logan, *The Betrayal of the Negro: From Rutherford B. Hayes to Woodrow Wilson* (New York: Da Capo, 1997).

3. Julius Thompson, *Black Life in Mississippi: Essays on Political, Social and Cultural Studies in a Deep South State* (Lanham, MD: University Press of America, 2001), 65.

4. In his classic study on the history of Black education, James Anderson provides an excellent and detailed treatment of the Hampton-Tuskegee model and the subversive ways in which youths and faculty, who grew increasingly militant, rejected the paternalistic and demeaning manner in which white authorities attempted to shape the boundaries of the Black college curriculum. See James Anderson, *The Education of Blacks in the South, 1860–1935* (Chapel Hill: University of North Carolina Press, 1988), 33–78.

5. Tougaloo received appropriations from the state of Mississippi from its founding until 1892. Its status as a private institution somewhat insulated the college from the demands of Mississippi legislators who attempted to extinguish any overt signs of radicalism at the other state-controlled colleges throughout the twentieth century and particularly during the rise of the modern civil rights

movement. For an analysis of Tougaloo's early years that includes budget details, curriculum development, summary of day-to-day operations, and faculty and administrative changes, see Clarice T. Campbell and Oscar Allan Rodgers Jr., *Mississippi: The View from Tougaloo* (Jackson: University Press of Mississippi, 1979).

6. The AMA was responsible for the founding of several Black colleges in the South. One of their primary goals was to bring "civility" and "morality" to a "benighted" people fresh from the bonds of slavery. By establishing these schools in the wake of the Civil War, they, along with their Black supporters, took deliberate care to ensure that southern whites did not perceive these schools as threats to the social structure. For more on the history of the AMA, see Augustus F. Beard, *A Crusade of Brotherhood: A History of the American Missionary Association* (Boston: Pilgrim, 1909); Joe M. Richardson, *Christian Reconstruction: The American Missionary Association and Southern Blacks, 1861–1890* (Athens: University of Georgia Press, 1986) and Ralph E. Luker, *The Social Gospel in Black and White: American Racial Reform, 1885–1912* (Chapel Hill: University of North Carolina Press, 1991).

7. James W. Loewen and Charles Sallis, eds., *Mississippi: Conflict and Change* (New York: Pantheon Books, 1974), 148–64; Campbell and Rodgers, *Mississippi*, 46.

8. Neil R. McMillen, *Dark Journey: Black Mississippians in the Age of Jim Crow* (Urbana: University of Illinois Press, 1989), 100.

9. James McPherson, "White Liberals and Black Power in Negro Education, 1865–1915," *American Historical Review* 75, no. 5 (June 1970): 1359.

10. Harlan Paul Douglass, *Christian Reconstruction in the South* (Boston: The Pilgrim Press, 1909), 162–63.

11. For more on the early development of Black Nationalism and its impact on African American institutions in the nineteenth century, see Leslie M. Alexander, *African or American? Black Identity and Political Activism in New York City, 1784–1861* (Urbana: University of Illinois Press, 2008); James Horton and Lois Horton, *In Hope of Liberty: Culture, Community, and Protest among Northern Free Blacks, 1700–1860* (Oxford: Oxford University Press, 1997); and Wilson Jeremiah Moses, *The Golden Age of Black Nationalism, 1850–1925* (Oxford: Oxford University Press, 1978).

12. "Dear News," *Tougaloo News*, February 1890.

13. Richardson, *Christian Reconstruction*, 208.

14. "Dear News."

15. Whitt, "Address before the Alumni."

16. Campbell and Rodgers, *Mississippi*, 116.

17. "The Christian Ministry among Our People," *Tougaloo Quarterly* 6, no. 1 (June 1889)

18. "The Christian Ministry among Our People."

19. "The Christian Ministry among Our People"; Campbell and Rodgers, *Mississippi*, 117.

20. For more on the long legacy of mobbing in the North and its racial undertones, see David Grimsted, *American Mobbing, 1828–1861* (Oxford: Oxford University Press, 1998); and Paul A. Gilje, *Rioting in America* (Bloomington: Indiana University Press, 1999).

21. Luker, *Social Gospel*, 15.

22. Campbell and Rodgers, *Mississippi*, 95.

23. "Public Sentiment," *Tougaloo Quarterly* 6, no. 1 (June 1889).

24. "Salutory Temperance," *Tougaloo Enterprise* 1, no. 1 (May 24, 1884).

25. Evelyn Brooks Higginbotham, *Righteous Discontent: The Women's Movement in the Black Baptist Church, 1880–1920* (Cambridge, MA: Harvard University Press, 1993), 14–15.

26. "Public Sentiment."

27. Historian Adam Fairclough has documented the fact that northern Louisiana was the most violent place in the state, and three counties in particular, Caddo, Ouachita, and Morehouse had more lynchings than any other place in America from 1889 to 1922, with the former date being the year that Aaron arrived to teach in that portion of the state. See Adam Fairclough, *Race and Democracy: The Civil Rights Struggle in Louisiana, 1915–1972* (Athens: University of Georgia Press, 1999), 9.

28. "Student's Correspondence," *Tougaloo Quarterly* 6, no. 2 (September 1889).

29. Historian Ralph Luker discusses the reaction of social gospel prophets to the idea of African colonization. Although the movement still remained influential and widely debated within prominent Black circles, many white ministers renounced the idea by the end of the nineteenth century for a variety of reasons. See Luker, *Social Gospel*, 30–56.

30. Luker, 5. Crummell and Turner were two of the most dedicated activists and proponents of emigration in the latter half of the nineteenth century. For more on both men, see Wilson Jeremiah Moses, *Alexander Crummell: A Study of Civilization and Discontent* (Oxford: Oxford University Press, 1989); J. R. Oldfield, *Civilization and Black Progress: Selected Writings of Alexander Crummell on the South* (Charlottesville: University of Virginia Press, 1995); Stephen Ward Angell, *Bishop Henry McNeal Turner and African American Religion in the South* (Knoxville: University of Tennessee Press, 1992); and Andre Johnson, *The Forgotten Prophet: Bishop Henry McNeal Turner and the African American Prophetic Tradition* (Lanham, MD: Lexington Books, 2014).

31. "Shall We Emigrate?," *Tougaloo Quarterly* 6, no. 2 (September 1889).

32. "Tougaloo University, Miss.," *Tougaloo News*, February 1890; "The News," *Tougaloo News*, December 1890; T. McCants Stewart, "Popular Discontent," *A.M.E. Church Review* 7, no. 4 (April 1891): 357–72.

33. "Notes," *Tougaloo News*, September 1891.

34. Moses, *Golden Age of Black Nationalism*, 198.

35. For more information on the voracious appetite for reading that early Black college students possessed, see Mollie E. Dunlap, "Recreational Reading of Negro College Students," *Journal of Negro Education* 2, no. 4 (October 1933): 448–59. See also Hortense Powdermaker, *After Freedom: A Cultural Study in the Deep South* (New York: Viking, 1939), 320.

36. The preeminent scholar Carter G. Woodson discusses difficulties early Black historians encountered as they sought to disseminate their work. Historian William Banks further highlights a particular dilemma that W. E. B. DuBois dealt with when a Mississippi plantation owner received funding from the Carnegie Institute

to conduct a study on race that had earlier been denied to DuBois. See Carter G. Woodson, "Negro Life and History in Our Schools," *Journal of Negro History* 4, no. 3 (July 1919): 278; and William M. Banks, *Black Intellectuals: Race and Responsibility in American Life* (New York: W. W. Norton, 1996), 39. For a more detailed analysis of the struggle of early Black scholars and the origins of the Black academy, see Stephen G. Hall, *A Faithful Account of the Race: African American Historical Writing in Nineteenth-Century America* (Chapel Hill: University of Chapel Hill Press, 2009), 188–226.

37. James Weldon Johnson, *Along This Way: The Autobiography of James Weldon Johnson* (New York: Viking, 1935), 79.

38. "Educational Work in the South," *American Missionary* 50, no. 12 (December 1896): 442.

39. In an essay written in 1908, Howard University professor Kelly Miller argued that it was "the spirit not the letter that maketh alive," thus advocating for a more compassionate approach to working with Black youths whom he saw as indispensable to the struggle for Black liberation. Later, famed sociologist E. Franklin Frazier would argue that appeals to the emotion of Black youths had relegated "the product of Negro education" to the sidelines of social activism during the age of the New Negro. See Kelly Miller, *Race Adjustment: Essays on the Negro in America* (New York: Neale, 1908), 273; and E. Franklin Frazier, "A Note on Negro Education," in *The Opportunity Reader: Stories, Poetry, and Essays from the Urban League's "Opportunity" Magazine*, ed. Sondra Kathyrn Wilson (New York: Random House, 1999), 462.

40. "The Change of Purpose in Education," *Tougaloo News*, November 1895. See also "The Spirit of the Teacher," *Tougaloo News*, January 1896.

41. "Anniversary Exercises," *The American Missionary* 50, no. 12 (December 1896): 222.

42. McMillen, *Dark Journey*, 120–21. For more on the whitecapping movement in Mississippi and beyond, see William F. Holmes, "Whitecapping: Agrarian Violence in Mississippi, 1902–1906," *Journal of Southern History* 35, no. 2 (1969): 165–85; and Steven Hahn, *A Nation under Our Feet: Black Political Struggles in the Rural South from Slavery to the Great Migration* (Cambridge, MA: Harvard University Press, 2003), 427–28.

43. "Notes from Graduates' Letters," *Tougaloo News*, April 1898.

44. "Illinois Woman's Home Missionary Union," *Advance* 62, no. 2399 (October 26, 1911): 533.

45. "A Student's Observation," *Tougaloo News*, December 1900; "Can the Negro Colonize?," *Tougaloo News*, April 1902.

46. Kenneth Marvin Hamilton, *Black Towns and Profit: Promotion and Development in the Trans-Appalachian West, 1877–1915* (Urbana: University of Illinois Press, 1991), 64.

47. Aurelius P. Hood, *The Negro at Mound Bayou: Being an Authentic Story of the Founding, Growth, and Development of the "Most Celebrated Town in the South"* ([Nashville, TN]: [printed by A.M.E. Sunday School Union for the author], 1909), 81, 89, 98, 109.

48. Booker T. Washington, *My Larger Education: Being Chapters from My Experience* (New York: Doubleday, 1911), 197.

49. For more on the financial struggles that confronted Tougaloo and other AMA schools at the turn of the century, see Joe M. Richardson and Maxine D. Jones, *Education for Liberation: The American Missionary Association and African Americans, 1890 to the Civil Rights Movement* (Tuscaloosa: University of Alabama Press, 2009), 119. For more on Booker T. Washington and the early challenges that marginalized the growth of Mound Bayou, see August Meier and Elliott Rudwick, *Along the Color Line: Explorations in the Black Experience* (Urbana: University of Illinois Press, 1976), 217–23.

50. "Alumni Notes," *Tougaloo News*, January 1903.

51. The early twentieth century witnessed the increased formation of new literary societies on Tougaloo's campus, the opening of the campus to wave after wave of speakers who were associated with the growing freedom struggle, and the final inclusion of Black faculty who were instrumental in the continued politicization of Tougaloo students. See Campbell and Rodgers, *Mississippi*, 129–40.

52. See the reference to Tougaloo as "Cancer College" in James Silver, *Mississippi: The Closed Society* (New York: Harcourt, Brace and World, 1963), 33.

53. McMillen, *Dark Journey*, 101.

54. Charles M. Payne, *I've Got the Light of Freedom: The Organizing Tradition and the Mississippi Freedom Struggle* (Berkeley: University of California Press, 1995), 405.

Chapter Three

1. Hattie Bailey, phone interview by the author, February 19, 2014.

2. "Head of Student Government Attends Congress," *Bennett Banner*, October 1937.

3. Erik Gellman, *Death Blow to Jim Crow: The National Negro Congress and the Rise of Militant Civil Rights* (Chapel Hill: University of North Carolina Press, 2012), 115.

4. Gunnar Myrdal, *An American Dilemma*, vol. 2, *The Negro Problem and Modern Democracy* (New Brunswick, NJ: Transaction, 1996), 818.

5. "Head of Student Government."

6. Lorenzo J. Greene, *Selling Black History for Carter G. Woodson: A Diary, 1930–1933*, ed. Arvarh E. Strickland (Columbia: University of Missouri Press, 1996), 68.

7. August Meier, *Negro Thought in America, 1880–1915* (Ann Arbor: University of Michigan Press, 1966), 67.

8. On the impact of segregation and the resulting damage to the Black psyche, see Daryl Michael Scott, *Contempt and Pity: Social Policy and the Image of the Damaged Black Psyche, 1880–1996* (Chapel Hill: University of North Carolina Press, 1997).

9. James Corrothers, *In Spite of the Handicap: An Autobiography* (New York: George H. Doran Co., 1916), 101–18.

10. Bennett College, *Bennett Belle 1973 Yearbook* (Greensboro, NC: graduating class of 1973), Bennett College Archives.

11. "The United Negro: His Problems and His Progress," (conference program), 1902, in Abraham H. Peeler Papers, MSS Collection No. 142, Series 7, Folder 5, Greensboro Historical Museum Archives.

12. "Bennett Mourns Death of Race Leader: Tribute to His Efforts," (newspaper clipping), 1915, in A. H. Peeler Papers, MSS Collection No. 142, Series 12, Folders 1, 4. Greensboro Historical Museum Archives.

13. Historian Wilson Jeremiah Moses documented the importance of literary societies to the advancement of Black nationalism and other militant ideas. These societies were created as forms of entertainment as well as a means to politicize African American readers. They were particularly popular on Black college campuses in the late nineteenth and early twentieth centuries. See Wilson Jeremiah Moses, *The Golden Age of Black Nationalism, 1850–1925* (New York: Oxford University Press, 1978), 198. For more information concerning the voracious appetite for reading that early Black college students possessed, see Mollie E. Dunlap, "Recreational Reading of Negro College Students," *Journal of Negro Education* 2 (October 1933): 448–59. See also Hortense Powdermaker, *After Freedom: A Cultural Study in the Deep South* (New York: Viking Press, 1939), 320.

14. J. Ormond Wilson, "Stewart Missionary Foundation for Africa in Gammon Theological Seminary," *Liberia*, no. 19 (November 1901).

15. Bennett College, *Bennett Belle 1973 Yearbook*.

16. Sarah Caroline Thuesen, *Greater Than Equal: African American Struggles for Schools and Citizenship in North Carolina, 1919–1965* (Chapel Hill: University of North Carolina Press, 2013), 20, 22.

17. Historian James Brawley documents the impetus behind Bennett's transition to a single-sex college. The move was made when the school partnership with the Woman's Home Missionary Society, also affiliated with the Methodist Episcopal Church, increased its influence through the domestic science department on campus. In 1926, with women already outnumbering men on campus by four to one, and the number of women enrolling in college across the nation steadily increasing, the decision was made to convert Bennett to a single-sex college. See James Brawley, *Two Centuries of Methodist Concern: Bondage, Freedom, and Education of Black People* (New York: Vantage, 1974), 162–64.

18. W. F. Steele, "A Work That Pays Big Dividends," *Epworth Herald,* 15, no. 36, February 4, 1905. The *Epworth Herald* was the official organ of the Epworth League, a Methodist young adult organization.

19. Stephanie Evans, *Black Women in the Ivory Tower, 1850–1954: An Intellectual History* (Gainesville: University Press of Florida, 2007), 43.

20. W. E. B. DuBois, *The Education of Black People: Ten Critiques, 1906–1960*, ed. Herbert Aptheker (Amherst: University of Massachusetts Press, 1973), 101.

21. Sondra Kathryn Wilson, ed., *The Opportunity Reader: Stories, Poetry, and Essays from the Urban League's "Opportunity" Magazine* (New York: Random House, 1999), 415, 462.

22. See Herbert Aptheker, "The Negro College Student in the 1920s—Years of Preparation and Protest: An Introduction," *Science and Society* 33, no. 2 (Spring 1969): 150–67; Raymond Wolters, *The New Negro on Campus: Black College Rebellions of the 1920s* (Princeton, NJ: Princeton University Press, 1975); and Ibram H. Rogers, *The Black Campus Movement: Black Students and the Racial Reconstitution of Higher Education, 1965–1972* (New York: Palgrave Macmillan, 2012), 29–49.

23. Raymond Gavins, *The Perils and Prospects of Southern Black Leadership: Gordon Blaine Hancock, 1884–1970* (Durham, NC: Duke University Press, 1977), 92. See also Mark Ellis, *Race Harmony and Black Progress: Jack Woofter and the Interracial Cooperation Movement* (Bloomington: Indiana University Press, 2013).

24. William Chafe, *Civilities and Civil Rights: Greensboro, North Carolina, and the Black Struggle for Freedom* (Oxford: Oxford University Press, 1981), 20.

25. "Negro Mass Meeting Monday Night, 8:30," (newspaper clipping), ca. 1929–1930, Bennett College Scrapbook, Bennett College Archives.

26. "The Phyllis Wheatley Literary Society of Bennett College for Women Presents the Freshman Oratorical Contest," March 19, 1931, Bennett College Scrapbook, Bennett College Archives; "Things Worth While," *Bennett Banner*, January 1931; "The Charlotte Hawkins Brown Literary Society" and "Student Inter-racial Movement Started," *Bennett Banner*, May 1931.

27. Junius Irving Scales and Richard Nickson, *Cause at Heart: A Former Communist Remembers* (Athens: University of Georgia Press, 2005), 60.

28. "Congressman De Priest Visits," "Dr. Johnson Speaks at Bennett College," and "Eighth Home-Making Institute Week," *Bennett Banner*, May 1934.

29. "David Dallas Jones," (obituary), *Journal of Negro History* 41, no. 2 (April 1956): 180–81.

30. Linda Beatrice Brown, *The Long Walk: The Story of the Presidency of Willa B. Player at Bennett College* (Greensboro, NC : Bennett College, 1998), 160–61.

31. "Interesting Chapel Programs Given," *Bennett Banner*, October 1937.

32. Robert Cohen, *When the Old Left Was Young: Student Radicals and America's First Mass Student Movement, 1929–1941* (New York: Oxford University Press, 1993), 223.

33. "Meeting of Theater Owners Opens Today," *Greensboro Daily News*, December 5, 1937; "Federal Regulation of Movies Opposed," *Greensboro Daily News*, December 7, 1937; "Hill Addresses Theater Group," *Greensboro Record*, December 7, 1937; "Resolution Adopted by Theater Owners," *Greensboro Daily News*, December 8, 1937; Lorraine Ahearn, "'37 Boycott Was Ahead of Its Time," *Greensboro News and Record*, February 3, 1994. For more on the legacy of Jeni LeGon and the plot and background of the film *Ali Baba Goes to Town*, see Nadine George-Graves, "Identity Politics and Political Will: Jeni LeGon Living in a Great Big Way," in *The Oxford Handbook of Dance and Politics*, eds., Rebekah J. Kowal, Gerald Siegmund, and Randy Martin (Oxford: Oxford University Press, 2017), 511–35.

34. "Greensboro Theater Boycotted by A&T and Bennett Students," Durham *Carolina Times*, January 15, 1938. The *Carolina Times* reported that "one thousand students joined in the boycott." It is not clear whether the number referred to signed pledges or indicated widespread picketing.

35. Rita Liberti, "'We Were Ladies, We Just Played like Boys': African American Women and Competitive Basketball at Bennett College, 1928–1942," in *The Sporting World of the Modern South*, ed. Patrick B. Miller (Urbana: University of Illinois Press, 2002), 160.

36. Theodore Kornweibel Jr., *"Seeing Red": Federal Campaigns against Black Militancy, 1919–1925* (Bloomington: Indiana University Press, 1998), 66.

37. Most of the demonstrations that transpired at Black colleges in the years prior to the Bennett boycott focused on internal campus issues. Students protested white paternalism, poor campus conditions, and infantilizing social policies that severely curbed their freedoms. Bennett College was fairly unique in staging off-campus protests and a boycott that focused on Jim Crow policies and white supremacy.

38. David Dallas Jones, "Cultural Obligations of the Faculty in a Negro Liberal Arts College," *Bulletin of the Association of American Colleges* 25, no. 1 (March 1939).

39. William Edward Farrison to W. E. B. Du Bois, March 3, 1934, W. E. B. Du Bois Papers (MS 312), Special Collections and University Archives, University of Massachusetts Amherst Libraries.

40. "Campus Commentary," *Bennett Banner*, December 1938; David C. Barnett, "Radio Show Chronicled Blacks' Harsh Realities," March 3, 2008, in *All Things Considered*, NPR, podcast, https://www.npr.org/templates/story/story.php?storyId =87780799; Kwame Anthony Appiah and Henry Louis Gates Jr., eds., *Arts and Letters: An A-to-Z Reference of Writers, Musicians, and Artists of the African American Experience*, Africana (Philadelphia: Running, 2005), 581–82.

41. WBIG first went on the air in 1926. In the 1930s, WBIG was owned and operated by the Jefferson Standard Life Insurance Company and became a CBS radio affiliate. The radio station also provided on-air space to North Carolina A&T as well. How university officials of both Bennett and A&T negotiated airtime with the station's owners is unclear and perhaps speaks more to the relatively progressive nature of the city. The city's first Black-owned and -operated radio station, WEAL, would not broadcast until 1962. For more on the history of WBIG, see Gayle Hicks Fripp, *Greensboro: A Chosen Center: An Illustrated History* (Sun Valley, CA: American Historical Press, 2001) and Jeffrey L. Rodengen and Richard F. Hubbard, *Jefferson Pilot Financial, 1903–2003: A Century of Excellence* (Fort Lauderdale, FL: Write Stuff Enterprises, 2003).

42. Reports of Bennett College Press Board, David Dallas Jones Papers, Box 15, Folder: Public Relations—Purchases, Bennett College Archives.

43. The Freedom Schools were an outgrowth of the Freedom Summer Project sponsored by the Student Nonviolent Coordinating Committee in 1964. The Freedom Schools combined elements of a curriculum that had long since existed in many historically Black colleges. Black college students were exposed to a communitas that heavily emphasized race consciousness, and much like the Freedom Schools, they were often provided with opportunities to hone their leadership skills and envision and practice participatory democracy through mock elections, student government, and various campus organizations. Countless students and alumni would utilize their exposure to the second curriculum to fuel both collective

and individual demands for Black equality. For more on the Freedom Schools, see Charles M. Payne, *I've Got the Light of Freedom: The Organizing Tradition and the Mississippi Freedom Struggle* (Berkeley: University of California Press, 1995); John Dittmer, *Local People: The Struggle for Civil Rights in Mississippi* (Urbana: University of Illinois Press, 1995); and William Sturkey and Jon N. Hale, eds., *To Write in the Light of Freedom: The Newspapers of the 1964 Mississippi Freedom Schools* (Jackson: University Press of Mississippi, 2015).

44. "Bennett College on the Air," February 16, 1945, David Dallas Jones Papers, Box 14, Folder: Public Relations—Radio, Bennett College Archives.

45. "Bennett Graduate Originates Radio Program," *Bennett Banner*, March 1942.

46. "Negro Americans," Report of Bennett College Press Board, David Dallas Jones Papers, Box 15, Folder: Public Relations—Purchases, Bennett College Archives.

47. "Plans for Summer Institute Announced," *Bennett Banner*, March 1942; "Recent Supreme Court Ruling in the Texas Primary Case Has Far Reaching Political Possibilities," *Bennett Banner*, April 1944; "Student Interracial Conference Held," *Bennett Banner*, November 1944.

48. "The Negro and the Postwar World," *Christian Advocate*, September 16, 1943.

49. Historian Sarah Thuesen does an excellent job of exposing the public and covert ways in which Black college administrators, particularly those who were heads of state, controlled institutions and handled the growing movement. While Shepard was known for adopting a public persona that was conservative, he also facilitated the growth of radicalism and militancy on his campus by giving limited but all-important space for the debate, discussion, and implementation of activist ideals. See Thuesen, *Greater Than Equal*, 118–26.

50. Raymond Gavins, "The NAACP in North Carolina during the Age of Segregation," in *New Directions in Civil Rights Studies*, ed. Armstead L. Robinson and Patrician Sullivan (Charlottesville: University of Virginia Press, 1991), 105–25.

51. Historian Bill Chafe illustrates the role that Black colleges played in ushering forth a new era of Black political empowerment in the city of Greensboro. Randolph Blackwell, a graduate of North Carolina A&T, which is located directly across the street from Bennett, was instrumental in helping to turn out the African American vote. Additionally, F. A. Mayfield, a former professor at A&T, made one of the first major runs at election to city office in 1947. Although Mayfield did not win, his success at netting 25 percent of the total votes cast gave African Americans in the city the boost of confidence needed to believe that change was inevitable. See Chafe, *Civilities and Civil Rights*, 24–28.

52. "How Much Do You Know?" *Bennett Banner*, October 1942.

53. For more on the increased comparison of Jim Crow and Nazism before and during World War II, see Carol Anderson, *Eyes Off the Prize: The United Nations and the African American Struggle for Human Rights, 1944-1955* (New York: Cambridge University Press, 2003), 8–58, and Johnpeter Horst Grill and Robert L. Jenkins, "The Nazis and the American South in the 1930s: A Mirror Image?" *Journal of Southern History 58* (November 1992): 667–94.

54. Valena E. Minor, "Editorially Speaking," *Bennett Banner*, January 1943.

55. J. D. Bragg to David Dallas Jones, February 5, 1944, Jones to Bragg, February 10, 1944, both in Folder—Church Board of Mission and Church Extension of the Methodist Church, Correspondence (1943–1947), Box 4, David Dallas Jones Papers, Bennett College Archives.

56. "Negro History Week Celebrated on Campus," *Bennett Banner*, February 1944; Ella Baker, interview by Casey Hayden and Sue Thrasher, New York, April 19, 1977, Interview G-0008, Southern Oral History Program Collection #4007, Series G, Southern Women, Manuscripts Department, University of North Carolina, Chapel Hill. For more on Baker's contributions to the freedom movement and her matriculation and orientation at Shaw University, see Barbara Ransby, *Ella Baker and the Black Freedom Movement: A Radical Democratic Vision* (Chapel Hill: University of North Carolina Press, 2003).

57. Megan Taylor Shockley, *"We Too Are Americans": African American Women in Detroit and Richmond, 1940–1954* (Urbana: University of Illinois Press, 2004), 60–62.

58. "Editorially Speaking," *Bannett Banner*, May 1944.

59. For more on the plight of working African American women during World War II and the Urban League's "Last Hired, First Fired" slogan, see Cheryl Lynn Greenberg, *To Ask for an Equal Chance: African Americans in the Great Depression* (Lanham, MD: Rowman and Littlefield, 2009); and Karen Tucker Anderson, "Last Hired, First Fired: Black Women Workers during World War II," *Journal of American History* 69 (June 1982): 82–97.

60. "Homemaking Institute Presents Interesting Problems," *Bennett Banner*, May 1944.

61. Alice Holloway, "Editorial," *Bennett Banner*, May 1944.

62. Barbara Seals Nevergold and Peggy Brooks Bertram, *Uncrowned Queens: African American Women Community Builders of Western New York* (Buffalo, NY: Uncrowned Queens, 2003), 2:100.

63. For more on the Student Interracial Ministry that evolved in the early 1960s, see David P. Cline, "Revolution and Reconciliation: The Student Interracial Ministry, Liberal Protestantism, and the Civil Rights Movement, 1960–1970" (PhD diss., University of North Carolina, 2010).

64. "Student Interracial Conference Held," *Bennett Banner*, November 1944.

65. Orial Ann Banks, "Woman's College Carries Extra in the Carolinian," *Bennett Banner*, December 1944.

66. "Deposed 'Flat Hat' Editor Invited to Join Banner Staff as Guest Writer" and "Freedom of Speech and Freedom of the Press," *Bennett Banner*, February 1945.

67. "Vesper Speakers," *Bennett Banner*, February 1945; Taylor Branch, *Parting the Waters: America in the King Years, 1954–1963* (New York: Simon and Schuster, 1988), 10; Patrick Louis Cooney, "At Home, 1944–1948," in *The Life and Times of the Prophet Vernon Johns: Father of the Civil Rights Movement*, Vernon Johns Society website, 1998, http://www.vernonjohns.org/tcal001/vjathome.html.

68. Racial violence and social tension swept across the country during World War II and heightened as the war drew to a close. For more on this phenomenon

and how Black war veterans were often targeted by racial pogroms, as well as how African Americans rallied to the cause of the Fair Employment Practice Committee, see Thomas Sugrue, *The Origins of the Urban Crisis: Race and Inequality in Postwar Detroit* (Princeton, NJ: Princeton University Press, 2005); Daniel Kryder, *Divided Arsenal: Race and the American State during World War II* (Cambridge: Cambridge University Press, 2000); Charles D. Chamberlain, *Victory at Home: Manpower and Race in the American South during World War II* (Athens: University of Georgia Press, 2003); Jennifer E. Brooks, *Defining the Peace: World War II Veterans, Race, and the Remaking of Southern Political Tradition* (Chapel Hill: University of North Carolina Press, 2004); David Welky, *Marching across the Color Line: A. Philip Randolph and Civil Rights in the World War II Era* (Oxford: Oxford University Press, 2014); Ira Katz Nelson, *When Affirmative Action Was White: An Untold History of Racial Inequality in Twentieth-Century America* (New York: W. W. Norton, 2006); and Merl E. Reed, *Seedtime for the Modern Civil Rights Movement: The President's Committee on Fair Employment Practice, 1941–1946* (Baton Rouge: Louisiana State University Press, 1991).

69. Katznelson, *When Affirmative Action Was White*, 5.

70. John Egerton, *Speak Now Against the Day: The Generation Before the Civil Rights Movement in the South* (New York: Alfred Knopf, 1995), 413.

71. "Inquiring Reporter," *Bennett Banner*, April 1945.

72. Reed, *Seedtime*, 172.

73. "Where Do We Go from Here?" and "The Inquiring Reporter," *Bennett Banner*, October 1945; "Yergan Denounces Imperialism" and "Nothing but Good Will Can Save America—Mayes Proclaims," *Bennett Banner*, November 1945.

74. "And You Call This Christianity" and "Opinion," *Bennett Banner*, November 1945.

75. "Minorities—A Challenge to American Democracy," *Bennett Banner*, December 1945.

Chapter Four

1. Joe Azbell, "At Holt Street Baptist Church," *Montgomery Advertiser*, December 7, 1955.

2. Division of Music, 1971, ASU Publications, Alabama State University Archives.

3. Jamila Jones, interview, April 27, 2011, Civil Rights History Project Collection, American Folklife Center, Library of Congress.

4. Jamila Jones, interview with the author, August 8, 2010.

5. Dr. Laurence Hayes obituary, May 20, 2006, Laurence Hayes Papers, Special Collections, Vertical File, Alabama State University Archives.

6. Jamila Jones, interview with the author, August 8, 2010.

7. William B. Paterson, the founder of what would later become ASU, reported having altercations with the Ku Klux Klan and using armed defense to ward away such hostilities. See W. B. Paterson to Booker T. Washington, January 5, 1887, Booker T. Washington Papers, Alabama Department of Archives and History; and Robert G. Sherer, "William Burn Paterson: Pioneer as Well as Apostle of Negro

Education in Alabama," *Alabama Historical Quarterly*, Volume 36, no. 2, Summer 1974, 129.

8. Editorial, *Montgomery Advertiser*, June 8, 1887.

9. Beverly worked another three years at ASU after stepping down from the presidency before retiring in 1923 at sixty-five years old. However, he surprisingly came out of retirement in that same year to accept a teaching position at Prairie View A&M in Texas, where he died on December 16, 1924, just one year after his arrival. He is buried in the Dexter Avenue Baptist Church cemetery, which was made famous for becoming a hub of the Montgomery bus boycott in 1955. It is unclear whether Beverly had distaste for administration and simply wanted to teach and continue his research or whether there were other forces that pushed him out of Alabama and ASU. For more on Beverly's life, see Robert G. Sherer Jr., "John William Beverly: Alabama's First Negro Historian," *Alabama Review* 26 (January 1973): 194–208; Thelma D. Perry, *History of the American Teachers Association* (Washington, DC: National Education Association, 1975), 108–9; and Agnes J. Lewis, "A Sketch of Professor J.W. Beverly," *State Normal Courier Journal*, February 1924, 11–12, Alabama State University Archives.

10. "He Must," Writings by George W. Trenholm, Harper Councill Trenholm Papers, Box 179–4, Moorland-Spingarn Research Center, Howard University.

11. While he was effective in the area of promoting equity for Black teachers, G. W. Trenholm was no firebrand. He may have taken a cue from Councill, who became notably conservative after his famous protest of segregation policies in Huntsville. But it is highly probable that his social and political moderation was a product of his place and time. He delivered a speech entitled "The Black Man's Burden" in Aldrich, Alabama. During his presentation, he spoke on the proliferation of ignorance, poverty, and crime among Blacks but failed to fully address the role of white supremacy and racial violence running rampant throughout the South. Scribbled in the margins of his speech is perhaps a clue as to why he restrained himself from making any comments concerning the harsh realities of Black life. He wrote, "Must not offend the Ransome's." While it is not clear who the Ransomes were, it is quite possible that they were local white landowners, politicians, or both who were looking in on Trenholm's speech. Surveillance such as this was common during Black gatherings. See George W. Trenholm, "The Black Man's Burden," G. W. Trenholm Papers, Section 6, Shelf 1, Box 5, Alabama State University Archives. For more on the early work of G. W. Trenholm, see Vivian Morris and Curtis Morris, *The Price They Paid: Desegregation in an African American Community* (New York: Teachers College Press, 2002); and Carol F. Karpinski, *A Visible Company of Professionals: African Americans and the National Education Association during the Civil Rights Movement* (New York: Peter Lang, 2008).

12. Frank Caffey to Harper Councill Trenholm, March 6, 1926, Harper Councill Trenholm Papers, Section 6, Shelf 3, Box 17, Moorland-Spingarn Research Center, Howard University.

13. Historian August Meier documents the development of cultural nationalism among New Negro thinkers, scholars, and activists at the turn of the century. The activity of these women and men helped to lay out the protest agenda and trajectory

of Black radical thought, which circulated through Black college campuses for much of the twentieth century. See August Meier, *Negro Thought in America, 1880–1915* (Ann Arbor: University of Michigan Press, 1966), 256–78.

14. Harper Councill Trenholm, untitled speech, January 1926, Harper Councill Trenholm Papers, Box 179–27, Folder 22, Moorland-Spingarn Research Center, Howard University.

15. "Acting President Trenholm Speaks at Huntsville: Madison County Stages a Big Emancipation Celebration," *State Normal Courier Journal* 4, no. 5 (January 23, 1926): 3.

16. "Summer School to Be Featured," *State Normal Courier Journal* 4, no. 7 (March 25, 1926): 2.

17. For more on the Delver's Literary Club and the participation of ASU faculty in Negro History Week, see "Community Items," *State Normal Courier Journal* 4, no. 3 (November 27, 1925): 4; "Community Items," *State Normal Courier Journal* 4, no. 4 (December 21, 1925): 4; and "Community Items," *State Normal Courier Journal* 4, no. 5 (January 23, 1926): 4.

18. "Founders Day," *State Normal Courier Journal,* 1, no. 1 (January 1928): 1.

19. "National Negro History Week," *State Normal Courier Journal* 5, no. 1 (February 9, 1927): 2.

20. "National Negro History Week," 3. Clayton was the daughter of William and Frazzie Clayton, owners of Montgomery's largest Black-owned mortuary. She later married Rufus Lewis, who was a force in the Montgomery civil rights movement. She died in 1958 in a car accident.

21. Solomon Seay Sr., *I Was There by the Grace of God* (Montgomery: S. S. Seay Sr. Educational Foundation, 1990), 69–70; and Martin Luther King Jr., *Stride toward Freedom: The Montgomery Story* (New York: Harper and Row, 1958), 73. Seay was a major force in the Montgomery movement. He was highly respected by Blacks in the city as one of the most outspoken advocates for civil rights. His autobiography gives a full account of his life and work in the movement.

22. The Scottsboro Boys case was a widely covered case involving charges of rape that were brought against nine young African American men. One of the two white women who first brought the charge soon recanted, but many of the boys (most of whom soon passed into adulthood) served out long sentences, and one escaped from prison and was later pardoned in 1976. For more on the Scottsboro Boys, see James E. Goodman, *Stories of Scottsboro* (New York: Vintage Books, 1995); Dan T. Carter, *Scottsboro: A Tragedy of the American South* (Baton Rouge: Louisiana State University Press, 2007); Glenda Elizabeth Gilmore, *Defying Dixie: The Radical Roots of Civil Rights, 1919–1950* (New York: W. W. Norton, 2008); and Robin D. G. Kelley, *Hammer and Hoe: Alabama Communists during the Great Depression* (Chapel Hill: University of North Carolina Press, 1990).

23. E. T. Belsaw to H. C. Trenholm, August 5, 1931, Harper Councill Trenholm Papers, Box 179, Folder 13, Moorland-Spingarn Research Center, Howard University.

24. H. C. Trenholm to E. T. Belsaw, August 7, 1931, Harper Councill Trenholm Papers, Box 179, Folder 13, Moorland-Spingarn Research Center, Howard University.

25. Randal Maurice Jelks, *Benjamin Elijah Mays, Schoolmaster of the Movement: A Biography* (Chapel Hill: University of North Carolina Press, 2012), 77.

26. "Kings Mountain Student Conference 1931," H. C. Trenholm Papers, Box 179–37, Folder 8, Moreland Spingarn Research Center, Howard University.

27. H. C. Trenholm to Carter G. Woodson, March 23, 1936, Harper Councill Trenholm Papers, Box 179, Folder 13, Moorland-Spingarn Research Center, Howard University.

28. Carter G. Woodson to H. C. Trenholm, July 2, 1936, H. C. Trenholm to Carter G. Woodson, July 11, 1936, and H. C. Trenholm to Carter G. Woodson, May 18, 1937, Harper Councill Trenholm Papers, Box 179–37, Folder 13, Moorland-Spingarn Research Center, Howard University.

29. Carter G. Woodson to H. C. Trenholm, February 9, 1935, Harper Councill Trenholm Papers, Box 179, Folder 13, Moorland-Spingarn Research Center, Howard University.

30. Ambrose Caliver to H. C. Trenholm, June 28, 1935, Harper Councill Trenholm Papers, Box 179, Folder 13, Moorland-Spingarn Research Center, Howard University.

31. Harper Councill Trenholm, "The Socio-economic Factor as a Determinant in the Program of the Negro College," February 1937, Harper Councill Trenholm Papers, Box 179–28, Folder 22, Moorland-Spingarn Research Center, Howard University.

32. Leila Mae Barlow, *Across the Years: Memoirs* (Montgomery: Paragon, 1959), 45.

33. Carl Sandburg, *The People, Yes* (New York: Harcourt, Brace, 1936), 254.

34. Karpinski, *Visible Company of Professionals*, 10.

35. Harper Councill Trenholm, "From the President," Harper Councill Trenholm Papers, Box 179–27, Folder 30, Moorland-Spingarn Research Center, Howard University.

36. Jo Ann Gibson Robinson, "George Eliot's Treatment of Sin" (MA thesis, Atlanta University, 1948).

37. "Lynched Negro Found in River," *Atlanta Constitution*, April 27, 1912; "Negro Was Lynched and Body Thrown in River," *Butts County Progress*, May 3, 1912.

38. For more on the history of lynching in Georgia, see W. Fitzhugh Brundage, *Lynching in the New South: Georgia and Virginia, 1880–1930* (Urbana: University of Illinois Press, 1993); and Julie Buckner Armstrong, *Mary Turner and the Memory of Lynching* (Athens: University of Georgia Press, 2011).

39. Harper Councill Trenholm, "The Negro Teacher Faces the Problems of the Present World Crisis," Harper Councill Trenholm Papers, Box 179–27, Folder 30, Moorland-Spingarn Research Center, Howard University.

40. Mary Fair Burks, "Trailblazers: Women in the Montgomery Bus Boycott," in *Women in the Civil Rights Movement: Trailblazers and Torchbearers, 1941–1965*, ed. Vicki L. Crawford, Jacqueline Anne Rouse, and Barbara Woods (Bloomington: Indiana University Press, 1993), 81.

41. L. D. Reddick, "A New Interpretation for Negro History," *Journal of Negro History* 22, no. 1 (January 1937): 27.

42. For more on Reddick's paper and how it helped to frame the future of Black studies as a field, see James Turner and C. Steven McGann, "Black Studies as an

Integral Tradition in African-American Intellectual History," *Issue: A Journal of Opinion* 6, no. 2/3 (Summer/Autumn 1976): 73–78.

43. Reddick, "New Interpretation for Negro History," 20.

44. Barlow, *Across the Years*, 33–34.

45. What started as a letter to the editor to express outrage regarding the glaring hypocrisies of American democracy resulted in a nationwide campaign widely embraced by African Americans to draw attention to racism throughout the country. In 1944 the adoption of the Servicemen's Readjustment Act, more popularly known as the GI Bill, brought numerous Black veterans to HBCU campuses, where many of them continued in their politicization and militancy. See James G. Thompson, letter to the editor, *Pittsburgh Courier*, January 31, 1942; and "The Courier's Double 'V' for a Double Victory Campaign Gets Country-Wide Support," *Pittsburgh Courier*, February 14, 1942. For more historical analysis of the *Pittsburgh Courier* and the Double V campaign, see Andrew Buni, *Robert L. Vann of the Pittsburgh Courier: Politics and Black Journalism* (Pittsburgh: University of Pittsburg Press, 1974); Patrick Washburn, *A Question of Sedition: The Federal Government's Investigation of the Black Press during World War II* (New York: Oxford University Press, 1986); and Charles W. Eagles, "Two Double V's: Jonathan Daniels, FDR, and Race Relations during World War II," *North Carolina Historical Review* 59, no. 3 (July 1982): 252–70.

46. Thelma Glass, interview by Randall Williams, n.d., Alabama State University Archives.

47. Like many Black fraternities, sororities, and civic groups, Alpha Phi Alpha was highly politicized and worked to shape policy concerning civil rights. Many of its members were at the forefront of the early civil rights movement, including Rufus Lewis. For more on Alpha Phi Alpha and its impact on the movement at large, see Robert E. Weems Jr., "Alpha Phi Alpha, the Fight for Civil Rights, and the Shaping of Public Policy," in *Alpha Phi Alpha: A Legacy of Greatness, the Demands of Transcendence*, ed. Gregory S. Parks, Stefan M. Bradley, and Michael A. Blake (Lexington: University Press of Kentucky, 2011). For direct evidence of Lewis's voter registration efforts and the correlation with the Alpha Phi Alpha campaign, see Jo Ann Gibson Robinson, *The Montgomery Bus Boycott and the Women Who Started It: The Memoir of Jo Ann Robinson* (Knoxville: University of Tennessee Press, 1987), 29. For more on the history of the Voteless People is a Hopeless People program see Jessica Harris and Vernon C. Mitchell Jr., "A Narrative Critique of Black Greek-Letter Organizations and Social Action," in *Black Greek-Letter Organizations in the Twenty-first Century*, ed. Gregory S. Parks (Lexington: University of Kentucky Press, 2008), 147.

48. J. Mills Thornton III, *Dividing Lines: Municipal Politics and the Struggle for Civil Rights in Montgomery, Birmingham, and Selma* (Tuscaloosa: University of Alabama Press, 2002), 30.

49. U.S. Department of Commerce, Bureau of the Census, *1950 United States Census of Population*, vol. 2, *Characteristics of the Population*, pt. 2, *Alabama* (Washington, DC: Government Printing Office, 1952), table 55, "Citizenship by Age, Color, and Sex, for the State and for Cities of 100,000 or More: 1950."

50. See "Four Hundred Vets at State" and "Enrollment Shows Steady Increase," *Hornet*, February 1950.

51. For more on the Cold War's impact on the civil rights movement, see John Egerton, *Speak Now against the Day: The Generation before the Civil Rights Movement in the South* (New York: Alfred A. Knopf, 1995); Mary Dudziak, *Cold War Civil Rights: Race and the Image of American Democracy* (Princeton, NJ: Princeton University Press, 2000); Manning Marable, *Race, Reform, and Rebellion: The Second Reconstruction in Black America, 1945–1990* (Jackson: University Press of Mississippi, 1991); Brenda Gayle Plummer, *Rising Wind: Black Americans and U.S. Foreign Affairs, 1935–1960* (Chapel Hill: University of North Carolina Press, 1996); Penny Von Eschen, *Race against Empire: Black Americans and Anticolonialism, 1937–1957* (Ithaca, NY: Cornell University Press, 1997); and Erik S. McDuffie, *Sojourning for Freedom: Black Women, American Communism, and the Making of Black Left Feminism* (Durham, NC: Duke University Press, 2011).

52. Gilmore, *Defying Dixie*, 414.

53. Danielle L. McGuire has composed a brilliant study of sexual violence against Black women in the South and how protest efforts surrounding this issue helped to set the tone for the modern civil rights movement. However, her assessment of the space that was afforded to Blacks in Montgomery leaves out the impact of venues such as ASU. While she acknowledges that many of the movement's participants worked at the institution, her suggestion that the politicization of Blacks in the city largely took place in civic groups, churches, and clubs leaves out the development of idealism and race consciousness at ASU and the role this played in developing local protest efforts. See Danielle L. McGuire, *At the Dark End of the Street: Black Women, Rape, and Resistance: A New History of the Civil Rights Movement from Rosa Parks to the Rise of Black Power* (New York: Vintage Books, 2010), 74.

54. For further analysis of the case, see Thornton, *Dividing Lines*, 30; and McGuire, *At the Dark End*, 69–70.

55. Robinson, *The Montgomery Bus Boycott and the Women Who Started It*, 110.

56. John Dittmer, *Local People: The Struggle for Civil Rights in Mississippi* (Chicago: University of Illinois Press, 1995), 225–26.

57. Created in an effort to oppose integration, the White Citizens' Council was formed in 1954 following the landmark decision in the *Brown v. Board of Education* case. With chapters across the south and thousands of dues-paying members, the WCC effectively marginalized would-be activists by using bold intimidation tactics intended to deprive Blacks of jobs, homes, and their constitutional rights. For a broad treatment of the White Citizens Council and its impact on the Civil Rights Movement, see Neil R. McMillen, *The Citizens' Council: Organized Resistance to the Second Reconstruction, 1954–64* (Urbana: University of Illinois Press, 1994).

58. Thelma Glass, interview with Randall Williams, (n.d.), Alabama State University Archives.

59. Robinson, *Montgomery Bus Boycott*, 8. Robinson too was subjected to the abusive nature of Jim Crow policies. During her first semester teaching at ASU, a white bus driver violently lashed out at her for sitting in the wrong seat on a segregated bus. She noted that it was this moment that heightened her commitment to bring down the Jim Crow policies of Montgomery's transportation system. For a

more detailed account of this incident, see David Garrow, "The Origins of the Montgomery Bus Boycott," *Southern Changes* 7 (October–December 1985), 21.

60. "'On Whitman Ave.' Presented at Fla. A&M. Dec. 5th," *Fresh-More*, December 1949. Abernathy went on to become a minister and outspoken leader of the civil rights movement, founding the Southern Christian Leadership Conference with Martin Luther King Jr. in 1957.

61. "Youth Council Plans Drive," *Hornet*, February 1952.

62. "Human Relations," *Fresh-More*, February 1954.

63. Carrie Brown, "Bama Students Cautioned by Noted Author," *Fresh-More*, February 1954; "Noted Author Speaks at College," *Alabama State College Alumni News* 4, no. 2 (March 1955); W. Edward Harris, *Miracle in Birmingham: A Civil Rights Memoir, 1954–1965* (Indianapolis: Stonework, 2004), 150. The Alabama Sovereignty Commission and the Alabama Legislative Commission to Preserve the Peace were set up in 1963 as a response to the increased number of protests occurring throughout the state. They worked in tandem to spy on the efforts of local activists and set up a ring of intimidation designed to curb movement activity.

64. "Reaction toward Inter-racial Affairs Heard by Social Studies Class," *Fresh-More*, February 1954.

65. "Did You Know," *Fresh-More*, February 1954.

66. Editorial, *Fresh-More*, December 1955.

67. Loretta Jean Thomas, "Is White Supremacy Faltering?," *Fresh-More*, December 1955.

68. "High Lights of Representative Adam Clayton Powell" and "Congressman Adam Clayton Powell Visits Campus," *Fresh More*, December 1955.

69. Franklin M. Gary, "Son Delivers Founders Day Address," *Fresh-More*, February 1958.

70. Charlie Varner Jr., "History Study Club," *Fresh-More*, February 1958.

71. For more on Jeremiah Reeve's case, see Phillip Hoose, *Claudette Colvin: Twice Toward Justice* (New York: Square Fish, 2010), 23–25; Rosa Parks and Jim Haskins, *Rosa Parks: My Story* (New York: Puffin Books, 1999), 85–86; Danielle L. McGuire, *At the Dark End of the Street*, 62–63.

72. "Negroes Protest," *The Fresh-More*, May 1958, Alabama State University Archives.

73. "Facts Relating to Recent Violence Inflicted upon Negro Citizens of Montgomery, Alabama," MIA Activism File, Box 3, Folder 4, Montgomery Improvement Association (MIA) Special Collection, Alabama State University Archives; Seay, *I Was There*, 213; Thornton, *Dividing Lines*, 93–94.

74. Othia M. White, "A Lady from Africa Visits State Campus," Pearlie Curry, "Mrs. Daisy Bates Speaks in City," and Joseph Laster, "Carter G. Woodson," *Fresh-More*, November 1958.

75. Martin Luther King Jr., *Stride toward Freedom*, 33.

76. "Editorial . . . ," *Fresh-More*, December 1955.

77. Taylor Branch, *Parting the Waters: America in the King Years, 1954–63* (New York: Simon and Schuster, 1988), 276.

78. Many students at ASU struggled with the idea of embracing indirect protest tactics or the nonviolent strategies espoused by King and others. When a caravan of white "commandoes began invading campus soon after the bus boycott, students ambushed one of the cars with bricks." See L. D. Reddick, "The Bus Boycott in Montgomery," in *Voices of Dissent: A Collection of Articles from "Dissent" Magazine*, ed. *Dissent* staff (New York: Grove, 1958), 177–78.

79. Septima P. Clark to S. S. Seay, March 22, 1960, Highlander Folk School File, Box 3, Folder 33, MIA Special Collection, Alabama State University Archives.

80. "City Leaders Issue Words of Warning," *Montgomery Advertiser*, February 26, 1960; "Statement Asserts Negroes to Continue 'Rights' Fight," *Montgomery Advertiser*, February 26, 1960; "Protest March May Be Staged on Monday," *Alabama Journal*, February 27, 1960.

81. "Students Petition the Governor," Harper Councill Trenholm Papers, Box 179–61, Folder 13, Moorland-Spingarn Research Center, Howard University.

82. Historian Martin Oppenheimer documents the fact that on March 14, student leaders delayed the boycotts of class that were organized shortly after the initial sit-in in an effort to tone down the rhetoric and limit the opportunities for violent exchanges with local law enforcement. This action was taken as a result of the on-campus conference of the Alabama State Teachers Association, the Black advocacy group that Trenholm had headed up for years. This type of deference was indicative of the respect that students had for Trenholm. See Martin Oppenheimer, *The Sit-In Movement of 1960* (New York: Carlson, 1989), 164.

83. Maylon Nicholson, "Students Jailed Here," *Alabama Journal*, March 8, 1960; Dick Hines and Arthur Osgoode, "City Police Arrest 37 Negro Agitators for Demonstrations," *Montgomery Advertiser*, March 9, 1960; "Faculty Member, Husband among 37 Jailed by Police," *Montgomery Advertiser*, March 9, 1960; Seay, *I Was There*, 220–21; Thornton, *Dividing Lines*, 113–14.

84. East Gadsden Brotherhood Club to S. S. Seay, July 1, 1960, MIA Activism File, Box 3, Folder 12, E. M. Williamson to Ralph Abernathy, May 11, 1960, MIA Activism File, Box 3, Folder 11, Bea Lazar to S. S. Seay, April 28, 1960, MIA Activism File, Box 3, Folder 9, S. S Seay to Charles D. Langford, August 25, 1960, MIA Activism File, Box 3, Folder 13, S. S. Seay to Dannie Grace, July 25, 1960, MIA Special Collection, Box 4, Folder 18, S. S. Seay to Collis Ivery, July 25, 1960, MIA Special Collection, Box 4, Folder 12, S. S. Seay to W. L. Harris, Lodge #784, July 12, 1960, MIA Special Collection, Box 4, Folder 15, Alabama State University Archives.

85. William "Meatball" Douthard, "I'll Never Forget Alabama Law." Originally published in *Liberal News* 6, no. 6 (February/March 1965).

86. Historian Hasan Jeffries's brilliant study on Lowndes County, Alabama, documents one of the state's and country's most notoriously violent regions. Though it eventually became a key battleground in the national movement for Black liberation, the fact that activists delayed going there until 1965 underscores how violence was used to repress movement activity. See Hasan Jeffries, *Bloody Lowndes: Civil Rights and Black Power in Alabama's Black Belt* (New York: New York University Press, 2009), 7–37.

87. Minutes of the meeting of the state board of education, March 25, 1960, Harper Councill Trenholm Papers, Box 179–61, Folder 22, Moorland-Spingarn Research Center, Howard University.

88. "Professor Fired after Patterson Cites Red 'Links,'" *Mobile Register*, June 15, 1960.

89. "Dismissal for President Also Hinted," *Birmingham Post-Herald*, June 15, 1960.

90. "Fired Prof Leaves for Africa," *Alabama Journal*, June 4, 1960.

91. Trezzvant W. Anderson, "Firing of Reddick Sparks Outcry at Ala. State College," *Pittsburgh Courier*, June 25, 1960. While Trenholm never offered public comment through the media, he did submit reports to the state board of education updating them on his efforts to curb the outgrowth of activism on campus. The extent to which he followed through on his written commitment to suppress activism on campus is unclear, but he did expel students and removed faculty when instructed to do so by state authorities. See "Report Submitted by Dr. H. Councill Trenholm, President of Alabama State College, at a Meeting of the Alabama State Board of Education," Administrative Files, Box SG014005, Folder 6, Alabama Department of Archives and History, July 20, 1960.

92. Karl Portera, "AAUP Denounces Patterson for Firing Negro Professor," *Montgomery Advertiser*, December 19, 1961.

93. Clayborne Carson et al., eds., *The Papers of Martin Luther King Jr., Volume V: Threshold of a New Decade, January 1959–December 1960* (Berkeley: University of California Press, 2005), 495n2.

94. "Lo, the Poor College Presidents," *Pittsburgh Courier*, July 2, 1960.

95. Robinson, *Montgomery Bus Boycott*, 169.

96. Harper Councill Trenholm to Hannah Trenholm, December 24, 1960, Harper Councill Trenholm Papers, Shelf 3, Box 18, Alabama State University Archives.

97. Oppenheimer, *Sit-In Movement*, 167.

98. Loretta Jean Thomas, "Is White Supremacy Faltering?," *Fresh-More*, December 1955.

Chapter Five

1. Margaret Walker Alexander, journal entry, August 12, 1957, Box 9, Folder 53, Margaret Walker Center, Jackson State University.

2. "The Younger Generation," *Time*, November 5, 1951.

3. George Swan, "College Represented at Youth Congress," *The Blue and White Flash*, December 1946, Jackson State University Archives.

4. Jackson State established a chapter of SNYC on their campus not long after Swan's return. However, by the end of the 1940s SNYC folded under the increasing pressure and scrutiny of the conservative right and the increased intimidation of white supremacists organizations. For more information on SNYC, see C. Alvin Hughes, "We Demand Our Rights: The Southern Negro Youth Congress, 1937–1949," *Phylon*, 48, no. 1, 1987; Johnetta Richard, "The Southern Negro Youth Congress:

A History" (Ph.D. Dissertation, University of Cincinnati, 1987), "Report of the Youth Section of the National Negro Congress," February 14–16, 1937, Reel 2, Part I, Papers of the National Negro Congress, Library of Congress, Washington, DC, "Report of Committee on Permanent Organization," Papers of the National Negro Congress, Reel 2, Part I, 29 Collections of the Manuscript Division, Library of Congress, Washington, DC.

5. Peoples was a 1950 graduate of Jackson State College and served as student government president and captain of the football team.

6. John Peoples, interview by the author, July 21, 2004.

7. Useful book-length studies underscoring the diversity, purpose, and mission of Black college faculty include James D. Anderson, *The Education of Blacks in the South, 1860–1935* (Chapel Hill: University of North Carolina Press, 1988); Charles Payne and Carol Strickland, *Teach Freedom: Education for Liberation in the African American Tradition* (New York: Teachers College Press, 2008); Adam Fairclough, *A Class of Their Own: Black Teachers in the Segregated South* (Cambridge, MA: Harvard University Press, 2007); and Gabrielle Edgcomb, *From Swastika to Jim Crow: Refugee Scholars at Black Colleges* (Malabar, FL: Krieger, 1993).

8. Joy Ann Williamson, *Radicalizing the Ebony Tower: Black Colleges and the Black Freedom Struggle in Mississippi* (New York: Teachers College Press, 2008), 34.

9. Margaret Walker Alexander, interview by Ann Allen Shockley, July 18, 1973, Fisk University Archives, John Hope and Aurelia Franklin Library, Fisk University.

10. Susie Baughns, "Join the Youth Council," *Blue and White Flash*, November 1942.

11. "Jackson College Represented at NAACP Conference," *Blue and White Flash*, November 1942.

12. Fairclough, *Class of Their Own*, 137.

13. Onezimae Clark, "A Prayer for the Class of '45," *Blue and White Flash*, May 1945.

14. Johnny Edwards, "Moving Forward to Serve Humanity," *Blue and White Flash*, May 1949.

15. "This I Believe," *Blue and White Flash*, March 1956.

16. "Columbia's First Negro Woman Ph.D. Joins Faculty Here," *Blue and White Flash*, January 1951.

17. Jane McAllister to Mark Starr, December 14, 1951, Jane McAllister Collection, Box 2, Jackson State University Archives.

18. Jane McAllister to Charles Hunt, January 15, 1952, Jane McAllister Collection, Box 1, Jackson State University Archives.

19. Ouida Kinnard, interview by the author, July 31, 2005.

20. Dorie Ladner, interview by the author, June 23, 2004.

21. Jane McAllister to Arthur Gray, March 15, 1957, Jane McAllister Collection, Talladega College File, Jackson State University Archives.

22. Margaret Walker Alexander, journal entry, July 22, 1949, Margaret Walker Alexander Journals, Box 5, Folder 34, Margaret Walker Alexander National Research Center.

23. Margaret Walker Alexander, journal entry, September 27, 1949, Margaret Walker Alexander Journals, Box 5, Folder 36, Margaret Walker Alexander National Research Center.

24. Margaret Walker Alexander, journal entry, January 12, 1950, Margaret Walker Alexander Journals, Box 5, Folder 38, Margaret Walker Alexander National Research Center.

25. Margaret Walker Alexander, journal entry, October 9, 1955, Margaret Walker Alexander Journals, Box 9, Folder 51, Margaret Walker Alexander National Research Center.

26. Walker, journal entry, October 9, 1955.

27. Walker's own life may have had some bearing on the main character, Vyry, in her acclaimed novel *Jubilee*. In the novel, Vyry makes the conscious decision to not escape the horrors of slavery in order to remain with her family. See Margaret Walker Alexander, *Jubilee* (Boston: Houghton Mifflin, 1966).

28. Margaret Walker Alexander, journal entry, August 12, 1957, Margaret Walker Alexander Journals, Box 9, Folder 53, Margaret Walker Alexander National Research Center.

29. Gloria Jean Douglas-Clemons, interview by the author, July 31, 2005.

30. Kinnard, interview.

31. Douglas-Clemons, interview.

32. Margaret Walker Alexander, journal entry, June 24, 1958, Margaret Walker Alexander Journals, Box 9, Folder 54, Margaret Walker Alexander National Research Center.

33. Fairclough, *Class of Their Own*, 378.

34. William Jones to Jacob L. Reddix, n.d.; Junius R. Sanders to Jacob L. Reddix, May 2, 1937; J. Nathaniel Smith to Jacob L. Reddix, June 12, 1937, Box 1, Folder 6, Jacob L. Reddix Papers, Jackson State University, H.T. Sampson Library, University Archives/Special Collections, Jackson, Mississippi.

35. John Hope II to Jacob L. Reddix, March 14, 1939, Box 1, Folder 6, Jacob L. Reddix Papers, Jackson State University, H.T. Sampson Library, University Archives/Special Collections, Jackson, Mississippi.

36. Maurice L. Sisson to Jacob L. Reddix, March 8, 1940, Box 1, Folder 6, Jacob L. Reddix Papers, Jackson State University, H.T. Sampson Library, University Archives/Special Collections, Jackson, Mississippi.

37. Charles H. Welch to Jacob L. Reddix, February 15, 1937, Box 1, Folder 6, Jacob L. Reddix Papers, Jackson State University, H.T. Sampson Library, University Archives/Special Collections, Jackson, Mississippi.

38. Reddix was the first president to preside over Jackson College after the state assumed control of the institution in 1940, ending sixty-three years of control by the American Baptist Home Mission Society. The society noted that Tougaloo College was adequately meeting the educational needs of African Americans in the area, therefore relinquishing their financial support for Jackson College. For more on the transition of Jackson College to state control, see Jacob L. Reddix, *A Voice Crying in the Wilderness: The Memoirs of Jacob L. Reddix* (Jackson: University Press

of Mississippi, 1974); and Lelia Rhodes, *Jackson State University: The First Hundred Years, 1877–1977* (Jackson: University Press of Mississippi, 1979).

39. Reddix, *Voice Crying*, 222.

40. Peoples, interview.

41. For more on the Tougaloo Nine incident and the legacy of activism at Tougaloo, see Clarice T. Campbell and Oscar Allan Rogers Jr., *Mississippi: The View from Tougaloo* (Jackson: University Press of Mississippi, 1979); John Dittmer, *Local People: The Struggle for Civil Rights in Mississippi* (Urbana: University of Illinois Press, 1995); David Sansing, *Making Haste Slowly: The Troubled History of Higher Education in Mississippi* (Jackson: University Press of Mississippi, 1990); and Williamson, *Radicalizing the Ebony Tower*.

42. Hattiesburg's most famous freedom fighters were local NAACP leader Dahmer and activist turned political prisoner Kennard, both of whom worked vigorously for change in Mississippi. Dahmer fought tirelessly for change in Hattiesburg until his assassination in 1966. Kennard's demise was equally upsetting to Black Mississippians. Kennard attempted to become the first Black to enroll in Mississippi Southern College (now the University of Southern Mississippi). Kennard's attempts were unsuccessful, as he was continually harassed by local and state law officials and was finally arrested and sentenced to a seven-year prison term at the state penitentiary on trumped-up charges of theft. During his incarceration, it was discovered that Kennard was suffering from cancer. He was eventually released but succumbed to cancer shortly afterward. Both men played critical roles in shaping the political consciousness of numerous young men and women—namely, Dorie and Joyce Ladner. For more on both Dahmer and Kennard, see Dittmer, *Local People*; Charles Payne, *I've Got the Light of Freedom: The Organizing Tradition and the Mississippi Freedom Struggle* (Berkeley: University of California Press, 1995); and Sansing, *Making Haste Slowly*, 148–54.

43. Ladner, interview.

44. "Jackson State College Students Stage Protest," *Clarion Ledger*, March 28, 1961.

45. "Jackson State College."

46. Ladner, interview.

47. "Jackson State College."

48. Jacob L. Reddix to Albert Jones, April 1, 1961, Mississippi State Sovereignty Commission Files, Mississippi Department of Archives and History.

49. Ladner, interview.

50. Ladner, interview.

51. Ladner, interview.

52. Margaret Walker Alexander, journal entry, July 9, 1961, Margaret Walker Alexander Journals, Box 10, Folder 61, Margaret Walker Alexander National Research Center.

53. "Report Classes Boycotted at Jackson State," *Jackson Daily News*, October 7, 1961.

54. One can easily conclude that environmental factors played a large role in both Tougaloo and Jackson State students' decision not to become involved in the

movement. The class factor represents a somewhat plausible theory in comparing Jackson State and Tougaloo but does not hold up in an analysis of other institutions involved in the Black student movement, most notably North Carolina A&T State University, where the movement started. As it was a state institution, students involved in the movement there had the same working-class background as many Jackson State students, yet they became pioneers of Black student activism in the 1960s. The less threatening political and social climate can perhaps be attributed to the boldness on behalf of the students from Greensboro.

55. Quoted in James Silver, *Mississippi: The Closed Society* (New York: Harcourt, Brace and World, 1963), 34.

56. Quoted in Silver, 8.

57. Jane McAllister to Miss Briffault, November 12, 1962, Jane McAllister Collection, Box 1, Jackson State University Archives.

58. Jane McAllister to Rosalie, March 4, 1963, Jane McAllister Collection, Box 1, Jackson State University Archives.

59. Jane McAllister to J. D. Williams, November 8, 1962, Jane McAllister Collection, Jackson State University Archives.

60. It is not clear why Robinson left Southern University for Jackson State if his intentions included support for student insurgency. These institutions resembled each other in the sense that they were both state institutions that were under the thumb of hard-line presidents who served at the behest of a white governing board. At Southern University 3,500 members of the student body marched to the state capitol in protest against Jim Crow policies, and 140 members of the Southern faculty signed a statement of support for their students. Such support ultimately cost Robinson his job, but Southern University became a hotbed of student protest throughout the decade, producing famous student activists such as Major Johns, Ronnie Moore, Eddie Brown, and his younger, outspoken brother, H. "Rap" Brown (Jamil Amin). For more on Southern University and the rise of student activism in Baton Rouge, see August Meier and Elliot Rudwick, *CORE: A Study in the Civil Rights Movement, 1942–1968* (New York: Oxford University Press, 1973); Adam Fairclough, *Race and Democracy: The Civil Rights Struggle in Louisiana, 1915–1972* (Athens: University of Georgia Press, 1999); and Major Johns and Ronnie Moore, *It Happened in Baton Rouge* (New York: Congress of Racial Equality, 1962).

61. The fact that the MSSC refused to inform Reddix that two of his employees were being interrogated, despite the fact that they had a working relationship with him, corroborates the testimony of John Peoples. In an interview with the author, Peoples stated that Reddix often was angered by the state's request and sometimes falsified information to MSSC investigators. See "Investigation of George Lee Robinson, Colored Male and Delores Catherine Toms Robinson, Colored Female," April 16, 1963, Mississippi State Sovereignty Commission Files, Mississippi Department of Archives and History; and John Peoples, interview.

62. Jane McAllister to Mabel Carney, November 3, 1964, Jane McAllister Collection, Box 1, Jackson State University Archives.

63. For documentation on the effects of white terrorism on Black communities, see Julius Thompson, *Black Life in Mississippi: Essays on Political, Social, and*

Cultural Studies in a Deep South State (Lanham, MD: University Press of America, 2001); Anne Moody, *Coming of Age in Mississippi* (New York: Dell, 1968); Neil R. McMillen, *Dark Journey: Black Mississippians in the Age of Jim Crow* (Urbana: University of Illinois Press, 1990); Silver, *Mississippi*; and James W. Loewen and Charles Sallis, eds., *Mississippi: Conflict and Change* (New York: Pantheon Books, 1974).

64. David Dennis, interview by the author, August 11, 2004. Dennis was the Congress of Racial Equality field secretary in Mississippi, and he loaned the car that he had been using to John Chaney, Michael Schwerner, and Andrew Goodman to go to Meridian and then on to Philadelphia, Mississippi, to start schools in the area and to investigate recent church bombings. The three young men were among the earliest participants in Freedom Summer. They were abducted, beaten, and murdered, which sent shockwaves throughout the country.

65. Ladner continued to say in the interview that although she was hurt by Mrs. Burks's accusation, she did not take it personally. She contended that it was part of a larger web of ignorance on the part of a few of the older generation who blamed activists and not the culture of intolerance and terrorism in which they lived. Ladner, interview.

66. Dennis, interview.

67. Dittmer, *Local People*, 161.

68. Dittmer, 160–69.

69. Ed King, interview by the author, June 30, 2004.

70. Adam Nossiter, *Of Long Memory: Mississippi and the Murder of Medgar Evers* (Reading, MA: Addison-Wesley, 1994), 57.

71. Moody, *Coming of Age in Mississippi*, 277.

72. Moody, 278. Reddix did not strike Ladner, nor did students mount an organized demonstration on campus after the incident. However, what is clear throughout Moody's book is the fact that during the early stages of the civil rights struggle in Mississippi, Jackson State students participated in movement activities, albeit in smaller roles and numbers than their peers at Tougaloo. Moody makes note of Jackson State student Doris Erskine, whom she served time with in jail and whom she also participated in the freedom struggle in Canton with. In an interview, Ladner discussed the shooting of her friend Marylene Burks, who was a student at Jackson State. Both sources provide examples of students from Jackson State who overtly or covertly participated in movement activity. What this suggests is that, though most students attending Jackson State between the years 1960 and 1963 were still reluctant to join in the movement openly, there were others who participated without reprisal from campus authorities.

73. "One Hundred Years of Progress?," *Blue and White Flash*, April 1963.

74. Jane McAllister to James A. Colston, July 27, 1963, Jane McAllister Collection, Box 1, Jackson State University Archives. McAllister's students were referencing a speech that was delivered on campus by James Colston, president of Knoxville College, a small, historically Black college in Tennessee. During his speech, Colston keenly relayed the ancient Greek story of Antigone to students. The classic tale speaks of Polyneices, a rebel who has been killed in battle. Polyneices has been denied proper burial by Creon, ruler of Thebes, and Polyneices's sister

Antigone has decided to defy Creon and bury her brother anyway. The story concludes with the gods punishing Creon for being on the wrong side of righteousness. Colston's delivery of such a story in the wake of Medgar Evers's assassination and the turmoil following his funeral was not lost on Jackson State students, who embraced the metaphors.

75. Ross R. Barnett to Jacob L. Reddix, February 21, 1967, Box 1, Folder 12, Jacob L. Reddix Papers, Jackson State University, H.T. Sampson Library, University Archives/Special Collections, Jackson, Mississippi.

Chapter Six

1. William Nelson Jr., who served on the faculty of Southern University during the late 1960s, was the first person to relay this story to me. The archival staff at Southern University later corroborated Nelson's account of Clark and the ritual and theatrics surrounding the event. Nelson became one of the pioneers and founders of the Black studies field in the late 1960s. Nevertheless, his colleague Mack Jones offered a counterbalance to Nelson's recollection of Clark. Jones was a former student at Southern University and was actually one of many students who were expelled by Clark at the beginning of the decade. Yet in a conversation I had with Jones, the retired professor emeritus of Clark Atlanta University remembered Clark as being something of a race man in the years before the overt protests of the 1960s, a topic that will be further explored and illustrated throughout this chapter. Jones reenrolled at Texas Southern University in Houston and went on to become a prolific scholar in the field of political science and one of the foremost authorities on the history of historically Black colleges and universities.

2. Adam Fairclough, *Race and Democracy: The Civil Rights Struggle in Louisiana, 1915–1972* (Athens: University of Georgia Press, 1999), 266, 270; Adam Fairclough, *A Class of Their Own: Black Teachers in the Segregated South* (Cambridge, MA: Harvard University Press, 2007), 380.

3. Felton G. Clark, "Administrative Control of Public Negro Colleges," *Journal of Negro Education* 3, no. 3 (April 1934): 247.

4. D'Army Bailey, *The Education of a Black Radical: A Southern Civil Rights Activist's Journey, 1959–1964* (Baton Rouge: Louisiana State University Press, 2009), 36.

5. Henry C. Dethloff and Robert R. Jones, "Race Relations in Louisiana, 1877–98," in *The Louisiana Purchase Bicentennial Series in Louisiana History*, vol. 11, *The African American Experience in Louisiana*, pt. B, *From the Civil War to Jim Crow*, ed. Charles Vincent (Lafayette: University of Louisiana at Lafayette, 2000), 507–8.

6. Roger A. Fischer, *The Segregation Struggle in Louisiana, 1862–77* (Urbana: University of Illinois Press, 1974), 154.

7. Greta de Jong, *A Different Day: African American Struggles for Justice in Rural Louisiana, 1900–1970* (Chapel Hill: University of North Carolina Press, 2002), 41–63.

8. Fairclough, *Race and Democracy*, 6.

9. "President Clark Speaks before Thousands at the South Louisiana State Fair at Donaldsonville, Louisiana," *Southern University Digest*, October 15, 1929.

10. "Dr. Clark Delivers Commencement Address at Ruston," *Southern University Digest*, June 1, 1930.

11. For details on the Williams lynching and its aftermath throughout the state, see Fairclough, *Race and Democracy*, 29–32; George I. Lovell, *This Is Not Civil Rights: Discovering Rights Talk in 1939 America* (Chicago: University of Chicago Press, 2012), 52–53; Herbert Shapiro, *White Violence and Black Response: From Reconstruction to Montgomery* (Amherst: University of Massachusetts Press, 1988), 223; and Paul Gelpi, "The Consequences of a Small Town Murder: The Lynching of W.C. Williams and Louisiana Politics" (paper presented at the annual meeting of the American Society of Criminology, Chicago, IL, November 14–17, 2012).

12. "President and Three Representatives of Our 'Y' Guests of White Conference at Monroe," *Southern University Digest*, March 25, 1929; "President Clark Addresses Tuskegee Farmers' Conference," *Southern University Digest*, December 16, 1929; "S.U. Annual Farmers' Conference—February 13 and 14, 1930—Great Program," *Southern University Digest*, January 15, 1930; "Fifteenth Southern University Farmers' Conference Convened in Two Day Session February 13–14, 1930" and "Committee Studies Problems of Negroes," *Southern University Digest*, February 15, 1930.

13. "President Clark Addresses L.S.U. Y.M.C.A. Men," *Southern University Digest*, January 15, 1930.

14. "How Do We Think?," *Southern University Digest*, December 16, 1929.

15. "Dr. Clark Speaks at Corner Stone Laying," *Southern University Digest*, November 25, 1931.

16. Untitled article, *Southern University Digest*, February 15, 1930.

17. "Alice Dunbar Nelson Visits Southern and Makes Talk," *Southern University Digest*, March 15, 1930; "President's Broadcast Remarks on Labor Day—Labor as It Concerns Us Today," *Southern University Digest*, October 1931.

18. "Noise," *Southern University Digest*, January 15, 1930; Thomas Aiello, "Calumny in the House of the Lord: The 1932 Zion Traveler Church Shooting," in *Louisiana beyond Black and White: New Interpretations of Twentieth-Century Race and Race Relations*, ed. Michael S. Martin (Lafayette: University of Louisiana at Lafayette Press, 2011), 23; "Sherman Briscoe," *Washington Afro-American*, November 6, 1979, 4.

19. Lee Sartain makes the case for women activists and educators who formed the lifeblood of Louisiana's NAACP branches and whose insistence on training youths in Black history served as a critical stopgap measure in reversing the psychological effects of white supremacy. See Lee Sartain, *Invisible Activists: Women of the Louisiana NAACP and the Struggle for Civil Rights, 1915–1945* (Baton Rouge: Louisiana State University Press, 2007), 87–98.

20. "Negro History Week Celebration," *Southern University Digest*, February 1, 1932; "Southern Joins Nation in Celebrating Negro Health Week," *Southern University Digest*, April 1, 1932; "Concerning Liberia" and "Lest We Forget," *Southern University Digest*, January 19, 1933; "Noted Historian Will Visit Our Campus during Negro History Week," *Southern University Digest*, February 1, 1933; "Dr. Carter G. Woodson Speaks before Packed House Here Sunday Evening—Great Historian Stirs Audience to Race Pride," "Sub-cousins Observe Negro History Week during

Chapel Hour," "Cousins Celebrate Negro History Week in Scotlandville," and "Class in Negro History Gives Play on Negro Life," *Southern University Digest*, February 16, 1933.

21. Sartain, *Invisible Activists*, 116.

22. "Youth Organize for Cooperation," *Southern University Digest*, October 15, 1938.

23. "Baton Rouge Youths Branch of NAACP Organized Recently," *Southern University Digest*, January 18, 1939; Emmett W. Bashful, interview, June 8, 1990, African American Political Scientists Oral History Project, Louie B. Nunn Center for Oral History, University of Kentucky Libraries; Sartain, *Invisible Activists*, 117.

24. Bashful, interview; Bruce Kuklick, *Black Philosopher, White Academy: The Career of William Fontaine* (Philadelphia: University of Pennsylvania Press, 2008), 45–48; "Science Class Holds Election" and "Southern Students Go Political Minded," *Southern University Digest*, February 28, 1940.

25. "What Should We Fight For Should War Come," *Southern University Digest*, October 6, 1939.

26. "Negro Progress," *Southern University Digest*, January 18, 1939; "What Are We Doing?," *Southern University Digest*, February 17, 1939; "Radical Idealism and the Negro," *Southern University Digest*, November 18, 1939; "Dr. DuBois to Speak Here Saturday," *Southern University Digest*, February 1, 1940.

27. "Southern University Should Be Represented!!," *Southern University Digest*, April 5, 1940; "Social Science Classes Publish Bulletin," *Southern University Digest*, April 24, 1940; "Students Are Talking About" and "Southern Represented at Youth Congress," *Southern University Digest*, May 22, 1940.

28. "Aggressive Pessimism," *Southern University Digest*, March 7, 1941; "The Negro and the National Defense," *Southern University Digest*, December 5, 1940; "The Poet's Sweat Shop," *Southern University Digest*, January 13, 1941; "Negro History Week Celebrated Here" and "Town Hall Discussion Initiated Here," *Southern University Digest*, February 20, 1941; "Southern and LSU Students Discuss Race Relations," *Southern University Digest*, April 4, 1941; "Last Town Hall Meeting Is Huge Success at Southern U," *Southern University Digest*, May 30, 1941.

29. "Baton Rougeans Protest Unwarranted Attacks on Citizenry by Policemen," *Louisiana Weekly*, June 28, 1941; "Baton Rouge Citizens Seek Federal Aid to Stop Police Brutal Attacks on Negroes," *Louisiana Weekly*, July 26, 1941, "Baton Rouge Grand Jury Completes 'Wrong Way' Police Brutality Probe," *Louisiana Weekly*, August 2, 1941; "Dr. Logan Speaks at Mixed Assembly," *Southern University Digest*, December 5, 1941.

30. Fairclough, *Race and Democracy*, 111; F. A. Brigham, "Negro Leadership," *Southern University Digest*, January 26, 1942; Marcus S. Cox, *Segregated Soldiers: Military Training at Historically Black Colleges in the Jim Crow South* (Baton Rouge: Louisiana State University Press, 2013), 68–98.

31. Oby Jefferson, "Our Town," *Southern University Digest*, March 31, 1942.

32. Oby Jefferson, "Jottings," *Southern University Digest*, March 31, 1942; "Baton Rouge Citizens Continue Their Fight against Police Brutality," *Louisiana Weekly*, January 23, 1943; "Christianity Has Failed Rebutted the Negative in Town Hall," *Southern University Digest*, August 5, 1943.

33. "Institution Head Petitions Authorities 'to Consider Negro Interest' in Problems Course," *Southern University Digest*, March 5, 1943; "Dr. Felton Clark Pleads for Return to Christian Idealism," *Southern University Digest*, October 15, 1943; "Prexy's Letter Box," *Southern University Digest*, March 15, 1944.

34. Patricia Sullivan, "Southern Reformers, the New Deal, and the Movement's Foundation," in *New Directions in Civil Rights Studies*, ed. Armstead L. Robinson and Patricia Sullivan (Charlottesville: University Press of Virginia, 1991), 86; "Senior Is Selected as NAACP Representative," *Southern University Digest*, October 15, 1943; "Junior NAACP Chapter Receives Compliments," *Southern University Digest*, March 1, 1944; "Junior Branch of NAACP Gets Charter," *Southern University Digest*, March 15, 1944; "Support the NAACP," *Southern University Digest*, May 4, 1944.

35. Sartain, *Invisible Activists*, 82; Fairclough, *Race and Democracy*, 62; Mary Jacqueline Hebert, "Beyond Black and White: The Civil Rights Movement in Baton Rouge, Louisiana, 1945–1972" (PhD diss., Louisiana State University, 1999), 45–51.

36. "Southern U. Professor Speaks His Mind," *Southern University Digest*, April 19, 1944; "Dr. Jackson Speaks at Dillard University," *Southern University Digest*, May 24, 1944; "Students Arrested for Attempt to Break Down Jim Crow in Greyhound Bus Station" and "FBI Investigates Alabama Vote Ban," *Southern University Digest*, October 9, 1944; "Enters Suit against Railroad as Refused Dining Car Service" and "Ala. Man Denied Right to Register Wins Major Point," *Southern University Digest*, October 23, 1944.

37. "Hardy Victim of White Fascist Uprising," *Southern University Digest*, December 7, 1944; "White Attitude toward Negro Must Change, for Peace," *Southern University Digest*, December 15, 1944. For a detailed account of the Hardy assault, see Fairclough, *Race and Democracy*, 89–90.

38. "A. Phillip Randolph Addresses Student Body and Faculty," *Southern University Digest*, March 29, 1945.

39. "Academic Matters," *Southern University Digest*, June, July, August 1945; "S.U. Students in the Post War World," *Southern University Digest*, October 1945; Willie J. Hodge, "Which Way World?," *Southern University Digest*, November 1945. Pertee continued to teach at Southern until 1952, when he was appointed as the principal at Southtown High School in Houma, Louisiana. In her memoirs, Louisiana native Catherine J. Carter recalls how Pertee recruited teachers from Southern, Grambling, Xavier, and Dillard to come teach at Southtown and how those teachers helped to craft the freedom dreams of generations of Black youths. See Catherine J. Carter, *I Bet You Have a Story* (Bloomington, IN: Authorhouse, 2013), 12–13.

40. For a detailed assessment of the NAACP's challenges in Louisiana, see Sartain, *Invisible Activists*, 120–44; Shannon Frystak, *Our Minds on Freedom: Women and the Struggle for Black Equality in Louisiana, 1924–1967* (Baton Rouge: Louisiana State University Press, 2009), 12–29; Fairclough, *Race and Democracy*, 48–49, 188–91; Dupuy Anderson, interview, January 5, 1994, T. Harry Williams Center for Oral History, Louisiana State University Libraries Special Collections.

41. Patricia Sullivan, *Lift Every Voice: The NAACP and the Making of the Civil Rights Movement* (New York: New Press, 2009), 249; Rachel Lorraine Emanuel and

Alexander P. Tureaud Jr., *A More Nobel Cause: A. P. Tureaud and the Struggle for Civil Rights in Louisiana* (Baton Rouge: Louisiana State University Press, 2011), 127–37; "Atty. Berry Speaks to Business Law Class Here," *Southern University Digest*, October 22, 1946.

42. "Southern University Teachers File Suits to Test Legality of Bus Jim Crow," *Pittsburgh Courier*, December 14, 1946; "2 College Teachers Sue La. Bus Co. for $12,000," *Afro American*, February 1, 1947; Frystak, *Our Minds on Freedom*, 62; "Mrs. Cochran Speaks at LSU Student Center," *Southern University Digest*, November 12, 1946.

43. "Dr. Rose Speaks at Negro History Week Convocation," *Southern University Digest*, February 24, 1950.

44. Jewell Prestage, interview, October 30, 1992, African American Political Scientists Oral History Project, Louie B. Nunn Center for Oral History, University of Kentucky Libraries; Fairclough, *Race and Democracy*, 156. For more on Georgia Johnson and the civil rights movement in Alexandria, see Sartain, *Invisible Activists*, 120–44; and Frystak, *Our Minds on Freedom*, 18–23.

45. "Three to Attend NSA Confab in Miami, Fla.," *Southern University Digest*, November 29, 1952; "Segregation Is on the Way Out," *Southern University Digest*, November 15, 1952.

46. Fairclough, *Race and Democracy*, 157–58; Emmett Buell, "The Politics of Frustration: An Analysis of Negro Leadership in East Baton Rouge Parish, Louisiana, 1953–1966" (MA thesis, Louisiana State University, 1967), 116.

47. Aldon Morris, *The Origins of the Civil Rights Movement: Black Communities Organizing for Change* (New York: Free Press, 1984), 19–21; Fairclough, *Race and Democracy*, 158–59; Frystak, *Our Minds on Freedom*, 64–66.

48. Buell, "Politics of Frustration," 116–23; Fairclough, *Race and Democracy*, 160–63; Morris, *Origins*, 24–25; Dean Sinclair, "Equal in All Places: The Civil Rights Struggle in Baton Rouge, 1953–1963," *Louisiana History: The Journal of the Louisiana Historical Association* 39, no. 3 (Summer 1998): 354.

49. Hebert, "Beyond Black and White," 28; Sartain, *Invisible Activists*, 111; "Business Pioneer Thompson Dies at 98," *Advocate* (Baton Rouge, LA), October 22, 2012.

50. "Brotherhood—The Road to Peace," *Southern University Digest*, February 20, 1954.

51. "University Enrollment Increase Gains Momentum during Summer," *Southern University Digest*, July 14, 1954; "Law Prof's Profile," "Negro Literature," and "Negro History to Be Offered," "NAACP Chapter Formed on Campus," *Southern University Digest*, December 2, 1955; "Government Classes Hold Mock Convention," *Southern University Digest*, December 16, 1955; "Henderson Asks for Civic Plans," *Southern University Digest*, March 29, 1956; "Mock Convention Held by Classes in Government," *Southern University Digest*, May 25, 1956.

52. "Histopolighaphecon Series Begins," *Southern University Digest*, November 16, 1956; "Montgomery Boycott Leader Visits Baton Rouge Church," *Southern University Digest*, December 1, 1956.

53. Felton Grandison Clark, "President Clark Encourages Digest Staff," *Southern University Digest*, September 30, 1955; "News Leader Praises Southern," *Southern*

University Digest, October 28, 1955; Hebert, "Beyond Black and White," 158. For more on the American Friends Service Committee, see Allan W. Austin, *Quaker Brotherhood: Interracial Activism and the American Friends Service Committee, 1917–1950* (Urbana: University of Illinois Press, 2012); and Mary Hoxie Jones, *Swords into Plowshares: An Account of the American Friends Service Committee, 1917–1937* (New York: Macmillan, 1937).

54. Alvin Aubert, "Our Leaders Are Failing Us," *Southern University Digest*, January 28, 1957. Aubert returned to Southern to teach shortly after graduating and taught there for ten years beginning in 1960. He later became one of the militant voices of the Black Arts movement in the late 1960s, and he remains a prolific poet and author, often writing short stories and poems that center on life in Louisiana.

55. "Hampton Students Boycott Local Theatres," *Southern University Digest*, December 21, 1956. For more on the Tallahassee boycott, see Glenda Alice Rabby, *The Pain and the Promise: The Struggle for Civil Rights in Tallahassee, Florida* (Athens: University of Georgia Press, 1999); Ana Maria Spagna, *Test Ride on the Sunnyland Bus: A Daughter's Civil Rights Journey* (Lincoln: University of Nebraska Press, 2010); William Chafe, *Civilities and Civil Rights: Greensboro, North Carolina, and the Black Struggle for Freedom* (Oxford: Oxford University Press, 1980), 61; and August Meier and Elliot Rudwick, *Along the Color Line: Explorations in the Black Experience* (Urbana: University of Illinois Press, 2002), 307.

56. Sinclair, "Equal in All Places," 358–59.

57. "Spark Struck May Soon Set African Continent Ablaze" and "Writer Reveals False Idea of Africa by Americans—Both White and Negro," *Southern University Digest*, March 26, 1959; "Belgians Say Congo Moving toward Freedom," *Southern University Digest*, May 1, 1959.

58. Interview with Mack H. Jones, July 15, 1994, African American Political Scientists Oral History Project, Louie B. Nunn Center for Oral History, University of Kentucky Libraries.

59. Major Johns and Ronnie Moore, *It Happened in Baton Rouge* (New York: Congress of Racial Equality, 1962), 1–2.

60. August Meier and Elliot Rudwick, *CORE: A Study in the Civil Rights Movement, 1942–1968* (New York: Oxford University Press, 1973), 107–8; Fairclough, *Race and Democracy*, 268.

61. Frystak, *Our Minds on Freedom*, 110.

62. Johns and Moore, *It Happened in Baton Rouge*, 4; Warmouth T. Gibbs, interview by Lewis Brandon, December 12, 1987, Lewis Brandon Personal Archives (transcript in author's possession); Fairclough, *Class of Their Own*, 380.

63. Fairclough, *Race and Democracy*, 269; H. Rap Brown, *Die Nigger Die!* (Chicago: Lawrence Hill Books, 1969), 63. Brown became the chairman of the Student Nonviolent Coordinating Committee (SNCC) in 1967. Both he and his brother, Ed Brown, were active in the Baton Rouge sit-in movement. Ed was expelled in 1960 and went on to enroll at Howard University, where his politicization continued. H. Rap Brown left Southern on his own terms after the summer of 1964.

64. "The Digest in Retrospect Evaluated the Past Years Work," *Southern University Digest*, May 25, 1961; "Press Censorship" and "Strolling the Campus," *Southern*

University Digest, October 14, 1961; "Strolling the Campus," *Southern University Digest,* November 4, 1961.

65. Meier and Rudwick, *CORE,* 3–72; David Dennis, interview by the author, August 11, 2004.

66. Fairclough, *Race and Democracy,* 289; "Registrar Emphasizes Out-of-State Student's Responsibility," *Southern University Digest,* November 25, 1961.

67. Meier and Rudwick, *CORE,* 166; Sinclair, "Equal in All Places," 363; Johns and Moore, *It Happened in Baton Rouge,* 5.

68. Fairclough, *Race and Democracy,* 290–91; Johns and Moore, *It Happened in Baton Rouge,* 6; "Letters to the Editor," *Southern University Digest,* January 15, 1962.

69. Johns and Moore, *It Happened in Baton Rouge,* 8; and Fairclough, *Race and Democracy,* 291. August Meier and Elliot Rudwick contend that one of the major failures of the Baton Rouge protests of the early 1960s was the strategy adopted by the local white establishment. The media essentially ignored the protests, thus robbing organizations like CORE and the students of Southern of the exposure and notoriety they needed in order to draw attention to the fallacy and injustice of Jim Crow policies. See Meier and Rudwick, *CORE,* 168.

70. "Faculty Student Committee Initiates Improvement Meetings Following Campus Demonstrations," *Southern University Digest,* February 17, 1962.

71. "Misinterpretations: Who's at Fault," *Southern University Digest,* February 17, 1962.

72. Ibid; Dennis, interview.

73. "Rev. King Asks Negroes to Take Defensive Actions," *Southern University Digest,* March 12, 1962; Dennis, interview. Historian Wesley Hogan provides a very detailed look at the unraveling of SNCC and the growing frustration brought on by government obstinacy at all levels. See Wesley Hogan, *Many Minds, One Heart: SNCC's Dream for a New America* (Chapel Hill: University of North Carolina Press, 2007), 71–77.

74. "Campus Pierian Club Features Panel" and "Defends Right of Teachers and Students to Join in Demonstrations for Good Causes," *Southern University Digest,* April 4, 1962; Martin Oppenheimer, *The Sit-In Movement of 1960* (New York: Carlson, 1989), 86–94.

75. "A Double Victory: Tennessee and Mississippi," *Southern University Digest,* November 20, 1962; "Political Science Department Cited as Outstanding Here," *Southern University Digest,* June 3, 1963.

76. "In Retrospect: The Student Senate Year," *Southern University Digest,* April 21, 1964; "On the Civil Rights Bill" and "Write Your Congressman," *Southern University Digest,* May 20, 1964; "Politically Speaking," *Southern University Digest,* October 17, 1964; "The Republicans Twenty-Third Psalm" and "Why the Nation's Elderly Should Fear Sen. Goldwater," *Southern University Digest,* November 5, 1964; "Tests in Bogalusa by Demonstrators Prove Successful; Services Rendered" and "Saga in Jonesboro," *Southern University Digest,* March 3, 1965; Hebert, "Beyond Black and White," 308–9. Edmonia Davidson was a professor at Southern University and was instrumental in educating students on the decolonization efforts of African people

and the struggle throughout the continent. She subscribed to *Africa Today* news magazine and kept copies in the library available for students' perusal.

77. ; "Malcolm X—The Man without the Mask," and "Howard Univ. President Addresses 51st Anniversary Convocation," *Southern University Digest*, April 7, 1965.

78. For more on the internal tension in organizations such as SNCC and CORE and the slow demise of both organizations, see Clayborne Carson, *In Struggle: SNC and the Black Awakening of the 1960s* (Cambridge, MA: Harvard University Press, 1981), 175–211; Charles M. Payne, *I've Got the Light of Freedom: The Organizing Tradition and the Mississippi Freedom Struggle* (Berkeley: University of California Press, 1995), 363–90; Hogan, *Many Minds, One Heart*, 197–225; Meier and Rudwick, *CORE*, 282–326; "Deltas Host Civil Rights Workshop," *Southern University Digest*, May 12, 1965.

79. "Communists Make Move to College Campuses," *Southern University Digest*, May 31, 1965; "Chucklin' with Chuck," *Southern University Digest*, August 6, 1965.

80. "Department of Political Science Holds 'Black Power' Seminar," *Southern University Digest*, November 4, 1966.

81. "Volunteer Tutors Needed for Anti-poverty Program," *Southern University Digest*, November 18, 1966; "Digest Spotlight," *Southern University Digest*, April 5, 1968.

Chapter Seven

1. "Howard Fuller Addresses Black Student Conference," *A&T Register*, October 10, 1969.

2. William Chafe has written the authoritative work on the civil rights movement in Greensboro. Chafe traces student activism in Greensboro back to the 1930s and gives several examples of students from Bennett College and North Carolina A&T actively participating in demonstrations against Jim Crow long before the famous sit-ins of 1960. However, Chafe's community study of Greensboro presents a partial view of campus life as it related to activism at A&T. His attention to cultural patterns, protest traditions, and community institutions throughout the city provides room for more detailed analysis of student life and the progenitors of insurgency at A&T. See William Chafe, *Civilities and Civil Rights: Greensboro, North Carolina, and the Black Struggle for Freedom* (New York: Oxford University Press, 1980).

3. Jibrell Khazan, interview by the author, July 8, 1999.

4. The story of this unique coalition across class lines in Greensboro diverges from the narratives of other communities on the front lines of the civil rights movement. For example, historian Hasan Kwame Jeffries documents that the Student Nonviolent Coordinating Committee campaign in Lowndes County, Alabama, featured Black professionals who failed to embrace a political agenda that included the plight of working-class and poor Blacks. For more on SNCC and Lowndes County, see Hasan Kwame Jeffries, *Bloody Lowndes: Civil Rights and Black Power in Alabama's Black Belt* (New York: New York University Press, 2009).

5. For more on the mass jail-ins in Greensboro, see August Meier and Elliot Rudwick, *CORE: A Study in the Civil Rights Movement, 1942–1968* (Urbana: University of Illinois Press, 1975); Chafe, *Civilities and Civil Rights*; and Tom Dent, *Southern Journey: A Return to the Civil Rights Movement* (New York: William Morrow, 1997).

6. Claude Barnes, interview by the author, December 23, 1998.

7. For more on the class background of A&T students and how this favored the growth of activism, see Dent, *Southern Journey*, 39–40; and Miles Wolff, *Lunch at the 5 and 10: The Greensboro Sit-Ins* (New York: Stein and Day, 1970), 68–69.

8. The term *white power structure* is used often in civil rights discourse. In Greensboro, as in many other American cities, the power structure included city hall, housing authorities, law enforcement, and financial institutions. Additionally, these various forms of more institutionalized racism were both explicitly and tacitly supported by a number of average white citizens, some of whom resorted to more violent forms of coercion. There are numerous studies that examine the transformation to Black Power within the Student Nonviolent Coordinating Committee. For more on this ideological evolution, see Clayborne Carson, *In Struggle: SNCC and the Black Awakening of the 1960s* (Cambridge, MA: Harvard University Press, 1981); John Dittmer, *Local People: The Struggle for Civil Rights in Mississippi* (Urbana: University of Illinois Press, 1995); Charles Payne, *I've Got the Light of Freedom: The Organizing Tradition and the Mississippi Freedom Struggle* (Berkeley: University of California Press, 1995); Cynthia Griggs Fleming, *Soon We Will Not Cry: The Liberation of Ruby Doris Smith Robinson* (Lanham, MD: Rowman and Littlefield, 1998); Stokely Carmichael, *Ready for Revolution: The Life and Struggles of Stokely Carmichael (Kwame Ture)*, with Ekwueme Michael Thelwell (New York: Scribner, 2005); Christopher Strain, *Pure Fire: Self-Defense as Activism in the Civil Rights Era* (Athens: University of Georgia Press, 2005); Wesley Hogan, *Many Minds, One Heart: SNCC's Dream for a New America* (Chapel Hill: University of North Carolina Press, 2007); Akinyele Omowale Umoja, *We Will Shoot Back: Armed Resistance in the Mississippi Freedom Movement* (New York: New York University Press, 2013); Charles E. Cobb Jr., *This Nonviolent Stuff'll Get You Killed: How Guns Made the Civil Rights Movement Possible* (New York: Basic Books, 2014); and Hasan Kwame Jeffries, *Bloody Lowndes*.

9. Chafe, *Civilities and Civil Rights*, 213.

10. Lula M. Pennix to Scarborough Realty Company, January 22, 1969, Greensboro Association of Poor People (GAPP) Papers, Lewis Brandon Personal Archives. I have been given access to the unprocessed papers of GAPP, a vital organization to the civil rights movement in Greensboro. Lewis Brandon, a former student at A&T and a longtime activist in Greensboro, has collected the GAPP papers over time. The GAPP papers are four boxes that contain memoirs, minutes, flyers, essays by local and national activists, and correspondence related to GAPP activity. They also contain papers relating to the SOBU. These papers contain copies of the SOBU newspaper, the *African World*; correspondence between activists; flyers; newsletters; and newspaper clippings.

11. For more on the Orangeburg Massacre at South Carolina State University, see Jack Bass and Jack Nelson, *The Orangeburg Massacre* (Macon, GA: Mercer University

Press, 2002); Cleveland Sellers, *The River of No Return: The Autobiography of a Black Militant and the Life and Death of SNCC* (Jackson: University Press of Mississippi, 1990); Dent, *Southern Journey*; and Ibram Rogers, *The Black Campus Movement: Black Students and the Racial Reconstitution of Higher Education, 1965–1972* (New York: Palgrave Macmillan, 2012).

12. John White, *Black Leadership in America: From Booker T. Washington to Jesse Jackson* (London: Longman, 1990), 138–39.

13. Students enrolled in the internship program represented a cross section of North Carolina colleges. Those students included Rosalyn Woodward (North Carolina A&T State University), Catherine Watson (Duke University), Peggy Richmond (Bennett College), Larry McCleary (Fayetteville State College), Charles Hopkins (Duke University), and Lacy Joyner (North Carolina College). All students were placed in Greensboro for their internship in community organizing, a factor that increased the possibility for continued use of Greensboro as a laboratory for social activism. See A. S. Webb to Paul Gezon, July 22, 1968, GAPP Papers, Lewis Brandon Personal Archives.

14. Greensboro Association of Poor People Fact Sheet, GAPP Papers, Lewis Brandon Personal Archives.

15. Barnes, interview.

16. Barbara Joyner, "Dowdy Proposes Black Store, Student 'Blow' Money Needed," *A&T Register*, November 9, 1968.

17. Luther Brown, "College Students of G-boro Stage Peaceful 'Teach-In,'" *A&T Register*, November 9, 1968. For more on Dowdy and his response to the mass jail-in campaign of 1962–63, see Chafe, *Civilities and Civil Rights*, 185.

18. Lillie Miller, "Students Aid Workers in Obtaining Demands," *A&T Register*, March 20, 1969.

19. Sociologist Aldon Morris defines the concept of "local movement centers," which refers to the generation of activism among an aggrieved population by a specific organization or entity. See Aldon Morris, *The Origins of the Civil Rights Movement: Black Communities Organizing for Change* (New York: Free Press, 1984).

20. Cohen N. Greene, "Police Open Fire on Students in Wake of Campus Disturbance," *A&T Register*, March 20, 1969.

21. Greene, "Police Open Fire."

22. Horace Ferguson, "From Plantation to Hunting Ground," *A&T Register*, March 28, 1969.

23. Beginning with the protest of the Orangeburg Massacre during the winter of 1968 and continuing through the violent attack of campus by the National Guard in May 1969, a heavy military presence remained throughout Greensboro. See Chafe, *Civilities and Civil Rights*, 172–202.

24. Leander Forbes, "Reflective Notes on May 1969 at North Carolina A&T State University," GAPP Papers, Lewis Brandon Personal Archives.

25. Nelson Johnson, "Projection in Blackness," GAPP Papers, Lewis Brandon Personal Archives.

26. David Lee Brown, "University to Be Site of First Conference for Black Students," *A&T Register*, May 2, 1969.

27. Chafe, *Civilities and Civil Rights*, 185.

28. Chafe, 186.

29. Nelson Johnson to Lewis Brandon, November 1, 1969, GAPP Papers, Lewis Brandon Personal Archives.

30. Ed Whitfield, testimony to the Greensboro Truth and Reconciliation Commission, public hearing no. 1, July 16, 2005.

31. "650 Troops Sweep A&T," *Greensboro Daily News*, May 23, 1969.

32. George Simpkins, interview by the author, July 12, 1999.

33. Vernice Wright, "Hearing Indicates Racist City," *A&T Register*, October 10, 1969.

34. North Carolina Advisory Committee to the U.S. Commission on Civil Rights, *Trouble in Greensboro: A Report of an Open Meeting concerning Disturbances at Dudley High School and North Carolina A&T State University* (Washington, DC: North Carolina Advisory Committee on Civil Rights, 1970) (CR1.2:T75), 14.

35. "Over 600 Attend SOBU Conference," *A&T Register*, November 7, 1969.

36. "Johnson Assails Student Press," *A&T Register*, September 26, 1969.

37. Whitfield, testimony. For more on the rise of the Black independent school movement, see Russell Rickford, *We Are an African People: Independent Education, Black Power, and the Radical Imagination* (Oxford: Oxford University Press, 2016).

38. Chafe, *Civilities and Civil Rights*, 220.

39. Quoted in Peniel Joseph, *Waiting 'til the Midnight Hour: A Narrative History of Black Power in America* (New York: Henry Holt, 2006), 280.

40. Position paper, July 1, 1970, GAPP Papers, Lewis Brandon Personal Archives.

41. Vincent Harding, "Toward the Black University," *Ebony*, August 1970, 156–59.

42. Ed Whitfield, testimony. The Sharpeville Massacre happened on March 21, 1960, in South Africa. Furious at apartheid demands for Black South Africans to carry "passbooks" to identify and distinguish themselves, thousands of protesters gathered at a local police station. Law enforcement consequently opened fire on the crowd, killing sixty-nine protesters. For more on the massacre, see Tom Lodge, *Sharpeville: A Massacre and Its Consequences* (Oxford: Oxford University Press, 2011); and Phillip Frankel, *An Ordinary Atrocity: Sharpeville and Its Massacre* (New Haven, CT: Yale University Press, 2001).

43. Quoted in Chafe, *Civilities and Civil Rights*, 181.

44. Transcription of speech delivered by Stokely Carmichael, March 21, 1971, GAPP Papers, Lewis Brandon Personal Archives.

45. Ed Whitfield, testimony.

46. Quoted in Sally Bermanzohn, *Through Survivors' Eyes: From the Sixties to the Greensboro Massacre* (Nashville: Vanderbilt University Press, 2003), 121.

47. Only twenty-four miles away from Greensboro was one of the strongest Black Panther Party chapters in the Southeast. The Winston Salem Black Panther Party blossomed under the leadership of Nelson Malloy and created a number of local initiatives that benefited the local Black population. Despite the fact that the Black Panther Party never strongly took root in Greensboro, the presence of the

party in Winston Salem made the Triad area a formidable stronghold for Black Power politics. For more on the Panthers in Winston Salem and the history of the organization's efforts to coordinate at the local level, see Curtis Austin, *Up against the Wall: Violence in the Making and Unmaking of the Black Panther Party* (Fayetteville: University of Arkansas Press, 2008), Judson L. Jeffries, *Comrades: A Local History of the Black Panther Party* (Bloomington: Indiana University Press, 2007); Judson L. Jeffries, *On the Ground: The Black Panther Party in Communities across America* (Jackson: University Press of Mississippi, 2010); Peniel Joseph, *Neighborhood Rebels: Black Power at the Local Level* (New York: Palgrave Macmillan, 2010); and Donna Jean Murch, *Living for the City: Migration, Education, and the Rise of the Black Panther Party in Oakland, California* (Chapel Hill: University of North Carolina Press, 2010).

48. Chafe, *Civilities and Civil Rights*, 181.

49. Anthony James Ratcliff, "Liberation at the End of a Pen: Writing Pan-African Politics of Cultural Struggle" (PhD diss., University of Massachusetts Amherst, 2009).

50. Youth Organization for Black Unity, "Proposal for Expansion of Printing Capabilities and the Establishment of a 'Marketplace' Operation," GAPP Papers, Lewis Brandon Personal Archives.

51. Cedric Johnson, *Revolutionaries to Race Leaders: Black Power and the Making of African American Politics* (Minneapolis: University of Minnesota Press, 2007), 137.

52. "African Liberation Day Coordinating Committee in Greensboro," GAPP Papers, Lewis Brandon Personal Archives.

53. "Dr. Stevenson Speaks on Revolution in the Black Community," *Carolinian*, May 8, 1970.

54. Chafe, *Civilities and Civil Rights*, 238; Randolph Blackwell, interview by William Chafe, May 5, 1973, Civil Rights Movement Collection, University of North Carolina.

55. "College Students of G'boro Stage Peaceful 'Teach-In,'" *A&T Register*, November 9, 1968.

56. "Director Cited in National Volume," *A&T Register*, September 20, 1968.

57. "Black Movements Show Similarity," *A&T Register*, November 14, 1969; "Mutunhu's Goal Is Cultural Knowledge," *Guilfordian*, January 30, 1979.

58. "Carmichael to Address Students," *A&T Register*, December 6, 1968; Joe Weixlmann, "A Tribute to Darwin T. Turner," *Black American Literature Forum* 25, no. 1 (Spring 1991): 8–9; Lewis Brandon, phone interview by the author, March 25, 2017; Nelson Johnson, phone interview by the author, March 26, 2017.

59. "Turner Commutes to Wis.; Lectures an Afro Course," *A&T Register*, May 2, 1969.

60. Taylor Branch, *Parting the Waters: America in the King Years, 1954–1963* (New York: Simon and Schuster, 1988), 92; Stephen C. Ferguson II, " Understanding the Legacy of Dr. Wayman Bernard McLaughlin: On the Problem of Interpretation in the History of African American Philosophy," *Newsletter on Philosophy and the Black Experience* 13, no. 2 (Spring 2014): 2–11; Brandon, interview; Nelson Johnson, interview; Joyce Glaise, *From Danville to Destiny: I Got Nerve: The Political Legacy*

of a Danville Native (Bloomington, IN: Trafford, 2016); Chafe, *Civilities and Civil Rights*, 219.

61. Carmichael, *Ready for Revolution*, 129.

62. Barnes, interview; "Joe Tex Talks about New Career with Islam," *A&T Register*, September 22, 1972.

63. "A&T Steps Up Interest in Solving Urban Concerns," *Carolina Peacemaker*, January 24, 1970.

64. "A&T Steps Up Interest"; minutes, board of trustees, February 23, 1972, Book 3, North Carolina A&T State University Archives.

65. Henry Ell Frye, oral history interview, February 18 and 26, 1992, Interview C-0091, Southern Oral History Program Collection #4007, Southern Historical Collection, Manuscripts Department, Wilson Library, University of North Carolina at Chapel Hill.

66. Ibid. "Eight Found Black Bank in Greensboro, NC," *Jet*, July 9, 1970.

67. H. Rap Brown, *Die Nigger Die*, 47; Jerry Watts, *Amiri Baraka: The Politics and Art of a Black Intellectual* (New York: New York University Press, 2001), 22–24.

68. "Atlanta University Position Paper on Racism and Violence in the United States," May 28, 1970, Dr. Mack H. Jones Personal Archives. Historian Martha Biondi documents the fact that students at Black colleges were more likely to sustain violence from local and state police and National Guard soldiers than students at predominantly white institutions. This reality resulted in violent outbreaks and often murder at South Carolina State University, North Carolina A&T, Howard University, Voorhees College, Jackson State, Texas Southern, and Southern University. See Martha Biondi, *The Black Revolution on Campus* (Berkeley: University of California Press, 2012), 157. For more concerning the creation of the SCBS program, see Richard Benson II, *Fighting for Our Place in the Sun: Malcolm X and the Radicalization of the Black Student Movement, 1960–1973* (New York: Peter Lang, 2015), 208–13; and Rickford, *We Are an African People*, 198–99.

69. "SOBU Delegates Conclude Rap Is Dead," *A&T Register*, April 20, 1970; Ron "Slim" Washington, "The Rise and Fall of the Revolutionary Workers League (RWL): Or as Was Said in *The Bronx Tale*, 'There's Nothing Worse Than Wasted Potential,'" *Encyclopedia of Anti-revisionism Online*, August 4, 2009, https://www.marxists.org/history/erol/ncm-1a/rwl-history.pdf.

70. "Julian Bond to Speak at 'Save Black Schools' Banquet," *A&T Register*, December 16, 1970.

71. "SGA Explains Procedures for Upcoming Student Body Elections," *A&T Register*, September 10, 1971. The rumor and threat of a merger between the two state institutions, which are located in the city of Greensboro less than two miles from one another, continued well into the 1990s and was a hot source of protests among students and alumni during that period. See "Subtle Attempts to Alter A&T?," *A&T Register*, November 16, 1990; "Open Letter on Alleged Merger Issue," *A&T Register*, February 4, 1991; "Fort Addresses Merger Allegations," *A&T Register*, February 8, 1991; "How the Merger Will Take Place," *Carolina Peacemaker*, August 20, 1992; and "A&T-UNCG Merger Only about Economics," *A&T Register*, January 31, 1998.

72. Position paper delivered by Howard Fuller at MXLU, GAPP Papers, Lewis Brandon Personal Archives.

73. Howard Fuller, interview by Akbar, December 1980, GAPP Papers, Lewis Brandon Personal Archives.

74. Devin Fergus, *Liberalism, Black Power, and the Making of American Politics, 1965–1980* (Athens: University of Georgia Press, 2009), 78.

75. "Controversial School Comes of Age," *Greensboro Record*, November 24, 1971; Fergus, *Liberalism*, 80–82. For more on the politics and vision of Charlotte Hawkins Brown, see Charlotte Hawkins Brown, *"Mammy": An Appeal to the Heart of the South—The Correct Thing to Do—to Say—to Wear* (Boston: G. K. Hall, 1995); and Charles W. Wadelington and Richard F. Knapp, *Charlotte Hawkins Brown and Palmer Memorial Institute: What One Young African American Woman Could Do* (Chapel Hill: University of North Carolina Press, 1999).

76. According to historian Devin Fergus, MXLU received a far different response and welcome when located in the more conservative Black community of Durham. Fergus contends that a strong sense of apathy existed among the students and faculty, resulting in low turnout for volunteerism or support. This is the opposite of the reaction MXLU received at A&T, where faculty came out to embrace the organization when it relocated and students helped to staff and operate the fledgling institution. See Fergus, *Liberalism*, 74–77.

77. "Building the North Carolina Black Assembly: An Organization Approach," October 14, 1972, GAPP Papers, Lewis Brandon Personal Archives.

78. Austin, *Up against the Wall*, 326.

79. Milton Coleman, "A Coming of Age," *African World*, August 1971. I benefited greatly from a dissertation and a master's thesis that provided exceptional scholarship on the ideological struggles of the Black Power era as it related to SOBU and the Pan-Africanist–Marxist divide. See Claude Barnes, "A Consideration of the Relationship between Ideology and Activism in the Black Nationalist Movement: A Case Study of the Rise and Fall of the Greensboro Association of Poor People" (MA thesis, Atlanta University, 1981); and Ratcliff, "Liberation." See also Benson, *Fighting for Our Place*, 198–207.

80. "Police Brutality Trial of the Greensboro Black Community," August 11, 1972, GAPP Papers, Lewis Brandon Personal Archives; "Placement Sponsors Three-Day Confab" and "Research Peaks $1.4 Million," *A&T Register*, September 28, 1973; Brandon, interview; and Nelson Johnson, interview. In August 1972 GAPP organized a "people's court" that heard a case against the Greensboro Police Department, which was charged with several instances of police brutality against the Black community. The case recognized episodes of violence that were inflicted against A&T students and other Black citizens.

81. Rod Bush, *We Are Not What We Seem: Black Nationalism and Class Struggle in the American Century* (New York: New York University Press, 1999), 160.

82. "A Proposal for a New Thrust—1974 and Beyond," GAPP Papers, Lewis Brandon Personal Archives.

Epilogue

1. Like numerous HBCUs, Florida Agricultural and Mechanical University has a long history of cultivating Black leadership and advancing the struggle for Black freedom within the city of Tallahassee and beyond. In May 1956, five months after the Montgomery bus boycott, two students from Florida A&M defied Jim Crow bus laws and took a stand against segregation. Their actions helped to launch a student-led boycott of the local bus system in the city. For more on this boycott and the legacy of Florida A&M in the civil rights movement, see Glenda Alice Rabby, *The Pain and the Promise: The Struggle for Civil Rights in Tallahassee, Florida* (Athens: University of Georgia Press, 1999); Ana Maria Spagna, *Test Ride on the Sunnyland Bus: A Daughter's Civil Rights Journey* (Lincoln: University of Nebraska Press, 2010); and Irvin Winsboro, *Old South, New South, or Down South? Florida and the Modern Civil Rights Movement* (Morgantown: West Virginia University Press, 2009).

2. Ira Katznelson, *When Affirmative Action Was White: An Untold History of Racial Inequality in Twentieth-Century America* (New York: W. W. Norton, 2005), 132. Katznelson's brilliant study on historic and systemic inequalities examines the barriers that prevented upward mobility for African Americans in the twentieth century, with a special focus on the rising white middle class that was solidified with the benefit of access to New Deal and post–World War II programs that routinely discriminated against Blacks. See also Sarah E. Turner and John Bound, "Closing the Gap or Widening the Divide: The Effects of the G.I. Bill and World War II on the Educational Outcomes of Black Americans," *Journal of Economic History* 63 (March 2003): 145–77.

3. For more on the history of integration in collegiate sports and its effects on HBCUs, see Michael Hurd, *Black College Football, 1892–1992: One Hundred Years of History, Education, and Pride* (Virginia Beach, VA: Donning, 1993); Samuel G. Freedman, *Breaking the Line: The Season in Black College Football That Transformed the Sport and Changed the Course of Civil Rights* (New York: Simon and Schuster, 2013); and William C. Rhoden, *$40 Million Slaves: The Rise, Fall, and Redemption of the Black Athlete* (New York: Three Rivers, 2006), 231–62.

4. Hollis Watkins, interview by author, August 9, 2004.

5. Deborah Gray White, *Lost in the USA: American Identity from the Promise Keepers to the Million Mom March* (Urbana: University of Illinois Press, 2017), 5.

6. David Hoffman, dir., *Making Sense of the Sixties: We Can Change the World*, PBS Video, 1991, video.

7. Cornell University, "Teaching Hip Hop," filmed November 1, 2008, YouTube video, 1:32:57, posted April 14, 2009, https://www.youtube.com/watch?v=S6lx EtOPTpk.

8. Richard M. Breaux, "Nooses, Sheets, and Blackface: White Racial Anxiety and Black Student Presence at Six Midwest Flagship Universities, 1882–1937," in *Higher Education for African Americans before the Civil Rights Era, 1900–1964*, ed. Marybeth Gasman and Roger L. Geiger (New York: Routledge, 2017), 44; Manny Fernandez and Richard Perez Pena, "As Two Oklahoma Students Are Expelled for

Racist Chant, Sigma Alpha Epsilon Vows Wider Inquiry," *New York Times,* March 10, 2015; Susan Svrluga, "OU: Frat Members Learned Racist Chant at National SAE Leadership Event," *Washington Post,* March 27, 2015; William C. Rhoden, "University of Missouri Football Players Exercise Power in Racism Protest," *New York Times,* November 8, 2015; Anemona Hartocollis, "Long after Protests, Students Shun the University of Missouri," *New York Times,* July 9, 2017; "Clemson's Black Student VP Impeached after Pledge Protest," *Washington Post,* October 26, 2017; Jeremy Bauer Wolf, "A Social Lynching: Clemson Student Government Vice President, Who Is Black, Says He Faces Impeachment Trial Because He Wouldn't Stand for the Pledge of Allegiance," *Inside Higher Ed,* October 30, 2017; Alex Thomas, "University of Hartford Student Arrested after Allegedly Poisoning Freshman Roommate," *Atlanta Journal Constitution,* November 1, 2017; Jonah Engel Bromwich, "Hartford Student Charged after Boasting about Contaminating Roommate's Belongings," *New York Times,* November 1, 2017.

9. Anemona Hartocollis, "Colleges Celebrate Diversity with Separate Commencements," *New York Times,* June 2, 2017; Douglas Ernst, "Harvard to Host First All-Black Graduation: 'This Is Not about Segregation,'" *Washington Times,* May 9, 2017. There have been a plethora of scholars who have published studies examining the hostilities that have often confronted students of color and other historically marginalized students on predominantly white college campuses and how those students have often negotiated and demanded the creation of space to support their matriculation. For more on this topic, see Dafina-Lazarus Stewart, *Black Collegians' Experiences in US Northern Private Colleges: A Narrative History, 1945–1965* (New York: Palgrave Macmillan, 2017); Shaun R. Harper, "Niggers No More: A Critical Race Counternarrative on Black Male Student Achievement at Predominantly White Colleges and Universities," *International Journal of Qualitative Studies in Education* 22, no. 6 (2009): 697–712; Shaun R. Harper, "Institutional Seriousness concerning Black Male Student Engagement: Necessary Conditions and Collaborative Partnerships," in *Student Engagement in Higher Education: Theoretical Perspectives and Practical Approaches for Diverse Populations,* ed. Shaun R. Harper and Stephen John Quaye (New York: Routledge, 2008), 137–50; Joy Gaston Gayles and Bridget Kelly, "Resistance to Racial/Ethnic Dialogue in Graduate Preparation Programs: Implications for Multicultural Competence," *College Student Affairs Journal* 29, no. 1 (2011): 77–87; Gina Garcia, "Complicating a Latina/o Serving Identity at a Hispanic Serving Institution," *Review of Higher Education* 40, no. 1 (2016): 117–43; Sylvia Hurtado and Andriana Ruiz, "The Climate for Underrepresented Groups and Diversity on Campus," *Higher Education Research Institute: Research Briefs,* University of California, Los Angeles, June 2012; and Daniel Solórzano, Walter R. Allen, and Grace Carroll, "Keeping Race in Place: Racial Microaggressions and Campus Racial Climate at the University of California, Berkeley," *Chicano Latino Law Review* 23 (Spring 2002): 15–111.

10. Charles Blow, "Race, College, and Safe Space," *New York Times,* November 16, 2015.

11. Smith has published extensively on what he refers to as "racial battle fatigue and its affect on Black students and faculty at predominantly white institutions.

See William A. Smith, "Challenging Racial Battle Fatigue on Historically White Campuses: A Critical Race Examination of Race-Related Stress," in *Faculty of Color: Teaching in Predominantly White Colleges and Universities*, ed. Christine A. Stanley (Bolton, MA: Anker, 2006), 299–327; William A Smith, "Toward an Understanding of Misandric Microaggressions and Racial Battle Fatigue among African Americans in Historically White Institutions," in *The State of the African American Male*, ed. E. M. Zamani-Gallaher and V. C. Polite (East Lansing: Michigan State University Press, 2010), 265–77; and William A. Smith, foreword to *Racial Battle Fatigue in Higher Education: Exposing the Myth of Post Racial America*, ed. Kenneth J. Fasching-Varner, Katrice A. Albert, Roland W. Mitchell, and Chaunda M. Allen (Lanham, MD: Rowman and Littlefield, 2015).

12. Ernst, "Harvard to Host." Following her bold statement on the history of Harvard, Woods enrolled in law school at Howard University, where she is matriculating as of this writing.

13. Roderick A. Ferguson, *We Demand: The University and Student Protests* (Berkeley: University of California Press, 2017), 84.

14. Melissa E. Wooten, *In the Face of Inequality: How Black Colleges Adapt* (New York: State University of New York Press, 2015), 110. For more on recent cases pursuing equity in funding for Black colleges, see Mary Beth Marklein, "Black Colleges Press Case for More Funding," *USA Today*, December 1, 2013; Eric Kelderman, "In Court, Group Seeks More State Support for Maryland's Black Universities," *Chronicle of Higher Education*, January 3, 2012; Talia Richman, "Attorneys for State's Historically Black Universities Propose Spending Millions to Remedy Segregation," *Baltimore Sun*, June 8, 2017; Tanzina Vega, "Where White Means Diversity: Maryland's Black Colleges Fight for Equity," *New York Times*, February 4, 2014; and Deborah Bailey, "Timeline of the Maryland HBCU Equality Lawsuit," *AFRO*, February 28, 2017.

15. Gerren Keith Gaynor, "Hampton University Business School Bans Dreadlocks," *Black Enterprise*, August 23, 2012; Elena Gaona, "Hampton University's Student Newspaper Confiscated by University," *Daily Press* (Newport News, VA), October 23, 2003; Elizabeth Gates, "Morehouse College's Gay Travesty," *Daily Beast*, October 20, 2009, https://www.thedailybeast.com/morehouse-colleges-gay-travesty; Jeremy Bauer Wolf, "A Work in Progress: Gay Rights Group Gathers Leaders of Black Colleges and Universities to Discuss Path to Making Them More Inclusive of LGBTQ Students," *Inside Higher Ed*, July 20, 2017, https://www.insidehighered.com/news/2017/07/20/historically-Black-colleges-universities-still-need-work-lgbtq-issues; Shaun R. Harper and Marybeth Gasman, "Consequences of Conservatism: Black Male Students and the Politics of Historically Black Colleges and Universities," *Journal of Negro Education* 77, no. 4 (2008): 336–51.

16. Walter Kimbrough, "What's Causing the Increased Enrollment at HBCUs?," interview by Michel Martin, September 17, 2016, in *All Things Considered*, NPR; Jason Johnson, "The Black Renaissance Is Real: HBCUs See Record Growth in 2017," *The Root*, October 25, 2017, http://www.theroot.com/the-black-renaissance-is-real-hbcus-see-record-growth-1819841936.

17. Mack Jones, "The Black College in the 21st Century: Plotting the Future," *The Hole Card: Race, Class, Gender, and American Life* (blog), September 29, 2015, http://theholecard.blogspot.com/.

18. Derrick White, *The Challenge of Blackness: The Institute of the Black World and Political Activism in the 1970s* (Gainesville: University Press of Florida, 2011), 9.

19. Barbara Ransby, "Black Lives Matter Is Democracy in Action," *New York Times*, October 21, 2017.

20. Transcription of speech delivered by Stokely Carmichael, March 21, 1971, Greensboro Association of Poor People Papers, Lewis Brandon Personal Archives.

Bibliography

Manuscript Sources

Alabama Department of Archives and History, Montgomery, AL
    Administrative Files
    Booker T. Washington Papers
Alabama State University Archives, Montgomery, AL
    Alabama State University Publicatons
    Laurence Hayes Papers
    Jo Ann Gibson Robinson Collection
    G. W. Trenholm Papers
    Harper Councill Trenholm Papers
    Levi Watkins Papers
    Montgomery Improvement Association (MIA) Special Collection
Bennett College Archives, Thomas F. Holgate Library, Greensboro, NC
    Bennett College Scrapbook
    David Dallas Jones Papers
Ferdinand Bluford Library Archives, North Carolina Agricultural and Technical
      State University, Greensboro, NC
    John Marshall Kilimanjaro (Stevenson) Papers
    Frederick A. Williams Papers
Lewis Brandon Personal Archives, Greensboro, NC
    Greensboro Association of Poor People (GAPP) Papers
    Student Organization for Black Unity (SOBU) Papers
John B. Cade Library Archives, Southern University, Baton Rouge, LA
    Dr. Rodney Higgins Papers
    Leon Netterville Papers
Cheyney State University Archives, Cheyney, PA
    William Dorsey Scrapbook
    Leslie Pinckney Hill Papers
Greensboro Historical Museum Archives, Greensboro, NC
    Allen-McFarland Papers
    A. H. Peeler Papers
Jan Hillegas Personal Archives, Jackson, MS
Historical Society of Pennsylvania, Philadelphia, PA
    American Negro Historical Society (ANHS) Collection
    Leon Gardiner Collection
    Jacob C. White Papers

Jackson State University Archives, Jackson, MS
   Jane McAllister Collection
   Jacob L. Reddix Papers
Dr. Mack H. Jones Personal Archives, Atlanta, GA
   Atlanta University Position Paper on Racism and Violence in
      the United States
Library of Congress, Washington, DC
   African American Pamphlet Collection
   Rayford Logan Papers
   Robert Moton Papers
   Papers of the National Negro Congress
Mississippi Department of Archives and History, Jackson, MS
   Council of Federated Organizations Papers
   Medgar Evers Papers
   John Garner Papers
   Mississippi State Sovereignty Commission Files
Moorland-Spingarn Research Center, Howard University, Washington, DC
   North Star
   Harper Councill Trenholm Papers
   Jacob C. White Collection
National Archives, Washington, DC
   Ambrose Caliver Papers
   Walter Daniel Papers
   Works Progress Administration Files
Special Collections and University Archives, University of Massachusetts Amherst
      Libraries, Amherst, MA
   W. E. B. Du Bois Papers
Tougaloo College Archives, Tougaloo, MS
Margaret Walker Center, Jackson State University, Jackson, MS
   Margaret Walker Alexander Journals

Interviews Conducted by the Author

Bailey, Hattie, Philadelphia, PA, February 19, 2014
Barnes, Claude, Greensboro, NC, December 23, 1998
Blackwell, Unita, Mayersville, MS, August 7, 2004
Brandon, Lewis, Greensboro, NC, March 25, 2017
Dennis, David, Jackson, MS, August 11, 2004
Douglas-Clemons, Gloria Jean, Jackson, MS, July 31, 2005
Fisher, Clarence, Charlotte, NC, August 27, 2018
Johnson, Nelson, Greensboro, NC, March 26, 2017
Jones, Jamila, Atlanta, GA, August 8, 2010
Khazan, Jibrell, New Bedford, MA, July 8, 1999
King, Ed, Jackson, MS, June 30, 2004
Kinnard, Ouida, Jackson, MS, July 31, 2005

Ladner, Dorie, Jackson, MS, June 23, 2004
Mclemore, Leslie, Jackson, MS, July 8, 2004
Peoples, John, Jackson, MS, July 21, 2004
Simpkins, George, Greensboro, NC, July 12, 1999
Watkins, Hollis, Jackson, MS, August 9, 2004
Young, Eugene "Jughead," Jackson, MS, July 15, 2004

Interviews Conducted by Others

Anderson, Dupuy, January 5, 1994, T. Harry Williams Center for Oral History, Louisiana State University Libraries Special Collections, Baton Rouge.

Baker, Ella, by Casey Haden and Sue Thrasher, New York, April 19, 1977, Southern Oral History Program Collection #4007, Series G, Southern Women, Manuscripts Department, Wilson Library, University of North Carolina at Chapel Hill.

Bashful, Emmett W., June 8, 1990, African American Political Scientists Oral History Project, Louie B. Nunn Center for Oral History, University of Kentucky Libraries, University of Kentucky, Lexington.

Blackwell, Randolph, by William Chafe, May 5, 1973, Civil Rights Movement Collection, University of North Carolina at Greensboro.

Dittmer, John, by John Jones, August 21, 1980, Mississippi Department of Archives and History, Jackson.

Frye, Henry Ell, oral history interview, February 18 and 26, 1992, Interview C-0091, Southern Oral History Program Collection #4007, Southern Historical Collection, Manuscripts Department, Wilson Library, University of North Carolina at Chapel Hill.

Fuller, Howard, by Akbar, December 1980, Greensboro Association of Poor People Papers, Lewis Brandon Personal Archives, Greensboro, NC.

Gibbs, Warmouth T., by Lewis Brandon, December 12, 1987, Lewis Brandon Personal Archives, Greensboro, NC.

Glass, Thelma, by Randall Williams, n.d., Alabama State University Archives, Montgomery.

Jones, Jamila, April 27, 2011, Civil Rights History Project Collection, American Folklife Center, Library of Congress, Washington, DC.

Jones, Mack H., July 15, 1994, African American Political Scientists Oral History Project, Louie B. Nunn Center for Oral History, University of Kentucky Libraries, University of Kentucky, Lexington.

Kimbrough, Walter, "What's Causing the Increased Enrollment at HBCUs?," interview by Michel Martin, September 17, 2016, in *All Things Considered*, NPR.

Prestage, Jewell, October 30, 1992, African American Political Scientists Oral History Project, Louie B. Nunn Center for Oral History, University of Kentucky Libraries, University of Kentucky, Lexington.

Walker Alexander, Margaret, by Ann Allen Shockley, July 18, 1973, Fisk University Archives, John Hope and Aurelia Franklin Library, Fisk University, Nashville, TN.

Films and Videos

California Newsreel. "SNCC 50th Reunion." Filmed April 2010. YouTube video, 2:43. Posted February 18, 2011. https://www.youtube.com/watch?v=aTPbNs Acy9s.

Cornell University. "Teaching Hip Hop." Filmed November 1, 2008. YouTube video, 1:32:57. Posted April 14, 2009. https://www.youtube.com/watch?v =S6lxEtOPTpk.

Hoffman, David, dir. *Making Sense of the Sixties: We Can Change the World*. PBS Video, 1991. Video.

Websites

Barnett, David C. "Radio Show Chronicled Blacks' Harsh Realities." March 3, 2008, in *All Things Considered*, NPR. Podcast. https://www.npr.org/templates /story/story.php?storyId=87780799.

Bauer-Wolf, Jeremy. "A Work in Progress: Gay Rights Group Gathers Leaders of Black Colleges and Universities to Discuss Path to Making Them More Inclusive of LGBTQ Students." *Inside Higher Ed*, July 20, 2017. https://www .insidehighered.com/news/2017/07/20/historically-Black-colleges-universities -still-need-work-lgbtq-issues.

Cooney, Patrick Louis. "At Home, 1944–1948." In *The Life and Times of the Prophet Vernon Johns: Father of the Civil Rights Movement*, Vernon Johns Society website, 1998. http://www.vernonjohns.org/tcal001/vjathome.html.

Douthard, William "Meatball." "I'll Never Forget Alabama Law." Originally published in *Liberal News* 6, no. 6 (February/March 1965). http://www.crmvet .org/nars/gadsden.htm.

Gates, Elizabeth. "Morehouse College's Gay Travesty." *Daily Beast*, October 20, 2009. https://www.thedailybeast.com/morehouse-colleges-gay-travesty.

Johnson, Jason. "The Black Renaissance Is Real: HBCUs See Record Growth in 2017." *The Root*, October 25, 2017. http://www.theroot.com/the-black -renaissance-is-real-hbcus-see-record-growth-1819841936.

Jones, Mack. "The Black College in the 21st Century: Plotting the Future." *The Hole Card: Race, Class, Gender, and American Life* (blog), September 29, 2015. http://theholecard.blogspot.com/.

Washington, Ron "Slim." "The Rise and Fall of the Revolutionary Workers League (RWL): Or as Was Said in *The Bronx Tale*, 'There's Nothing Worse Than Wasted Potential.'" *Encyclopedia of Anti-revisionism Online*, August 4, 2009. https://www.marxists.org/history/erol/ncm-1a/rwl-history.pdf.

Government Publications

North Carolina Advisory Committee to the U.S. Commission on Civil Rights. *Trouble in Greensboro: A Report of an Open Meeting concerning Disturbances at*

Dudley High School and North Carolina A&T State University. Washington, DC: North Carolina Advisory Committee on Civil Rights, 1970.

U.S. Department of Commerce, Bureau of the Census. *1950 United States Census of Population.* Vol. 2, *Characteristics of the Population,* pt. 2, *Alabama.* Washington, DC: Government Printing Office, 1952.

Whitfield, Ed. Testimony to Greensboro Truth and Reconciliation Commission. Public hearing no. 1, July 16, 2005. https://www.greensborotrc.org/whitfield .doc.

Newspapers and Other Serials

A&T Register (Greensboro, NC)

African World

Afro-American

Alabama Journal

Alabama State College Alumni News (Montgomery, AL)

A.M.E. Church Review

Atlanta Constitution

Baltimore Daily Herald

Baltimore Sun

Bennett Banner (Greensboro, NC)

Birmingham Post-Herald

Black Enterprise

Blue and White Flash (Jackson, MS)

Butts County Progress (Jackson, GA)

Carolina Peacemaker (Greensboro, NC)

Carolina Times (Durham, NC)

Carolinian (Greensboro, NC)

Clarion Ledger (Jackson, MS)

Fresh-More (Montgomery, AL)

Greensboro (NC) Daily News

Greensboro (NC) News and Record

Guilfordian (Greensboro, NC)

Hornet (Montgomery, AL)

Jackson (MS) Daily News

Jet

Louisiana Weekly (New Orleans, LA)

Mobile (AL) Register

Montgomery Advertiser

Montgomery Examiner

New York Times

Pittsburgh Courier

State Normal Courier Journal (Montgomery, AL)

Southern University Digest (Baton Rouge, LA)

Time
Tougaloo Enterprise (Jackson, MS)
Tougaloo News (Jackson, MS)
Tougaloo Quarterly (Jackson, MS)
USA Today
Washington Afro-American
Washington Post
Washington Times

Dissertations and Theses

Barnes, Claude. "A Consideration of the Relationship between Ideology and Activism in the Black Nationalist Movement: A Case Study of the Rise and Fall of the Greensboro Association of Poor People." MA thesis, Atlanta University, 1981.

Buell, Emmett. "The Politics of Frustration: An Analysis of Negro Leadership in East Baton Rouge Parish, Louisiana, 1953–1966." MA thesis, Louisiana State University, 1967.

Burke, Dawne Raines. "Storer College: A Hope for Redemption in the Shadow of Slavery, 1865–1955." PhD diss., Virginia Polytechnic Institute and State University, 2004.

Cline, David P. "Revolution and Reconciliation: The Student Interracial Ministry, Liberal Protestantism, and the Civil Rights Movement, 1960–1970." PhD diss., University of North Carolina, 2010.

Covington, Morris, and Mary Covington. "A Historical Calendar of Tougaloo College." MA thesis, California State University, Dominguez Hills, 1987.

Hebert, Mary Jacqueline. "Beyond Black and White: The Civil Rights Movement in Baton Rouge, Louisiana, 1945–1972." PhD diss., Louisiana State University, 1999.

Morris, Tiyi. "Black Women's Civil Rights Activism in Mississippi: The Story of Womanpower Unlimited." PhD diss., Purdue University, 2002.

Ratcliff, Anthony James. "Liberation at the End of a Pen: Writing Pan-African Politics of Cultural Struggle." PhD diss., University of Massachusetts Amherst, 2009.

Richard, Johnetta. "The Southern Negro Youth Congress: A History." PhD diss., University of Cincinnati, 1987.

Robinson, Jo Ann Gibson. "George Eliot's Treatment of Sin." MA thesis, Atlanta University, 1948.

Articles and Books

Aiello, Thomas. "Calumny in the House of the Lord: The 1932 Zion Traveler Church Shooting." In *Louisiana beyond Black and White: New Interpretations of Twentieth-Century Race and Race Relations*, edited by Michael S. Martin, 17–34. Lafayette: University of Louisiana at Lafayette Press, 2011.

Alexander, Leslie M. *African or American? Black Identity and Political Activism in New York City, 1784–1861.* Urbana: University of Illinois Press, 2008.

Alexander, Shawn Leigh. *An Army of Lions: The Civil Rights Struggle before the NAACP.* Philadelphia: University of Pennsylvania Press, 2011.

Anderson, Carol. *Eyes off the Prize: The United Nations and the African American Struggle for Human Rights, 1944–1955.* Cambridge: Cambridge University Press, 2003.

Anderson, James D. *The Education of Blacks in the South, 1860–1935.* Chapel Hill: University of North Carolina Press, 1988.

Anderson, Karen Tucker. "Last Hired, First Fired: Black Women Workers during World War II." *Journal of American History* 69 (June 1982): 82–97.

Angell, Stephen Ward. *Bishop Henry McNeal Turner and African American Religion in the South.* Knoxville: University of Tennessee Press, 1992.

"Anniversary Exercises." *American Missionary* 50, no. 1 (January 1896): 222.

Appiah, Kwame Anthony, and Henry Louis Gates Jr., eds. *Arts and Letters: An A-to-Z Reference of Writers, Musicians, and Artists of the African American Experience.* Africana. Philadelphia: Running, 2005.

Aptheker, Herbert. "The Negro College Student in the 1920s—Years of Preparation and Protest: An Introduction." *Science and Society* 33, no. 2 (Spring 1969): 150–67.

Armstrong, Julie Buckner. *Mary Turner and the Memory of Lynching.* Athens: University of Georgia Press, 2011.

Atlanta University. *The College-Bred Negro American.* The Atlanta University Publications, no. 15. New York: Arno, 1968.

Austin, Allan W. *Quaker Brotherhood: Interracial Activism and the American Friends Service Committee, 1917–1950.* Urbana: University of Illinois Press, 2012.

Austin, Curtis. *Up against the Wall: Violence in the Making and Unmaking of the Black Panther Party.* Fayetteville: University of Arkansas Press, 2008.

Bacon, Jacqueline, and Glen McClish, "Reinventing the Master's Tools: Nineteenth-Century African-American Literary Societies of Philadelphia and Rhetorical Education." *Rhetoric Society Quarterly* 30, no. 4 (Autumn 2000): 19–47.

Bailey, D'Army. *The Education of a Black Radical: A Southern Civil Rights Activist's Journey, 1959–1964.* Baton Rouge: Louisiana State University Press, 2009.

Ball, Wendy, and Tony Martin. *Rare Afro-Americana: A Reconstruction of the Adger Library.* Ann Arbor: University of Michigan Press, 1981.

Banks, William M. *Black Intellectuals: Race and Responsibility in American Life.* New York: W. W. Norton, 1996.

Barlow, Leila Mae. *Across the Years: Memoirs.* Montgomery: Paragon, 1959.

Bartley, Numan. *The Rise of Massive Resistance: Race and Politics in the South during the 1950s.* Baton Rouge: Louisiana State University Press, 1969.

Bass, Jack, and Jack Nelson. *The Orangeburg Massacre.* Macon, GA: Mercer University Press, 1984.

Beard, Augustus F. *A Crusade of Brotherhood: A History of the American Missionary Association.* Boston: Pilgrim, 1909.

Bell, Howard Holman, ed. *Minutes of the Proceedings of the National Negro Conventions, 1830–1864*. New York: Arno, 1969.

Benson, Richard, II. *Fighting for Our Place in the Sun: Malcolm X and the Radicalization of the Black Student Movement, 1960–1973*. New York: Peter Lang, 2015.

Bermanzohn, Sally. *Through Survivors' Eyes: From the Sixties to the Greensboro Massacre*. Nashville: Vanderbilt University Press, 2003.

Biddle, Daniel R., and Murray Dubin. *Tasting Freedom: Octavius Catto and the Battle for Equality in Civil War America*. Philadelphia: Temple University Press, 2010.

———. "Who Was O. V. Catto?" *Philadelphia Inquirer Magazine*, July 6, 2003.

Bilbo, Theodore G. *The War; Constitutional Government; and the Race Issue— America's Greatest Unsolved Domestic Problem*. Washington, DC: Government Printing Office, 1944.

Biondi, Martha. *The Black Revolution on Campus*. Berkeley: University of California Press, 2012.

Birmingham, Stephen. *Certain People: America's Black Elite*. Boston: Little, Brown, 1977.

Blackett, Richard. "Martin Delany and Robert Campbell: Black Americans in Search of an African Colony." *Journal of Negro History* 62, no. 1 (January 1977): 1–25.

Blackett, R. J. M. *Beating against the Barriers: Biographical Essays in Nineteenth-Century Afro-American History*. Baton Rouge: Louisiana State University Press, 1986.

Blair, Lewis. *Southern Prophecy: The Prosperity of the South Dependent upon the Elevation of the Negro*. Boston: Little, Brown, 1964.

Bond, Horace Mann. *Education for Freedom: A History of Lincoln University, Pennsylvania*. Princeton, NJ: Princeton University Press, 1976.

———. *The Education of the Negro in the American Social Order*. New York: Octagon Books, 1966.

Bradley, Stefan M. *Harlem vs. Columbia University: Black Student Power in the Late 1960s*. Urbana: University of Illinois Press, 2009.

Branch, Taylor. *Parting the Waters: America in the King Years, 1954–1963*. New York: Simon and Schuster, 1988.

———. *Pillar of Fire: America in the King Years, 1963–65*. New York: Simon and Schuster, 1998.

Brawley, James. *Two Centuries of Methodist Concern: Bondage, Freedom, and Education of Black People*. New York: Vantage, 1974.

Breaux, Richard M. "Nooses, Sheets, and Blackface: White Racial Anxiety and Black Student Presence at Six Midwest Flagship Universities, 1882–1937." In *Higher Education for African Americans before the Civil Rights Era, 1900–1964*, edited by Marybeth Gasman and Roger L. Geiger, 43–74, New York: Routledge, 2017.

Brisbane, Robert. *The Black Vanguard: Origins of the Negro Social Revolution, 1900–1960*. Valley Forge, PA: Judson, 1969.

Brooks, F. Erik. *Tigers in the Tempest: Savannah State University and the Struggle for Civil Rights*. Macon, GA: Mercer University Press, 2014.

Brooks, Jennifer E. *Defining the Peace: World War II Veterans, Race, and the Remaking of Southern Political Tradition*. Chapel Hill: University of North Carolina Press, 2004.

Brown, Charlotte Hawkins. *"Mammy": An Appeal to the Heart of the South—The Correct Thing to Do—to Say—to Wear*. Boston: G. K. Hall, 1995.

Brown, H. Rap. *Die Nigger Die!* Chicago: Lawrence Hill Books, 1969.

Brown, Linda Beatrice. *The Long Walk: The Story of the Presidency of Willa B. Player at Bennett College*. Danville, VA: McCain, 1998.

Brown, Nikki. *Private Politics and Public Voices: Black Women's Activism from World War I to the New Deal*. Bloomington: Indiana University Press, 2006.

Brundage, W. Fitzhugh. *Lynching in the New South: Georgia and Virginia, 1880–1930*. Urbana: University of Illinois Press, 1993.

Bullock, Henry Allen. *A History of Negro Education in the South: From 1619 to the Present*. Cambridge, MA: Harvard University Press, 1970.

Buni, Andrew. *Robert L. Vann of the Pittsburgh Courier: Politics and Black Journalism*. Pittsburgh: University of Pittsburg Press, 1974.

Burin, Eric. *Slavery and the Peculiar Solution: A History of the American Colonization Society*. Gainesville: University Press of Florida, 2008.

Burke, Dawne Raines. *An American Phoenix: A History of Storer College from Slavery to Desegregation*. Pittsburgh: Geyer, 2006.

Burks, Mary Fair. "Trailblazers: Women in the Montgomery Bus Boycott." In *Women in the Civil Rights Movement: Trailblazers and Torchbearers, 1941–1965*, edited by Vicki L. Crawford, Jacqueline Anne Rouse, and Barbara Woods, 71–84. Bloomington: Indiana University Press, 1993.

Bush, Rod. *We Are Not What We Seem: Black Nationalism and Class Struggle in the American Century*. New York: New York University Press, 1999.

Butchart, Ronald. "'Outthinking and Outflanking the Owners of the World': A Historiography of the African American Struggle for Education." *History of Education Quarterly* 28, no. 3 (Autumn 1988): 333–66.

Caliver, Ambrose. "Certain Significant Developments in the Education of Negroes during the Past Generation." *Journal of Negro History* 35, no. 2 (April 1950): 111–34.

Campbell, Clarice T., and Oscar Allan Rogers Jr. *Mississippi: The View from Tougaloo*. Jackson: University Press of Mississippi, 1979.

Carmichael, Stokely. *Ready for the Revolution: The Life and Struggles of Stokely Carmichael (Kwame Ture)*. With Ekwueme Michael Thelwell. New York: Scribner, 2005.

Carson, Clayborne. *In Struggle: SNC and the Black Awakening of the 1960s*. Cambridge, MA: Harvard University Press, 1981.

Carson, Clayborne et al., eds. *The Papers of Martin Luther King Jr., Volume V: Threshold of a New Decade, January 1959–December 1960*. Berkeley: University of California Press, 2005.

Carter, Catherine J. *I Bet You Have a Story*. Bloomington, IN: Authorhouse, 2013.

Carter, Dan T. *Scottsboro: A Tragedy of the American South.* Baton Rouge: Louisiana State University Press, 2007.

Cashin, Sheryll. *The Agitator's Daughter: A Memoir of Four Generations of One Extraordinary African American Family.* New York: Perseus Books, 2008.

Chafe, William. *Civilities and Civil Rights: Greensboro, North Carolina, and the Black Struggle for Freedom.* Oxford: Oxford University Press, 1980.

Cha-Jua, Sunidata Keita, and Clarence Lang. "'The Long Movement' as Vampire: Temporal and Spatial Fallacies in Recent Black Freedom Studies." *Journal of African American History* 92, no. 4 (Fall 2007): 265–88.

Chamberlain, Charles D. *Victory at Home: Manpower and Race in the American South during World War II.* Athens: University of Georgia Press, 2003.

Clark, Felton G. "Administrative Control of Public Negro Colleges." *Journal of Negro Education* 3, no. 3 (April 1934): 245–56.

Clark Hine, Darlene, and Kathleen Thompson. *A Shining Thread of Hope: The History of Black Women in America.* New York: Broadway Books, 1999.

Cobb Jr., Charles E. *This Nonviolent Stuff'll Get You Killed: How Guns Made the Civil Rights Movement Possible.* New York: Basic Books, 2014.

Cohen, Robert. *When the Old Left Was Young: Student Radicals and America's First Mass Student Movement, 1929–1941.* Oxford: Oxford University Press, 1993.

Conyers, Charline Howard. *A Living Legend: The History of Cheyney University, 1837–1951.* Cheyney, PA: Cheyney University Press, 1990.

Coppin, Fanny Jackson. *Reminiscences of School Life, and Hints on Teaching.* Philadelphia: A.M.E. Book Concern, 1913.

Cornelius, Janet Duitsman. "'We Slipped and Learned to Read': Slave Accounts of the Literacy Process." *Phylon* 44 (3rd qtr., 1983): 171–86.

——. *When I Can Read My Title Clear: Literacy, Slavery, and Religion in the Antebellum South.* Columbia: University of South Carolina Press, 1991.

Corrothers, James. *In Spite of the Handicap: An Autobiography.* Ann Arbor: University of Michigan Press, 1916.

Couto, Richard. *Ain't Gonna Let Nobody Turn Me Round: The Pursuit of Racial Justice in the Rural South.* Philadelphia: Temple University Press, 1991.

Cox, Marcus S. *Segregated Soldiers: Military Training at Historically Black Colleges in the Jim Crow South.* Baton Rouge: Louisiana State University Press, 2013.

Curry, J. L. *A Brief Sketch of George Peabody, and the History of the Peabody Educational Fund through Thirty Years.* New York: Negro Universities Press, 1969.

Curry, Leonard. *The Free Black in Urban America, 1800–1850: The Shadow of a Dream.* Chicago: University of Chicago Press, 1981.

Curti, Merle, and Roderick Nash. *Philanthropy in the Shaping of American Higher Education.* New Brunswick, NJ: Rutgers University Press, 1965.

Davies, Carol Boyce. *Left of Karl Marx: The Political Life of Black Communist Claudia Jones.* Durham, NC: Duke University Press, 2008.

Davis, Allison. *Children of Bondage: The Personality Development of Negro Youth in the Urban South.* New York: Harper and Row, 1964.

Davis, Hugh. *"We Will Be Satisfied with Nothing Less": The African American Struggle for Equal Rights in the North during Reconstruction.* Ithaca, NY: Cornell University Press, 2011.

Davis, Townsend. *Weary Feet, Rested Souls: A Guided History of the Civil Rights Movement.* New York: W. W. Norton, 1998.

DeBoer, Clara. *His Truth Is Marching On: African Americans Who Taught the Freedmen for the American Missionary Association, 1861–1877.* New York: Garland, 1995.

de Jong, Greta. *A Different Day: African American Struggles for Justice in Rural Louisiana, 1900–1970.* Chapel Hill: University of North Carolina Press, 2002.

Delany, Martin R., and Robert Campbell. *Search for Place: Black Separatism and Africa, 1860.* Ann Arbor: University of Michigan Press, 1969.

Dent, Tom. *Southern Journey: A Return to the Civil Rights Movement.* New York: William Morrow, 1997.

Dethloff, Henry C., and Robert R. Jones. "Race Relations in Louisiana, 1877–98." In *The Louisiana Purchase Bicentennial Series in Louisiana History,* vol. 11, *The African American Experience in Louisiana,* pt. B, *From the Civil War to Jim Crow,* edited by Charles Vincent, 507–8. Lafayette: University of Louisiana at Lafayette, 2000.

Dittmer, John. *Local People: The Struggle for Civil Rights in Mississippi.* Urbana: University of Illinois Press, 1995.

Dixon, Charles. *African America and Haiti: Emigration and Black Nationalism in the Nineteenth Century.* Westport, CT: Greenwood, 2000.

Dollard, John. *Caste and Class in a Southern Town.* New York: Doubleday Anchor Books, 1957.

Douglass, Harlan Paul. *Christian Reconstruction in the South.* Boston: The Pilgrim Press, 1909.

Drewry, Henry, and Humphrey Doermann. *Stand and Prosper: Private Black Colleges and Their Students.* Princeton, NJ: Princeton University Press, 2001.

DuBois, W. E. B. *Darkwater: Voices from within the Veil.* Mineola, NY: Dover, 1999.

———. "Does the Negro Need Separate Schools?" *Journal of Negro Education* 4, no. 3 (June 1935): 328–35.

———. *The Education of Black People: Ten Critiques, 1906–1960.* Edited by Herbert Aptheker. Amherst: University of Massachusetts Press, 1973.

———. *The Philadelphia Negro: A Social Study.* New York: Shocken Books, 1967.

———. *Report of the First Conference of Negro Land-Grant Colleges for Coordinating a Program of Cooperative Social Studies.* Atlanta: Atlanta University Publications, 1943.

———. *The Souls of Black Folks.* New York: Signet Classic, 1995.

Dudziak, Mary. *Cold War Civil Rights: Race and the Image of American Democracy.* Princeton, NJ: Princeton University Press, 2000.

Dunlap, Mollie E. "Recreational Reading of Negro College Students." *Journal of Negro Education* 2, no. 4 (October 1933): 448–59.

Eagles, Charles W. "Two Double V's: Jonathan Daniels, FDR, and Race Relations during World War II." *North Carolina Historical Review* 59, no. 3 (July 1982): 252–70.

Earle, Jonathan H. *Jacksonian Antislavery and the Politics of Free Soil.* Chapel Hill: University of North Carolina Press, 2003.

Edgcomb, Gabrielle. *From Swastika to Jim Crow: Refugee Scholars at Black Colleges.* Malabar, FL: Krieger, 1993.

"Educational Work in the South." *American Missionary* 50, no. 12 (December 1896): 442.

Edwards, Harry. *Black Students.* New York: Free Press, 1970.

Egerton, John. *Speak Now against the Day: The Generation before the Civil Rights Movement in the South.* New York: Alfred A. Knopf, 1995.

Ellis, Mark. *Race Harmony and Black Progress: Jack Woofter and the Interracial Cooperation Movement.* Bloomington: Indiana University Press, 2013.

Emanuel, Rachel Lorraine, and Alexander P. Tureaud Jr. *A More Noble Cause: A. P. Tureaud and the Struggle for Civil Rights in Louisiana.* Baton Rouge: Louisiana State University Press, 2011.

Evans, Stephanie. *Black Women in the Ivory Tower, 1850–1954: An Intellectual History.* Gainesville: University Press of Florida, 2007.

Fairclough, Adam. *A Class of Their Own: Black Teachers in the Segregated South.* Cambridge, MA: Harvard University Press, 2007.

———. *Race and Democracy: The Civil Rights Struggle in Louisiana, 1915–1972.* Athens: University of Georgia Press, 1999.

———. *Teaching Equality: Black Schools in the Age of Jim Crow.* Athens: University of Georgia Press, 2001.

Farmer, James. *Lay Bare the Heart: An Autobiography of the Civil Rights Movement.* New York: Plum Books, 1985.

Faulkner, Carol. "The Root of the Evil: Free Produce and Radical Antislavery, 1820–1860." *Journal of the Early Republic* 27 (Fall 2007): 377–405.

Fergus, Devin. *Liberalism, Black Power, and the Making of American Politics, 1965–1980.* Athens: University of Georgia Press, 2009.

Ferguson, Roderick A. *We Demand: The University and Student Protests.* Berkeley: University of California Press, 2017.

Ferguson, Stephen C., II. "Understanding the Legacy of Dr. Wayman Bernard McLaughlin: On the Problem of Interpretation in the History of African American Philosophy." *Newsletter on Philosophy and the Black Experience* 13, no. 2 (Spring 2014): 2–11.

Finkelman, Paul. "Prelude to the Fourteenth Amendment: Black Legal Rights in the Antebellum North." *Rutgers Law Journal* 17 (Spring/Summer 1986): 415–82.

Fischer, Roger A. *The Segregation Struggle in Louisiana, 1862–77.* Urbana: University of Illinois Press, 1974.

Fleming, Cynthia Griggs. *Soon We Will Not Cry: The Liberation of Ruby Doris Smith Robinson.* Lanham, MD: Rowman and Littlefield, 1998.

Forman, James. *The Making of Black Revolutionaries.* New York: Macmillan, 1972.

Fosdick, Raymond. *Adventure in Giving: The Story of the General Education Board, a Foundation Established by John D. Rockefeller.* New York: Harper and Row, 1962.

Frankel, Phillip. *An Ordinary Atrocity: Sharpeville and Its Massacre.* New Haven, CT: Yale University Press, 2001.

Franklin, V. P. *Black Self-Determination: A Cultural History of African-American Resistance.* New York: Lawrence Hill, 1992.

———. "'They Rose or Fell Together': African American Educators and Community Leadership, 1795–1954." In *The Sage Handbook of African American Education,* edited by Linda Tillman, 35–54. Thousand Oaks, CA: Sage, 2008.

Franklin, V. P., and James Anderson, eds. *New Perspectives on Black Educational History.* Boston: G. K. Hall, 1978.

Frazier, E. Franklin. *Black Bourgeoisie.* New York: Free Press Paperbacks, 1997.

Freedman, David. "African-American Schooling in the South prior to 1861." *Journal of Negro History* 84, no. 1 (Winter 1999): 1–47.

Freedman, Samuel G. *Breaking the Line: The Season in Black College Football That Transformed the Sport and Changed the Course of Civil Rights.* New York: Simon and Schuster, 2013.

Freire, Paulo. *Pedagogy of the Oppressed.* New York: Bloomsbury, 2000.

Frystak, Shannon. *Our Minds on Freedom: Women and the Struggle for Black Equality in Louisiana, 1924–1967.* Baton Rouge: Louisiana State University Press, 2009.

Funke, Loretta. "The Negro in Education." *Journal of Negro History* 5, no. 1 (January 1920): 1–21.

Gaines, Kevin. *Uplifting the Race: Black Leadership, Politics, and Culture in the Twentieth Century.* Chapel Hill: University of North Carolina Press, 1996.

Garcia, Gina. "Complicating a Latina/o Serving Identity at a Hispanic Serving Institution." *Review of Higher Education* 40, no. 1 (2016): 117–43.

Gardner, Eric. *Unexpected Places: Relocating Nineteenth-Century African American Literature.* Jackson: University Press of Mississippi, 2009.

Garibaldi, Antoine, ed. *Black Colleges and Universities: Challenges for the Future.* Westport, CT: Praeger Publishers, 1984.

Garrow, David, ed. *Atlanta, Georgia, 1960–1961: Sit-Ins and Student Activism.* New York: Carlson, 1989.

———. *Bearing the Cross: Martin Luther King, Jr., and the Southern Christian Leadership Conference.* New York: HarperCollins, 1986.

———. "The Origins of the Montgomery Bus Boycott." *Southern Changes* 7 (October–December 1985): 21–27.

Gatewood, William B., Jr. *Aristocrats of Color: The Black Elite, 1880–1920.* Fayetteville: University of Arkansas Press, 2000.

Gavins, Raymond. *The Perils and Prospects of Southern Black Leadership: Gordon Blaine Hancock, 1884–1970.* Durham, NC: Duke University Press, 1977.

Gayles, Joy Gaston, and Bridget Kelly. "Resistance to Racial/Ethnic Dialogue in Graduate Preparation Programs: Implications for Multicultural Competence." *College Student Affairs Journal* 29, no. 1 (2011): 77–87.

Gellman, Erik. *Death Blow to Jim Crow: The National Negro Congress and the Rise of Militant Civil Rights.* Chapel Hill: University of North Carolina Press, 2012.

Gilje, Paul A. *Rioting in America.* Bloomington: Indiana University Press, 1999.

Gilmore, Glenda Elizabeth. *Defying Dixie: The Radical Roots of Civil Rights, 1919–1950.* New York: W. W. Norton, 2008.

Glaise, Joyce. *From Danville to Destiny: I Got Nerve: The Political Legacy of a Danville Native.* Bloomington, IN: Trafford, 2016.

Goodman, James E. *Stories of Scottsboro.* New York: Vintage Books, 1995.

Gordon, Vivian Verdell. "A History of Storer College, Harpers Ferry, West Virginia." *Journal of Negro Education* 30, no. 4 (Autumn 1961): 445–49.

Gore, Dayo F. *Radicalism at the Crossroad: African American Women Activists in the Cold War.* New York: New York University Press, 2011.

Graham, Lawrence Otis. *Our Kind of People: Inside America's Black Upper Class.* New York: Harper Perennial, 1999.

Greenberg, Cheryl Lynn. *To Ask for an Equal Chance: African Americans in the Great Depression.* Lanham, MD: Rowman and Littlefield, 2009.

Greenberg, Polly. *The Devil Has Slippery Shoes: A Biased Biography of the Child Development Group of Mississippi.* London: Macmillan, 1969.

Greene, Lorenzo J. *Selling Black History for Carter G. Woodson: A Diary, 1930–1933.* Edited by Arvarh E. Strickland. Columbia: University of Missouri Press, 1996.

Gregory, James. *The Southern Diaspora: How the Great Migrations of Black and White Southerners Transformed America.* Chapel Hill: University of North Carolina Press, 2005.

Griffin, Henry H. *The Trial of Frank Kelly for the Assassination and Murder of Octavius V. Catto, on October 10, 1871.* Philadelphia: Daily Tribune, 1888.

Grill, Johnpeter Horst, and Robert L. Jenkins. "The Nazis and the American South in the 1930s: A Mirror Image?" *Journal of Southern History* 58, no. 4 (November 1992): 667–94.

Grimsted, David. *American Mobbing, 1828–1861.* Oxford: Oxford University Press, 1998.

Gundaker, Grey. "Hidden Education among African Americans during Slavery." *Teachers College Record* 109, no. 7 (July 2007): 1591–612.

———. *Signs of Diaspora, Diaspora of Signs: Literacies, Creolization, and Vernacular Practice in African America.* New York: Oxford University Press, 1998.

Hahn, Steven. *A Nation under Our Feet: Black Political Struggles in the Rural South from Slavery to the Great Migration.* Cambridge, MA: Harvard University Press, 2003.

Halberstam, David. *The Children.* New York: Random House, 1998.

Hall, Jacquelyn Dowd. "The Long Civil Rights Movement and the Political Uses of the Past." *Journal of American History* 91, no. 4 (March 2005): 1233–63.

Hall, Stephen G. *A Faithful Account of the Race: African American Historical Writing in Nineteenth-Century America.* Chapel Hill: University of North Carolina Press, 2009.

Hamilton, Kenneth Marvin. *Black Towns and Profit: Promotion and Development in the Trans- Appalachian West, 1877–1915.* Urbana: University of Illinois Press, 1991.

Hampton, Henry, and Steve Fayer, eds. *Voices of Freedom: An Oral History of the Civil Rights Movement from the 1950s through the 1980s.* New York: Bantam Books, 1991.

Harding, Vincent. "Toward the Black University." *Ebony,* August 1970, 156–59.

Harper, Shaun R. "Institutional Seriousness concerning Black Male Student Engagement: Necessary Conditions and Collaborative Partnerships." In *Student Engagement in Higher Education: Theoretical Perspectives and Practical Approaches for Diverse Populations,* edited by Shaun R. Harper and Stephen John Quaye, 137–50. New York: Routledge, 2008.

———. "Niggers No More: A Critical Race Counternarrative on Black Male Student Achievement at Predominantly White Colleges and Universities." *International Journal of Qualitative Studies in Education* 22, no. 6 (2009): 697–712.

Harper, Shaun R., and Marybeth Gasman. "Consequences of Conservatism: Black Male Students and the Politics of Historically Black Colleges and Universities." *Journal of Negro Education* 77, no. 4 (2008): 336–51.

Harris, Jessica and Vernon C. Mitchell Jr., "A Narrative Critique of Black Greek-Letter Organizations and Social Action." In *Black Greek-Letter Organizations in the Twenty-first Century,* edited by Gregory S. Parks, 143–68. Lexington: University of Kentucky Press, 2008.

Harris, Sheldon. *Paul Cuffe: Black America and the African Return.* New York: Simon and Schuster, 1972.

Harris, W. Edward. *Miracle in Birmingham: A Civil Rights Memoir, 1954–1965.* Indianapolis: Stonework, 2004.

Higginbotham, Evelyn Brooks. *Righteous Discontent: The Women's Movement in the Black Baptist Church, 1880–1920.* Cambridge, MA: Harvard University Press, 1993.

Hobson, Maurice J. *The Legend of the Black Mecca: Politics and Class in the Making of Modern Atlanta.* Chapel Hill: University of North Carolina Press, 2017.

Hoffschwelle, Mary. *The Rosenwald Schools of the American South.* Gainesville: University Press of Florida, 2006.

Hogan, Wesley. *Many Minds, One Heart: SNCC's Dream for a New America.* Chapel Hill: University of North Carolina Press, 2007.

Holmes, Dwight O. *The Evolution of the Negro College.* New York: Arno, 1969.

Holmes, William F. "Whitecapping: Agrarian Violence in Mississippi, 1902–1906." *Journal of Southern History* 35, no. 2 (1969): 165–85.

Hood, Aurelius P. *The Negro at Mound Bayou: Being an Authentic Story of the Founding, Growth, and Development of the "Most Celebrated Town in the South."* [Nashville, TN]: [printed by A.M.E. Sunday School Union for the author], 1909.

hooks, bell. *Teaching to Transgress: Education as the Practice of Freedom.* New York: Routledge, 1994.

Horton, James, and Lois Horton. *In Hope of Liberty: Culture, Community, and Protest among Northern Free Blacks, 1700–1860.* Oxford: Oxford University Press, 1998.

Huggins, Nathan, Martin Kilson, and Daniel M. Fox, eds. *Key Issues in the Afro-American Experience*. Vol. 1, *To 1877*. New York: Harcourt Brace Jovanovich, 1971.

Hughes, Langston. "Cowards from the Colleges." *Crisis* 41 (August 1934): 226–28.

Hurd, Michael. *Black College Football, 1892–1992: One Hundred Years of History, Education, and Pride*. Virginia Beach, VA: Donning, 1993.

Hurtado, Sylvia, and Andriana Ruiz. "The Climate for Underrepresented Groups and Diversity on Campus." *Higher Education Research Institute: Research Briefs*, University of California, Los Angeles, June 2012.

Jeffries, Hasan Kwame. *Bloody Lowndes: Civil Rights and Black Power in Alabama's Black Belt*. New York: New York University Press, 2009.

Jeffries, Judson L. *Comrades: A Local History of the Black Panther Party*. Bloomington: Indiana University Press, 2007.

———. *On the Ground: The Black Panther Party in Communities across America*. Jackson: University Press of Mississippi, 2010.

Jelks, Randal Maurice. *Benjamin Elijah Mays, Schoolmaster of the Movement: A Biography*. Chapel Hill: University of North Carolina Press, 2012.

Johns, Major, and Ronnie Moore. *It Happened in Baton Rouge*. New York: Congress of Racial Equality, 1962.

Johnson, Andre. *The Forgotten Prophet: Bishop Henry McNeal Turner and the African American Prophetic Tradition*. Lanham, MD: Lexington Books, 2014.

Johnson, Cedric. *Revolutionaries to Race Leaders: Black Power and the Making of African American Politics*. Minneapolis: University of Minnesota Press, 2007.

Johnson, Charles S. *Growing Up in the Blackbelt: Negro Youth in the Rural South*. Washington, DC: American Council on Education, 1941.

Johnson, Daniel M. *Black Migration in America: A Social Demographic History*. Durham, NC: Duke University Press, 1981.

Johnson, James Weldon. *Along This Way: The Autobiography of James Weldon Johnson*. New York: Viking, 1968.

Johnston, Erle. *Mississippi's Defiant Years*. Forest, MS: Lake Harbor, 1990.

Jones, Angela. *African American Civil Rights: Early Activism and the Niagara Movement*. Santa Barbara, CA: Praeger, 2011.

Jones, David Dallas. "Cultural Obligations of the Faculty in a Negro Liberal Arts College." *Bulletin of the Association of American Colleges* 25, no. 1 (March 1939): 62–68.

Jones, Jacqueline. *Soldiers of Light and Love: Northern Teachers and Georgia Blacks, 1865–1873*. Athens: University of Georgia Press, 2004.

Jones, Mary Hoxie. *Swords into Plowshares: An Account of the American Friends Service Committee, 1917–1937*. New York: Macmillan, 1937.

Joseph, Peniel. *Neighborhood Rebels: Black Power at the Local Level*. New York: Palgrave Macmillan, 2010.

———. *Waiting 'til the Midnight Hour: A Narrative History of Black Power in America*. New York: Henry Holt, 2006.

Karpinski, Carol F. *A Visible Company of Professionals: African Americans and the National Education Association during the Civil Rights Movement*. New York: Peter Lang, 2008.

Katznelson, Ira. *When Affirmative Action Was White: An Untold History of Racial Inequality in Twentieth-Century America*. New York: W. W. Norton, 2006.

Kelderman, Eric. "In Court, Group Seeks More State Support for Maryland's Black Universities." *Chronicle of Higher Education*, January 3, 2012.

Kelley, Robin D. G. *Hammer and Hoe: Alabama Communists during the Great Depression*. Chapel Hill: University of North Carolina Press, 1990.

Kilson, Martin. *Transformation of the African American Intelligentsia, 1880–2012*. Cambridge, MA: The President and Fellows of Harvard College, 2014.

King, Kenneth James. *Pan-Africanism and Education: A Study of Race Philanthropy and Education in the Southern States of America and East Africa*. Oxford: Oxford University Press, 1971.

King, Martin Luther, Jr. *Stride toward Freedom: The Montgomery Story*. New York: Harper and Row,1958.

Kornweibel, Theodore, Jr. *"Seeing Red": Federal Campaigns against Black Militancy, 1919–1925*. Bloomington: Indiana University Press, 1998.

Kryder, Daniel. *Divided Arsenal: Race and the American State during World War II*. Cambridge: Cambridge University Press, 2000.

Kuklick, Bruce. *Black Philosopher, White Academy: The Career of William Fontaine*. Philadelphia: University of Pennsylvania Press, 2008.

Lane, Roger. *Roots of Violence in Black Philadelphia, 1860–1900*. Cambridge, MA: Harvard University Press, 1986.

——. *William Dorsey's Philadelphia and Ours: On the Past and Future of the Black City in America*. New York: Oxford University Press, 1991.

Lau, Peter. *Democracy Rising: South Carolina and the Fight for Black Equality since 1865*. Lexington: University Press of Kentucky, 2006.

Lawson, Steven, and Charles Payne. *Debating the Civil Rights Movement, 1945–1968*. Lanham, MD: Rowman and Littlefield, 1998.

Lefever, Harry G. *Undaunted by the Fight: Spelman College and the Civil Rights Movement, 1957–1967*. Macon, GA: Mercer University Press, 2005.

Lewis, David Levering. *W. E. B. Du Bois: Biography of a Race, 1868–1919*. New York: Henry Holt, 1993.

——. *When Harlem Was in Vogue*. Oxford: Oxford University Press, 1989.

Liberti, Rita. "'We Were Ladies, We Just Played like Boys': African American Women and Competitive Basketball at Bennett College, 1928–1942." In *The Sporting World of the Modern South*, edited by Patrick Miller, 153–74. Urbana: University of Illinois Press, 2002.

Little, Monroe. "The Extra-curricular Activities of Black College Students, 1868–1940." *Journal of Negro Education* 65, no. 2 (Spring 1980): 135–48.

Litwack, Leon. *Been in the Storm So Long: The Aftermath of Slavery*. New York: Random House, 1980.

——. *Trouble in Mind: Black Southerners in the Age of Jim Crow*. New York: Knopf, 1998.

Locke, Alain, ed. *The New Negro: Voices of the Harlem Renaissance*. New York: Touchstone, 1997.

Lodge, Tom. *Sharpeville: A Massacre and Its Consequences*. Oxford: Oxford University Press, 2011.

Loewen, James W., and Charles Sallis, eds. *Mississippi: Conflict and Change*. New York: Pantheon Books, 1974.

Logan, Rayford. *The Betrayal of the Negro: From Rutherford B. Hayes to Woodrow Wilson*. New York: Da Capo, 1997.

Lovell, George I. *This Is Not Civil Rights: Discovering Rights Talk in 1939 America*. Chicago: University of Chicago Press, 2012.

Luker, Ralph E. *The Social Gospel in Black and White: American Racial Reform, 1885–1912*. Chapel Hill: University of North Carolina Press, 1991.

Magness, Phillip, and Sebastian Page. *Colonization after Emancipation: Lincoln and the Movement for Black Resettlement*. Columbia: University of Missouri Press, 2011.

Major, Gerri, and Doris Saunders. *Black Society*. Chicago: Johnson, 1977.

Marabel, Manning. *Race, Reform, and Rebellion: The Second Reconstruction in Black America, 1945–1990*. Jackson: University Press of Mississippi, 1991.

Marabel, Manning, and Leith Mullings, eds. *Let Nobody Turn Us Around: Voices of Resistance, Reform, and Renewal*. Lanham, MD: Rowman and Littlefield, 2003.

Martin, Michael S. *Louisiana beyond Black and White: New Interpretations of Twentieth-Century Race and Race Relations*. Lafayette: University of Louisiana at Lafayette, 2011.

Martin, Tony. "The Banneker Literary Institute of Philadelphia: African American Intellectual Activism before the War of the Slaveholders' Rebellion." *Journal of African American History* 87 (Summer 2002): 303–22.

Martinson, David L. "'Defeating the Hidden Curriculum': Teaching Political Participation in the Social Studies Classroom." *Clearing House* 76, no. 3 (January–February 2003): 132–35.

Mays, Benjamin E. *Born to Rebel: An Autobiography*. Athens: University of Georgia Press, 2003.

McAdam, Doug. *Political Process and the Development of Black Insurgency, 1930–1970*. Chicago: University of Chicago Press, 1982.

McGuire, Danielle L. *At the Dark End of the Street: Black Women, Rape, and Resistance: A New History of the Civil Rights Movement from Rosa Parks to the Rise of Black Power*. New York: Vintage Books, 2010.

McDuffie, Erik. *Sojourning for Freedom: Black Women, American Communism, and the Making of Black Left Feminism*. Durham, NC: Duke University Press, 2011.

McHenry, Elizabeth. *Forgotten Readers: Recovering the Lost History of African American Literary Societies*. Durham, NC: Duke University Press, 2002.

McMillen, Neil R. *Dark Journey: Black Mississippians in the Age of Jim Crow*. Urbana: University of Illinois Press, 1989.

McPherson, James. "White Liberals and Black Power in Negro Education, 1865–1915." *American Historical Review* 75, no. 5 (June 1970): 1357–86.

Meier, August. *Negro Thought in America, 1880–1915*. Ann Arbor: University of Michigan Press, 1966.

———. *A White Scholar and the Black Community, 1945–1965*. Amherst: University of Massachusetts Press, 1992.

Meier, August, and Elliot Rudwick. *Along the Color Line: Explorations in the Black Experience*. Urbana: University of Illinois Press, 2002.

———. *CORE: A Study in the Civil Rights Movement, 1942–1968*. Urbana: University of Illinois Press, 1975.

Miller, Kelly. *Race Adjustment: Essays on the Negro in America*. New York: Neale, 1908.

Moody, Anne. *Coming of Age in Mississippi*. New York: Dell, 1968.

Moore, Jacqueline. *Leading the Race: The Transformation of the Black Elite in the Nation's Capital, 1880–1920*. Charlottesville: University of Virginia Press, 1999.

Morris, Aldon. *The Origins of the Civil Rights Movement: Black Communities Organizing for Change*. New York: Free Press, 1984.

Morris, Robert C. *Reading, 'Riting, and Reconstruction: The Education of Freedmen in the South, 1861–1870*. Chicago: University of Chicago Press, 2010.

Morris, Vivian, and Curtis Morris. *The Price They Paid: Desegregation in an African American Community*. New York: Teachers College Press, 2002.

Moses, Wilson Jeremiah. *Alexander Crummell: A Study of Civilization and Discontent*. Oxford: Oxford University Press, 1989.

———, ed. *Classical Black Nationalism: From the American Revolution to Marcus Garvey*. New York: New York University Press, 1996.

———. *The Golden Age of Black Nationalism, 1850–1925*. Oxford: Oxford University Press, 1978.

Murch, Donna Jean. *Living for the City: Migration, Education, and the Rise of the Black Panther Party in Oakland, California*. Chapel Hill: University of North Carolina Press, 2010.

Murray, Pauli. *The Autobiography of a Black Activist, Feminist, Lawyer, Priest, and Poet*. Knoxville: University of Tennessee Press, 1989.

Myrdal, Gunnar. *An American Dilemma*. Vol. 2, *The Negro Problem and Modern Democracy*. New Brunswick, NJ: Transaction, 1996.

Nash, Gary. *Forging Freedom: The Formation of Philadelphia's Black Community, 1720–1840*. Cambridge, MA: Harvard University Press, 1999.

Neverdon-Morton, Cynthia. *Afro-American Women of the South and the Advancement of the Race, 1895–1925*. Knoxville: University of Tennessee Press, 1991.

Nevergold, Barbara Seals, and Peggy Brooks Bertram. *Uncrowned Queens: African American Women Community Builders of Western New York*. Vol. 2. Buffalo, NY: Uncrowned Queens, 2003.

Newman, Richard, Patrick Rael, and Richard Lapsansky, eds. *Pamphlets of Protest: An Anthology of Early African American Protest Literature, 1790–1860*. New York: Routledge, 2001.

Noble, Stuart. *Forty Years of the Public Schools in Mississippi: With Special Reference to the Education of the Negro*. New York: Teachers College Press, Columbia University, 1918.

Norrell, Robert J. *Reaping the Whirlwind: The Civil Rights Movement in Tuskegee.* Chapel Hill: University of North Carolina Press, 1998.

Nossiter, Adam. *Of Long Memory: Mississippi and the Murder of Medgar Evers.* Reading, MA: Addison-Wesley, 1994.

Oates, Stephen. *To Purge This Land with Blood: A Biography of John Brown.* Amherst: University of Massachusetts Press, 1984.

Oldfield, J. R. *Civilization and Black Progress: Selected Writings of Alexander Crummell on the South.* Charlottesville: University of Virginia Press, 1995.

Oppenheimer, Martin. *The Sit-In Movement of 1960.* New York: Carlson, 1989.

Patterson, Orlando. *The Ordeal of Integration: Progress and Resentment in America's "Racial" Crisis.* Washington, DC: Civitas, 1997.

Payne, Charles. *I've Got the Light of Freedom: The Organizing Tradition and the Mississippi Freedom Struggle.* Berkeley: University of California Press, 1995.

Payne, Charles, and Carol Strickland. *Teach Freedom: Education for Liberation in the African American Tradition.* New York: Teachers College Press, 2008.

Payne, Daniel. *Recollections of Seventy Years.* New York: Arno, 1968.

Peoples, John. *To Survive and Thrive: The Quest for a True University.* Jackson, MS: Town Square Books, 1995.

Perkins, Alfred. *Edwin Rogers Embree: The Julius Rosenwald Fund, Foundation Philanthropy, and American Race Relations.* Bloomington: Indiana University Press, 2011.

Perkins, Linda M. *Fanny Jackson Coppin and the Institute for Colored Youth, 1865–1902.* New York: Garland, 1987.

Perry, Thelma D. *History of the American Teachers Association.* Washington, DC: National Education Association, 1975.

Plummer, Brenda Gayle. *Rising Wind: Black Americans and U.S. Foreign Affairs, 1935–1960.* Chapel Hill: University of North Carolina Press, 1996.

Porter, Dorothy. "The Organized Educational Activities of Negro Literary Societies, 1828–1846." *Journal of Negro Education* 5, no. 4 (October 1936): 555–76.

Powdermaker, Hortense. *After Freedom: A Cultural Study in the Deep South.* New York: Viking, 1939.

Quarles, Benjamin. *Allies for Freedom: Blacks and John Brown.* Oxford: Oxford University Press, 1974.

———. *Black Abolitionists.* New York: Oxford University Press, 1969.

———. *Blacks on John Brown.* Champagne: University of Illinois Press, 1972.

Rabby, Glenda Alice. *The Pain and the Promise: The Struggle for Civil Rights in Tallahassee, Florida.* Athens: University of Georgia Press, 1999.

Ransby, Barbara. *Ella Baker and the Black Freedom Movement: A Radical Democratic Vision.* Chapel Hill: University of North Carolina Press, 2003.

Reddick, L. D. "The Bus Boycott in Montgomery." In *Voices of Dissent: A Collection of Articles from "Dissent" Magazine,* edited by Dissent staff, 107–17. New York: Grove, 1958.

———. "A New Interpretation for Negro History." *Journal of Negro History* 22, no. 1 (January 1937): 17–28.

Reddix, Jacob L. *A Voice Crying in the Wilderness: The Memoirs of Jacob L. Reddix.* Jackson: University Press of Mississippi, 1974.

Reed, Merl E. *Seedtime for the Modern Civil Rights Movement: The President's Committee on Fair Employment Practice, 1941–1946.* Baton Rouge: Louisiana State University Press, 1991.

Reynolds, David S. *John Brown, Abolitionist: The Man Who Killed Slavery, Sparked the Civil War, and Seeded Civil Rights.* New York: Vintage Books, 2006.

Rhoden, William C. *$40 Million Slaves: The Rise, Fall, and Redemption of the Black Athlete.* New York: Three Rivers, 2006.

Rhodes, Lelia. *Jackson State University: The First Hundred Years, 1877–1977.* Jackson: University Press of Mississippi, 1979.

Richardson, Joe M. *Christian Reconstruction: The American Missionary Association and Southern Blacks, 1861–1890.* Tuscaloosa: University of Alabama Press, 2009.

Richardson, Joe M., and Maxine D. Jones. *Education for Liberation: The American Missionary Association and African Americans, 1890 to the Civil Rights Movement.* Tuscaloosa: University of Alabama Press, 2009.

Rickford, Russell. *We Are an African People: Independent Education, Black Power, and the Radical Imagination.* Oxford: Oxford University Press, 2016.

Ripley, Peter C., ed. *The Black Abolitionist Papers.* Vol. 4. Chapel Hill: University of North Carolina Press, 1991.

Robeson, Paul. *Here I Stand.* New York: Beacon, 1998.

Robinson, Jo Ann Gibson. *The Montgomery Bus Boycott and the Women Who Started It: The Memoir of Jo Ann Robinson.* Knoxville: University of Tennessee Press, 1987.

Rogers, Ibram. *The Black Campus Movement: Black Students and the Racial Reconstitution of Higher Education, 1965–1972.* New York: Palgrave Macmillan, 2012.

Rudwick, Elliot M. "The Niagara Movement." *Journal of Negro History* 42, no. 3 (July 1957): 177–200.

Sanborn, F. B., ed. *The Life and Letters of John Brown.* New York: New American Library, 1969.

Sandburg, Carl. *The People, Yes.* New York: Harcourt, Brace, 1936.

Sansing, David. *Making Haste Slowly: The Troubled History of Higher Education in Mississippi.* Jackson: University Press of Mississippi, 1990.

Sartain, Lee. *Invisible Activists: Women of the Louisiana NAACP and the Struggle for Civil Rights, 1915–1945.* Baton Rouge: Louisiana State University Press, 2007.

Scales, Junius Irving, and Richard Nickson. *Cause at Heart: A Former Communist Remembers.* Athens: University of Georgia Press, 2005.

Scott, Daryl Michael. *Contempt and Pity: Social Policy and the Image of the Damaged Black Psyche, 1880–1996.* Chapel Hill: University of North Carolina Press, 1997.

Seay, Solomon, Sr. *I Was There by the Grace of God.* Montgomery: S. S. Seay Sr. Educational Foundation, 1990.

Sellers, Cleveland. *The River of No Return: The Autobiography of a Black Militant and the Life and Death of SNCC.* Jackson: University Press of Mississippi, 1990.

Shapiro, Herbert. *White Violence and Black Response: From Reconstruction to Montgomery.* Amherst: University of Massachusetts Press, 1988.

Shaw, Stephanie. *What a Woman Ought to Be and to Do: Black Professional Women Workers during the Jim Crow Era.* Chicago: University of Chicago Press, 1996.

Sherer, Robert G., Jr. "John William Beverly: Alabama's First Negro Historian." *Alabama Review* 26 (January 1973): 194–208.

Sherman, Joan R., ed. *African-American Poetry of the Nineteenth Century: An Anthology.* Urbana: University of Illinois Press, 1992.

Shockley, Megan Taylor. *"We Too Are Americans": African American Women in Detroit and Richmond, 1940–1954.* Urbana: University of Illinois Press, 2004.

Silcox, Harry. "Philadelphia Negro Educator: Jacob C. White, Jr., 1837–1902." *Pennsylvania Magazine of History and Biography* 97 (January 1973): 75–98.

Silver, James. *Mississippi: The Closed Society.* New York: Harcourt, Brace and World, 1963.

Sims, David Henry. "Religious Education in Negro Colleges and Universities." *Journal of Negro History* 5, no. 2 (April 1920): 166–207.

Sinclair, Dean. "Equal in All Places: The Civil Rights Struggle in Baton Rouge, 1953–1963." *Louisiana History: The Journal of the Louisiana Historical Association* 39, no. 3 (Summer 1998): 347–66.

Singh, Nikhil Pal. *Black Is a Country: Race and the Unfinished Struggle for Democracy.* Cambridge, MA: Harvard University Press, 2004.

Smith, Eric Ledell. "To Teach My People: Fanny Jackson Coppin and Philadelphia's Institute for Colored Youth." *Pennsylvania Heritage* 29 (Winter 2003): 6–11.

Smith, William A. "Challenging Racial Battle Fatigue on Historically White Campuses: A Critical Race Examination of Race-Related Stress." In *Faculty of Color: Teaching in Predominantly White Colleges and Universities,* edited by Christine A. Stanley, 299–327. Bolton, MA: Anker, 2006.

——. Foreword to *Racial Battle Fatigue in Higher Education: Exposing the Myth of Post-Racial America,* edited by Kenneth J. Fasching-Varner, Katrice A. Albert, Roland W. Mitchell, and Chaunda M. Allen, xi–xii. Lanham, MD: Rowman and Littlefield, 2015.

——. "Toward an Understanding of Misandric Microaggressions and Racial Battle Fatigue among African Americans in Historically White Institutions." In *The State of the African American Male,* edited by E. M. Zamani-Gallaher and V. C. Polite, 265–77. East Lansing: Michigan State University Press, 2010.

Solórzano, Daniel, Walter R. Allen, and Grace Carroll. "Keeping Race in Place: Racial Microaggressions and Campus Racial Climate at the University of California, Berkeley." *Chicano Latino Law Review* 23 (Spring 2002): 15–111.

Spagna, Ana Maria. *Test Ride on the Sunnyland Bus: A Daughter's Civil Rights Journey.* Lincoln: University of Nebraska Press, 2010.

Steele, W. F. "A Work That Pays Big Dividends." *Epworth Herald* (Chicago), February 4, 1905.

Sterling, Dorothy, ed. *Speak Out in Thunder Tones: Letters and Other Writings by Black Northerners, 1787–1865.* New York: Doubleday, 1973.

Stewart, Dafina-Lazarus. *Black Collegians' Experiences in US Northern Private Colleges: A Narrative History, 1945–1965.* New York: Palgrave Macmillan, 2017.

Stewart, James Brewer. "The Emergence of Racial Modernity and the Rise of the White North." *Journal of the Early Republic* 18 (Summer 1998): 181–217.

Strain, Christopher. *Pure Fire: Self-Defense as Activism in the Civil Rights Era.* Athens: University of Georgia Press, 2005.

Stuckey, Sterling. *The Ideological Origins of Black Nationalism.* Boston: Beacon, 1996.

Sugrue, Thomas. *The Origins of the Urban Crisis: Race and Inequality in Postwar Detroit.* Princeton, NJ: Princeton University Press, 2005.

Sullivan, Patricia. *Lift Every Voice: The NAACP and the Making of the Civil Rights Movement.* New York: New Press, 2009.

——. "Southern Reformers, the New Deal, and the Movement's Foundation." In *New Directions in Civil Rights Studies,* edited by Armstead L. Robinson and Patricia Sullivan, 81–104. Charlottesville: University Press of Virginia, 1991.

Talbert, Horace. *The Sons of Allen: Together with a Sketch of the Rise and Progress of Wilberforce University.* Xenia, OH: Aldine, 1906.

Teal, Christopher. *Hero of Hispaniola: America's First Black Diplomat, Ebenezer Bassett.* Westport, CT: Praeger, 2008.

Thomas, Lamont D. *Rise to Be a People: A Biography of Paul Cuffe.* Urbana: University of Illinois Press, 1986.

Thompson, Cleopatra. *The History of the Mississippi Teachers Association.* Washington, DC: NEA Teachers Rights, 1973.

Thompson, Julius. *Black Life in Mississippi: Essays on Political, Social, and Cultural Studies in a Deep South State.* Lanham, MD: University Press of America, 2001.

Thompson, Patrick. *The History of Negro Baptists in Mississippi.* Jackson, MS: W. H. Bailey, 1898.

Thornton, J. Mills, III. *Dividing Lines: Municipal Politics and the Struggle for Civil Rights in Montgomery, Birmingham, and Selma.* Tuscaloosa: University of Alabama Press, 2002.

Thuesen, Sarah. *Greater Than Equal: African American Struggles for Schools and Citizenship in North Carolina, 1919–1965.* Chapel Hill: University of North Carolina Press, 2013.

Thurman, Howard. *With Head and Heart: The Autobiography of Howard Thurman.* New York: Harcourt Brace, 1979.

Tye, Larry. *Rising from the Rails: Pullman Porters and the Making of the Black Middle Class.* New York: Holt Paperbacks, 2005.

Turner, James, and C. Steven McGann. "Black Studies as an Integral Tradition in African-American Intellectual History." *Issue: A Journal of Opinion* 6, no. 2/3 (Summer/Autumn 1976): 73–78.

Turner, Sarah E., and John Bound. "Closing the Gap or Widening the Divide: The Effects of the G.I. Bill and World War II on the Educational Outcomes of Black Americans." *Journal of Economic History* 63 (March 2003): 145–77.

Turner, Victor. *The Ritual Process: Structure and Anti-structure*. Ithaca, NY: Cornell University Press, 1969.

Umoja, Akinyele Omowale. *We Will Shoot Back: Armed Resistance in the Mississippi Freedom Movement*. New York: New York University Press, 2013.

Von Eschen, Penny M. *Race against Empire: Black Americans and Anticolonialism, 1937–1957*. Ithaca, NY: Cornell University Press, 1997.

Wadelington, Charles W., and Richard F. Knapp. *Charlotte Hawkins Brown and Palmer Memorial Institute: What One Young African American Woman Could Do*. Chapel Hill: University of North Carolina Press, 1999.

Walker Alexander, Margaret. *Jubilee*. Boston: Houghton Mifflin, 1966.

Walker, Vanessa. *Their Highest Potential: An African American School Community in the Segregated South*. Chapel Hill: University of North Carolina Press, 1996.

Washburn, Patrick. *A Question of Sedition: The Federal Government's Investigation of the Black Press during World War II*. New York: Oxford University Press, 1986.

Washington, Booker T. *My Larger Education: Being Chapters from My Experience*. New York: Doubleday, 1911.

Washington, Booker T., et al. *The Negro Problem: A Series of Articles by Representative American Negroes of Today*. New York: AMS Press, 1970.

Watkins, William H. *The White Architects of Black Education: Ideology and Power in America, 1865–1954*. New York: Teachers College Press, Columbia University, 2001.

Watson, Harry L. *Liberty and Power: The Politics of Jacksonian America*. New York: Hill and Wang, 2006.

Watts, Jerry. *Amiri Baraka: The Politics and Art of a Black Intellectual*. New York: New York University Press, 2001.

Webber, Thomas. *Deep like Rivers: Education in the Slave Quarter Community, 1831–1835*. New York: Norton, 1978.

Weems, Robert E., Jr. "Alpha Phi Alpha, the Fight for Civil Rights, and the Shaping of Public Policy." In *Alpha Phi Alpha: A Legacy of Greatness, the Demands of Transcendence*, edited by Gregory S. Parks, Stefan M. Bradley, and Michael A. Blake, 233–62. Lexington: University Press of Kentucky, 2011.

Weixlmann, Joe. "A Tribute to Darwin T. Turner." *Black American Literature Forum* 25, no. 1 (Spring 1991): 8–9.

Welky, David. *Marching across the Color Line: A. Philip Randolph and Civil Rights in the World War II Era*. Oxford: Oxford University Press, 2014.

Wells, Ida B. *Southern Horrors and Other Writings: The Anti-lynching Campaign of Ida B. Wells, 1892–1900*. Boston: Bedford Books, 1997.

Wharton, Vernon. *The Negro in Mississippi, 1865–1890*. Chapel Hill: University of North Carolina Press, 1947.

White, Deborah Gray. *Lost in the USA: American Identity from the Promise Keepers to the Million Mom March*. Urbana: University of Illinois Press, 2017.

White, Derrick. *The Challenge of Blackness: The Institute of the Black World and Political Activism in the 1970s*. Gainesville: University Press of Florida, 2011.

White, John. *Black Leadership in America: From Booker T. Washington to Jesse Jackson*. London: Longman, 1990.

Whitfield, Stephen. *A Death in the Delta: The Story of Emmett Till.* Baltimore, MD: Johns Hopkins University Press, 1988.

Williams, Kidada E. *They Left Great Marks on Me: African American Testimonies of Racial Violence from Emancipation to World War I.* New York: New York University Press, 2012.

Williamson, Joy Ann. *Radicalizing the Ebony Tower: Black Colleges and the Black Freedom Struggle in Mississippi.* New York: Teachers College Press, 2008.

Wilson, Charles, Sr. *Education for Negroes in Mississippi since 1910.* Newton, MA: Meador, 1947.

Wilson, J. Ormond. "Stewart Missionary Foundation for Africa in Gammon Theological Seminary." *Liberia*, no. 19 (November 1901): 7.

Wilson, Sondra Kathryn, ed. *The Opportunity Reader: Stories, Poetry, and Essays from the Urban League's "Opportunity" Magazine.* New York: Random House, 1999.

Winch, Julie. *Philadelphia's Black Elite: Activism, Accommodation, and the Struggle for Autonomy, 1787–1848.* Philadelphia: Temple University Press, 1988.

Winsboro, Irvin. *Old South, New South, or Down South? Florida and the Modern Civil Rights Movement.* Morgantown: West Virginia University Press, 2009.

Wolff, Miles. *Lunch at the 5 and 10: The Greensboro Sit-Ins.* New York: Stein and Day, 1970.

Wolters, Raymond. *The New Negro on Campus: Black College Rebellions of the 1920s.* Princeton, NJ: Princeton University Press, 1975.

Woodson, Carter G. *The Education of the Negro prior to 1861.* New York: Arno, 1968.

———. "Negro Life and History in Our Schools." *Journal of Negro History* 4, no. 3 (July 1919): 273–80.

Wooten, Melissa E. *In the Face of Inequality: How Black Colleges Adapt.* New York: State University of New York Press, 2015.

Wright, Richard. *Black Boy: A Record of Childhood and Youth.* New York: Harper and Row, 1937.

Young, Richard, ed. *Roots of Rebellion: The Evolution of Black Politics and Protest since World War II.* New York: Harper and Row, 1970.

Zaki, Hoda M. *Civil Rights and Politics at Hampton Institute: The Legacy of Alonzo G. Moron.* Urbana: University of Illinois Press, 2007.

Zinn, Howard. *SNCC: The New Abolitionists.* Boston: Beacon, 1965.

Index

Note: Photographs and illustrations are indicated by page numbers in *italics*.

Gibbs, Warmouth T., 189
GI Bill, 240–41, 286n45
Gilmore, Glenda Elizabeth, 115–16
Glaise, Joyce, 223
Glass, Thelma, 115–16
Gooden, Earl, 138
Goodman, Andrew, 295n64
Grandison, Charles N., 71–73
Grant, Ulysses, 43–44
Gray, Fred, 129
Gray, Freddie, *251*
Great Depression, 76, 109, 164–65
Green, Alfred, 40
Green, Sam, 116
Greene, Cohen N., 207
Greene, Percy, 157
Greensboro Association of Poor People
  (GAPP), 203–8, 211, 216, 234–36,
  304n10
Greensboro College, 86, 93–94
Greensboro National Bank, 226–27
Gregory, James, 11
Grimes, Willie, 212
Guilford College, 221–22
Guinn, Chandra, 264n10
Gulfside Assembly, 75

Haitian Revolution, 122
Hall, Jacquelyn Dowd, 261n2
Hall, Scott, 212
Hampton-Tuskegee model, 272n4
Hampton University, 186
Harding, Vincent, 214–15
Hardman, Flossie, 116
Hardy, J. Leo, 176
Harper's Ferry, 2–3, 34
Hartford Baptist Church (Detroit), 134
Harvard University, 312n12
hate crimes, 246, 249
Hayes, Laurence, 101–2, 116, 132
Haynes, E. H., Jr., 54
Hedgemon, J. J., 191
Henry, Alexander, 35
Higginbotham, Evelyn Brooks, 60
Higgins, Rodney, 161

Hill, Charles, 134
Hill, Leslie Pinckney, 110, 248
Hill, Montgomery S., 78–79
hip-hop generation, 242–43, 246
historically Black colleges and universities (HBCUs): activism and, 7–8;
  American Missionary Association
  and, 273n6; and "brain-drain," 239;
  communitas at, 5–8; as control
  mechanism, 3; GI Bill and, 240–41;
  hip-hop generation and, 242–43, 246;
  "second curriculum" at, 5, 7; Student
  Nonviolent Coordinating Committee
  and, 2; tolerance of, 3; and white
  sentiment toward Blacks, 161–62; as
  workspaces, 206–7
history, black, 64, 78, 90, 105–6, 110,
  114, 166, 185, 297n19
Hodge, Willie J., 178
Hodges, Luther, 186
Hogan, Wesley, 264n10
"Hold Your Job" campaign, 92–93
Holloway, Alice, 93
Home Defense Workshop in Commu-
  nity Leadership, 86
Hood, R. W., 67
Hood, Samuel, 67
Hoover, J. Edgar, 80
Hope, John, II, 144–45
Hopkins, Andy, 155
Hopkins, Charles, 305n13
Hornet (newspaper), 117–18, 125
Horton, James, 23, 26
Horton, Lois, 23, 26
Houston, Charles Hamilton, 178
Howard University, 8–9, 70, 222, 308n68
Huggins, Horne, 179
Hughes, Langston, 10, 87, 110, 140,
  265n23
Humphreys, Richard, 25, 266n1
Hurston, Zora Neale, 110

IBW. *See* Institute of the Black World
  (IBW)
ICY. *See* Institute for Colored Youth (ICY)

public relations, 242
Purvis, Robert, 32–33

Quarles, Benjamin, 28, 35

race men, 7, 90, 98, 131
race women, 7, 90, 98, 131. *See also* Bennett College; women
"racial battle fatigue," 247, 311n11
racial uplift, 6, 9, 134, 252; and Bennett College, 71, 73, 84; Bennett College and, 71; education and, 152; and Institute for Colored Youth, 12, 32, 43, 46–47; and Tougaloo College, 49, 52–54, 56–57, 60–61, 63
radicalism, 11, 88, 104, 169–71, 190–91
radio, 82–85, *83*, 279n41
Rakim (musician), 237
Randolph, A. Philip, 92, 177–78
Rankin, John, 96
Ransby, Barbara, 250
Reason, Charles Lewis, 26–30, 48, 269n37
Reconstruction, 50, 52, 103
Reddick, Lawrence Dunbar, 108, 114, 129–30
Reddix, Jacob L., 14, 144–48, 151–52, 157–58, 160, 292n38, 295n72
Red Scare, 115
Red Summer, 73–74
Reed, Adolph, 193
Reed, Mattye, 223
Reed, Merl, 97
Reeves, Jeremiah, 122–23
Reform Convention, 24–25
Reid, Ira, 94
religious education, 50
Remond, Charles, 32
respectability politics, 8, 60–61, 63, 231
Revels, Hiram, 52
Rice, Leon, 127
Richmond, Peggy, 305n13
"Right of Suffrage, The" (Johnson), 21–22
riots, 150–51. *See also* protests

Robeson, Paul, 97–98
Robinson, Delores, 154–55
Robinson, George Lee, 154, 294n60
Robinson, Jackie, *202*
Robinson, Jo Ann, 112–13, 116–19, *124*, 287n59
Robinson, Marvin, 189
Robson, Maurice J., 8
Rogers, Oscar, 56
Roosevelt, Franklin, 92, 96, 109, 177
Rose, Arnold, 179–80
Rudwick, Elliot, 302n69

Sadaukai, Owusu, 219. *See also* Fuller, Howard
Samuel Crowther Friends of Africa, 73
Sandburg, Carl, 110
Sartain, Lee, 297n19
Save and Change Black Schools (SCBS), 228–29
Scales, Junius, 76–77, 79
SCBS. *See* Save and Change Black Schools (SCBS)
Schomburg, Arthur A., 108, 114
School Daze (film), 238
Schwerner, Michael, 295n64
Scott, A. J., 170
Scott, Rachel Pepper, 66
Scottsboro Boys trial, 10, 108, 265n23, 284n22
Seay, Solomon, Sr., 106–7, 126, 129
second curriculum: at Alabama State University (ASU), 105–6, 118–19; at historically Black colleges and universities (HBCUs), 5, 7; at Jackson State University, 135–38; at Tougaloo College, 64–65, 67–69
segregation: in Baton Rouge, 179, 181–83; in Greensboro, 71–72, 98; hypocrisy of, 91–92, 96, *99*; Minor on, 89–90; in Montgomery, 287n59; in Philadelphia, 40–43; and World War II, 172. *See also* integration; Jim Crow
Seiber, Hal, 225
separatism, 165

CPSIA information can be obtained
at www.ICGtesting.com
Printed in the USA
LVHW092035050121
675792LV00010B/2173

9 781469 661445